WRECK DIVERS &
ARCHAEOLOGISTS

A History *of* Maritime Archaeology *in* California

by
Thomas N. Layton
and
James P. Delgado

SOCIETY *for*
HISTORICAL
ARCHAEOLOGY

A Society for Historical Archaeology Publication

Wreck Divers & Archaeologists:
A History of Maritime Archaeology in California

by Thomas N. Layton and James P. Delgado

©2024 by Society for Historical Archaeology
ISBNs:

    978-1-957402-57-4 ~ Print (BW)

    978-1-957402-56-7 ~ Print (color)

    978-1-957402-58-1 ~ eBook (ePUB, reflowable)

Library of Congress Control Number: 2024943314

Layout & cover design by knic pfost and render jemis

Society for Historical Archaeology
13017 Wisteria Drive, #395 Germantown, MD 20874, U.S.A.
www.sha.org

Benjamin Ford, SHA Special Publication Editor

Figure 1. Della Scott-Ireton. (Photo by Nicole Grinnan, 2022, Courtesy Florida Public Archaeology Network.)

Preface

Della A. Scott-Ireton

But, if we allow the interested public to become involved in meaningful ways, we'll do much better than we're doing now.

Larry Pierson, this volume

These insightful words from wreck diver Larry Pierson, who went on to become a professional archaeologist, sum up the purpose of this latest wonderful book centered on the *Frolic* shipwreck as well as the point of citizen science and community engagement in modern archaeology, underwater and terrestrial. Learning to embrace the "public" (that is, anyone who is not a formally trained archaeologist), not only as interested audiences for lectures and tours, but also as collaborators and partners in research, has been a long, hard voyage for maritime archaeologists. And sometimes the waters still are rough. Thomas Layton and James Delgado describe in these pages the foundations of underwater archaeology in California and include the invaluable interview contributions of some of the first sport divers to investigate historical shipwrecks along that coast, in particular the unique *Frolic*. The overarching memories are of divers becoming alienated, sometimes prosecuted, and eventually estranged from researching the sites they found and first explored, but also plundered for souvenirs and items to sell, thus running afoul of preservation laws intended to protect submerged heritage sites. The most important part of this book, however, is that Tom and Jim then go on to explain and describe how archaeologists have worked and continue to work toward an understanding with sport divers, realizing that the best way to protect these fragile and nonrenewable heritage resources is through working together for their preservation.

We archaeologists, generally speaking, have had a hard time embracing non-practitioners as fellow researchers. We have seen shipwrecks absolutely ravaged by treasure hunters, both professional "commercial salvors" and weekend collectors, until nothing is left to see or enjoy or learn from or to serve as habitat for marine life.

And I say that as both an archaeologist and a sport diver. But the vast majority of sport divers are, I think, just as interested in the story of the shipwreck—from where it came, how it was wrecked, the stories of the crew and passengers—as are archaeologists. The diving public is possessed of burning curiosity, wild enthusiasm, unquenchable interest, and mad skills—they just require a little training, some direction, and a productive mission to fulfill. Archaeologists need, as Larry says, to enable the public, divers, and landlubbers to become involved in meaningful ways that transcend the simple pleasure of merely collecting by empowering the production of knowledge.

Archaeologists are getting there, and sport divers are eager to learn and engage. Currently, such programs as the Maritime Archaeological Society, Diving with a Purpose, Maritime Archaeological and Historical Society, and the Nautical Archaeology Society, as well as numerous others, are dedicated to partnering divers and archaeologists for further research, preservation, social justice, and educational goals. This is community activism and engagement at its best, where "communities" includes local people, visitors, youth, professionals, avocationals, divers, beachcombers, history buffs—really anyone who loves old shipwrecks.

The outreach and promotional products developed as part of the *Frolic* project exemplify this community involvement. In addition to lectures, books, educational programs, and even a film, the local group, Friends of the *Frolic*, produced newsletters and public information, while artifacts from the ship and its cargo were featured in five different exhibits at five different museums. A play based on stories inspired by cargo artifacts, *Voices from the* Frolic *and Beyond*, and even an adult beverage, *Frolic* Shipwreck Ale, are especially illustrative of the meaningful and creative outreach strategies developed to attract and engage people with this shipwreck. Everyone should all take note.

In *Wreck Divers and Archaeologists: A History of Maritime Archaeology in California*, Tom and Jim describe underwater archaeology in California as a process that has come, essentially, full circle with wreck divers. From reminiscences with "old-time" divers, who remember what it was like to discover a wreck littered with artifacts and then become obsessed with learning about it, to Jim's excellent history of how underwater archaeology developed as a discipline in the Golden State (mostly from his own experiences, because he was there!), and Tom's superb use of the *Frolic* shipwreck project as a case study for community archaeology, this volume is a shining example of what can be accomplished when archaeologists and sport divers work together. They also do not shy away from frank discussion of the polarizing disagreements, leading in some cases to bitter enmity that developed between wreck divers and archaeologists. Fortunately, the *Frolic* project has contributed immensely toward reconciliation.

So, this book has it all—exploits of early wreck finders, the excitement of discovery underwater and in archives, research that leads to dead ends and fascinating answers, arguments, partnerships, friendships made and destroyed, names famous and infamous (if you are a diver), artifacts collected and returned, lessons taught, and lessons learned. Readers, particularly those with some familiarity of the ongoing animosity between science-based archaeologists and commerce-minded salvors, may wonder at the inclusion of narratives from both perspectives in this one book. But these intertwined histories are crucial to understanding the long journey of *Frolic*, from her wrecking in 1850 to her modern place in the annals of archaeology as a success story of community engagement.

Now, join Tom and Jim and their old friends for a tale unlike any other, though one that should serve as an example for all maritime archaeologists and sport divers, because aren't we all, really, wreck divers?

Introduction

∼

Thomas N. Layton

The Past is never dead. It's not even past,
William Faulkner, *Requiem for a Nun (1951)*

It may seem strange that Jim Delgado and I should speak of wreck divers and underwater archaeologists in the same sentence without a rolling of the eyes and clearing of the throat, or that we have dared to juxtapose the seemingly impossible—their two awkwardly intertwined histories—in one volume.

However, the story of the 1850 wreck of the *Frolic* at Point Cabrillo on the north coast of California has enabled us to accomplish that. It is a story of making the best of a scientific tragedy, for the *Frolic* was not only among the very oldest shipwrecks discovered on the coast of California, but it was also among the most completely pillaged. Only then, through the cooperation of wreck divers and archaeologists, did it become the most completely studied shipwreck on the west coast of North America.

But the underlying truth of the following history is that a network of California wreck divers had become technically proficient and sufficiently research-savvy to locate many of the sunken vessels along the California coast and to carry out a systematic pillage of those vessels long before professional archaeologists had either the skills or the institutional backing to manage or to document their remains.

Looking back, it seems equally strange that, when I wrote my review article, "The Status of California Archaeology in 1984," for the *Journal of California and Great Basin Anthropology*, I made no mention of California's underwater heritage. I am now struck by the irony, for it was during that very summer, as I was completing that article, that my San Jose State University archaeology field-class students began excavating Chinese porcelain sherds from a Pomo village site on a remote ridge in Mendocino County, and my attempt to explain those potsherds would lead to the *Frolic* Shipwreck Project.

This volume is not a story of good guys and bad guys, but it documents a time, starting during the early 1960s, in which both state and federal agencies lacked the staff and the expertise to respond to multiple opportunities to preserve not only the *Frolic* shipwreck, but many other underwater sites as well. However, it also documents the growth of a subsequent culture of stewardship for those underwater treasures by those same agencies, and a generation of archaeologists that trained themselves to conduct underwater research.

That first generation included John Foster, who, in 1980, became the de facto state underwater archaeologist at the California Department of Parks and Recreation, and James Delgado, who about the same time was struggling to convince his superiors at the National Park Service in San Francisco to allow him to document the underwater vessels and beached wrecks under their jurisdiction.

So much has happened since the California Department of Parks and Recreation, the National Maritime Museum in San Francisco, and San Jose State University all refused to receive the "stolen" *Frolic* artifacts returned by the wreck divers. Since that time, Parks and Recreation, under the leadership of Foster, funded a 2003–2004 expedition, led by Sheli O. Smith, to map and analyze what remains of the *Frolic*,

and the Maritime Museum used the story of the *Frolic* to frame their California Gold Rush sesquicentennial exhibit. And, finally, in this volume, we have been able to present the *Frolic* Shipwreck Project as a kind of metaphor or touchstone to present the much broader story of underwater archaeology in California.

In Part 1 of this volume, James Delgado presents a formal history of underwater archaeology in California.

Part 2 of this volume presents a less-formal history of both California wreck diving and underwater archaeology as told by the wreck divers and the archaeologists themselves. The overarching theme of this section is that each narrator "touched" the *Frolic* in a meaningful way, either during its pillage or in the subsequent efforts to put the pieces back together. In addition to Delgado's formal history, both Delgado and Foster supplied personal narratives for this portion of the volume. As a specialist in prehistoric archaeology I should note that this volume does not treat the offshore prehistoric archaeological record, mostly obscured by Holocene sea-level rise —a record that is likely to be revealed in decades to come.

PART 1

The Early Years of Underwater / Maritime / Nautical / Marine Archaeology in California: A Personal Perspective

James P. Delgado

Introduction: A Personal Tao of Maritime Archaeology

Something that has occasionally struck me, as an anthropologically based archaeologist, is how even scholars who study systems can be caught up in the patterns of behavior inherent in the development of systems. Archaeologists are perfect examples of this. What I also find fascinating is looking at the field through the training I received and perceptions I developed as an early career historian; archaeologists can be poor historians, particularly in regard to their own discipline. Add to that mix the lessons of a course I took at San José State on comparative religions nearly five decades ago, and the sense I have of archaeology as practiced underwater, as well as on ships, is influenced by those three threads of my own experience, scholarship, and belief.

Referring to the narrative about my life and career that appears later in this volume, my perspectives are also influenced by a precocious approach as a young man to engage with, discuss, and learn from the generations before my own, an approach that persisted throughout my career until I was no longer young. Part of that, as I have said, came from being raised from ages two to five by my grandparents, which left me with values and perspectives that better fit those of the generation before my own. While 14, I was engaged in archaeology, interviewed and befriended octogenarian descendants of my hometown's pioneers, and, in time, turned that focus to archaeology. Unafraid to approach them, introduce myself respectfully, and begin to ask for guidance, advice, and then to hear their stories, the ability to listen then gave me the gift of knowing, hearing, and, in many cases, befriending the archaeological and maritime archaeological generation before my own.

Thanks to asking and listening, I was fortunate to hear, one on one, firsthand accounts from George Bass, Ann Bass, Honor Frost, Peter Throckmorton, and Claude Duthuit about Cape Gelidonya; I also learned more about Marsala from Honor Frost. I learned of Cosa from Anna Marguerite McCann; about the Spanish Armada's wrecks from Colin Martin; *Mary Rose* from Margaret Rule; London's buried ships from Peter Marsden; Florida's early sites from George Fischer; Warm Mineral Springs from Sonny Cockrell (which included a dive on the site); more on Florida's sites, and, in time, Pearl Harbor and many other sites from Dan Lenihan and Larry Murphy; Canada's wrecks from Robert Grenier; about USS *Cairo* from Edwin C. Bearss; shipwreck anthropology from Dick Gould; maritime cultural landscapes from Christer Westerdahl; USS *Monitor* from Gordon Watts; *Vasa* from Carl Olof Cederlund; Australia's shipwrecks and the archaeology of *Batavia* and other sites from Graeme Henderson and Michael "Mack" McCarthy; *Titanic* from Bob Ballard; *Hunley* and other wrecks from Clive Cussler; and about many other sites from so many others around the world.

I also interviewed and had discussions with pioneering wreck divers and treasure hunters, and sat down and discussed their careers and finds with Mel Fisher, Robert Marx, legendary diver and wreck salvager Fred Rogers of British Columbia, and George Tulloch of RMS *Titanic*, among others. The key point is not to whom I was able to talk as some measure of how connected I was as a young professional; I want to encourage young scholars to do exactly what I did—walk up, introduce themselves, express their interest to older, established figures in the field, and then sit down and listen. What follows draws in part on those discussions and that perspective of an archaeologist who was granted the opportunity to span the field's first and second generations, or, as I have quietly joked, to be a "Version 1.5" instead of a "Version 2.0" maritime archaeologist.

Archaeology is the child of antiquarianism, relic-seeking, and outright looting. It only follows that the wet and ship side of the house was born of the same traditions. Add to that mix the centuries-old belief that the sea and sunken ships are the source of lost riches. The recovery of lost riches and the exploitation of other resources in the sea (such as pearls) played an influential role in the development of technologies (diving bells, "submarine armor," submersibles, scuba) to enable human beings to journey beneath the water to explore and to recover that which they found down there. The other factor to consider is the very human belief that subsequent generations are smarter and know better than previous ones. The apocryphal Mark Twain quote most pertinent to this begins: "When I was a boy of fourteen, my father was so ignorant I could hardly stand to have the old man around," sentiments you can find in any discipline, underwater archaeology being just one. Where we find ourselves now, as a discipline, and I see this in my own belief, is the second half of the quote: "But when I got to be twenty-one, I was astonished at how much he had learned in seven years."

In looking back on my own career, I certainly see that to be true in my own beliefs and actions. The start of my career saw me rescuing artifacts and burials being bulldozed, and, of course, there was a temptation to keep a projectile point or a mortar, which I did not, but that was because of a strong sense, imbued in my upbringing, that you did not keep that which was not yours, as well as taking to heart what the books I read told me archaeology was all about. However, when I worked at the New Almaden Museum, when Connie Perham could not pay me in cash, she did allow me to work to acquire surplus artifacts, such as one of the oldest, first-generation, cast-iron mercury flasks from the 1845–1849 initial development of the mines. I kept that flask until 2020, when I gifted it to another archaeologist who studies that period and knows those mines.

I always comforted myself with the knowledge that the flask was non-archaeological and had been kept by the mining company, along with hundreds of others, until they ceased operations after World War II, but the reality is that I felt a connection to the past through the flask, and it always was there to remind me of the mining history of California and my first job in the field of history and culture. It is a human response, part of our culture, and, for me, items and artifacts can be as powerful a mnemonic as a piece of music, a scent, or a place. As I write this, on the shelf in my office is an engraved stone given to me by the hospital chaplain while my brothers and I sat together as our mother slowly died; each of us three boys has one with a different inscription. I look at it, I pick it up, and the details of that moment come flooding back. Resting nearby on the shelf, a crushed Styrofoam cup from my submersible dive to *Titanic* in 2000, warped and compressed by thousands of pounds of pressure, fills me with memories of that dive and a vivid memory of being inside a 6 ft. diameter nickel-steel sphere falling into the darkness, as beads of water, the condensation of our breath, formed on the cold steel and began to run in tiny rivulets down the inner curve of the submersible.

So, as much as some (many?) archaeologists do not want to admit it, we understand at some level those who wish to collect. Some feel the compulsion themselves, but the training and the harsh experience of knowing what happens when collecting, not science, takes hold of a site, with so much lost information, separates the archaeologist from the collector. Having said that, I am sure a number of colleagues, when pressed, can see the point when Mick Jagger sings: "just as every cop is a criminal and all the sinners saints" in "Sympathy for the Devil," that that line can be a thin one. That brings me back to religion; if, metaphorically, archaeology was born of paganism and is now Judeo-Christian, we can see how it has gone through its own Councils of Nicaea, undergone its own purges of heretics, banished certain publications as apocrypha, and created various sects and faiths, the underwater/marine/maritime/nautical faith, as I have parsed it, having its own sectarian divisions.

It should come as no surprise that in the reactions of some of my maritime archaeological colleagues to wreck divers, collecting and treasure hunting is a modern version of the medieval Catholic rite for exorcism's prayer "Vade retro Satana!" (Go back, Satan!). The biblical origin of the phrase, when Christ rebukes Peter when he objects to Jesus' sacrifice of his own life: "Get behind me Satan! You are a stumbling block to me; you do not have in mind the concerns of God, but merely human concerns," (Matthew 16:23) is for me another allegorical example of how some colleagues feel and act when confronted by the collector and the collections.

The Origins of Underwater/Nautical/Maritime Archaeology in California, 1950–1970

So we turn to the origins of underwater archaeology and, in particular, the origins of underwater archaeology in California. The origins of underwater archaeology in California are interrelated with the story of global underwater archaeology. That also means they are interrelated with the story of wreck diving and treasure hunting. The first national magazine dedicated to diving, *Skin Diver*, debuted in California in December 1951. At that time the Cousteau-Gagnan regulator had been on the market for five years, marketed as the Aqua-Lung by U.S. Divers, which licensed the patent from Cousteau. One of the advertisements in the first issue was for Mel Fisher's Fisher Sporting Goods in Torrance, later moved and reopened as Mel's Aqua Shop in Redondo Beach before he went to Florida in the early 1960s to begin treasure hunting.

The 1950s were the pioneer era for scuba diving, and salvage of shipwrecks largely remained the domain of old-school hard-hat divers, but by the early 1960s that changed as the ranks of scuba divers increased. The first dive courses leading to certification of divers began in Los Angeles in 1955 through the county's Department of Parks and Recreation. The National Dive Patrol, later renamed the National Association of Underwater Instructors (NAUI), was founded in 1960 and incorporated in California in 1961. PADI, the Professional Association of Dive Instructors, was founded in 1966. When I attended dive school at the Presidio of San Francisco it was a NAUI course, and NAUI certification remains the standard for most military divers as well as the National Park Service and the National

Oceanic and Atmospheric Administration (NOAA).

Scuba-diver participation in serious salvage and recovery remained small; the major shipwreck projects of the late 1950s and early 1960s, such as the recovery of *Vasa* in 1961 and USS *Cairo* in 1964, were not done as archaeological recoveries, but as marine-salvage jobs with hard-hatted divers in standard dress. Cousteau and his team had excavated, though not archaeologically, the ancient Mediterranean wreck at Grand-Congloué in 1952, but it was not until 1960 that Honor Frost, George Bass, Joan Du Plat Taylor, and Peter Throckmorton led the first complete excavation of an ancient shipwreck on the seabed by archaeologists at Cape Gelidonya on the Anatolian coast of Turkey.

A key figure in nascent underwater archaeology in the United States at the same time was John M. Goggin, a professor at the University of Florida, founder of the Florida Anthropological Society, whose work had broad implications, not only in Florida and colonial-era historical archaeology, but also underwater archaeology. *Sports Illustrated* featured Goggin in July 1959, noting that the "43-year-old professor-turned-skin diver" had converted scuba diving into "[a] new academic discipline" with students as he led underwater expeditions into the Suwannee and Ichtucknee rivers. Goggin's article, "Underwater Archaeology: Its Nature and Limitations," published in *American Antiquity* in the January 1960 issue is a seminal piece of writing (Goggin 1960). Stressing that it was limited to shallow depths, noting early work in submerged springs, such as the Fig Springs Site in

A PERSONAL PERSPECTIVE

Figure 2. George Bass and Peter Throckmorton at Gelidonya. (Photo courtesy of the Institute of Nautical Archaeology 1960)

Florida starting in 1950, but also noting that "New World activity in this area cannot compare in volume or scope with the worked carried out in the Mediterranean," Goggin then addressed the fact that much of the focus and attention in "underwater archaeology" had been on "the diving techniques and the artifacts found rather than with the archaeological results" (Goggin 1960:348).

At that stage, Goggin hit the nail squarely on the head when it came to the salvaging and collecting origins of the field, whether done by Cousteau and his chief diver, Phillipe Diolé, or in his critical review of the salvage of the wreck of HMS *Looe* in the Florida Keys by Mendel Peterson of the Smithsonian, a project that troubled him because it had a "professional aura" because of the Smithsonian, but "an examination of their techniques reveals them to be unacceptable to professional archaeologists" (Goggin 1960:349). He also noted the work done by Stephan Borhegyi at Lake Amatitlán in Guatemala, reported on by Borhegyi in *Natural History* in 1958 as "Aqualung Archaeology," "although Borhegyi did not dive" (Goggin 1960:349). He roundly criticized Cousteau for the excesses of his divers and for playing jokes on the archaeologists who "observed" on the deck of Cousteau's ship, although "no criticism of the archaeologists for not being underwater is implied; many people simply cannot dive" (Goggin 1960:349). Another observation was that "probably most of what has been called "underwater archaeology" to date is really salvage" (Goggin 1960:353).

That being said, Goggin firmly asserted that underwater archaeology should be defined as "the recovery and interpretation of human remains of the past from underwater by *archaeologists*" (Goggin

1960:350, emphasis in original). The gauntlet then was thrown down; sites underwater "are just as significant as those on land and they should be handled by trained archaeologists, not by sport or professional divers" (Goggin 1960:350). Having stressed that there was no excuse to *not* do good archaeology underwater, a point which the excavators at Cape Gelidonya had also expressed and which George Bass would hammer home in his book *Archaeology under Water* (Bass 1966), Goggin laid out an initial, well-thought-out typology of underwater sites of all types, not just shipwrecks and cenotes.

At the dawn of the sport-diving era, modern treasure hunting, and underwater archaeology, a tension arose, not only in terms of how work was conducted and whether people got to take artifacts home, but also the question of diving competency. George Bass had never dived when selected by Rodney Young to represent and lead the excavation at Gelidonya for the University of Pennsylvania; he quickly started a diving class at the YMCA, but had only progressed through the classroom work when the time came to depart for Turkey. When he notified his instructor that he was about to dive to a site more than a 100 ft. deep and dig, the instructor quickly took him to the pool, showed him how to use his gear, and, as George later told me, told him to remember to not hold his breath.

When George got to Turkey, he found diving difficult and could not clear his ears, but Claude Duthuit, who was then a working salvage diver who joined the Gelidonya project, and later became a founding director of the Institute of Nautical Archaeology, took George on what was his first real dive. They started very shallow, and Claude slowly moved George along, finally stopping and showing him on the depth gauge that he had passed 30 ft. George was not alone, and I fully remember, as a brand-new NAUI-trained diver, going to my first project in California at Tennessee Cove in 1980 and horrifying seasoned wreck-diver Dave Buller, who was sure that I would die if he did not step in. A consistent complaint I heard for decades was that archaeologists did not know how to dive; but that was, in its own way, when not true, a means to push back against the disdain and dismissal directed at exceptionally qualified divers by archaeologists.

In the 1950s and 1960s a key figure known to all was John Huston of San Francisco; Mr. Huston was the founder of the Council on Underwater Archaeology; George Bass, Peter Throckmorton, and others I knew often spoke of him. It was to John Huston that Peter Throckmorton turned when he returned from Turkey to find support and an archaeologist to work with on Cape Gelidonya Wreck excavation. John Huston introduced him to Rodney Young at the University of Pennsylvania, and Dr. Young shouted for George Bass to come over and meet Peter. And, thus, history was made (Bass 1966:136, 1976:12).

A "retired businessman" who was a real-estate speculator in San Francisco, Mr. Huston's interest in underwater archaeology began in the 1950s and was to prove transformative, as it would be Mr. Huston's Advisory Council, formally created in 1959, that initially united the interested parties in the U.S.—divers, archaeologists, and historians—in creating a new discipline that moved past salvage and collecting to conducting archaeology underwater with the same standards as on land (Kennell 2019:54–56). The

late Anna Marguerite McCann always spoke warmly about John Huston, noting in her major scholarly monograph on the Roman port of Cosa that Mr. Huston "made a major contribution to this field by bringing together underwater archaeologists, scientists, and divers at a number of international conferences" (McCann et al. 1987:3).

While working tirelessly nationally and internationally, John Huston led what was probably the first professionally organized maritime archaeological project in California when he directed (and I believe partly sponsored) fieldwork at Drakes Bay in 1965 aided by a small grant from the National Park Service. The search for California's oldest known wreck was part of his interest in locating and studying that which lay close to home. *San Agustin* was then, as it would continue to be in the 21st century, an aspirational goal in the state's underwater archaeology. Bob Marx told me that John Huston had first discussed *San Agustin* with Adan Treganza and Paul Schumacher of the National Park Service in December 1953 when talking about doing a survey in Drakes Bay to find the galleon, and he followed up on it two years later, finding a pattern of anomalies that they all thought were shipwreck related.

This all fits with a fascinating note in an *Oakland Tribune* column on underwater archaeology in 1960 that asked readers:

> *If you discover something which you believe could be of archaeological or historical value while diving, get in touch with John Huston, secretary of the Council on Underwater Archeology at 41 Sutter St., San Francisco, BEFORE you remove anything. The council will keep your find confidential, but will assist you with*

information which will result in the proper recovery or recording of the objects discovered.

(Ferris 1960:40)

The column also pointed out that "there are a number of shipwrecks of historical significance off the California coast. Divers have also come across Indian metates, from 500 to 1,300 years old in waters near la Jolla" (Ferris 1960:40). The 41 Sutter Street address was where Mr. Huston kept his office, in a high-rise commercial building.

The first proceedings of a conference on underwater archaeology, held at the Minnesota Historical Society in St. Paul on 26–27 April 1963, were cosponsored by Huston's nonprofit Council on Underwater Archaeology with the Minnesota Historical Society; the proceedings open with a note about the council by Mr. Huston, noting it was founded as a clearinghouse, sponsor, and an educational organization, and was allied with the Archaeological Institute of America and the Underwater Society of America.

The council's leadership, as of 1964, was John Huston; George Bass, then working in Turkey as he concluded his Ph.D. studies; James B. Pritchard; Rodney S. Young (all from the University of Pennsylvania at that time); and Andreina Becker-Colonna, professor of Mediterranean Archaeology at San Francisco State College. Drs. Young and Pritchard were eminent East Coast archaeologists of the Far East; James Pritchard focused on the ancient Near East and Biblical archaeology and was notable for excavating the Phoenician city of Sarepta in Lebanon; and Dr. Young, a classical archaeologist and curator of the University Museum's

Mediterranean section, was famous for excavating Gordium, home of the fabled King Midas, founded the university's graduate program in Mediterranean archaeology, and was George Bass's advisor and mentor.

The triad of Young, Pritchard, and Bass reflected the growing sense that the Mediterranean would be where scientific underwater archaeology would flourish, as well as, I suspect, the sense that ancient and classical sites would dominate interest and gain wider support than more "modern" wrecks that were, at that time, within the sphere of interest of antiquarians and treasure hunters. Dr. Becker-Colonna, as another classical scholar, provided links to Egyptology, but, also, perhaps, as a San Franciscan, may have had a link to or sponsorship from the San Francisco–based John Huston.

Dr. Becker-Colonna cofounded the classics department at San Francisco State with Richard Trapp in 1965–1966. One of her other major achievements was acquiring and moving the Adolph Sutro Egyptian Collection out of the soon-to-be-closed Sutro Baths at Lands End (San Francisco) just before the building burned down in 1966. When I transferred to San Francisco State in 1978, Dr. Becker-Colonna had been a professor emerita for three years; her primary work was Egypt, but archaeology and mentoring were very important to her, and her influence on the department was still significant. I never had a chance to speak to Dr. Becker-Colonna and learn how she became engaged with underwater archaeology, but suspect it came through a passion for archaeology and advancing the cause, as she had done in saving a significant local collection for the university. I would be remiss if I did not note that she translated and offered

A PERSONAL PERSPECTIVE

—Examiner Photo by Frant Ortiz.

MRS. ANDREINA BECKER-COLONNA
. . . finding windows on the past

Figure 3. Andreina Becker-Colonna, as featured in the *San Francisco Examiner*, on 15 March 1964. (Photo by Fran Ortiz)

commentary on the ancient Egyptian manuscript, the "Story of the Shipwrecked Sailor," from the 11th or 12th Dynasty of the Middle Kingdom (Becker-Colonna 1968).

At this stage, I note how fascinating it is that interest in underwater archaeology by California archaeologists was not widespread, and it did not seem to have made much of an impact at the University of California or Stanford despite early interaction with shoreside remains from the wrecked Manila galleon *San Agustin*. *San Agustin* is the oldest known European shipwreck on the Pacific Coast of North America (Wagner 1924; Sanchez 2001), and it also played a central role in some of the earliest efforts to conduct underwater

archaeology in California. It also was the setting for the first major battle over "treasure" from a shipwreck in California.

In the 1940s, Robert F. Heizer of the University of California excavated burials from the local Coast Miwok tribes and, in burials and habitation contexts, found material from the wreck, including glass made into projectile points, ceramic "bead blanks," and iron ship fasteners. That work was followed by additional excavations at sites in and around Drakes Bay in the 1950s and 1960s by University of California Los Angeles pioneering archaeologist Clement Meighan and then, Adán Treganza and, then, Thomas F. King and W. F. Upson (Meighan 1950, 2002; Meighan and Heizer 1952; Treganza 1959; Treganza and King 1968; King and Upson 1970). Adán Treganza, who joined the faculty of San Francisco State College in 1947, founded its Department of Anthropology in 1948/1949, and was instrumental in the growth of the future cultural-resource-management (CRM) "salvage archaeology" in the face of ongoing development in California. He also founded the college's anthropology museum, which now bears his name. Dr. Treganza's contributions to California's prehistoric and historic-period archaeology were immense (Hohenthal 1969:463). I suspect he might have been more active in the first stirrings of underwater archaeological interest in the mid-1960s, but for the fact that he was in poor health with heart problems and died of a coronary in September 1968.

When I attended San Francisco State and balanced my two competing interests of study, finally crossing the threshold to earn a B.A. in history, I was a regular in the anthropology department, taking classes from Gary Pahl, Rodger Heglar, and Marley Brown, and saw my first shipwreck

Figure 4. Scrapbook of images from Robert Heizer's 1941 excavations at Drakes Bay, "Marin County Site Binder." University of California Archaeological Survey, University of California, Berkeley. (Images courtesy of the Regents of the University of California, Phoebe A. Hearst Museum of Anthropology, UC Berkeley)

A PERSONAL PERSPECTIVE

artifacts there in the form of fragment of *San Agustin* porcelain from Dr. Treganza's excavations. Any accounting of early maritime archaeology in California needs to acknowledge the land-based work that documented the cultural contact and impact of the wreck as excavated and studied by those archaeological pioneers. I am not appropriating them as "maritime archaeologists," but acknowledging that, in addition to the galleon itself, *San Agustin*'s presence in the middens of Drakes Bay can now be seen within the larger context of maritime archaeological theory, including maritime cultural landscapes as well as world systems.

As long as I am "appropriating" older scholars as posthumous maritime archaeologists, it would be remiss not to note that, in addition to his 1941 work at Drakes Bay encountering *San Agustin* artifacts, Robert F. Heizer's other maritime connection was his analysis of the presumed gravestone of Spanish maritime explorer Juan Rodriguez Cabrillo, who died on Spain's initial voyage of maritime exploration of the California coast in 1543 (Heizer 1972). In 1972, Dr. Heizer published an account of his analysis of the marker, a sandstone slab excavated by Phillip Mills Jones on Santa Rosa Island in 1901 and first studied in 1956 by Heizer with Albert Elsasser at the Lowie Museum of Anthropology at UC Berkeley (another repository for *San Agustin* artifacts from Heizer's excavations). Dr. Heizer was careful to present his findings and not argue for what the stone might represent; his title, "California's Oldest Historical Relic?" purposely ends with a question mark. But, as a "maritime" subject I view through a maritime cultural landscape perspective, Robert Heizer's work on that stone was another early example of what

we now would call maritime (not underwater, marine, or nautical) archaeology.

Drakes Bay is also the setting for ongoing debate on whether it was the landing site of Francis Drake's *Golden Hinde* in 1579. Without getting into the debate, archaeological work by the Drake Navigators Guild, notably by historian Raymond Aker and archaeologist Edward Von der Porten, were early projects, as was work by retired National Park Service western region historian and state historian for the California State Parks System's Division of Beaches and Parks, V. Aubrey Neasham, who argued for a site he was excavating at Bolinas (Von der Porten 1968, 1972; Aker et al. 1974; Shangraw and Von der Porten 1981). While, again, a series of proposed "land sites," the context for the Drake landing site of 1579 is undeniably maritime, albeit again not underwater.

I was regularly entangled in the Drake issue many times in my own National Park Service (NPS) career from 1978 to 1991, as I was based in San Francisco, successively as the assistant regional historian, as the park historian for the Golden Gate National Recreation Area (GGNRA), and finally as the maritime historian of the NPS. I knew these three men very well, valued their mentoring and friendship, and, not only respected Aubrey Neasham, but also knew his wife Irene, who ran the Wells Fargo Bank History Room. In later years I also ended up consulting on and looking at evidence for a British Columbia Drake landing by Samuel Bawlf, and an Oregon landing by Melissa Darby, and have consistently stayed out of the argument. I never told any of these senior colleagues that, like at least 50,000 other people, maybe more, I am a nondirect descendant of Francis's brother Thomas Drake, who was on that voyage and landed somewhere on the Pacific Coast of North America in 1579 before heading home to start a vast extended family that, 17 generations later, I would join.

Back to the 1960s: the conference proceedings from that first meeting on underwater archaeology at the Minnesota Historical Society in St. Paul in April 1963 include a variety of papers from early pioneers. Goggin was to have been there, but he tragically died of cancer the year before. Among the attendees was Stephan Borhegyi; another was my former boss, NPS chief historian Edwin C. Bearss, who spoke about the recovery of USS *Cairo*; George Bass; Donald Jewell on "limnoarchaeology in California"; Mendel Peterson; Andres Franzen; and Ole Crumlin-Pederson. Don Jewell was a California archaeologist, and his paper was on what today we call inundation studies, as he spoke about sites flooded by reservoir construction. His 1961 paper on "fresh-water archaeology" was a pioneering effort; he also did work on sites such as those associated with Oroville Dam Spillway, and he was another pioneer I had the privilege to meet and talk with in later years.

At that stage, "underwater archaeology" was growing at an exponential pace in the Mediterranean, in the Baltic, in various parts of Europe, and in the United States. It remained a mix of salvage, treasure hunting, and actual archaeology through the 1970s and into the 1980s, when the first symbolic "casting out of heretics" took place at the Society for Historical Archaeology conference at Reno in 1988. California efforts stalled after 1966, however, largely because John Huston died. With him went the impetus and, I suspect, the core funding for the first Council on Underwater Archaeology. The council, headed by Mr. Huston, organized the first

conference on underwater archaeology in Toronto at the Royal Ontario Museum in 1965, followed by the third conference, held in Miami in 1967 and sponsored by the University of Miami.

After a brief illness, John Huston died in March 1968 at age 54, leaving his wife Patricia and three small children, Jenny, Katina, and Reece. While he is remembered as a "retired businessman" by some, he "divided his time in recent years between his real estate investment and management business and in research, exploration and recovery of ancient under water artifacts" (*Sunday Examiner and Chronicle* 1968). His obituary noted how key he was in the establishment of underwater archaeology overall; the key point I took away from this was that, at the start, a Californian and what some would call an "amateur" archaeologist had been one of the now forgotten creators of the field well beyond the society and conferences.

He led an excavation party off Minturno, Italy, in 1966 and 1967, and also joined in a survey off New Corinth, Greece, with the University of Chicago in 1966. Among other studies conducted by the council, an affiliate of the American Institute of Archaeology, was a survey of classical underwater sites in the western Peloponnesus. It was also cosponsor of the team that made an excavation of a Bronze Age ship off Izmir, Turkey (*Sunday Examiner and Chronicle* 1968).

The obituary also noted that Mr. Huston "owned a rare collection of classical and renaissance antiquities" (*Sunday Examiner and Chronicle* 1968). In reading this, what struck me as a one-time president of George Bass's Institute of Nautical Archaeology (INA) was how much Mr. Huston fit the profile of a number of dedicated, passionate, and archaeology-focused

A PERSONAL PERSPECTIVE

trustees of INA, some of them formerly collectors, who not only sponsored field-work, but conservation, laboratory analysis, publication, and INA's infrastructure, and, seeing John Huston as a sponsor for Gelidonya, I suspect he may have helped inspire George's vision for INA when he founded it in 1972.

In 1969, an early National Park Service report on underwater archaeology noted that

> [t]he Council of Underwater Archaeology in San Francisco has been active in coordinating activities in the field, and has also conducted investigations for the Service at Point Reyes National Seashore. Since the death of the Council's President, John Huston, the organization has become inactive and it is not presently known whether it will again have a significant influence.

(Fisher and Riggs 1969:14)

It was not until 1973, at a Society for Historical Archaeology meeting, that a new Advisory Council on Underwater Archaeology was formed out of an informal gathering of conference attendees who worked on or were interested in underwater sites, and, after that, subsequent SHA/ACUA meetings have been held every year (Marx 1978).

The San Francisco Maritime Museum

While underwater archaeology went into a quiet hiatus in California in the late 1960s to the late 1970s, what I see as the origins of California maritime archaeology emerged at the San Francisco Maritime Museum through the drive and initiative of founder Karl Kortum and the research of Albert Harmon and Harlan Soeten, the museum's librarian and the museum's curator, respectively. The origins of the museum in 1941 were traditional, with a displayed collection of art, relics, and models in the San Francisco Museum of Science and Industry. Freshly returned from sea on the bark *Kaiulani*, the Petaluma, California-born Karl Kortum, able-bodied seaman and maritime history enthusiast, contacted the sponsor, Alma de Bretteville Spreckels, in 1948. Kortum was a firm believer that the concept of a maritime museum as a place where historic ships, on display and open to the public following the model of Mystic Seaport, would be of greater interest to the public and a more viable business model. With Mrs. Spreckels's initial sponsorship and ongoing support, Kortum began to build a coalition, and, in January 1950, they formed the San Francisco Maritime Museum Association. On 27 May 1951 they opened the San Francisco Maritime Museum in the Aquatic Park building on San Francisco's northern waterfront.

Like many other maritime museums being opened around the country, the San Francisco Maritime Museum built up a collection that included artwork; wheels, bells, and fittings from ships; ship models; and iconic relics, such as the figurehead from the clipper *David Crockett*. Kortum, however, had other goals, which included saving and displaying historic ships and entire sections and working gear from vessels that could not be saved in their

Figure 5. Karl Kortum, Gordon Fountain, and Gordon Riehl aboard *C. A. Thayer*, 1957. (Photo courtesy of San Francisco Maritime National Historical Park, SAFR 21374, P93-065, Series 1, File Unit 9, Item A09.38795)

entirety, a concept pioneered in the 1930s at the Stockholm Maritime Museum in Sweden (Throckmorton 1987:212). While models and paintings made up part of the new museum, what Kortum sought and fought to acquire was the "real thing," which ranged from floating historic ships to sections of and equipment from ships that lay abandoned, hulked, or rotting away on mudflats. The San Francisco Maritime Museum's collection thus began to grow, as windlasses, sections of masts and yards, and even entire portions of vessels were rescued from hulks on mudflats and from ships nearing the ends of their lives.

Because Karl was a photographer as well as a nascent oral historian, the museum's collections include large-format black-and-white negatives of old sailing ships at the ends of their lives, some alone, others in ship graveyards. The hulk of the wooden barkentine *Galilee*, beached on the foreshore of Richardson Bay off Sausalito, riddled with dry rot and slowly collapsing, was one of these vessels. The last visible remnant of the prodigious work of Pacific-coast shipbuilder Matthew Turner, *Galilee* had been beached as a houseboat and, by the late 1950s, was about to collapse. Harlan Soeten and a team from the museum documented the remains and then cut free the stern and took it to the museum to preserve it; they did the same with the stern of the wooden-hulled scow schooner *Charles W.*

They were not archaeologists, and their standards of documentation were different from those of several decades later. But they made a major contribution to saving the last tangible physical remains of ships. They saved not only figureheads and ship's bells, but items like a sternwheel from a steamboat, the pumps from a large sailing ship, and the entire mechanism from a waterfront ropewalk that manufactured rigging and hawses. They collected from buildings about to be torn down and from ships nearing their ends of days as hulks

26

Figure 6. Left to right: Lou Goldblatt, Piero Patri, and Harlan Soeten standing on remnants of *Galilee's* deck. Harlan Soeten (San Francisco Maritime Museum curator), Lou Goldblatt (ILWU executive and San Francisco Maritime Museum board member), and Piero Patri (San Francisco architect). (Photo courtesy of San Francisco Maritime National Historical Park, SAFR 21374, P93-065, Series 2, File Unit 8, Item B08.23185.10.)

as far north as a breakwater made out of hulks at Royston, British Columbia. Their approach was revolutionary and inspired maritime museums and ship preservationists around the world.

The museum's approach excited visitors, but had less appeal to more genteel supporters of the painting-and-ship-model school of maritime museums. Among these was Alma Spreckels. Kortum, the museum's staff, and their supporters pushed for a more realistic depiction of

the maritime world in all its aspects, particularly in the saving, not only of pieces of ships, but also of historic ships themselves. The drive to acquire, restore, and preserve the three-masted, steel-hulled ship *Balclutha* was their first success.

Purchased in 1954 by the museum association, *Balclutha* was then known as *Pacific Queen* and was near the end of its days, displayed as a "pirate ship." Volunteers, largely led by veteran rigger Jack Dickerhoff, brought the ship back to its

Figure 7. Restoration crew onboard *Balclutha*, ca. 1955. Left to right: Harry Dring, Al Hatt, Jack Shickell, Karl Kortum, Jack Dickerhoff, Bill Bartz. and "Chick." (Photo courtesy of San Francisco Maritime National Historical Park, SAFR 21374, P93-065, Series 1, File Unit 9, Item A09.16127)

earliest days as the full-rigged *Balclutha*. The ship opened to the public at Pier 41 near Fisherman's Wharf in 1955, part of a growing national movement, inspired by Kortum and allies like Peter Stanford, founder of the South Street Seaport Museum in Manhattan, to save the world's last historic ships before they disappeared. Inside the ship the San Francisco Maritime Museum staff placed a variety of exhibits about maritime history, *Balclutha*, and the type of ships and trades it represented.

Kortum in San Francisco and Stanford in New York were joined in their work by women who cared and worked, including their wives, Jean Kortum and Norma Stanford; and men, including Dickerhoff, who also rigged and helped save the historic ships *Star of India* in San Diego and *Falls of Clyde* in Honolulu; and Harrison "Harry" Dring in San Francisco. Another ally was pioneering marine archaeologist Peter Throckmorton, who worked with the museums as well as others to rescue all or part of historic ships that lay more or less preserved on mudflats or in the near-Antarctic conditions of the Straits of Magellan and the Falkland Islands. Among those initiatives was the successful recovery of a portion of the downeaster *St. Mary* from the Falklands in 1978–1981 and the bow of the clipper ship *Snow Squall*, also from the Falklands, in 1987 (Throckmorton 1987:212). Not all of these endeavors were successful; efforts to save the Falkland hulks *Champigny*, *Charles Cooper*,

A PERSONAL PERSPECTIVE

and *Vicar of Bray* in time faltered. However, a trend had been set and was being followed, both in the United States and also internationally.

The next major push for Kortum and the museum was to create a collection of historic ships that would have worked and been dockside in San Francisco at the end of the 19th century. Lobbying the State of California with support from industry, philanthropists, and the editorial backing of the *San Francisco Chronicle*, which had been a proponent of the museum since its beginning, they achieved success when a bill was passed by the California State Legislature that called for the purchase of the three-masted, wooden-hulled schooner *C. A. Thayer* and the wooden-hulled steamer *Wapama*, and also created the San Francisco Maritime State Historic Park. The wooden-hulled steam ferry *Eureka* and scow schooner *Alma* were acquired (1958–1959), and, in 1960, the state public-works board approved the expenditure of $75,000 for the creation of an authentic Victorian park. San Francisco Maritime State Historic Park opened close to the museum at nearby Hyde Street Pier in 1963. Within the next years, the steel-hulled screw tug *Hercules* was saved, restored, and put on display.

I cannot emphasize enough what this work in California did, even if it was not maritime archaeology, to greatly benefit the cause of maritime archaeology. I will start by acknowledging that some colleagues can look back and criticize the stripping of fittings and structure from hulks in ship graveyards; it was with some interest that I assisted the documentation of one of those hulks, the largely collapsed remains of the 1876 iron-hulled, three-masted ship *Melanope* in the graveyard/breakwater made up of half-sunk hulks

at Royston, decades after the San Francisco Maritime Museum had salvaged fittings from it (R. James 2004:14–19). The recovery of the equipment in the 1950s essentially saved the artifact, preserving details that otherwise might have been lost or discerned only through extensive conservation, and, one can argue, the process of maritime preservation as Kortum and colleagues practiced it seven decades ago, while no longer followed, is in and of itself now historical and part of an ongoing process of anthropogenic impacts. In the case of what the museum saved, it did not recover and then sell what they did save from scrap. The artifacts were placed on display and interpreted, as were the entire ships they saved. Perhaps, not ironically, but to the point, another of the Royston hulks, the 1894-built, three-masted steel ship *Riversdale* was stripped of 14 tons of fittings, "including the bollards, fairleads, windlass, and capstan" in 1970 to restore the 1885-built ship *Wavertree* at New York's South Street Seaport, where *Wavertree*, a National Register–listed ship, remains, in 2021, on display afloat on the East River (R. James 2004:46).

At the very end of *Galilee*'s "life" the hulk had deteriorated to just the top of the bow, attached to a worm-eaten stem about to fall. I was then, in 1986, working on an archaeological project to document and list the shipyard where *Galilee* had been built, then a forgotten archaeological site in Benicia, California. As part of that project, working with the Benicia city historian, local politicians, the local museum in Benicia, and a philanthropic marine-salvage operator of the old school—known affectionately to the historian as the "pirate"—named Joe Garzke, we cut free the bow after slinging it to a crane of Garzke's barge and took it back to Benicia, where it is now displayed at the city's historical museum. I stand by that decision to this day. It was the right thing to do and far superior to making detailed drawings of a collapsed bow structure on a mudflat as an archaeologist. It is preserved in a museum and accessible as both physical data and as a teaching tool, while the site of the beached *Galilee*, subsequently redeveloped, with nothing done to mitigate the impact to the site except avoidance as a new marina was put in, leaves an empty patch in that marina, now turned to marsh, with no evidence of the buried lower hull of *Galilee* nor any interpretation at the site.

I put it plainly that way because of what the San Francisco Maritime Museum, now San Francisco Maritime National Historical Park, represents in the maritime world and, specifically, for maritime archaeology. In addition to archives, books, and small artifacts, the larger artifacts, including the historic ships, were an invaluable, tangible teaching resource for me as a young maritime archaeologist. My early work benefited powerfully from my knowing those ships and their construction; from wood to iron and steel, from sail to 19th-century steam engines, and all the nuances of fittings, fasteners, gear, and equipment, when I was working on the ships as a NPS ranger and interpreter, and, subsequently, as the park's historian, my hands-on, three-dimensional understanding of them translated into my work as a maritime archaeologist.

Those experiences in 1978–1979, as the ships were regularly maintained and restored by expert shipwrights and riggers, were more valuable to me in time than much of my classroom learning. I was there to see the ships not as dead hulks, but as actively used displays and interpretive platforms. I sailed on *Alma*, steamed on *Hercules*, helped run overnight school programs on *C. A. Thayer* where we stood watch, stowed cargo, cooked in the ship's galley, taught celestial navigation, and lowered a ship's boat with elementary school students. I saw firsthand as seams were caulked, lines spliced, standing rigging tarred, and planks were replaced by the riggers and shipwrights. I also spent many long hours, arriving to work hours early, and I remember many gray mornings, as the foghorns moaned and cold water dripped from the rigging, while I sat with a mug of thick, hot black coffee in the wheelhouse of *Eureka* by Harry Dring's desk (the inshore wheelhouse was his office), as he mentored me because he saw and supported my keen interest to learn.

As my career advanced and I worked on shipwreck sites, first in my own park, the Golden Gate National Recreation Area, and then in others—Channel Islands National Park, Cape Hatteras National Seashore, Cape Cod National Seashore, Fort Jefferson National Park (now Dry Tortugas National Park)—my understanding of what I was seeing on the bottom, even in fragments, was tremendously assisted by the time with those ships. On a hard-hat dive to the wreck of the four-masted steel-bark *Goldenhorn* off the Channel Islands, I catalogued the wreckage as Larry Murphy swam along filming it.

I did the same with the Windjammer site, the ship *Avanti*, in the Dry Tortugas and, seeing extensive damage to the windlass and no chain in the locker, pointed out how the wreck had come after the anchors were dragged and lost and the windlass torn out, pulling out the chain. The crew, at the last, just before the wreck, had taken its last anchor and a short section of chain (that I found stretched tight with the

A PERSONAL PERSPECTIVE

Figure 8. NOAA R/V *Fulmar* during the Greater Farallones National Marine Sanctuaries three-year mission at the wreck site of *USS Conestoga* off the Farallones. (Photo courtesy of NOAA/Robert Schwemmer, 2013)

anchor dug deep into the coral) as the ship hit the reef and broke into three pieces. I knew what to look for and had an intuitive sense of what had happened because of my experiences and hands-on learning at the museum.

Decades later, while at NOAA, I was on the R/V *Fulmar*, with a team that included West Coast maritime heritage coordinator Bob Schwemmer, conducting a maritime archaeological survey off the Farallones. We had deployed a remotely operated vehicle (ROV) in those shark-infested waters, dropped 180 ft., and were approaching a sonar target that represented a hitherto uncharted, unexplored wreck with a strong outline that indicated it was metal-hulled. As the ROV approached the wreck, Bob asked: "What kind of bow is that?" As the ROV maneuvered around, I blurted out: "It's a tugboat." I asked the operator to run the ROV aft, and, while the superstructure was gone, saw the

exposed triple-expansion steam engine in the hold, and, on the aft deck, the tow winch. As I looked, I told the team: "This is early 20th century at the latest, at least in terms of when it was built." I got a few looks of "sure ...," and then we continued on the survey.

At the end of the survey and on our last day, I took the team for a drive from Sausalito, where we docked *Fulmar* and went to the maritime museum and the historic ships. I had called ahead and asked them if they could open up *Hercules*, then closed to the public, for me to take our team on a tour. As we walked up the pier and approached the bow of *Hercules*, Bob turned around and looked at me. I smiled and said: "I walked by that bow for years." As we toured *Hercules*, the layout and equipment of that perfectly preserved 1907 steam tug were a very close match to what we had all just seen in 180 ft. of water, corroded and covered with marine

Figure 9. The steam tug *Hercules* towing the five-masted schooner *W. J. Pirrie*. (Photo courtesy of San Francisco Maritime National Historical Park, SAFR 21374, P93-065, Series 10, File Unit 3, Item J05.28407, c. 1910)

Figure 10. On the wreck site of *USS Conestoga* with family members, NOAA crew and the U.S. Navy. (Photo courtesy of NOAA/Paul Chetirkin, 2014)vv

A PERSONAL PERSPECTIVE

life. Bob Schwemmer took it all in, especially the layout. Taking the ROV footage, including some from a GoPro strapped to the bottom of the ROV, and with a tangible sense of scale, he went through it all and found a series of matches to the plans of a tug supposedly lost thousands of miles away, the 1904-built, steel-hulled tugboat USS *Conestoga*, which went missing after steaming out of the Golden Gate in March 1921.

A follow up mission confirmed the identity, especially when Bob spotted the tug's very diagnostic armament and we were able to make out a few of the letters not obscured on the fantail that spelled out part of the tug's name (Delgado, et al. 2020). It solved one of the great mysteries of U.S. Navy ships that disappeared with all hands and brought closure to families who still felt the loss and the pain that had rippled forward through generations. Once again, the pioneering efforts of the San Francisco Maritime Museum's founders had proved a benefit to maritime archaeology.

It also reinforced the career-transformative power of the opportunity that came to me as a young historian and archaeologist to transition from the park to the Washington office to launch and head the NPS Maritime Heritage Program, then known as the National Maritime Initiative. For four years, a nationwide tour, to every state, with detailed inspections of over 300 historic ships, hundreds of lighthouses, life-saving stations, waterfront communities, museums, and archaeological shipwreck projects with the Submerged Resources Center gave me an intensive education that came from being out there and seeing so many ships and sites. After my NPS years, taking the same approach in Canada and then around the world did more than offer the broadening of the mind that comes with travel.

It is just as important as staying up to date with the literature in the field, and, most recently, at the end of 2020 I was working on another project, in the field, documenting the wooden structure of a Civil War ironclad in close detail as we dismantled it in preparation for conservation. While guided by a sense of what I had seen in years past with other wooden vessels, including the restoration and rebuilding of several, the fantail of the CSS *Jackson* was another in-depth, pardon the pun, course in maritime technology and naval architecture as illuminated by an archaeological approach.

Back to San Francisco and the museum: the museum's leadership was never engaged in underwater archaeology, and I heard from many divers that Karl Kortum had little to no time for them and few artifacts recovered from early wreck dives made it into the museum's collections. Karl was fascinated by the history, and the museum gathered huge files on shipwrecks, complete with a collection of shipwreck images unrivaled on the coast. One of my prized possessions is an offprint from an illustrated publication Karl did with historian Roger Olmsted, at that time a curator at the maritime museum. "... *It Is a Dangerous Looking Place*" told the story of sailing on the Redwood Coast north of San Francisco, and the image of a dismasted schooner washed up against the rocks, half flooded and breaking apart, is powerful (Kortum and Olmsted 1971). But ask Karl if he wanted to look for that wreck site and document it? No.

The museum's intersection with maritime archaeology came from finds on land, similar in a way to how the visible hulks and laid-up ships in backwaters and on mudflats had filled out the collections of the nascent museum. I have previously called this "urban archaeology's intersection with maritime archaeology" (Delgado 2009:23). The maritime aspects of the California Gold Rush were a major interest of the museum's staff, and that interest was spurred by the fact that the former waterfront of San Francisco, dating from 1849 to the mid-1850s, had been filled in, burying ships and waterfront infrastructure. This phenomenon is not unique; many major waterfront cities have similar archaeological sites ranging from antiquity to the industrial era, notably buried ships with, at times, exceptional levels of preservation (Delgado 2011). Early finds and excavations of these sites, especially in London, are early and significant events in the history of nautical archaeology, as were the late 19th – and 20th-century excavations of ships used as sepulchers for Viking and Saxon royalty, such as the Gokstad, Oserberg, Tune, and Sutton Hoo ships. The museum's librarian, Al Harmon, gathered accounts of the Gold Rush waterfront and with curator Harlan Soeten and Karl Kortum compiled a detailed, magnificent large-format scrapbook on the buried Gold Rush fleet that included, based on their research, a map showing the location of those sites superimposed on modern streets (Harmon et al. 1963).

With the potential for as many as 40 ships still lying beneath downtown, the map was a powerful interpretive tool in the museum's displays. More important,

it was the first comprehensive effort to identify the probable locations of what we now know to be a major archaeological site composed of the partially burned and buried waterfront devastated by fire in May 1851 and quickly filled over in anaerobic conditions, as well as subsequent deposits and ships overtaken by the rapid pace of landfilling from 1851 to 1855. The 1963 map served as the basis of subsequent maps, including a more accurate and detailed one done by the San Francisco Maritime National Historic Park staff in an effort led by then-curator of exhibits Richard Everett that takes into account discoveries and archaeology done since 1963. The City and County of San Francisco also created a GIS database that incorporates the buried ships as part of a comprehensive record of all San Francisco archaeological sites and sensitivity zones. Like the early map, the GIS is a tool for predicting possible exposures of sites (Delgado 2009:120).

The maritime museum's staff, especially Harlan Soeten, often found itself being called when construction "hit something." This included finds made with the Golden Gateway and Embarcadero Center developments, which began in 1965; the subsequent tunneling through downtown for the Bay Area Rapid Transit system; as well as the San Francisco Municipal Railway through the mid-1970s. The museum team was almost always beaten to the scene by the local bottle-hunting community, but what Harlan and Karl sought, in addition to smaller artifacts, were anchors and large wooden pieces of Gold Rush ships spurned by the collectors. Cleaned of mud and dried out, these pieces were displayed in a new gallery constructed by Harlan and

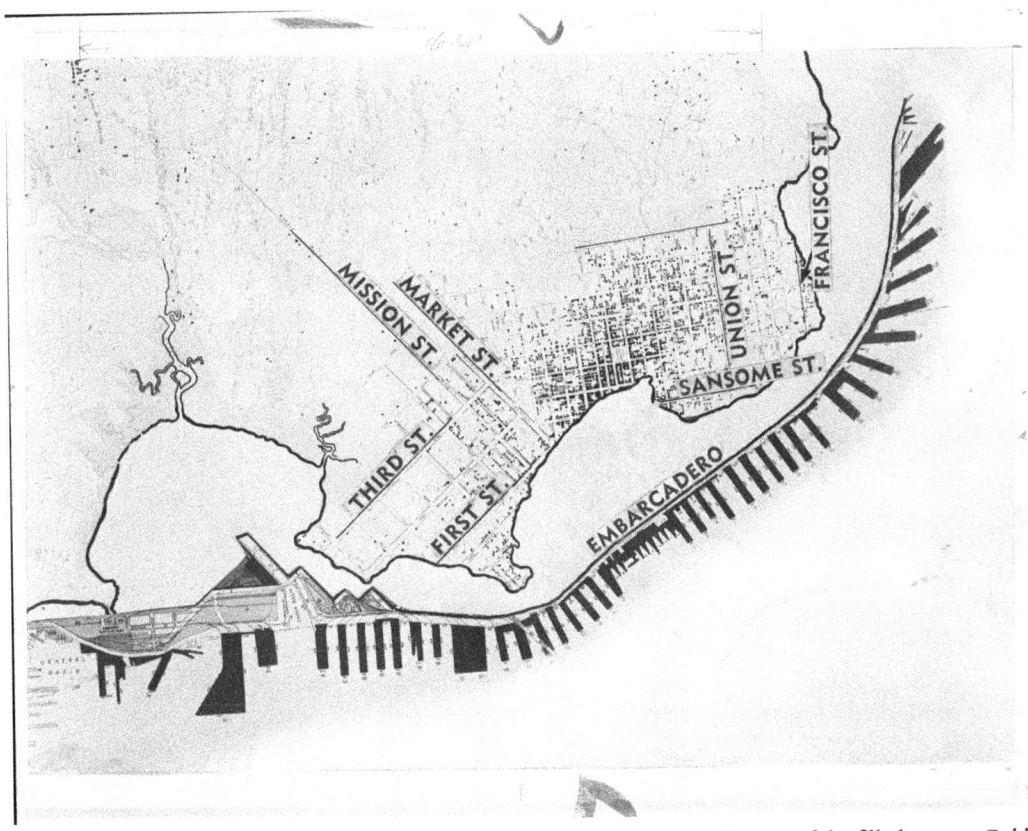

Figure 11. This 1957 map, created by the San Francisco Chronicle, shows the area of the filled-in pre–Gold Rush waterfront. (Photo courtesy of San Francisco Maritime National Historical Park, SAFR 21374, P93-065, Series 1, File Unit 11, Item A11.15005)

team in the 1960s that used the artifacts as an exciting means to connect visitors to the beginnings of San Francisco as a world port (Delgado 2009:120–121). It was a powerful influence on me as well as others who would walk downtown, map in hand, and picture a near-intact hulk two stories below the sidewalk. At the same time, the museum called for greater awareness and advocated for archaeology.

The first *maritime* archaeological excavation in California came thanks to the maritime museum's advocacy and response to a major discovery at Clay and Sansome streets in May 1978. One of the ships on the museum's map, *Niantic*, was known to have been situated on the shore of the now-buried Yerba Buena Cove in July 1849, had burned in 1851, and was subsequently encountered in construction at the site in 1872 and 1907. It was not certain that remains of *Niantic* would be encountered during a new high-rise project at the site in 1978, and the laws at that stage were inadequate to respond if that did happen. The excavation of the site reached down over 20 ft. and exposed the bottom of the hull, with an area near the bow still laden with goods stored in it during the Gold Rush. Through the good graces of the project developer, J. Patrick Mahoney, the maritime museum was invited to do an emergency excavation that was overseen by staff member Isabel Bullen, who had had archaeological training (Bullen 1979).

The emergency nature of the find and the fact that the ship had to be removed

Figure 12. The stem and knee of the head from a Gold Rush hulk, recovered from the Embarcadero Center construction site in 1973 and being lifted into position for display at the San Francisco Maritime Museum. (Photo courtesy of the San Francisco Maritime National Historical Park, SAFR 21374, P93-065, Series 1, File Unit 10, Item A10.30392, c. 1974)

Figure 13. Allen Pastron, Roger Olmsted, and Harlan Soeten at the *Lydia* site, 1978. (Photo Courtesy of the National Park Service, 1980)

A PERSONAL PERSPECTIVE

for construction to continue brought in support from the National Trust for Historic Preservation and the NPS. Mr. Mahoney's company paid to remove a cross-section of the hull and the stern for the museum, and those major pieces, along with the windlass, were donated to the museum along with all of the artifacts from the excavation (less those things that were disappeared at night by the bottle collectors). *Niantic's* unplanned find, as noted, resulted in the first full-scale maritime archaeological excavation, albeit on land. The maritime museum at that stage was about to become part of the GGNRA, and so, in addition to support from the NPS conservation laboratory at Harper's Ferry, the emergency excavation had an onsite visit by Fonda Thompson of the DeSoto Wildlife Refuge, home of the recently completed salvage excavation of the river steamer *Bertrand* from a field that had been, at one time, the river channel.

Coming quickly after that, as a brand-new employee whose archaeological experience of the past several years had been a mix of prehistoric and Spanish/Mexican colonial sites, I was assigned by the NPS to prepare a nomination of the site to the National Register of Historic Places. As part of that, I assisted in the initial cataloguing and assessment of the *Niantic* assemblage. That's how I came to be involved in maritime archaeology. The National Trust funded a more complete study of the assemblage by graduate student Mary Hilderman Smith (1981). The stern is now stabilized and displayed at the visitor center for San Francisco Maritime National Historical Park along with selected artifacts; the others are in museum storage at the park.

The city and county stepped up laws and regulations, especially as, within a month, work on a new waterfront sewer project trenched through another mid-19th-century ship buried at the foot of King Street. Ultimately determined to be the whaler *Lydia*, abandoned at the site and filled over around 1907, through detailed research by Roger and Nancy Olmsted (Roger was no longer with the museum and, with his wife, another highly qualified and capable historian, had started consulting) and Ray Aker of the Drake Navigators Guild, the double whammy of two buried ships being hit had a dramatic effect. I was again called out with NPS regional archaeologist Roger Kelly and my boss, regional historian Gordon Chappell, and watched as the team cleared the exposed remains; like *Niantic*, the very nature of the find was so exciting that my archaeological interests were starting to shift, not only to maritime, but also Gold Rush archaeology.

The Olmsteds and Ray Aker were consultants to archaeologist Allen Pastron, whose firm, Archeo-Tec, took the lead on San Francisco's historical archaeology CRM projects for the next three decades. Much of that was Gold Rush–related, and it included buried ships as well as collapsed structures on the 1851 waterfront. In late 1979, augur testing at the site of a new waterfront development known as Levi's Plaza struck what appeared to be another buried ship. That led to a February 1980 text excavation that came straight down onto the forecastle deck of the intact vessel. The bulwarks were in place, still rigged with iron chainplates. I was invited by the Olmsteds and Archeo-Tec's Pastron to participate, and the experience of being at the bottom of the test unit, gently scraping away thick blue-black mud to reveal solid deck planks and the coaming of the hatch

Figure 14. Roger Olmsted excavating alongside the bulwarks of *William Gray* at Levis Plaza. (Photo by James Delgado, 1980)

A PERSONAL PERSPECTIVE

that led into the forecastle made up my mind to pursue matters maritime.

Work by Roger, Nancy, and Ray determined that the hulk was likely the small ship *William Gray*, a Gold Rush arrival turned into a floating storeship, like *Niantic*, and subsequently converted into a rock-filled landing stage for the warehouse of Frederick Griffing, which was built on landfill next to the ship; the landfill, in short order, swallowed "Griffings Wharf," which lay over the hulk, and when we excavated it in 1980 it sat more than 10 ft. below the street level. A few years later, while researching another project, I found a very rare document—a hand-drawn map of the area depicting the various hulked vessels around the wharf, including *William Gray*, that helped cinch the identification. I also used the map to nominate that site to the National Register. Karl Kortum

Figure 15. Media-release photo from the press kit from the Hoff's Store excavation showing Allen Pastron with artifacts from the site. (Photo by Jerre Kosta, Archeo-Tec, 1986)

was advocating complete excavation and the displaying of the ship, but his public statements and lobbying angered Levi's officials, on whose property we were working, and so the work was stopped short, and they built a large fountain there that still stands on the site, sealing the tomb of *William Gray*.

These three buried ships, all the subject of excavations in 1978–1980, were the first of a handful of maritime archaeological excavations that would follow in the decades to come. The focus was nautical more than maritime; the history and the characteristics of the ships and their role in the Gold Rush were the focus. That was fascinating, and, decades later, I was able to work with a descendant of *William Gray*'s owner as he wrote his biography of the ship (Hill 2016). Far more significant than the individual sites, Archeo-Tec, especially in the working relationship with the Olmsteds, added substantially to the archaeology of San Francisco's emergence as a city, as a port, and as a diverse community; the major studies were San Francisco Waterfront: Report on Historical Cultural Resources (R. Olmsted et al. 1977) and *Behind the Seawall*, which incorporated a multitude of data into three amazing volumes (including *William Gray* and *Lydia*) (Pastron, Prichett et al. 1981).

Subsequent maritime archaeological projects downtown, for which I was able to join Allen's team on the excavations and in the analysis, include the partially burned, collapsed ship chandlery of William C. Hoff, which had been lost in the May 1851 fire and buried in a sealed anaerobic context until construction of Embarcadero Center Five encountered it. That time, thanks to new laws and pre-construction testing, we had a good idea about what was down there. The site was quintessentially maritime, at least to me, but the lively internal scholarly debate on it as an urban and mining site made for a substantial special publication by the Society for Historical Archaeology (Pastron and Hattori 1990). Following that, the next excavation was at a site next to the Hills Brothers Coffee company's historic complex, where we unearthed the remains of a number of dismantled Gold Rush ships, all part of a shipbreaking yard operated by an entrepreneur named Charles Hare and the local Chinese fishing community, whose village was nearby (Delgado 1981; Pastron and Delgado 1991).

Following that, in the same year (1987), we excavated an area adjacent to the Rincon Annex Post Office and documented a sailors' boardinghouse with an associated Chinese-run laundry. The site was fascinating and instructive, as the boardinghouse was in operation from 1887 until it was destroyed in the 1906 earthquake and fire. The range of material culture spoke to the lives of unmarried sailors in the coastal and South Seas trades, with a wide array of patent-medicine bottles, some alcoholic beverages (but not as many as one might expect), and souvenirs that included seashells and coral (Pastron and Delgado 1991). That was my last major participation in an Archeo-Tec job until 2001, as I moved to Washington, D.C., to take up my duties as the NPS's maritime historian, and then moved to Vancouver to run the maritime museum there. In 2001, Allen asked me down, and I came, *pro bono*, to be the maritime archaeologist for the excavation of the storeship *General Harrison*, moored in the mud aft of *Niantic* and burned in the same May 1851 fire.

The work on *General Harrison* brought me, as a maritime archaeologist, full circle, 23 years later and a block away from the

Niantic site. The work on *General Harrison* was a major shift in my perspective. I assessed the ship and its assemblage through the theoretical lenses of world systems and maritime cultural landscapes, as well as the ever-evolving perspectives of maritime archaeology. The thousands of artifacts and the remains of the hull, as well as all the other maritime work done on sites that represented the fire-ravaged and buried waterfront of 1851 (including a site not excavated by Archeo-Tec at 343 Sansome Street) became the basis of my dissertation, as I had at last returned to school in my 40s to get that doctorate, and it subsequently formed the basis for an academic-press book and subsequent musings (Delgado, Pastron et al. 2007; Delgado 2009, 2011, 2017).

The number of CRM projects being done in San Francisco back then (and continuing to this day) have led to an incredible library of largely gray literature at the Northwest Information Center (NWIC) at Sonoma State University, where all CRM project reports, site files, and maps from 18 counties, including San Francisco, are kept. The Department of Planning for the City and County of San Francisco also retains full copies of the various CRM reports. A careful perusal of those records will find a very strong, even if not fully identified or stated, maritime archaeological component in many of the San Francisco site files. These include reports on a site along Howison's Pier that encompassed the collapsed office of a pioneering stevedore firm that owned a nearby storeship (Dames & Moore 1989); William Self Associates' (WSA) work, led by Jim Allan, on Tichenor's Ways (William Self Associates 1999) and the buried Gold Rush ship *Rome* (William Self Associates 1996); 555 Washington Street (Pastron,

A PERSONAL PERSPECTIVE

Figure 16. William Self Associates archaeologists excavate the stern of the whaler *Candace*. (Photo courtesy of the National Park Service, 2006)

Figure 17. The fully exposed stern of the whaler *Candace*. (Photo courtesy of the National Park Service, 2006)

Figure 18. The excavation of *General Harrison* in downtown San Francisco, 2002. (Photo by Thomas Layton)

A PERSONAL PERSPECTIVE

Figure 19. William Self Associates archaeologists excavate the Gold Rush–era lighter south of Market Street, San Francisco. (Photo courtesy of the National Park Service, 2013)

Ambro et al. 2007); Clark's Wharf and Warehouse, destroyed in the May 1851 fire (Pastron and Ambro 2007); and more recent work, such as WSA's (now incorporated into PaleoWest) ongoing excavations off Rincon Point as well as at other sites in more recent years.

The Pioneer Era of Exploration of California's Changing Shoreline and Its Drowned Sites

While maritime archaeology in California was emerging from landfill in the 1970s, underwater archaeological interest continued through Don Jewell's "limnoarchaeology" and research by others interested in submerged prehistory, including coastal sites drowned by sea-level rise as well as sites covered by reservoir construction (Taylor and Cooley-Reynolds 1982). Garrison and Hale (2020:3) have written an excellent summary of the origins and early years of submerged-site archaeology (prior to 1990) in the U.S. and note early finds off La Jolla and Santa Barbara pre-1950 that would not be reported until the 1970s. After 1950 and into the 1960s, pioneering work by N. F. Marshall and James R. Moriarty assessed sites off California (Marshall and Moriarty 1964), but there were few published results, and much of the work "was taken up by scientists who were not formally trained archaeologists" (Garrison and Hale 2020:4), but who made significant contributions, such as marine biologist and prolific author Peter Howorth, whose knowledge of the Channel Islands area is encyclopedic.

Increased academic and government interest and support, particularly in the Channel Islands and off Point Conception, came in the 1970s with work by James R. Moriarty, Travis Hudson, and Jim Muche (Marshall and Moriarty 1964; Moriarty 1969, 1981; Moriarty et al. 1975; Hudson 1976, 1979; Muche 1982; Garrison and Cook 2020:6–7). In the 1980s, Peter Howorth, working with Travis Hudson for NOAA under contract, conducted a major study of the shipwrecks in the Channel Islands, capping 20 years of his research, and also incorporated a discussion by Travis Hudson on submerged prehistoric sites (Hudson and Howorth 1985). That study laid the groundwork for would become a highly active maritime archaeological program carried out jointly by the National Park Service and the NOAA.

Travis Hudson's untimely death at age 44 in 1985 cut off what would have been fascinating new approaches, as Travis Hudson pursued his studies with an uncommon vigor. I suspect that some colleagues outside California might have thought that Hudson was quintessentially "Californian," in the stereotypical way, with studies some thought were either outlandish or outré at the time, such as his work in Chumash archaeoastronomy, building a replica Chumash *tomol* and

recreating other aspects of Chumash material culture drawn from his extensive study of the unpublished notes and research of J. P. Harrington, and, of course, underwater archaeology. In reading a fond obituary of him as I prepared this, I wish I had known him, as I get the sense we were kindred spirits, especially as some of what was related reflects my behavior in the 1970s and 1980s.

His obituary described him as high energy, a practical joker, a storyteller, a traveler, a believer in getting into the field and in publishing and "getting it out, knowing that while some interpretations would be controversial, at least the work would be available to others so that knowledge could be advanced" (Timbrook 1985:148–149). He also did not have it easy as a child, being raised "in a confusing succession of step-families in a poor neighborhood of Los Angeles," to which I can relate, though my own circumstances were not so bad, but I also see that I followed his path in other ways without realizing it:

> "[H]e read whatever he could get his hands on and began purchasing projectile points and other artifacts from mail-order catalogs. By the time he was in high school he had compiled a meticulous inventory of the hundreds of objects he had acquired"
>
> (Timbrook 1985:148).

Federal and State Agencies Get Interested

The 1980s were an intense decade in terms of underwater/maritime/nautical/marine archaeology in California, and, for me, a whirlwind busy time in which maritime archaeology firmly took hold and changed my career path and life, as well as those of many friends and colleagues. The overarching themes that emerged in the decade were increased attention from and action by government, a greater number of discoveries and projects on beaches because of storm erosion, battles between archaeologists and treasure hunters (though not on the scale of Florida), and initial efforts to work with the sport-/wreck-diving community that collapsed at the end of the decade.

Government interest focused, at first, on the basic goals of CRM: (1) finding out what the potential was by developing inventories, (2) physical surveys, (3) site investigations, and (4) setting priorities, which for most of us involved the question of eligibility for listing in the National Register of Historic Places. The National Park Service's coastal presence in the 1960s was not insignificant, with Channel Islands National Monument, then defined as Anacapa and Santa Barbara islands (established in 1938), Point Reyes National Seashore (established in 1962), and Redwood National Park (established in 1968), and it had supported the early survey for *San Agustin* at Point Reyes National Seashore in 1965, but had no internal capacity to conduct underwater archaeological fieldwork.

The 1970s brought significant change in both areas; the Golden Gate National Recreation Area was established in 1972, and Channel Islands National Park, a vastly larger area of eight islands and the ocean surrounding them, was established at the end of the decade, March 1980. While shipwrecks were not specifically called out, nor were underwater archaeological sites, the fact they existed in the waters off these parks was known to some. Under the National Historic Preservation Act the NPS had a legal responsibility to survey and assess cultural resources in each park, and that would, ostensibly, lead to

internal NPS efforts to do so. As with all things, perhaps, responsibility aside, this came through individual interest and initiative. In the NPS the overall interest in archaeology underwater was fostered by George Fischer, Calvin Cummings, and Daniel Lenihan.

From small individual efforts, NPS underwater archaeology took a big step forward in the 1970s. The service began a comprehensive study of the effects of inundation on a variety of sites. That effort, the National Reservoir Inundation Study led by Dan Lenihan, was based out of the NPS's Southwest Regional Office in Santa Fe, New Mexico, and within a few years and following the publication of the final study became a more formal NPS underwater archaeology program. The program was then known as the Submerged Cultural Resources Unit (SCRU), which Dan, when we first met, shared that it was one of the "finest acronyms in government" (Lenihan 2002:11). Formally established in 1980, SCRU started with work in the Florida Keys, then in the Pacific, Isle Royale on Lake Superior, and, in time, throughout the entire National Park System (Lenihan 2002:54–57).

My first encounter with Dan Lenihan came in 1980 when I was the park historian for the GGNRA. As the first historian for the park working with its first archaeologist, Martin "Marty" Mayer, and with an understanding boss, Doug Nadeau, we had set out to do more-detailed surveys of historical and archaeological resources, which brought us, in 1980, to a Gold Rush shipwreck in the park, the steamship *Tennessee*. Coming fresh out of the *Niantic*, *Lydia*, and *William Gray* buried-ship experiences in San Francisco, I had been fired up by the maritime side of the California Gold Rush. When Harlan Soeten

Figure 20. Wreck of *SS Tennessee*, 1853. (Photo courtesy of the National Park Service)

Figure 21. Cross tail from the engine of *SS Tennessee* at Tennessee Cove, 1981. (Photo by James Delgado)

A PERSONAL PERSPECTIVE

told me of how in 1965 he had gone to Tennessee Cove's beach, 4 mi. north of the Golden Gate, to clear sand off a piece of the steamer's engine with the help of a local Boy Scout troop and then shared his drawing of it, that was all it took for me to head to the cove with Marty to look for it.

That sparked a project to assess what was left of an 1853 wreck on a small sand cove in an otherwise rocky, surf-lashed coast. The outcomes were test excavations, recovery of a few hundred artifacts, listing the site on the National Register of Historic Places (the key NPS goal), public outreach, and working with volunteers as a public archaeology project. That project also introduced me to Dave Buller, an extremely knowledgeable wreck diver with a keen sense of history. The other was the decision, spurred by reading the latest maritime archaeological scholarship, to prepare a research design for the *Tennessee* project. That research design was reviewed by Roger Kelly, the western regional archaeologist, and by Dan Lenihan, who I would meet shortly after as he made a tour of various parks. We talked a great deal about potential sites at Golden Gate and the difficulties in working them, as it was not an easy area to dive given tides, currents, sharks, and that Marty and I were about to go to dive school at the Presidio; even then our status as new divers meant we were not up to the conditions, and I did not dive on an NPS project until 1982. Meanwhile, I made as much as I could of the *Tennessee* project, small as it was (Delgado and Bennett 1981, Delgado 1983a, 1994), and have just completed a 40-year anniversary, honest look back at it (Delgado 2021).

That project was the SCRU's work at Point Reyes to conduct a comprehensive remote-sensing survey of the entire bay and to document as many of the wrecks as could be located and dived. While *San Agustin* was one of the proposed targets, other wrecks known to exist were the steamer *Munleon*, the tanker *Richfield*, the steam schooner *Pomo*, the steam schooner *Hartwood*, and the steam schooner *Shasta*. Historical records suggested over a dozen vessel losses. This was, as far as I can tell, the first comprehensive maritime archaeological survey in California, and, perhaps, on the Pacific coast (Murphy 1984; Delgado 2002a:223; Lenihan 2002:264–265). Prior to this, smaller-scale underwater surveys had been done, including one by archaeologist Roy Pettus off San Diego's Ballast Point, the site of a Spanish fortification, the Castillo de Guijarros (Pettus et al. 1981; Pettus 1982b). The underwater survey there was part of a larger effort led by archaeologist Ronald V. May of the Fort Guijarros Museum Foundation, established in 1981, and Ron's work continued through the next few decades up to 1996 (May 1982, 1985a, 1985b, 1988, 1990, 1994, 1995, 1996). In addition to his work on Fort Guijarros, Ron also focused on shore whaling at Ballast Point, all indicative of and pioneering what we now call maritime cultural landscape-focused archaeology (May 1985c). Other early surveys included work by Charles Rozaire, Jack Hunter, and Patricia Masters, as well as Roy Pettus, but these were small-scale surveys (Rozaire 1962; Hunter 1979; Hunter and Pierson 1980; Masters 1983, 1985; Pettus 1981, 1982a:73).

The Drakes Bay project, which had two annual seasons in 1982 and 1983, headed by Dan Lenihan and Larry Murphy, included archaeologist Ron Ice and scientific illustrator Jerry Livingston, all from SCRU. The overall coordinator was western regional archaeologist Roger Kelly,

Figure 22. Roger Kelly and Daniel Lenihan deploying the magnetometer at Point Reyes, 1982. (Photo courtesy of the National Park Service)

A PERSONAL PERSPECTIVE

who was and remained a consistent supporter of maritime and underwater archaeology throughout his career. On the water, wreck diver Dave Buller; Dave's wife and fellow diver, Noreen Buller (Dave's knowledge was invaluable and both Bullers' diving was exemplary and very instructive for me as new diver); volunteer Robert Bennett, a land archaeologist who had been an integral partner in the work on the *Tennessee* wreck; and John Foster from California State Parks. Marty Mayer and I, as well as a large number of the park staff and volunteers, also worked on the survey. The first season also included fellow archaeologist and longstanding friend Ervan "Erv" Garrison, then with Texas A&M.

A large area was surveyed, with a number of anomalies, the various wrecks mentioned were dived and assessed, with *Munleon* and *Hartwood* in the rocks directly below the promontory of Point Reyes being exceptionally rough rides (I did not dive on them, being too inexperienced). *Pomo*, close to the beach at the entrance to Drakes Estero and off the tip of Limantour Spit, was clearly marked by its triple-expansion marine steam engine rising out of the surf; that was rough water, too, and on dive I ended up head first in the largest cylinder, which was missing its cap. Scattered wreckage from *Pomo* lay across the spit, but we did not have time to examine it in 1982 and 1983. In 1984, a number of us returned to Drakes Bay for the third season. With Dan and Larry on another project, that field season was directed by archaeologist Toni Carrell from SCRU, and we were joined by Don Morris, the recently arrived park archaeologist for Channel Islands National Park (Carrell 1984; Kelly 1988b).

Figure 23. Divers in the National Park Service 36 motor lifeboat on Drakes Bay: Noreen Buller is at the bow, the next diver is unidentified, Ranger Jack Ohanessian is tending to a dive tank, and James Delgado is speaking with Dave Buller. (Photo courtesy of the National Park Service, 1982)

Prior to Don's arrival at Channel Islands, Dan Lenihan had visited there and dived the wreck of the Gold Rush steamer *Winfield Scott*, among other sites, with superintendent Bill Ehorn. The "Winnie" was well known to regional wreck divers, had yielded gold coins, and was one of many popular dive sites in a newly established national park that was also a new national marine sanctuary. As responsible government managers, the NPS needed to conduct surveys, learn more about the archaeological sites, including the shipwrecks, and assess them, especially to determine whether they were significant. Dan's recommendations were followed up by a visit to the park by Marty and me in 1981. Bill Ehorn conducted my National Park Service dive-certification check-out dive, and we began with an initial mapping of *Winfield Scott*. Dave Buller, who had dived the wreck, was not with us, but he provided access to his research and to his collection of artifacts, which he donated to the park (all of them collected before it was a park or sanctuary). I was chagrined to learn that Dave's donation was not acknowledged.

Based on the work we had done, having just completed the successful nomination and listing of SS *Tennessee*, I prepared the nomination for *Winfield Scott* and an academic history article (Delgado 1983b). The nomination immediately ran into problems. It also ended up being a national game-changer, and, a fact probably not well known is how a California wreck, *Winfield Scott*, ended up being the critical turning point for the National Register and shipwrecks. The National Register staff was concerned that a broken, scattered, and partially buried wreck, with much of its wooden components claimed by the marine environment, did not have

sufficient architectural or structural integrity to be listed. There was also the question of what were appropriate research questions to be asked and potentially answered through archaeology on the site. That led to some serious discussions, and a seeming impasse was headed off when Dan Lenihan and Ed Bearss convened a working-group meeting in conjunction with the NPS Washington Office at SCRU's offices in Santa Fe.

Chief historian Ed Bearss attended, as did other Washington staff, and, as the historian for Golden Gate, with several recent historic-ship nominations, including one wreck (*Tennessee*) successfully nominated and listed, I was handed the task of preparing a "white paper" on the topic. I had previously presented a paper, based on the experience of translating the National Register's nomination requirements for the historic ships in our park, at a 1985 special meeting of the Association of Preservation Technology held at our park. Coming out of the Santa Fe workshop and with considerable work done by Toni Carrell, our group drafted a much larger paper that I was then tasked with turning into a formal bulletin for the National Register. Thanks to the work of many and extensive review comments and corrections, the result was *Nominating Historic Ships and Shipwrecks to the National Register of Historic Places* (Delgado and National Park Service Maritime Task Force 1987). It effectively cleared the deck, so to speak, for subsequent nominations.

At Channel Islands, work by SCRU started with a 1985 session with a group of NPS divers, myself included, on Truth Aquatic's *Conception* to assess and map wrecks; *Winfield Scott* and the metal-hulled *Aggi* and *Goldenhorn* were the sites on which we dived. Larry Murphy headed up the archaeology. Steve Barsky, a veteran California diver with a long and significant career, was testing the latest helmet from Diving Systems International. I was given a chance to try on the helmet and narrate my way through the wreck on a dive with Murphy. Having come from my park with the square-rigger *Balclutha* and knowing *Balclutha* (one of my first assignments in the park was an interpreter's guide for all of us know-nothing park rangers so we would be able to tell fore from aft, port from starboard, and aloft from alow), I got to play tour guide with Larry as I sketched a map and he photodocumented while we played "pin the name on the wreckage" of *Goldenhorn*, as I mentioned previously.

Subsequent work by Don Morris and the park, and by SCRU's Matthew Russell, gathered more documentation, including work by Matt on a beached wreck site, the wreck of the schooner *Comet*, whose wooden and metal wreckage was occasionally exposed by beach erosion on the shores of San Miguel Island along with the remains of the schooners *J. M. Coleman* and *Dora Bluhm* (Russell 2004a, 2004b). Another important project was the beach survey and test excavation of the beached wreck of *Jane L. Stanford* by the *San Agustin* Institute under the direction of Marco Meniketti (Meniketti 1996). NOAA, meanwhile, was also involved, funding the initial database and assessment of potential and known shipwrecks and archaeological sites, which was completed that same year (Hudson and Howorth 1985). That work would increase dramatically,

and, ultimately, Don Morris and Jim Lima completed a major NPS study in 1996 that updated the inventory and summarized all work done to that point (Morris and Lima 1996). At that stage, Jim Lima was with Troy State University in Alabama and not a federal employee; this was all part of the ongoing NPS commitment to work with nongovernment archaeologists. Jim is now with the Bureau of Ocean Energy Management as of 2021.

Matt Russell's work on *Comet*, like all projects, involved many in the fieldwork, among them Don Morris, Jim Bradford, Ian Williams, Hank Silka, Georgia Fox, Patrick Smith, Bob Schwemmer, Tom Harris, Bill Harris, Jack Carraher, and Mark Linder. These projects were part of the ongoing working relationship with NOAA (Bob Schwemmer) but also volunteers. Some of them were expert divers with long association and knowledge, including the late Patrick "Pat" Smith. Pat's extensive experience and research had, was then and would be invaluable to many projects. Pat Smith's work had already resulted in a must-have history and archaeology book with diving pioneer, wreck diver, journalist, and author Bonnie J. Cardone for the diving and non-diving public on the wrecks of Southern California (Cardone and Smith 1989). A key point that needs to be made, if not already apparent, is that the archaeology done on all these projects would not have been accomplished without the knowledge and support of the diving public. This situation was not unique to California, and it needs to be explicitly recognized and acknowledged.

The other aspect of the *Comet* project was that it represented a theme that had been a key part of maritime archaeology on the California coast in the 1980s, with projects documenting the remains of ships exposed on beaches and in intertidal zones after storm-induced erosion. My first project, at Tennessee Cove, was punctuated by an extreme erosional event in March 1981 that exposed over 200 artifacts. In December 1982 a substantial portion of the wooden hull of the two-masted schooner *Neptune*, exposed by storms on San Francisco's Ocean Beach, was my second maritime archaeology project in the GGNRA (Delgado 1986a). As noted earlier, the experience gained by working at and being in close proximity to the historic ships of the park was a boon. The wreck "looked very familiar" and, with help from Ray Aker in determining it was likely *Neptune*, had been lost at the same spot in August 1900. The familiar aspect became clear as *Neptune* was built in 1882 by the same shipbuilder in the same yard that had launched the park's 1895-built three-masted schooner *C. A. Thayer*. As I said before, those years spent in the park and the regular contact with its historic ships and the maritime museum, as well as subsequent experience with other ships and other museums, were at least equal to my graduate degrees.

The storms of December 1982 continued, one after another, well into the first quarter of 1983. They exposed another wreck on Ocean Beach and, in time, the full outline of its intact lower hull, which we were able to identify as the 1856-built medium clipper *King Philip*, which went ashore at the exact spot in 1878. The wreck drew large crowds, as Marty and I

documented it with the help of volunteers, including the San Francisco Fire Department, which sent a pumper to the highway above to give us pressure to hydraulically probe the interior of the hull. We found it still loaded with stone ballast. The erosion also exposed timbers, wire rigging, and the bobstays from the bowsprit of the three-masted schooner *Reporter*, which in 1901 had wrecked on the beach next to *King Philip*'s exposed bones (Delgado 1985c). Ongoing work with *King Philip* continued through 1985, while, at the same time, Marty and I responded to the discovery of a washed-up piece of the stern of a small 19th-century wreck north of the Golden Gate on the park's Rodeo Beach.

The same storms also stripped sand off the *Pomo* wreck at Drakes Bay, and in March 1983 Marty, volunteer archaeologists Greg Brown and Rebecca La Fontaine (who had also been part of the *King Philip* team), and I went back up to assist Point Reyes National Seashore in the absence of SCRU, then on a project in another park, documenting the scattered pieces of *Pomo* and establishing that there was a pattern in which the pieces of the steam schooner had moved up and down 3 mi. from where *Pomo* had hit the beach—the spot still marked by that engine block I knew so well. Our report was made into an appendix in the second volume of the report by SCRU on the Drakes Bay survey (Carrell 1984). Beached wrecks accounted for much of a report I made in 1984 on shipwreck archaeology in California (Delgado 1984).

Larry Murphy and I followed up on all of that with surveys on Ocean Beach for the likely buried remains of the 1851 wreck of the U.S. revenue cutter *C.W.*

Figure 24. The schooner *Neptune* wrecked on Ocean Beach, 1900. (Photo courtesy of the National Park Service)

Figure 25. The remains of *Neptune* in the rocks (Photo by James Delgado, 1982)

A PERSONAL PERSPECTIVE

Lawrence, and that work included not only surf work off a coast-guard motor lifeboat, but also a systematic gridded survey of Ocean Beach with a handheld magnetometer. That was followed up, after I left California in 1987, with a contracted survey of Ocean Beach done by Robert Gearhart, then with Espey, Huston and Associates (Gearhart 1988), and with another survey and test excavations by Larry Murphy in the 1990s. Sand replenishment covered *King Philip* so thoroughly that it was not seen again until the 21st century.

While we were chasing wooden wrecks up and down storm-washed beaches, other projects undertaken by colleagues grappled with the ongoing discoveries made through erosional events. The major find, and the biggest headline grabber, was the 1981 discovery, after a storm stripped away the sand, of five iron cannon on the beach at Goleta by a local beachcomber. John Foster, as the state's underwater archaeologist, responded to the find, as did archaeologist Jack Hunter, a friend and colleague then working as the archaeologist for Caltrans. Jack conducted a magnetometer survey off the beached cannons' location (Hunter 1981). John, already mentioned, with more to come, was a key ally and a strong proponent for archaeology underwater, and when I left California in 1987 to run a national program John stayed in California and made a vast and profound difference. John is the leading and longest-standing key figure in the maritime, underwater, marine, and nautical archaeology of California.

The site's attention came from the realization that the cannon were old—potentially 16th century—which put them into contention for being from the time of Francis Drake, an ever-contentious topic in West Coast history and archaeology (Hanna 1979). At the same time as the guns were found, stone bowls, representing Indigenous habitation that had been

Figure 26. Martin Mayer plotting the location of *King Philip's* bow. (Photo courtesy of the National Park Service, 1984)

Figure 27. James Delgado and Kaea Morris plotting the curve of the bow of *King Philip*, 1986. (Photo courtesy of the National Park Service)

Figure 28. The wreck of *Atlantic* on Ocean Beach, 1886. (Photo courtesy of the San Francisco Maritime National Historical Park, SAFR 21374, P93-065, Series 1, File Unit 3, Item A03.01440)

A PERSONAL PERSPECTIVE

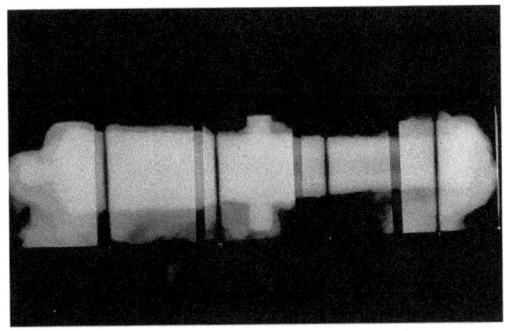

Figure 29. X-ray image of cannon recovered from Goleta beach. (Photo courtesy of Jack Hunter, 1982)

submerged by sea-level rise, were also noted in the same area, as Travis Hudson had reported a single bowl in 1976 (Hudson 1976). Whether the guns had been cast off a ship, were from a shipwreck, or represented guns left behind to fortify the spot was difficult to discern (Gimore and Hunter 1983). John Foster did tremendous work in seeing the guns archaeologically documented in situ, recovered, and conserved (the latter by Shirley Gotelipe). The guns were also extensively studied by local historian Justin Ruhge and a team led by Pandora Snethkamp, as well as by Jack Hunter and local historian Jim Gilmore (Foster, Hunter et al. 1983; Gilmore and Hunter 1983; Ruhge 1984, 1987; Snethkamp et al. 1990). Snethkamp et al. (1990:89) determined the guns were likely more recent than the 16th century based on radiocarbon analysis of a fragment of rope associated with one of the cannon that had been encased in concretion that yielded an age of 120 ± 50 ^{14}C B.P. Based on trunnion markings, Ruhge (1987:225–226) contends that the guns are 18th-century weapons.

Another find at that time that grabbed fewer headlines, but was still a significant maritime archaeological revelation, took place farther north. The Año Nuevo State Reserve, south of Half Moon Bay,

had been the setting from a number of 19th-century wrecks, one of them the clipper *Sir John Franklin*, whose 1865 loss had drowned the captain and most of the crew. The bodies of four seamen were buried near the wreck site, and, in 1980, a winter storm exposed human remains that seemingly came from the graves of Sir John Franklin's crew. In 1982 California State Parks had authorized the archaeological excavation of the burials, another reminder that maritime archaeology can encompass more than the remains of a ship that has been wrecked. The work, done by the San José State Department of Anthropology's Alan Leventhal and Robert Jermain, excavated four burials.

On a visit I made to the lab at San José State right after the 1982 excavation, Alan and Bob showed me the remains, which included compelling forensic evidence of the hard life of a sailor, including the wear and tear on back vertebrae, repeated injuries to tibias, and chronic disease. Ultimately, a search for additional remains on the site was conducted in 1993, and, in 1997, following another exposure of remains, California State Parks archaeologists Pete Schulz, Lee Motz, and Richard Hastings directed an excavation in 1999. The additional burials likely were from an 1866 wreck, *Coya*, and/or an 1868 wreck, *Hellespont*, which altogether killed 38 people, at least 13 of whom had been buried at the point (Hykelma 2018).

After those severe storms along the entire California coast that lasted from December 1982 to March 1983, three pieces of wooden shipwreck remains were exposed at the mouth of the Little River, near Trinidad, by record high tides and heavy seas, and documented by local historian Melvin Krei. Mel shared his report, sketches, and photos of his find with Ray Aker and with me, and to Ray the style of construction suggested an earlier 19th-century vessel, possibly the bark *Acadia*, wrecked in 1861, or the schooner *Union Forever*, wrecked in 1866, both close to the site of the exposed remains. At the same time, in March 1983, the buried outline of a wooden hull had been exposed on Pismo Beach in Southern California and spotted by all-terrain-vehicle riders (that section of the beach was specially designated as an ATV recreation area). Unfortunately, it was too far south for Marty and me to drive to and well outside any NPS area, so we had no excuse.

Closer to home, however, we did not need an excuse. That busy winter of 1982/1983 also resulted in a serendipitous discovery in which, in a rare circumstance, the wreck "told us its name." Storm run-off washing down a creek and high tides and surf rushing up the mouth of a creek at Año Nuevo State Reserve, south of San Francisco, exposed a section of the bow of a wooden wreck, partially covered in mud as the water receded. With our friends from California State Parks who had called to share the news, Marty and I went to the site at the mouth of Greenoaks Creek where it flowed across the beach and into the Pacific. Marty jumped on down, waded into the stream, and started clearing mud and vegetation off the hull. The rest of us followed.

As we started clearing the timber, it was stunning to see the paint still in place clinging to the planking and then the thickness of a strake, which, when I looked at it, had some lettering visible. Above it was the complete name of the vessel. About that time, John Foster or Pete Schulz or Lee Motz asked what type of vessel it was, and I looked up and said: "It's the *Point Arena*." That was the name

carved on the bow, preserved when torn free as the steamer wrecked at the point on 9 August 1913. The bow fragment, stood up between bracing, was a prominent landmark at a trailhead until 2016, when it was moved to the Pigeon Point Lighthouse, where it stands still. The storm-exposed wrecks of 1982/1983 and subsequent work on *King Philip* sparked my next maritime archaeological passion (in addition to the Gold Rush), "environmentally exposed shipwreck remains." Larry Murphy and I worked together on assessing what we thought was going on and developed a nomenclature and presented our preliminary sense of it all at the Society for Historical Archaeology conference at Williamsburg, Virginia, in January 1984 (Delgado and Murphy 1984).

When I went East for a year in 1984, on leave without pay from the NPS to attend East Carolina University and work on my M.A., my major field project was a follow up on the environmentally exposed wrecks question, surveying a 60 mi. stretch of Cape Hatteras and Cape Lookout National seashores. The area was strewn with beached shipwrecks whose remains were dramatically exposed, as I deliberately timed my field survey in early September with Hurricane Diana, as I recall, a big storm (Category 2) that lashed the coast. Tom Hartman, the superintendent of Cape Hatteras National Seashore, after conferring with my boss in San Francisco, agreed to cover my salary for the two-week period, and so I returned to active duty, donned my uniform, and was given a patrol vehicle.

That brought other responsibilities, including traffic duty at the height of the hurricane and closing the highway as heavy seas washed over the dunes and across Highway 12, taking it out. I had

Figure 30. Martin Mayer clears silt from the bow of *SS Point Arena* at Ano Nuevo. (Photo by James Delgado, 1983)

Figure 31. The exposed starboard bow of *SS Point Arena*. (Photo by James Delgado, 1983)

Figure 32. Part of the name of the steam schooner exposed on the bow of *SS Point Arena*. (Photo by James Delgado, 1983)

some of my fellow graduate students working with me on the project and in the vehicle. As they stayed put, I went out onto the surf-covered highway that buckled and collapsed as I headed in to rescue a family whose truck had tried to outrace the waves. Kevin Foster ran the winch at the front of my patrol vehicle as I did a triple wrap of wire rope around my middle and headed in with a baton. The truck was dead, sinking into the sand and with water up to the windows. The family could not get the windows open, and so I went to the offshore side, broke out the driver's window, had him pass me his wife and child, and then Kevin reeled us in. I then went back, got the driver, and, exhausted, soaked, and sandy on the bluff, looked back to see his truck start to go over with his dog still tied down in the back. That dog was paddling like mad to keep his head above water. I went back in, cut the line, grabbed the dog, and Kevin reeled me back in for the third time.

That part of that project gave me a first-hand sense of what it had to be like to be in a wreck that hit the beach and the forces at play; two days later, as the seas died down, we found over a dozen new sites where buried sections of wooden ships were newly exposed. I wrote a detailed overview of the sites with individual sites numbered and documented, and submitted it to Richard Lawrence and Mark Wilde-Ramsing of the North Carolina Division of Archives and History to help build the state's archaeological site files. They had done a tremendous amount of work already, but a hurricane-focused one had not yet been done. I also joined SCRU for a project at Cape Cod National Seashore, where we also studied beached wrecks, including the iron-hulled ship *Frances*, which at times was buried by the beach and at other times was underwater, scoured by surf and exposed. Larry Murphy and I went into the surf zone, slipped under the deck, and were able to get into the forecastle, which had been filled with sand that was then washed out. The view was worth the ride; the wooden bunks were still there, collapsed, with a lidless and empty seaman's chest from one of the crew. All of that work on beached wrecks notwithstanding, my M.A. thesis focused on *SS Tennessee*, as the Gold Rush was still my first and true love in maritime archaeology.

60

As the storms stripped sand from beaches and exposed the skeletons of ships, maritime archaeology in California took a substantial leap forward in the 1980s, thanks to the interest and activities of John Foster, state underwater archaeologist and with California State Parks; his counterpart in the state historic preservation office (SHPO), Nicholas "Nick" Del Cioppo; and a series of projects that focused on the Gold Rush ships in the Sacramento River. California's State Parks System started its underwater parks program in 1968 and, five decades later, had established 19 state underwater parks (Dodds and Jaffke 2014). John Foster was a key part and a major driver, going into the field and documenting sites. While this was part of a CRM strategy, it also brought attention to hitherto "unseen" and underappreciated resources.

In 1981, John started work at Fort Ross State Historic Park, which, while well known for his history and role as a Kashaya Pomo, Aleut, and Russian site, had a significant 19th – and 20th-century role in the establishment of coastal ranching and the maritime lumber trade. Just the year before, State Parks had published a pioneering study of sites like Fort Ross, but north of the fort's Sonoma County location in neighboring Mendocino County (Sullenberger 1980). The report, *Dogholes and Donkey Engines: A Historical Resources Study of Six State Park System Units on the Mendocino Coast*, while not delving underwater, was a pioneering effort in what we now identify as maritime cultural landscapes toward defining maritime archaeological potential on maritime-related land sites. John's initial work at Fort Ross was a magnetometer survey of

the cove with a U.S. Navy Mobile Diving and Salvage Unit (MDSU) (Foster 1981, 1984). This was the first systematic State Parks underwater archaeological survey (Foster 2016:170).

One of the artifacts was an anchor known to local divers (the cove was well known as a good spot for breath-held abalone dives), and Marty and I had done a check-out dive there for our dive-school training and had "bounce-dived" to the anchor. John's major focus was the one big wreck at Fort Ross, the 1908 wreck of the coastal steamer *Pomona*. Marty and I later accompanied John and Fort Ross ranger Bill Walton on *Pomona*, where I focused on a slow dive to hand map and draw the propeller shaft. John's focus on *Pomona* brought in other partners, including Jack Hunter and Franklin Fisher in 1989, and a decade later, Charles "Charlie" Beeker from Indiana State University (Hunter and Fisher 1989). Charlie's research was more than the archaeology, also focusing on better access to and understanding of wreck sites as underwater museums in the sea, which back then was revolutionary and, as such, absolutely the right thing to do. In that California was again at the cutting-edge of trends that would emerge as key aspects of the field (Beeker 2005). John and Charlie, with Marianne Simoulin from San José State University, conducted a one-week site assessment and mapping with limited artifact recovery in 1998 (Simoulin 2000). The site plan prepared by Charlie, John, and their team in 2007 was provided as a roadmap for visiting divers (Beeker and Foster 2007). The other aspect that was very significant was the preparation of a National Register nomination and listing *Pomona* in the

National Register (Simoulin 2000; Beeker 2008, Dodds and Jaffke 2014:188–190).

Other work by John and Charlie included work with Annalies Corbin and Sheli Smith of the PAST Foundation, with projects at Crystal Cove State Park that documented a 1946 wreck of a U.S. Navy F4U Corsair and work on barges and small recreational craft at Emerald Bay in Lake Tahoe (S. Smith 1991, 2005a; Beeker and S. Smith 2005; Dodds and Jaffke 2014:190–193). Fort Ross and the various doghole ports remained a strong interest for John and California State Parks, and in 2016 the work picked up again, this time in cooperation with the NOAA's Maritime Heritage Program and Greater Farallones National Marine Sanctuary; that project will be discussed in more detail later.

Figure 33. Lake Tahoe, Emerald Bay Underwater Park crew, 1990. Left to right: Jim Barry, Jack Hunter, Dick Swete, Monica Hunter, John Foster, Sheli Smith, and Carol Barry. The submerged mini-fleet of recreational boats as well as the lumber barges were recorded. (Photo by Kathy A. Foster, 1990)

Gold Rush Hulks in the Sacramento River

John Foster's focus included the waters of the Sacramento River below Old Sacramento State Historic Park, where he knew at least one sunken ship from the Gold Rush, the bark *LaGrange*, had sunk and subsequently been hit in 1972 by a dredge cutting a trench across the river for a telephone cable. Following the recovery of an anchor illegally raised from the river by a salvager and seeing the anchor had the date 1844 incised in it, in 1985 John invited Marty Mayer and me to come to Sacramento to see the anchor; that led to us all diving on the wreck of the brig *Sterling* at the foot of J Street (Foster 2016). In 1984, Jack Hunter had conducted a survey of the site from which the anchor came and identified two historic wooden wrecks, one possibly *LaGrange* and the other most likely the brig *Sterling*, another Gold Rush hulk that had been moored and later sank in place at the foot of J Street (Hunter et al. 1984; James 1986b; Foster 1988a). In our dive on that wreck, it was powerful to see the still copper-sheathed bow sticking out of the riprap that defined the riverbank, chainplates for the foremast still in place, and, for me, being able to go into the hull and crawl under deck beams to reach the stub of the foremast.

That work, thanks to John Foster's interest, Jack's excellent work, and the fact that the wrecks were Gold Rush era, sparked a series of important projects in the mid-1980s. At this point it is important to note that another key player in all of this was the archaeologist from the State Historic Preservation Office, Nicholas Del Cioppo. Nick was present at many of the various projects done by the

state, by our NPS team, and by the various CRM firms that encountered maritime resources, and he brought the advice of his office with him in addition to his support as a fellow archaeologist. He also was (and is) a great friend, whose humor lightened up many hard and long field days. The river on the stretch between the Tower and Pioneer bridges was the focus of concurrent surveys and assessments. Funded by the Sacramento Housing and Development Agency, Steve James, then with Espey, Huston & Associates, conducted surveys in February and June 1986 (James 1986a, 1986b). John Foster, Pete Schulz, and I assisted Steve and the project.

The dive and survey boat was provided by Bob Taylor of Advanced Divers; Bob was another pioneer, a great diver and a good man, and I got to know him not only through this project, but also from his reserve status as a U.S. Navy diver with the MDSU detachment that assisted the NPS

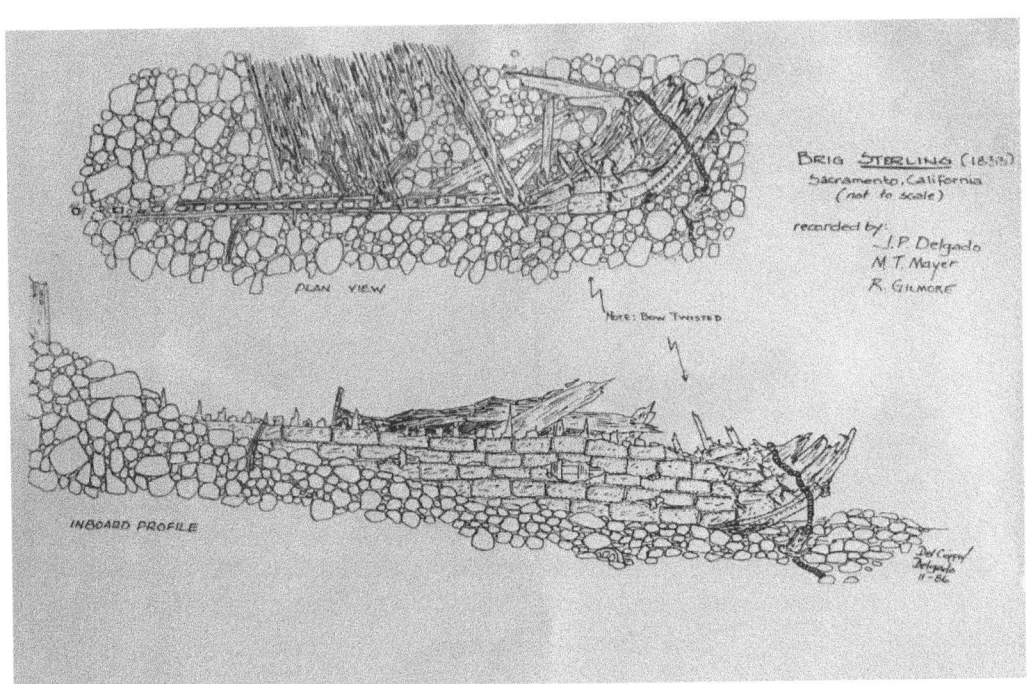

Figure 34. Drawings by Nicholas Del Cioppo and James Delgado of the J Street Wreck, believed to be the brig *Sterling*, 1985.

on a few projects, including an underwater survey of Alcatraz's shores that Marty and I had planned and participated in. The 1986 work began with the remote-sensing survey in February and in June shifted to diving on 16 targets identified by the survey (James 1986a). Those surveys located two sections of an early to mid-19th-century wooden wreck that was in the location of *LaGrange*'s known mooring; the other wreck, farther down the river, was the articulated lower hull of another 19th-century wooden wreck that we suspected was either *Dimon* or *Ninus*, two Gold Rush–era hulks that had ended their days in close proximity to the site of this wreck (James 1986b, 1987; Foster 2016).

As I was regularly researching at the National Archives, I was able to get Steve copies of the registries for the various Gold Rush ships that had ended as hulks, which were helpful, as we had a primary source to check against the physical remains. Despite the limited visibility and the mud crawling at the bottom of the Sacramento River, I enjoyed the project and appreciated the collegial invitation to join and help. I was glad to have had the experience of having worked on documenting the recovered remains of *Niantic* and *Lydia* and assisting in the excavation of the Levi's Plaza ship, as it helped interpret what we were seeing down there. Fellow river-diving archaeologists on the project were Jack Irion, Jim Duff, Bob Gearhart, Shirley Gotelipe, Todd Hannahs, and Franklin Fisher. The entire project was exceptionally well done thanks to Steve and the team.

That project was followed up by a third, in September and October 1987, when Steve returned, with funding from California Parks and Recreation to conduct a detailed study of the possible *LaGrange*

site. Steve had left Espey, Huston and had formed a small company with Sheli O. Smith, Jack Hunter, and Monica Reed, the Underwater Archaeological Consortium. Sheli's addition brought her back to her native California. Her training at Texas A&M with George Bass was a boon, and we shared common experience with buried ships, as Sheli and Warren Riess had conducted the 1982 project to excavate and recover the Ronson ship in Lower Manhattan. That was a race against a construction timeclock as we had done with the Levi's Plaza Ship the year before (but we did not recover, only documented).

The 1987 project, led by Sheli and Steve, also included John Foster, Jack Hunter, Franklin Fisher, and me. It was an important project, as the conclusion was that this was likely *LaGrange*, that it was the ship hit in the 1972 cable-dredging incident (and, despite that, significant sections and artifacts remained), and it was likely eligible for the National Register (S. Smith et al. 1988). The other important aspect of the project conducted by Sheli and Monica was to document the work and produce an educational video. That aspect of sharing the story and the excitement of archaeology and, especially, education—a consistent theme in Sheli's and Monica's careers—is absolutely essential, but, back then, very few folks in the field were thinking about it or, more to the point, doing it. I fondly remember sitting down with them for an interview about the Gold Rush on the replica Gold Rush hulk *Globe*, moored just down from where we were working, with me suffering from a bad cold and Monica rescuing me with a large fresh-squeezed orange juice before we started filming.

A PERSONAL PERSPECTIVE

In between these projects I had gone to East Carolina University (ECU) in 1984, returning to GGNRA in May 1985 before my final classroom work, which was a survey by ECU of a ship graveyard at Tranter's Creek and then test excavations on the Civil War wreck USS *Picket* off Little Washington, North Carolina. I returned to San Francisco and to the park at the end of the summer of 1985, but with a new special assignment from Ed Bearss. The NPS had just signed a memorandum of agreement with the NOAA to assist with USS *Monitor*. Dan Lenihan, Larry Murphy, and Cal Cummings were working on an archaeological research design, while I was assigned to coordinate special history studies and to conduct the National Historic Landmark (NHL) study for *Monitor* as the first specially commissioned NHL for a shipwreck. That process was not only tremendously assisted by leading scholars, but it was also like going back to graduate school, as I was able to work with leading historians and anthropologists, among them Bill Dudley, Harold Langley, Richard Gould, Bill Still, and Dan and Larry. It was a tremendous boost to my out-of-classroom education.

That work expanded in response to a directive from Congress, put into the appropriations bill for the NPS, to essentially sort out the scope and significance of the nation's historic maritime resources and develop standards for preservation, as well as determine priorities for preservation. What followed was the major shift in my career that I previously mentioned, when I transitioned from being the park historian for the GGNRA to leading what became known as the National Maritime Initiative (NMI) and, in that, successfully competing for the job of being the NPS's first maritime historian (Delgado 1991). While running the NMI from an interim office at GGNRA headquarters in historic Fort Mason in San Francisco, I was able to take a more active role in maritime archaeology in the state, still working with Marty Mayer. That included interacting with Tom Layton as he was actively moving forward with his research on the brig *Frolic* and diving that site, the ongoing work on Sacramento's Gold Rush hulks (as previously noted), responding to regional shipwreck finds, and conducting field projects, the documentation of the Matthew Turner/ James Robertson Shipyard in Benicia (with its rescue of the bow of *Galilee*); test excavation of the bark *Stamboul*, lying off the shipyard site; and a weekend project at Candlestick Point State Recreation Area with John Foster.

Channeling my love of the Gold Rush with my always present archaeo-activism, I asked if I could test the new NRHP bulletin with a thematic study of Gold Rush maritime archaeological sites, and Ed Bearss and Ben Levy, who ran the National Historic Landmark Program in the History Division in Washington, agreed. I started with an historical context study on the maritime aspects of the California Gold Rush, building on what I had done for my M.A. thesis on SS *Tennessee*, but also on other aspects that had come through other research. While at East Carolina I had tackled a major project on the side that was unrelated to my thesis but was burning a hole in my figurative scholarly "pocket." One of the buried ships in downtown San Francisco, the ship *Apollo*, was another 1849 arrival that had become a floating storeship or hulk on the

Figure 35. Documenting the wreck of the steam schooner *Daisy Gadsby* at Candlestick Point SRA. (Photo by James Delgado, 1987)

A PERSONAL PERSPECTIVE

San Francisco waterfront. Moored close to *Niantic*, it was successively hemmed in by wharves and waterfront structures built atop pilings, trapped in the middle of what Chilean gold seeker and writer Benjamin Vicuña Mackenna would call a "Venice Built of Pine." Like *Niantic* and *General Harrison*, *Apollo* burned to the waterline in a 3–4 May 1851 fire that destroyed much of the city and was quickly filled over and largely forgotten until later construction dug deep into the landfill and hit those charred oaken bones.

The construction that unearthed *Apollo* was for the Federal Reserve Bank of San Francisco. It was completely exposed, chopped on, and reburied, and hit again with the digging of an underground garage and an elevator shaft in the 1920s. Fascinated by the skeleton under the building, Federal Reserve officials retained artifacts from the ship, including a piece of its stem and souvenirs carved from wood from the hull, as well as a series of notebooks in which Joseph Perkins Beach, son of *Apollo*'s owner and supercargo on the voyage to California, had kept his personal log of *Apollo*'s passage to California. In 1979, Harlan Soeten of the maritime museum told me about the artifacts and the log.

At that stage I was assigned to Hyde Street Pier, working as an interpretive ranger in between my assignment to the Western Regional Office and to GGNRA headquarters. I was laid up with my right leg in a cast after being injured in a rescue when heavy winds pushed a sailboat up against the pier. Bored stiffer than that leg in a cast after a few weeks of being off on sick leave, I called up the Federal Reserve, put on my uniform, and took the bus downtown on crutches. The bank officials were gracious; the artifacts and journals were displayed in the boardroom,

not open to the public. As we talked and I examined everything, they asked if the maritime museum might want it all, as the bank was moving to a new building on Market Street.

Without hesitating, I answered yes and then went home and wrote a memo to Harlan explaining it all. A true museum professional with love at heart for the subject, he also said yes and went downtown to sign the papers. Bank officials made the donation in front of the museum at a press conference, and I was allowed to attend in April 1980. "Allowed" is the right word. I had been spotted in uniform and on crutches by an unnamed fellow NPS employee, also downtown that day, and turned in because I was on sick leave. The reprimand was verbal, but I was told my punishment was that I would have to stand in the back of the crowd on the day of the donation. I did not get it then, but, years later, promoted in rank and with a staff, I realized why my enthusiasm and commitment, while appreciated at some times, also exposed the park to possible liability, as in being on sick leave but in uniform and not in the park.

Before I headed east to Greenville to start my studies at ECU, I packed a xerox copy of the journals made by the museum, the files I had gathered, and a number of books. My plan was to perhaps make the journals and *Apollo* my thesis topic. However, *Apollo*'s "archaeology" was scanty, and I had a larger obligation to write up *Tennessee*. *Apollo* became my side project, and many evenings I would sit in my home office, at the front of the house we'd rented from an ECU professor, transcribing the journals. I then started a focused annotation, which included not only explanations of maritime terms, places, and other ships encountered, but also identified

Property/Site Name	County	NRIS Number
Apollo	San Francisco	91000561
Bow of *Niantic*	San Francisco	91000563
Griffing's Ship / *William Gray* / Levi's Plaza Ship	San Francisco	82002248
J Street Wreck/*Sterling*	Sacramento	91000562
SS *Tennessee*	Marin	81000102
SS *Winfield Scott*	Ventura	87002111
SS *Yankee Blade*	Santa Barbara	91000564
Frolic	Mendocino	91000565
LaGrange	Sacramento	Not listed
Vicar of Bray	N/a	Not listed
Snow Squall	N/a	Not listed

Table 1 The maritime connotations of the California Gold Rush Thematic Group nominations

the source of many literary and poetical quotes Beach had inserted into his journal with some, but often no, attribution. The university library was a blessing, as I could go when my children were asleep and work in the stacks, pulling now-obscure literary journals and poetry compendia. I wrote as detailed a contextual history of the ship as I could find, summarized the archaeological importance of the still-buried hull, and included an inventory of all known artifacts.

When it was all done, after we returned home to San Francisco I turned the manuscript in to the publications committee of the Book Club of California (BOC); the executive director, Joan Redington, had opened its library to me for research earlier, and the BOC's journal had published a few articles I did on the buried ships. The committee approved it, and *The Log of the Apollo* was beautifully published in a cloth-bound limited edition of 500 copies for the club by the Arion Press (Delgado 1986b).

Drawing on that, I knew the maritime-context study needed to include voyages around Cape Horn, the ships involved in that, whether buried or sunk, as well as the Panama steamers, the Sacramento River steamboats and the city's hulks, and any wrecks that spoke to regular trade, either coastal or transpacific. With all of those contexts discussed, I turned to the writing of National Register nominations. In all, I prepared 11 nominations, with some as collaborative work with colleagues like Tom Layton. Not every site nominated was listed after review, especially as I stretched the boundaries by including two U.S.-owned hulks in the Falkland Islands with Gold Rush connections, *Vicar of Bray* and the clipper *Snow Squall*, but a precedent had been set for a thematic group of shipwrecks and buried ships to be listed.

The National Register's guidance has shifted to multiple-property nominations now; the thematic structure I applied was the approach taken by the National Historic Landmarks (NHL) Program. I was

A PERSONAL PERSPECTIVE

not able to advance the cause for Gold Rush–shipwreck NHLs, however, but was successful in the NHL studies for USS *Monitor*, USS *Arizona*, and USS *Utah* being designated as NHLs by the secretary of the interior; they were the first three individual wrecks to become NHLs (out of nine currently designated). In 2001 I nominated *General Harrison* as part of the group, but the SHPO returned the nomination; I was more successful in nominating and listing the steamer *Brother Jonathan* in 1995. There are other sites that warrant nomination in addition to resubmitting *General Harrison*: the Clarksburg Wreck, the steamer S.S. *Lewis*, and, if I were as radical as I once was and with limitless energy, I would try for a multiple-property archaeological district spanning the entirety of the burned and filled-over waterfront of 1851 in San Francisco's Financial District.

The nomination of *Frolic* and its listing came about because of Tom Layton's incredible work on that site. Starting from his excavations at Three Chop Ridge in 1984 to Tom's connecting the artifacts to the wreck; his interviews with the wreck divers, gaining their trust; to determining the identity of the wreck; starting an archaeological project; writing reports, articles, books, one of which won the James Deetz Award from the Society for Historical Archaeology for its approachable, public-friendly nature and solid scholarship; museum partnerships; temporary and permanent displays and exhibitions; a Chautauqua-inspired play; *Frolic* ale; and television documentaries, Tom's energy and his inspirational leadership in pursuing *Frolic* offers a national and international role model for maritime archaeological projects that connect with communities. Listing the wreck in the National Register was the right thing to do, and it was an honor to coauthor the nomination with Tom.

Another powerful aspect of the project was how much it demonstrated the interconnectivity among the California

Figure 36. John Foster and Fritz Hanselmann preparing to dive a Gold Rush–era Clarksburg shipwreck in the Sacramento River. (Photo by Sheli O. Smith, 2007)

wreck-diving, archaeological, and museum communities; *Frolic* is probably the most powerful contender for being named the state's "Kevin Bacon of shipwrecks." For me, the connections include Dave Buller and other wreck divers; among my archaeological friends and colleagues, John Foster, Charley Beeker, and Sheli Smith; and, from my museum days, Richard Everett at San Francisco Maritime National Historical Park and many others. It was fun to dive the wreck for Tom with John Foster, even if the conditions were like being in a washing machine on spin cycle, looking through artifacts at Tom's lab at San José State with Richard Everett and identifying maritime fittings, and sitting on the panel assembled by Sandy Metzler and Mark Rawitsch to help define a program for public engagement.

Tom likes to tell the story of how I picked up a sherd of porcelain, adopted an accent, and channeled my inner ship's captain of the Gold Rush era, followed by other personas. That suggested a framework for Sandy and the others to tell the story, and it was some kind of powerful (and a moment of pride) to see actors on stage holding the artifact and connecting to each other's stories through it—just as François Girard did with a red violin in his 1998 film. At the time of that meeting, I had been a maritime-museum director for several years and more actively engaged in public interpretation; I had also returned to the NPS as a volunteer at Fort Vancouver National Historical Site in Vancouver, Washington. That outpost of the maritime fur trade, operated by the Hudson's Bay Company (HBC) from 1829 to 1845, had literally been resurrected through archaeology and reconstruction. The volunteers, working with historian and curator David Hansen and ranger Rick

Edwards, interpreted the site in character and accurate clothing, especially each year at the annual candlelight tour of the fort. The meals were prepared based on documentary records and the archaeological evidence, notably the faunal remains; the table was set with modern reproductions of the porcelain and ceramics and glassware also found in the archaeological excavations at the fort.

My role, honed from my NPS experience at Hyde Street Pier, was that of Captain James Allen Scarborough, the English-born commander of the HBC's schooner *Cadboro*, based at the fort with his indigenous wife, Paley Temaikamae Tchinouk, or, as she was called at the fort, Elizabeth Ann. With an exquisitely tailored uniform, leather sea boots, sword, and a small period telescope, I would join the other gentlemen for dinner at the chief factor's home at the fort. David and volunteers worked for days to prepare a full period meal, roasting, baking, and then serving us all at the table as we talked of the events of 1845, the coming season, talk of possible war with the Americans, and of the "trade," as furs were capital.

Also at the table was Captain Thomas Baillie, RN, in command of HMS *Modeste*, then at anchor off the fort. Thomas Ballie was played by Nick Peck, a charming, highly educated gentleman and a *real* Englishman. With some help from Nick and a few hints from watching Rex Harrison as the spectral Captain Daniel Gregg in *The Ghost and Mrs. Muir*, Nick and I, as captains Baillie and Scarborough, had a roaring good time at those dinners, regaling the other guests with tales of coastal storms, foggy mornings on the Inside Passage, crossing the bar of the Columbia River, quelling incipient mutinies, and trading with the tribes, all with great delight and augmented with high-octane brandy advertised to the table as *"aguardiente"* acquired through trade with the Mexicans in Alta California. What this means is that what Tom saw at that meeting was the ghost of Captain Scarborough picking up that sherd. If archaeology is about people, and artifacts connect us to people in the past, then a little poetic license and a flair for a good story is a good thing in archaeological interpretation.

I strongly believe in the National Register and its powerful role in historic preservation. That comes in part from understanding, from my nearly 14 years in the National Park Service, that it is effective, as it has set criteria, increasingly high standards in research, documentation, and contextualizing significance, in evolving from 1966 to today. One of my first NRHP tasks was updating the documentation and forms for the schooner *C. A. Thayer* and later doing its NHL study, and in the course of my career I revised and added to nominations I had done for the National Register to then prepare the higher-standard assessment for NHL studies. That included historic ships, lighthouses, life-saving stations, and other properties from my own park (GGNRA), as well as the years of travel, documentation, and assessment of the nation's historic ships and maritime sites, with occasional forays into other aspects, such as the historic ranches in the Olema Valley north of San Francisco, the Adolph Sutro Historic District and Aquatic Park in San Francisco, and coauthoring the NHL study for the Lou Henry Hoover House at Stanford University.

In addition to focus and assessment through uniform criteria, National Register status confers certain levels of legal protection, and, for management purposes,

NRHP-listed properties and NHLs have higher priority for preservation action. In the aftermath of the accidental sewer trenching through the buried wreck of *Lydia* in San Francisco in 1978, Roger Olmsted prepared a successful nomination in 1981 to underscore its significance in case of any future work that might impact the site. *Tennessee*, listed on 15 April, and *Lydia*, listed on 16 July 1981, were the first National Register–listed maritime archaeological sites in California. That's why the first focus of historic preservation at GGNRA was to assess resources through context studies followed by nominations. The context studies for GGNRA were a massive set of volumes on the history of the area's seacoast fortifications, on Alcatraz, and on the various historical themes represented in the park.

National Register listing is probably the most crucial factor in assessing mitigation of impacts and hence a useful tool for federal, state, and local governments. That was key in my decision to prepare the nominations for the wrecks in the park—*Tennessee*, *King Philip*, and *Reporter*—and, in the aftermath of the news that a treasure-hunting group had located the wreck of SS *City of Rio de Janeiro*, the most tragic marine disaster off San Francisco, to nominate and list it. I also nominated *San Agustin* while the NPS was battling Robert Marx, who from the NPS perspective only wanted to treasure salvage that wreck. It was at first individually listed; it was then incorporated into the Drakes Bay Historical and Archaeological District in 2011. When treasure hunters were fighting the State of California to solely possess and salvage the steamship *Brother Jonathan*, the California State Lands Commission's Peter Pelkofer reached out, and I prepared

Property/Site Name	County	NRIS Number
SS *Brother Jonathan*	Del Norte	02000535
SS *City of Rio de Janeiro*	San Francisco	88002394
USS *Conestoga*	San Francisco	16000358
King Philip/Reporter	San Francisco	86001014
Lydia	San Francisco	81000173
USS *Macon*	Monterey	09001274
SS *Montebello*	Orange	16000636
SS *Pomona*	Sonoma	07000306
Turner/Robertson Shipyard	Solano	Not listed
Goldenhorn	Santa Barbara	Not listed

Table 2 Other NRHP-nominated and – listed maritime archaeological sites in California

a successful nomination for that wreck in 1995.

Other nominations were for the wreck of *Stamboul*, off Benicia at the Matthew Turner/ James Robertson Shipyard site, with a separate nomination for the shipyard site. Yet another, also in Benicia, was for the Yuba Manufacturing Company facility on the waterfront, which incorporated the last standing buildings and archaeological remains associated with the Gold Rush–era depot of the Pacific Mail Steamship Company. Neither nomination succeeded. A separate nomination for the wreck of *Goldenhorn* at Channel Islands National Park also did not result in it being listed. The SHPO recommended that the Turner/Robertson Shipyard site be rewritten for consideration as a California State Landmark, and it was accepted and listed as landmark No. 973 along with the wreck of *Stamboul*. Subsequent National Register maritime archaeological nominations now listed in California are the tanker *Montebello*, torpedoed and sunk in World War II, the SS *Pomona* at Fort Ross, the deep-sea wreck of the airship USS *Macon*, and the wreck of USS *Conestoga* (Table 2).

As this was happening, in addition to occasionally assisting Allen Pastron and Archeo Tec, I had also started to focus on another aspect of maritime archaeology, ship graveyards. That interest grew out of the Gold Rush work and specifically when Allen Pastron asked me to join his team in excavating the Charles Hare Shipbreaking Yard site south of Market Street in San Francisco. As previously noted, the site was the location of the ship graveyard of the Gold Rush fleet that had been laid up in the south end of Yerba Buena Cove in the lee of Rincon Point. The graveyard slowly gave way to shipbreaking by Charles Hare, who worked with the local Chinese community at a nearby fishing village. Because of an earlier publication (Delgado 1981) and more recent work together on the Hoff Store site, Allen asked me to join the team as they initially deployed in early 1987 and to assist in the excavation and documentation of the site as construction opened up the entire lot and dug down to the original bay floor in mid-1988.

Figure 37. James Delgado and Robert Schwemmer at the USS *Conestoga* memorial ceremony at the National Navy Memorial in Washington, D.C. (Photo courtesy of NOAA, 2016)

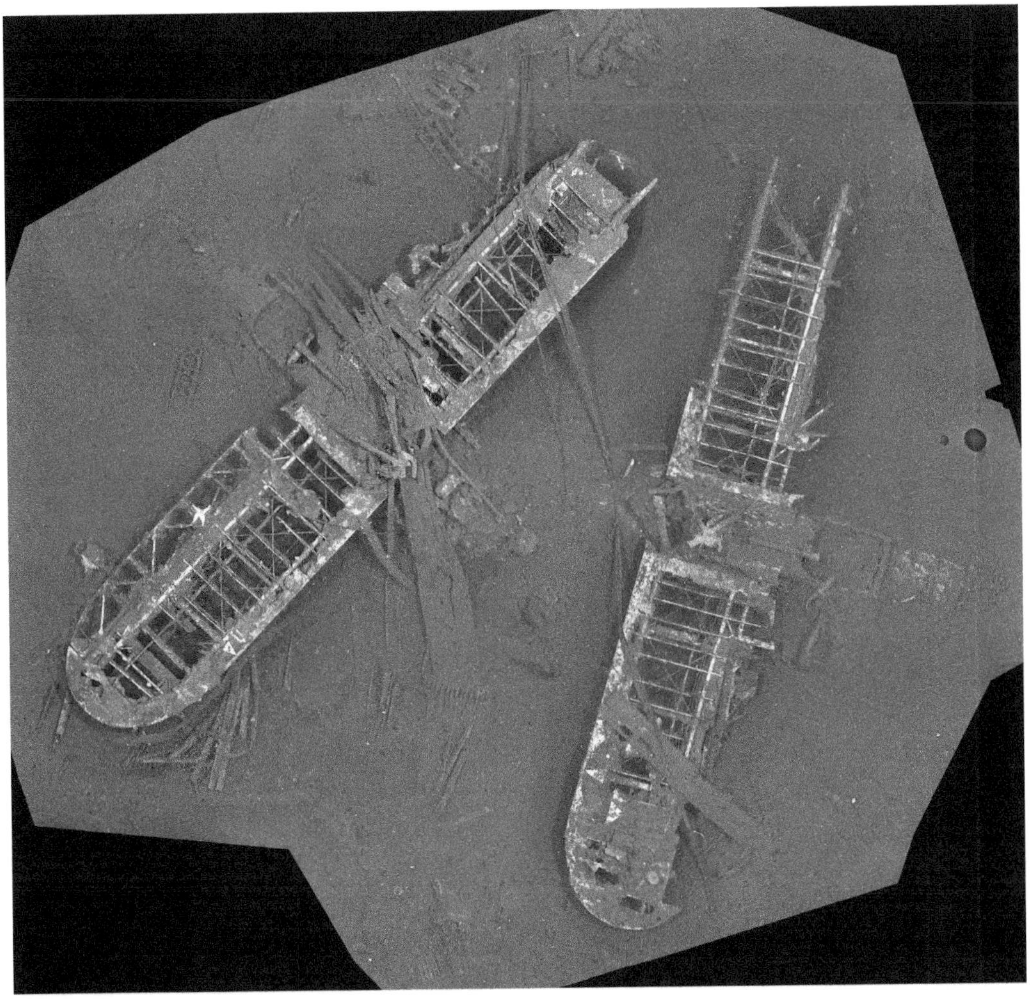

Figure 38. A photomosaic of Sparrowhawk aircraft on the wreck of *USS Macon* in Monterey Bay National Marine Sanctuary (Images courtesy of OET/NOAA, 2015)

Over 80 pieces of ship timber and a range of artifacts, including tools used to break apart the vessels, were found (Archeo-Tec 1987; Pastron and Delgado 1991). Not all of the site was excavated, as it lay under adjacent property lots. Jim Allan's team at William Self Associates excavated the adjacent lot in March–October 2005 and uncovered and documented the other half of the Hare Yard, locating the foundation of Hare's residence and office, more timbers, and the partially dismantled stern of what appeared to be an early 19th-century, copper-sheathed wooden vessel (Strother et al. 2007). Following the excavation, Jim Allan invited me to look at the timbers and assist in analysis and to also examine the recovered stern. Working with Jim, together we were able to initially identify it as the stern of one of the vessels noted in a contemporary February 1857 newspaper report of the shipbreakers' last work at the site, either the 1818-built bark *Candace* or the 1826-built bark *Harvest*, but more likely *Candace* (Strother et al. 2007:96–97).

Subsequent work on the stern in the laboratory found a set of whale's teeth cached between the floors at the stern, which, with damage to the rudder consistent with ice "nipping" from being trapped in Arctic ice, confirmed the stern was from *Candace*, damaged by ice while engaged in Arctic whaling, condemned as unfit, and sold to Hare. Subsequent to that project, Archeo-Tec did additional excavations at the site of the Chinese fishing village and found small pieces of ship timbers brought back in order to recover small copper and bronze fasteners (Pastron and Ambro 2007).

The work on that project sparked an interest shared with John Foster to examine the then-visible shoreside remains of

ships that had been hauled to a graveyard near Candlestick Point. There they were scrapped after being set on fire; when the fires were out, the salvagers recovered the metal fasteners. The graveyard's history and a preliminary inventory of vessels known to have been scrapped there was documented by historian Raymond Hillman (Hillman 1985). A mid-20th-century aerial photograph clearly showed the partially submerged outlines of the lower hulls of eight vessels: a "coal collier," the iron-hulled steamers SS *City of Peking* and SS *City of Sydney*, and the wooden-hulled steam schooners *Raymond*, *Grays Harbor*, *Carmel*, *Georgina Rolph*, and *Greenwood*. Following a report in early 1986 that the outline of a ship was visible on the shoreline at low tide, John Foster proposed a survey of the wreck, which lay within the boundaries of Candlestick Point State Recreational Area. I looked at the site with John and state archaeologist Herb Dallas on 30 April 1986, and John completed a site registration form, first in the state park database, and then with the trinomial CA-SFR-111H. We were eager to do more, and so working with John, we were able to plan a return with volunteers.

The California Academy of Sciences agreed to host an adult education course on maritime archaeology focused on the partial excavation and documentation of SFR-111H. I was the course instructor, and we were successful in enrolling 14 students. The class met on evenings, followed by a field trip to document the floating historic schooner *C. A. Thayer* at Hyde Street Pier to gain hands-on familiarity with the architecture of a West Coast–built ship, and then we went out to Candlestick with John Foster on 16 May 1987 and spent a long, muddy day documenting the wreck, probing its buried outline, and

A PERSONAL PERSPECTIVE

digging three 5 × 5 ft. units to determine the nature of the scrapping (fire) as well as how well preserved the lower hull was and to gain as accurate a set of measurements as could be done.

As a result, we were able to determine that the wreck was that of the 1907-built wooden-hulled steam schooner *Grays Harbor* based on its dimensions, position (using the labeled 1950s aerial photograph), and noting shoreline changes that had buried some of the other ships. Seven members of the class remained enthusiastic after the class ended on 19 May and substantially assisted in writing a final report on the project (Delgado, Babal et al. 1987). One of those "students" was fellow archaeologist René Péron, an instructor at Santa Rosa Junior College. René attended the 1988 SHA meetings in Reno and presented a paper on anthropological perspectives, specifically noting how Tom Layton's work on *Frolic* was a perfect example (Péron 1988). Another one of the adult education students from the class, Gerry Long, also attended the 1988 Reno meeting and presented a paper on *Grays Harbor*.

The 1988 meeting also included a paper by Nick Del Cioppo on a new state law to protect shipwrecks, and a paper by Roger Kelly also focused on protection and cooperation among Pacific Rim nations (Del Cioppo 1988; Kelly 1988a). Marco Meniketti, soon to join San José State, also attended and presented a paper on the need for archaeologists to understand political science. At that stage, a fierce battle was being waged in California between Bob Marx and the National Park Service, and, with Roger Kelly, I was in the forefront of the fight as the NPS representatives and spokespersons. That fight spilled into the meeting, as Bob Marx was

there along with a number of us from the National Park Service. As the underwater chair, I took that battle to the SHA board and held an open meeting to call out the ongoing presentation of treasure-hunting papers at SHA/CUA meetings and that Bob used his unelected role as a founder of the Advisory Council on Underwater Archaeology in his permit applications to salvage *San Agustin* and also work as a treasure hunter on other sites.

It was a contentious meeting, but it ended with a commitment to gradually shift the ACUA to an all-elected board and Bob's resignation from the ACUA; it was also the last SHA-CUA meeting in which papers considered for presentation did not undergo peer review with the authors agreeing to abide by archaeological ethics, i.e., reporting on sites where the artifacts were going to be sold. The year before, at the annual meetings in Savannah, Bob Marx had presented a paper on Manila galleons that spoke of the incredible riches carried in them, and a number of us, at least in the NPS, saw it as Bob using a professional conference to give a thinly disguised marketing paper and cloak it with an air of respectability as an academic paper. He was not alone in doing that at conferences.

To continue the discussion on ship graveyards, in 1987 dredging of the Coyote Point Marina adjacent to Candlestick Point hit the submerged and partially buried lower hull of the steam schooner *Daisy Gadsby*. The steam schooner, built in 1911, had been half sunk as part of a breakwater to form the marina in 1948. The dredging brought up big chunks of the wreck. Marty Mayer and I went out to Coyote Point document it and asked the maritime museum team if they wanted to save a representative piece, but Karl Kortum demurred, so the admittedly muddy, worm-eaten, and malodorous remains were hauled off to the dump. In 1989, sewer construction along the bay-shore side of Highway 101 as it passed Candlestick Point struck the buried remains of one of the scrapped ships; I was visiting and was invited to the site by Allen Pastron as Archeo-Tec was monitoring the work. Going back to Hillman's research (Hillman 1985) and looking at the remains, I identified the wreck for Allen as SS *City of Sydney*. Another construction project in February 2011 encountered two other buried ships from the graveyard, a scow schooner and a flat-bottomed barge, which were documented by Rebecca Allen and Scott Baxter of Past Forward (Delgado 2013:133). I was able to assist them remotely and sent references and the Hillman report.

As Garrison and Cook Hale (2020) noted with submerged site archaeology, the 1970s, 1980s, and 1990s saw a rapid expansion of projects spurred by technological advances and new methodologies and theoretical perspectives, exemplified by such seminal works as Muckelroy's *Maritime Archaeology* and Gould's edited volume, *Shipwreck Anthropology*. The 1980s also brought published CUA proceedings and a bibliography of underwater archaeology up to mid-decade, all produced by James F. Muche and A. Lani Low Muche (1984). The growth of the field, as the graduate programs at Texas A&M and East Carolina began graduating students with master's degrees in nautical archaeology (A&M) and maritime history and underwater research, later maritime studies (ECU). Both programs included a number of Californians. The focus also began to expand from localized sites to a more regional view of sites and contexts

(Delgado and Haller 1989a, 1989b; Pierson and Schiller 1989) and inspired discussions on the need for surveys in northern California as well as in the south (Simpson 1998).

In the federal family of agencies, the Minerals Management Service (MMS) began to focus more on offshore cultural resources, a process that would blossom into a major leadership role by them in the 21st century as a reorganized agency now known as the Bureau of Ocean Energy Management (BOEM), and the U.S. Army Corps of Engineers also began to focus more on maritime archaeological resources, both in assessing risks to them under the National Historic Preservation Act, but also in mitigation when Army Corps projects impacted them (Schwartz 1989, 1991). The project in question followed an earlier corps-funded cultural resources survey by Jack Hunter and Larry Pierson (1980) and focused on recovery of the steam engine of an historic ferry boat, SS *Sierra Nevada*, and its documentation to the standards of the Historic American Engineering Record (HAER).

Prior to that, the interest of the Army Corps was more often the interest and support of individual corps archaeologists, such as Richard Stradford of the San Francisco District, who, like Nick Del Cioppo, was a frequent visitor to various projects and participated in a number of them on his own initiative. Richard also brought his archaeological focus and process to Corps reviews of projects, a daunting task as his military superiors did not always appreciate cultural resources getting in the way of needed projects (Stradford 1998). Richard was a key player and a good colleague to work with throughout my federal years.

The period between 1960 and 2000 also saw California examples of evolutionary struggle, as underwater archaeology evolved from being something defined by its environment (wet) into archaeology that focused on various research themes, such as prehistoric, maritime, or nautical; the development and application of new technologies; the push for acceptance in the larger archaeological community; gain of support and commitment from various government agencies; and the internal struggle that divided a community of divers, wreck divers, treasure hunters, and the growing number of professional archaeologists.

In the U.S., much of the fight between treasure hunters and archaeologists was in Florida, but it also took place in California. The increased awareness of submerged sites and wrecks and the growing pace of asserting stewardship and regulation that collided with wreck divers who wished to continue their own recoveries also extended to California. The most dramatic example of the latter was the California Wreck Divers case in Southern California. I was caught up in that, disheartened after feeling that the overtures to work together in the Channel Islands were followed by a cruise advertised in *Nautical Brass* to visit and collect from wrecks in the national park and sanctuary. After alerting NPS officials, I did not hear more until after the undercover operation on the vessel—the same one we had chartered in 1985 for the NPS Saltwater Workshop—resulted in a series of charges and a court case. I traveled back to California to make a damage-assessment dive on the wreck of *Winfield Scott* with Larry Murphy and then worked with NOAA attorney Ted Buettler as the civil trial went forward before an administrative judge. That included time on the stand there as well as in a subsequent criminal case in Ventura County.

This followed and was also concurrent with being involved as an expert witness in the ongoing litigation over the gold recovered from the Panama Route steamer *Central America* off the coast of the Carolinas, the fights over *San Agustin* and Bob Marx seeking a permit, assisting California in a proposed salvage of SS *Yankee Blade*, as well as the proposal to salvage a reputed silver cargo (which did not exist, the metal ingots in the wreck being tin) from SS *City of Rio de Janeiro*, but prior to the win by the treasure hunters in the case of SS *Brother Jonathan*. My desire to try to work with and involve divers notwithstanding, my role as a government official led to showdowns that ruptured my friendship with Dave Buller and led to a falling out with John Foster that lasted for a while. Healing that relationship began with Tom Layton's ongoing work with wreck divers on *Frolic* and his interviews of a number of us in 1994. As Tom shared his transcripts with many of us, for me the commonality of the experiences and the thin line that separated the archaeologists from the wreck divers was a wake-up call to reach out and to move forward without making the debates personal.

Less contentious but passionately pursued as a topic of debate was the question of where Drake had landed, and that argument has yet to be settled, even as the NPS finally accepted the research and position taken by the Drake Navigators Guild's Ray Aker and Edward Von der Porten that Drakes Bay was the site and made it a National Historic Landmark district in

2011, also including *San Agustin* and the evidence of Cermeño's landing and interactions with the Coast Miwok (Wright and Von der Porten 2019). The question of the previously mentioned Goleta cannon, initially part of the debate as possibly being from that time period, was resolved and determined not to be from Drake's time.

The question of other early wrecks included work by James Muche, who in 1978 claimed he had found a Spanish Manila galleon, which he thought be *San Pedro*, off Santa Catalina Island (J. Muche 1981). The project ended with uncertainty that persists to this day, with one theory being that Howard Hughes used his assets to salvage the entire vessel and its treasure for the CIA, a reminder that Clive Cussler scenarios for shipwreck adventures and misadventures are always out there. That brings us to the case of the Palos Verdes stones. Local divers (and legendary scuba pioneers) Bob Meistrell and Wayne Baldwin had found the stones in 1975 and quietly invited archaeologists to take a look. Then all hell broke loose when the archaeologists called them stone "anchors," as the more than 30 stones had holes seemingly bored through them. Whether they were human-made was not the initial controversy. Considerable publicity and controversy ensued when Larry Pierson and James R. Moriarty announced that the stones might be Chinese stone anchors and evidence of pre-European maritime visitation by a "Chinese Columbus" from ca. 2250 B.C. (Pierson and Moriarty 1980, 1981).

The controversy raged for a while, long before Gavin Menzies published *1421: The Year China Discovered America*, with a rebuttal coming from Frank J. Frost of the University of California, Santa Barbara, who published an article in *Archaeology* suggesting they came from 19th-century Chinese fishermen's ships (Frost 1982). Another theory, advanced by Paul G. Chace (1983), was they were weights used to hold whale carcasses in position off shore whaling camps. Jack Hunter also got dragged into the controversy, rebutting a theory they were naturally formed, but were hand-carved, and, as Jack asserted, were not thousands of years old. Otto Orzech, a Navy Reserve dive officer and scientist who worked closely with Dan Lenihan and Larry Murphy, gave a paper he had jointly authored with Dan McCaslin on the controversy at the 1986 SHA meetings in Sacramento that John Foster chaired (McCaslin and Orzech 1988). John Foster visited in 1994, diving the site with Meistrell and Baldwin, and wrote a report with Jack Hunter in 1997 (Hunter and Foster 1997). In 2020, John Foster returned to the subject, laid out all of the theories, and reminded all of us who read that the mystery of what actually lay down there had yet to be definitively addressed, noting that California State Parks is now studying shore whaling-station sites off Pigeon Point and Point Lobos on the north-central coast, so if there are similar stones found, then perhaps the mystery will be solved (Foster 2020).

In December 1987, I left California and headed to Washington, D.C., to take up my duties there as the head of the National Maritime Initiative. I remained in Washington through April 1991, when, with the family, we headed back west to Vancouver, British Columbia, where I took up new duties as the executive director of the Vancouver Maritime Museum. I thought I'd return home to California at some stage, and while many visits followed in the intervening three-and-half decades, that has not happened yet. Among the tasks I finished in the National Park Service was a comprehensive submerged cultural-resources assessment for GGNRA, Point Reyes National Seashore, and Gulf of the Farallones National Marine Sanctuary with Steve Haller, who had succeeded me as the park's historian (Delgado and Haller 1989b). Steve and I also coauthored a more publicly accessible book on the shipwrecks off the Golden Gate (Delgado and Haller 1989a).

Meanwhile, I had become more active with the Submerged Cultural Resources Unit, joining in work at Pearl Harbor; at Bikini Atoll, where we documented some of the ships sunk in the 1946 atomic-bomb tests; and my final NPS archaeological project, leading a small team from SCRU to Mexico to jointly document the wreck of the U.S. Navy brig *Somers* off Veracruz with Pilar Luna Erreguereña and her team from INAH. While my focus turned to museum management and fundraising and I largely took a hiatus from active archaeological work, I gradually was able to return to a more "active" status, although then more focused on maritime archaeology in the Pacific Northwest and in the Arctic. The interest in and love of California maritime archaeology and history remained keen.

The ongoing work in California was exciting to see from a distance and at SHA conferences, as Marco Meniketti and Matt Russell, Ed Von der Porten, and Dan Lenihan and Larry Murphy all returned to conduct more detailed assessments at Drakes Bay with an emphasis on *San Agustin*, while John Foster, Sheli Smith, and Charley Beeker extensively documented SS *Pomona* at Fort Ross and also assessed the wrecks in Lake Tahoe at Emerald Bay. The major find of the Gold Rush vessel at Clarksburg in the Sacramento River, which also introduced me for the first time to the name of Fritz Hanselmann, soon to be introduced in person at an SHA by Charley Beeker, was a major discovery with ongoing potential. It was downright exciting to watch from afar and wish to be there, as Jim Allan and William Self Associates worked in a pressurized caisson in downtown San Francisco with the buried hulk of *Rome* after underground construction encountered it when drilling the Municipal Railway tunnel on San Francisco's Embarcadero.

It was also very satisfying to watch through the 1990s and into the new millennium as downtown San Francisco's buried sites, spanning the port and city's maritime heritage from prehistory to the city destroyed in the 1906 earthquake and fire, were regularly encountered during an increasingly fast-paced redevelopment of the city. Among those sites were early ship – and boatbuilding sites from the post–Gold Rush period, more work on the shipbreakers' yard, waterfront boardinghouses, and more Gold Rush sites. I was able to participate more as the decade came to an end, working from afar with Allen Pastron and Archeo-Tec, and also Jim Allan and WSA, as they occasionally reached out for background research and input into research designs and proposals.

The treasure salvage of SS *Brother Jonathan* in 1995, as previously noted, had me focus on the National Register nomination as a favor for California State Lands, working to describe the site as best I could from murky video and not being able to dive the wreck. Like *San Agustin*, *Brother Jonathan* was both a long-sought target by salvagers and legendary (Powers 2006). The case was a critical point in the state's management of its submerged cultural resources. Deep Sea Research, Inc., filed a suit in federal admiralty court to contest the state's ownership of *Brother Jonathan* in order to salvage the steamer's gold shipment. Deep Sea Research prevailed in the case, which was a blow to the state's oversight, but the State Lands Commission, which had increasingly stepped up to stewardship and shifted from what I'd seen as salvage at any costs by Bob Marx with *San Agustin* to inventories, evaluation (hence the NRHP nomination for *Brother Jonathan*), and insisting on mitigation when the court ruled for Deep Sea Research. Peter Pelkofer and Pamela Griggs at the SLC did tremendous work in this regard.

The Deep Sea Research salvage reportedly recovered $6 million in gold, but it is not clear whether that was an estimated value or the amount received through sale of the gold. The State Lands Commission, working with Jim Allan through his nonprofit Institute for Western Maritime Archaeology, acted as the state's archaeological consultant. The large cast – and wrought-iron "walking beam" from the steamer's engine was recovered, and in 2000 Deep Sea Research recovered an intact large wooden crate. When it was found to not have gold in it, Deep Sea Research turned it over to the state. Jim Allan arranged for the crate to go to the Conservation Research Laboratory at Texas A&M, where the crate was excavated and its contents studied and conserved by graduate student Carrie Sowden.

The crate contained a shipment from the Russell & Erwin Manufacturing Company of San Francisco. Carrie Sowden's work offers a convincing conclusion that the crate was likely intended "for a small, but well-established town with a base of customers from town as well as those that did not live directly in town. This could have been destined for any of the small settlements north of California" (Sowden 2006:158). This was excellent work in all regards, with the caveat that treasure hunters had seized a publicly owned asset in the name of free enterprise, obtained a flawed judgment from the court, made their money on grabbing the gold, and dumped the cost of preserving it and studying it on the state, and, if not for the ability of Texas A&M's laboratory and the opportunity to make it a student thesis, it might have cost more. The walking beam fared worse; it ended up being left in seawater off a dock in passive storage without conservation funds, and, as I was later told, was subsequently dredged up and discarded. The treasure hunters benefited from a beautifully illustrated book that I feel was done as a marketing piece for the gold (Bowers 1999). As of 2021, much of the site remains unknown, uncharacterized, and the extent of the work done and any damage unascertained. For me, *Brother Jonathan* represents not only the costs of treasure hunting, but also what we would have faced and lost if permits had been issued to allow treasure hunting with *San Agustin*.

Fitting California's Maritime Heritage and Underwater Archaeology into the Larger Picture

Akey point that had emerged earlier in regard to how best to parse "California" underwater and maritime archaeology is the fact that, while a site may be in a specific location and seemingly have "only" local or regional connotations, that's not always correct. The nature of the maritime world is the connectivity that comes through the movement of people, goods, and ideas by water. *San Agustín* spoke to emerging new global-trade patterns that linked Asia to the Americas and to Europe, and the Gold Rush was a global event. What was delightful to see was the growing assertion in maritime archaeology that the state's maritime history and archaeology, while significant, were neither unique nor isolated, just as evolving exploration and charting disproved the Elizabethan assumption that California was an island (Wagner 1937:144–147).

For me, that realization grew as I grew older and also matured as a scholar. It started as a natural process of physically leaving California. The extensive and intensive introduction to the maritime heritage of the United States and then the rest of the world helped make the connections to other scholars and scholarships, similar issues and sites, and the interconnectivity inherent in the maritime world. It was far more than seeing that other states and countries had wrecks on beaches, buried ships, or frontiers opened by ships.

There is a risk of parochialism in history and archaeology, especially for those of us maritime archaeologists who study a shipwreck site as a tree and not as part of the forest. A key part of my own journey was watching how Tom Layton made the story of *Frolic* and its history and archaeology far

more than a single ship. Another, frankly, was going back to school in my 40s to finish the academic journey and get a Ph.D. Working with a committee composed of Dave Burley, Margie Purser, George Nicholas, Ross Jamieson, Warren Gill, and Mark Staniforth was essential to properly characterizing and assessing the burnt, buried, and submerged waterfront of San Francisco's Gold Rush period as more than local history, an essay on the naval architecture of early to mid-19th-century ships, or a catalog of material culture (Delgado 2009, 2017). That in time led me to reassess the initial work I'd done with the Panama Route. The first inklings of the larger significance of the steamers came with early correspondence with Mark Staniforth as he studied the wreck of SS *Monumental City*, a Gold Rush steamer sent by its owners across the Pacific to Australia in response to the discovery of gold there and the subsequent rush to Down Under. What became abundantly clear was that the maritime world was more connected than my own parochial views had allowed in 1981, even while acknowledging that the Gold Rush was a global event.

The next important spur to rethink my earlier work on the Panama Route solely through the California wrecks and maritime sites (even my look at the former Pacific Mail Depot buildings in Benicia in 1987 was locally focused) came thanks to the work by Deborah (Dede) Marx, then a graduate student at East Carolina, on the wreck of *Winfield Scott*. Dede's thesis, completed in 2002, reflected her detailed research, significant additional fieldwork, and the integration of new perspectives, such as site-formation process as well the questions surrounding site management (D. Marx 2002). Dede also took a wider view of the steamer and its context in comparison to other steamers and its role on the East Coast prior to the Gold Rush.

What was also refreshing was to see her work point out mistakes and misinterpretations the NPS teams had made, myself included. Dede's thesis on *Winfield Scott* was a significant step forward in that it also it highlighted the role of sport divers, especially Pat Smith and CMAR, in the ongoing documentation of the site from 1995 forward, and the increasing role of NOAA as Channel Islands National Marine Sanctuary assumed a larger role in assessing, protecting, and interpreting the maritime heritage of the park and sanctuary. Looking back, what is clear in hindsight is that *Tennessee*, as my first maritime archaeological project, had sparked an interest in the Panama Route, and I had pursued that interest. The pursuit had also come from the realization that, in a way, the Gold Rush steamers were the California equivalent of Florida's 1622, 1715, and 1733 *flota* wrecks as targets for treasure hunters.

While some of that had taken place on a more individual scale, as savvy wreck divers dug for and found gold on *Winfield Scott*, *Yankee Blade*, and S.S. *Lewis*, the thought of greater riches through full salvage, initially rearing its head with *Yankee Blade*, was also a potential threat later realized with the "holy grail" Gold Rush–era steamer wreck, *Brother Jonathan*. My interests were both scholarly and resource-management focused, and so my energy was focused on the nomination of the steamer wrecks where I had sufficient information to complete a National Register form; SS *Lewis*'s location was unknown, as was *Brother Jonathan*'s, and

so the point was moot until they were "found" and marked. That came with *Brother Jonathan*, as noted, in 1995, four years after I left the NPS but retained my resource-management focus. That focus has been honed even sharper through several years of ongoing consultation as an expert witness for the insurance firms battling the treasure hunters in the ongoing admiralty court cases involving the SS *Central America*, the iconic Panama Route treasure wreck off the Carolina coast.

The shift to a more academic approach to the Panama Route and its archaeology came after 2000 and the first of what would be numerous visits to Panama, fieldwork on an 1866-built American submersible used to harvest pearls in the Islas de las Perlas off the Pacific coast of Panama, and finally fieldwork at the mouth of the Chagres River, a key site in the history of trans-isthmian transit and, thus, in the Gold Rush (Delgado, Hanselmann et al. 2011; Delgado 2013). That work introduced me to Panamanian colleagues and their work, not so much with wrecks but with the historical archaeology of Panama. I also met fellow maritime archaeologists in Mexico and El Salvador and shared observations on their Panama Route wrecks. Through that cross-fertilization of scholarship, I was getting to "know" the isthmus and its sites. I also learned by being in the field in Panama, hiking the same trails and heading up the same rivers as the gold seekers of the mid-19th century.

That work, done through two field seasons at the mouth of the Chagres, which, in addition to two reports and articles, culminated in a scholarly book. That coauthored volume on the maritime cultural landscape of Panama addressed the more globally significant scope and span of that landscape. It included sites beyond

A PERSONAL PERSPECTIVE

Panama, including the wrecks off California and the Benicia Depot of the Pacific Mail Steamship Company (Delgado, Mendizábal et al. 2016). I feel that, at last, for now at least, the wreck of *Tennessee*, first encountered on a Marin County beach in the park where I worked, can be looked at in a less particularistic and parochial way. That's why a scholar constantly has to accept challenges, and challenge their own scholarship and rethink it and rewrite it with fresh perspectives and new data.

Looking back to California now in 2021, 34 years after I moved east from San Francisco to Washington, D.C., and environs, to Vancouver, back to Washington, D.C., to Jacksonville, Florida, and now once again in the Washington, D.C. area, what has emerged in the state over that three-decade span follows the pattern of the field as a whole: evolving theoretical perspectives, connecting the dots globally, the decline of treasure hunting, the increased participation of government agencies in research and projects, and in the creation of new state underwater parks and the expansion of the National Marine Sanctuary system, the growth of partnerships with divers and others as part of citizen science, and the embrace and smart use of new technologies.

On the theoretical side, adopting the holistic approach of maritime cultural landscapes took a major step forward in California thanks to the leadership of Margie Purser at Sonoma State University. The track record of theses in the Cultural Resources Management Program of the anthropology department at Sonoma State is impressive, speaking to a broader and inclusive view of the maritime in maritime archaeology with seamen's burials, maritime households, and assessing Central Valley, San Francisco Bay, and coastal maritime cultural landscapes, as well as shipwrecks (Esser 1999; McCarthy 1999; Simpson 2001; McClellan 2015; Rockefeller 2015; Field 2017; Faycurry 2018). Over the last four decades, East Carolina University has graduated seven master's students with California-focused theses: two focus on shipyard sites (Allen 1993; Cooper 1995), one on shore whaling sites (Dickens 1998), one on Indigenous craft and seafaring (Hough 2018), one on beached shipwreck sites (Russell 1996), and two on Panama Route steamship wrecks (Delgado 1985a; D. Marx 2002). There is another on a Gold Rush steamer that, after California service, worked and wrecked in Australia (Warren 1998). The Nautical Archaeology Program at Texas A&M University graduated two students whose theses focused on two other Pacific wooden steamers of the post–Gold Rush period with California connections: SS *Brother Jonathan*, previously mentioned (Sowden 2006), and SS *Great Republic*, wrecked at the mouth of the Columbia River in Oregon (Roberts 2008). *Great Republic* regularly steamed from San Francisco to Japan and China after the Civil War.

At San José State, Marco Meniketti's active role in *San Agustin* and larger context studies of the Manila galleons and maritime cultural landscapes continued through the decade, as did mentoring students and his recent work applying forensic science through the XRF analysis of the Drakes Bay porcelains (Meniketti 2014, 2017; Gusick et al. 2019). One maritime thesis supervised by Marco focuses on the larger landscape and industrial aspects of often-overlooked smaller ports, in this case Aptos and Alviso (Spitzer 2015). I also want to emphasize the importance of the contribution made in Marco's latest publication, which integrates the social, labor, and maritime aspects through his study through archaeology of the timber industry at the Loma Prieta Mill. I was hooked at the start by the title of the introduction: "The Industrial Landscape of Timber" (Meniketti 2020). Most recently, Marco edited a comprehensive volume on the archaeology and social histories of California's maritime cultural landscapes, which is a major contribution with a number of leading scholars whose chapters range from prehistory to the industrial age and some of the state's ethnic communities (Meniketti 2023).

The previously mentioned work in the Channel Islands lives up to the active stewardship role that emerged as a need following the Channel Islands Wreck Diver Case at the end of the 1980s. The work of the NPS, as demonstrated by the ongoing work of Don Morris, the Submerged Resource Center projects, the work on the beached wrecks, and the development of the NOAA West Coast presence of the system-wide Maritime Heritage Program by Bob Schwemmer has seen extensive work with annual research cruises, ongoing surveys to locate and document shipwrecks and sunken aircraft, an extensive database, and the partnership with the Santa Barbara Maritime Museum and its interpretive displays, as well as public programs.

Bob Schwemmer's participation and support includes work outside of the Channel Islands, including projects at the Gulf of the Farallones, at Olympic Coast NMS in Washington State, in the Arctic, and in Hawaii. Bob, a former wreck diver, does not have an archaeology degree; as the former director of NOAA's Maritime Heritage Program, I saw this not as an obstacle, but as a plus, given his other skills, passion, and self-taught knowledge. When occasional criticism arose, I reminded people that the leading scholar in ship reconstruction, J. Richard "Dick" Steffy, also did not have an archaeology degree. That did not stand in the way of his exceptional career with the Institute of Nautical Archaeology, as a founding member of the Nautical Archaeology Program at Texas A&M, or in his selection for a MacArthur Fellowship. There are multiple examples of colleagues like Dick and Bob. Closer to home for Bob, in the Channel Islands, the strong role of wreck divers, exemplified by Patrick Smith and the Coastal Maritime Archaeology Resources Group (CMAR) is another powerful example.

Outside the park and sanctuary, the work by Gary Fabian and his colleagues with the rediscovery of the World War I prize submarine UB-88 offers another example. Gary Fabian is a highly skilled researcher and interpreter of sonar imagery, and many shipwreck discoveries, including UB-88, owe their discovery to him; at NOAA we worked closely with Gary. Individual wreck projects continue, both by California State Parks and also by NOAA, which followed up on the discovery of the deep-water wreck of the dirigible USS *Macon* with a series of research cruises and dives to document this unique submerged site. Assessing wrecks of historic significance that might pose a risk to the environment through leaking oil has included deep dives to the tanker *Montebello*, torpedoed by a Japanese submarine off Southern California in World War II, as well as the recent survey to locate and identify the wreck of the U.S. Coast Guard steam cutter *McCulloch*. In the CRM world, Andrew D. W. Lydecker of Panamerican Consultants, Inc., documented the substantial remains of the Clarksburg auto ferry, stripped and scuttled on the Sacramento River in advance of levee repair at Clarksburg (Lydecker 2010).

In 2010 I transitioned from the Institute of Nautical Archaeology to NOAA, returning to federal service as the director of the Maritime Heritage Program. As part of that nationwide program in the various sanctuaries, the time came to return to California to develop, lead, and also participate in several major initiatives then emerging as NOAA priorities: assessing potentially polluting wrecks; integrating maritime cultural landscapes, not only as a theoretical perspective, but also as a management tool; encouraging the ongoing inventory of sites and nominating significant ones to the National Register; and utilizing the newest deep-water tools and techniques in cooperation with NOAA's office of Ocean Exploration and Research, the three California sanctuaries, the state, and Bob Ballard's Ocean Exploration Trust.

The Monterey Bay Aquarium Research Institute (MBARI) pioneered California deep-water maritime heritage assessment in 1990 with the discovery of USS *Macon* in 442 m of water off the coast near Monterey and within the boundaries of Monterey Bay National Marine Sanctuary (Lickliter-Mundon et al. 2015:12). The images of the wreck site, with *Macon*'s fabric-covered, brightly painted Sparrowhawk spotter aircraft, published in *National Geographic* just five years after the discovery of *Titanic*, offered an exciting look at what lay deep off California. In the aftermath of the discovery, MBARI's Chris Grech and his team returned to the site and worked closely with NOAA to document the wreck in 2006, leading to a successful National Register nomination (Grech

2007). In partnership with NOAA and with NOAA funding, the redeployment by Dr. Ballard and the Ocean Exploration Trust of their vessel E/V *Nautilus* and its robotic systems opened the opportunity for a new mission utilizing the most recent technology to conduct a new assessment and comprehensive site map.

Maritime archaeologist Megan Lickliter-Mundon, then completing Ph.D. studies at Texas A&M University with an emphasis on submerged aviation archaeology, was working as a summer intern with the Maritime Heritage Program in 2013. As plans moved forward for a 2015 *Macon* mission, we selected Megan to be the lead principal investigator for the mission, working with co-PIs NOAA maritime historian Bruce Terrell, Bob Schwemmer, Alexis Catsambis from the Naval History and Heritage Command, and Michael Brennan, then with the Ocean Exploration Trust as its archaeologist and expedition leader. The new photomosaics, with high resolution, provided fresh insights and cleared the way for the pending final publication on *Macon*'s history and archaeology. *Macon* also formed a major portion of Megan's dissertation (Lickliter-Mundon 2018). Another major aspect of the mission was live broadcast over the Internet of the entire mission, utilizing telepresence to interpret the site, the technology, and deep-water archaeological assessment (Delgado, Brennan, Elliott et al. 2018).

The 2015 Ocean Exploration Trust Pacific Coast mission followed a series of earlier NOAA missions that assessed known and potential maritime archaeological sites in California's deep water. During the shakedown cruise for the newly acquired and refitted NOAA vessel *Okeanos Explorer*, a multi-beam survey conducted under the supervision of the ship's executive officer, Jeremy Weirich, pinpointed a sonar anomaly that was likely the nuclear-damaged aircraft carrier USS *Independence*. After surviving two nuclear blasts, *Independence* became a floating laboratory for ongoing study of radiation and as a training facility for the now emerging "Atomic Navy" at Hunter's Point Naval Shipyard in San Francisco. No longer needed, *Independence* sank after being scuttled with explosive charges off the coast in 1951.

Research suggested that the wreck lay deep within the waters of Monterey Bay National Marine Sanctuary. An earlier survey of the area by the U.S. Geological Survey mission to map the seabed with side-scan sonar had picked up an anomaly that might be the sunken carrier. Jeremy and I had been corresponding on the subject of *Independence* for a few years, as I was keen to follow up on a project I'd just finished as part of a team from the NPS Submerged Resources Center at Bikini and Kwajalein atolls with other wrecks from the 1946 "Operation Crossroads" atomic tests. We had completed documenting the wrecks in 1989–1990, while at the same time the USGS had done its survey and announced the possible finding of *Independence*'s wreck. That set into motion a slow, intermittent conversation through the years with Jeremy and with Kelley Elliott of NOAA and the resurvey of the target by *Okeanos Explorer*.

The larger maritime cultural landscape of Operation Crossroads includes several target ships brought back to California for study and progressive tests of decontamination measures that were subsequently scuttled. I wanted to see if *Independence* could be found in the sanctuary, as did Jeremy and Kelley Elliott. During those years Kelley completed her M.A. thesis on the potential archaeology of *Independence* (Elliott 2008). That opportunity came through the NOAA Office of Exploration and Research and a mission in 2015 to test Boeing's *Echo Ranger* autonomous underwater vehicle. That project, codirected

Figure 39. The NOAA and Ocean Exploration Trust team on E/V *Nautilus* conduct one of the archaeological dives on the wreck of *USS Independence* by ROV. (Photo by Julye Newlin, courtesy of OET/NOAA, 2016)

A PERSONAL PERSPECTIVE

with Frank Cantelas and Bob Schwemmer, resulted in a closer flyover of the wreck and mapping it with multi-beam sonar; there was no doubt that it was *Independence*, upright on the seabed in 828 m of water, damaged, but substantially intact, and with what appeared to be an aircraft in the forward elevator pit. We published the results, with a declassified series of documents and commentary by colleagues, in a special issue of the *Journal of Maritime Archaeology* (Delgado, Elliott et al. 2016; Delgado, Cantelas et al. 2016; Delgado, Brennan, Roletto et al. 2017; Delgado, Roletto, Brennan et al. 2017; Delgado, Roletto et al. 2017; Delgado, Brennan, Cantelas et al. 2018; Delgado, Brennan, Elliott et al. 2018).

The next phase was a series of dives, 30 hours in total bottom time, on the wreck from the E/V *Nautilus* with the Ocean Exploration Trust in 2016. A detailed characterization of the wreck with Bob Ballard, Mike Brennan, Russ Matthews, Kelley Elliott, Megan Lickliter-Mundon, and USS *Independence*'s official historian, John G. Lambert, who had also been part of the 2015 mission, documented its exterior, entered the hangar deck at the forward elevator and through a hole in the flight deck amidships, located the remains of two aircraft and barrels used to pack and discard irradiated laboratory equipment and clothing, measured for ambient radiation (there was none left from the atomic tests), and assessed biological colonization of the wreck, all published in another special issue of the *Journal of Maritime Archaeology* (Delgado, Brennan, Elliott et al. 2018; Delgado, Matthews et al. 2018). It was also broadcast live through telepresence, and, like all Ocean Exploration Trust and NOAA telepresence missions, the public had the opportunity write in with questions that the science team answered while working on the site (Delgado, Brennan, Cantelas et al. 2018).

The USS *Independence* missions coincided with a longstanding desire to return to California to continue work on the offshore wrecks and the larger maritime cultural landscape with Bob Schwemmer and other colleagues. Despite being an avowed trekkie, all we could do was a three-year, not a five-year mission. Starting in 2013, the Greater Farallones National Marine Sanctuary Maritime Heritage Assessment ran through 2016 and was codirected with Bob Schwemmer and Jan Roletto of GFNMS. The survey was a cooperative project with Greater Farallones National Marine Sanctuary (headquartered in San Francisco), Cordell Bank National Marine Sanctuary, and Monterey Bay National Sanctuary to assess a series of sonar targets provided by Gary Fabian through his prodigious research into archived sonar data and reinterpretation of that data.

Revisiting and Revising the Gulf of the Farallones with a New Perspective

The 2013–2016 mission literally brought me home again to where I had started a journey to become a maritime archaeologist in 1980. At that time, the NOAA Maritime Heritage Program was working closely with the Marine Protected Areas (MPA) Center, whose advisory committee, assembled by Valerie

Grussing, had prepared a white paper on maritime cultural landscapes for managing MPAs (MPA 2011). The Office of National Marine Sanctuaries had started shifting our program to work with the National Marine Sanctuary System to integrate MCLs into the management of the various sanctuaries (Barr 2013). One of the key members of the MPA advisory group, Dave Ball of BOEM, had spearheaded much work in California and up the coast from his Southern California office; Dave joined us on the missions.

The overall mission concluded in 2016 with a series of dives on some of the deeper targets with E/V *Nautilus* and the Ocean Exploration Trust team, when Mike Brennan joined as a co-PI. We moved beyond the Gulf of the Farallones's main area to go north to the Sonoma coast, where we documented the never-before-seen 1938 wreck of the lumber-trade freighter *Dorothy Wintermote*. Closer to the Golden Gate, the fieldwork discovered and documented the offshore wreck sites of the clipper ship *Noonday* (1863), SS *Selja* (1910), SS *Ituna* (1920), USS *Conestoga* (1921), and several unidentified

shipwrecks, including one modern fishing vessel with a partially obscured name. Joining us were partners from the NPS, BOEM, the Naval History and Heritage Command, and California State Parks (Dodds and Hawley 2019). The Navy participation came when one of Gary Fabian's targets was determined to be the wreck of USS *Conestoga*, found at last after going missing in 1921 and becoming a naval mystery for nearly a century (Delgado and Schwemmer 2016). The discovery and documentation of this very significant wreck, the grave of its entire crew, led to its successful nomination to the National Register by Dede Marx.

Some of the missions came as "targets of opportunity" through work with San Francisco Fire and Rescue, Coda Octopus (to test its three-dimensional mapping system), Bay Marine Services, and Hibbard Inshore. Those individual projects also included working with local partners from NOAA's Office of Coast Survey's Navigation Response Team, headquartered in the Bay Area. Wrecks located and documented included SS *City of Chester* (1889) and a relocation of SS *City of Rio de Janeiro*

Figure 40. ROV footage of the engine room of *SS Ituna* off Point Reyes. (Photo courtesy of the OET/NOAA, 2016)

A PERSONAL PERSPECTIVE

Figure 41. NOAA poster by Robert Schwemmer on the discovery of the wreck of *SS City of Chester* inside the Golden Gate. (Photo courtesy of NOAA, 2016)

(1901), both in the main shipping channel at the Golden Gate, and the 1951 wreck of the freighter *Fernstream*, a close-by and potentially polluting wreck. Yet another was a daring close-to-shore three-dimensional scan of the wrecks of the tankers *Frank H. Buck* and *Lyman Stewart*, sister ships that wrecked at the same location off San Francisco's Lands End. The wrecks are so shallow that their engines were sticking above the sea directly below the cliffs. Vitad Pradith of NOAA and his team practically surfed in and out on a very calm day. The other survey, a smaller-scale effort with Jim Allan in the shallows of Tomales Bay, north of San Francisco in Marin County, probed for and relocated the buried, partially teredo-consumed remains of the 1850 wreck of the ship *Oxford*.

The results of the various surveys, all parsed and reinterpreted through the theoretical perspective of MCLs as a maritime cultural landscape, were published in 2020 (Delgado, Schwemmer et al. 2020). It brought my own California maritime archaeological journey to, not a close, but to a new beginning nearly four decades after my first project. The final day of the survey, therefore, had to be taking the M/V *Fulmar* into the flat, calm waters of Tennessee Cove, following the track of the ill-fated *Tennessee* as it had steamed in and wrecked on 6 March 1853. Onboard with us was my friend and colleague John Martini, who had worked on that and many other projects with me in the 1980s, as well as Richard Everett of the maritime museum.

The last stage of the overall project was a cooperative venture with California State Parks on the Sonoma County coast. That coast, lined with redwood forests, is a maritime cultural landscape with a broad range of resources, Fort Ross being the most famous. As the waters off the coast had just been added to Greater Farallones and Cordell Banks National Marine Sanctuaries, I'd flown to Sacramento to discuss

Figure 42. James Delgado and James Allan probing for the wreck of the Gold Rush wreck *Oxford* in Tomales Bay, 2016. (Photo courtesy of James Delgado)

a joint project with California State Parks' Leslie Hartzell and Rick Fitzgerald, and, happily as well, with John Foster, who came in for the meeting. The project, jointly funded, was a comprehensive survey on land and water of the various "doghole ports" on the Sonoma County coast. The ports got their generic name as being small, tight landings where ships would anchor just out of the breakers and load and discharge lumber and freight, including ranchers' produce, using wooden chutes and later suspended wires. In 1980, CSP had kicked off the study and recognition of the dogholes with an assessment of the known ports in Mendocino County (Sullenberger 1980), and John Foster had done considerable work at Fort Ross, but in the last several years not much had been done as different priorities demanded attention.

The project included every known and suspected doghole, some in state parks (including Fort Ross) as well as on private property. It was yet another return to earlier projects and places for John, me, and others, and included Matt Lawrence and

Dede Marx, both then with NOAA, John Foster, Rick Fitzgerald, Scotty Greene, Richard Everett, Denise Jaffke, and Tricia Dodds, and it involved scrambling down cliffs, dangling above surf lines, water surveys, and diving from the R/V *Fulmar*. The team covered a tremendous amount of ground (and water) and documented a wide range of sites. It resulted in a major report (Delgado, Borgens et al. 2021) and

Figure 43. Taking notes during the Sonoma Coast Doghole Ports Survey. (Photo courtesy of California State Parks, 2016)

A PERSONAL PERSPECTIVE

is now being followed up on with a National Register of Historic Places multiple-property submission with detailed nominations for the various dogholes, all being completed by Dede Marx, who is a prodigious and exceptional veteran of NRHP maritime nominations. Margie Purser also joined us with two of her students who were completing theses on maritime cultural landscapes, and, one of them, Jessica Faycurry, focused hers on the Sonoma dogholes (Faycurry 2018).

If a project is to be done, and done well, ideally it has multiple outputs; Jessica's thesis was one, the report was another, the nominations yet another, and there was also some significant community outreach and interpretation through the good offices of the Fort Ross State Park's nonprofit foundation as well as through the gracious contributions of time, knowledge, and perspectives of the Kashia Pomo and local historians. The consultation with the Kashia was and is part of a concerted effort we'd started with various tribes as part of NOAA's partnership with BOEM. Dave Ball, as part of his engagement with the MPA Center's maritime cultural landscapes initiative, had sought and obtained funding from his agency for a special study on characterizing tribal cultural landscapes.

The process involved considerable consultation, working with three tribes: the Makah in Washington, the Grande Ronde in Oregon, and the Yurok in California. Valerie Grussing headed up the effort for NOAA. The results were a strong step forward in collaboration with the tribes to develop a proactive approach to working with Indigenous communities to identify areas of tribal significance that need to be considered in management and planning by federal agencies (Ball et al. 2017). There was and is more work to be done, and, as part of that, with Val, I'd started more outreach and discussed cooperation with other tribes, and so, with the

Figure 44. The doghole-ports team at a doghole port. (Photo courtesy of California State Parks, 2016)

Figure 45. Richard Everett at a windlass repurposed as a winch on the clifftop at Fisk Mill Cove doghole port. (Photo courtesy of California State Parks, 2016)

Figure 46. Pre-dive briefing on R/V *Fulmar* during the doghole ports survey. (Photo courtesy of NOAA, 2016)

Figure 47. Deborah Marx diving on the wreck of *SS Pomona* in Fort Ross Cove during the doghole ports survey. (Photo courtesy of NOAA, 2016)

doghole ports, the Kashia's ongoing, millennia-spanning presence on the coast was essential to recognize.

That aspect of the study remains to be done or has been done by the Kashia as per those guidelines, and if the state or NOAA plan a management action or activity that impinges on or might impact a tribal cultural property, the Kashia will let them know. This initiative was only one of several highly significant actions taken by BOEM and specifically by Dave Ball; in addition to updated inventories of potential historic shipwrecks, Dave had also funded and overseen studies on the potential for submerged environments and sites on the outer continental shelf drowned by sea-level rise at the end of the last great ice age. This is the latest significant and ongoing development in underwater archaeology in California. Appropriately, it takes us back to the earliest work on the California coast and in underwater archaeology overall, the question of "prehistoric" sites in the sea.

Indigenous Perspectives: From the Ice Age to Colonial Encounters

The archaeology of ice-age California and the people here at that time has evolved from scuba dives to robotic mapping and exploration some 100 m deep from the former shoreline. Taking into account the complexities of geological changes that leave a record is not as simply determined as a simple calculation of sea rise, but instead factors in variables, such as isostatic rebound and plate tectonics. Models of the Pacific coast as it was during and after the ice age and ongoing work have defined the Channel Islands area as a center for ongoing research by colleagues

Jon Erlandson, Amy Gusick, Torben Rick, Todd Braje, Loren G. Davis, and others. I am fascinated by the ongoing work and watch with great interest, but, with a different academic focus, honestly do not follow the expanding scholarly literature as much as I should with the needs of my own academic focus and workload. To attempt a moderately comprehensive bibliographic essay would fall short. I simply note that watching "underwater" archaeology coming full circle to this aspect of archaeology is exciting. The 21st century's great archaeological breakthroughs will in time be seen to include a rewriting of the story of the human past that incorporates the drowned world of humanity's ice-age ancestors.

As is the case with other aspects of archaeology, maritime work in California now incorporates more interdisciplinary science, such as the work of Cyler Conrad and his colleagues (Conrad et al. 2015) and other voices and perspectives from previously ignored groups. The maritime world never was exclusively white and male, and, in California, the spread of European colonial ambition incorporated California at first peripherally, but with impacts on its Indigenous inhabitants. To see the scholarship of the wreck of *San Agustin* increasingly focus on that has been an exciting development, especially thanks to Matt Russell and Kent Lightfoot's focus and interpretations. The aspect of cultural contact and impact is a key aspect of Tom Layton's work on the wreck of *Frolic*, again reflecting what happens when anthropologists get involved and when people start listening to Indigenous voices.

California did not begin with the Gold Rush, but that event was profound in the changes it brought to the region and the world in many ways. *Frolic* speaks to colonial-era contact and change, but it also speaks to how California and its

Figure 48. Chumash paddle a modern tomol through the waters of Channel Islands National Marine Sanctuary. (Photo by Robert V. Schwemmer; courtesy of NOAA)

A PERSONAL PERSPECTIVE

archaeology reflect the massive shifts in human civilization toward a global community and economy with, as yet, not fully realized consequences for both humanity and the world itself, as we firmly reside in this space and time in the Anthropocene epoch, a phase in the planet's evolution that is in itself an artifact of human activity. I suspect this macro-artifact will prove deadlier than the likely presence of deeply buried microscopic plutonium particles from the atomic bomb blasts at Bikini in the rusted hull of USS *Independence* off the coast of California.

Therefore, understanding the last 500 years and the role of maritime activity is where my academic interests have come, as the same has been true for other colleagues. I'm still fascinated by site-formation processes of ships wrecked on beaches, on the archaeology of discard and recycling inherent in ship graveyards, and in the theoretical construct of maritime cultural landscapes. But the overarching focus is global. The essentially maritime nature of the emerging global economy or, as Immanuel Wallerstein termed it, the "World System," brought increased cultural contact from ca. 1450 to 1850 to "distant" parts of the world; Wallerstein called them "peripheral zones," as they were outside of the European political and economic zones of influence. The nature of those contacts and the various reasons for them as extensions of economic, political, and cultural domination of Europe, as well as the consequences, are an oft-told aspect of scholarship and popular literature. Modern scholarship has challenged and amended Wallerstein's thesis, especially in regard to other systems that arguably were, if not global, extensive. Asian systems, Islamic systems, and Indigenous trade systems offer a more balanced and less Eurocentric view (Berrocal and Tsang 2017a, 2017b).

Within this discussion, however, is the undeniable drama and fascination with the concept of "first contact." The story of this aspect of the American experience (by this I mean the continental North and South and the Caribbean) has attracted considerable attention and has been the focus of much scholarship, starting with the 1960s discussion of drift voyages from Asia several thousand years ago and more recent work on Polynesian/South American cultural contact. More recently, the narratives have shifted to include the Indigenous experience and reinterpret some of these encounters as something more than a strange set of aliens with advanced technology landing on the beach. A recent project, previously mentioned, with the wreck of the ship *Oxford* in Tomales Bay to me is a perfect example of this evolution in archaeological thinking and practice, not in the work done by the maritime archaeologists, myself included, but in how the analysis and interpretation of specific artifacts were integrated into a larger and more significant perspective by Tsim Schneider and his colleagues.

The former packet ship *Oxford*, inbound with a cargo of whiskey, ice, and merchandise for Gold Rush San Francisco, stranded in the mudflats of Tomales Bay, about 50 mi. north of the Golden Gate, when the captain mistook his bearings. The cargo was salvaged, but *Oxford* was left to the tide. The vessel remained visible, stranded in the mud, for decades and was noted in U.S. Coast Survey charts through the 1870s. With Jim Allan I relocated the wreck while with NOAA, first georectifying the old chart data and then probing the site to find the mollusk-eaten, crunchy bits of *Oxford* under a mud-covered sand bar that lies atop the wreck. It is within Greater Farallones National Marine Sanctuary. From a CRM perspective, we had "marked the spot," and now it can be factored into planning and management decisions as a potentially National Register–eligible archaeological site. However, our work on *Oxford*, such as it was, is not the most significant archaeology to incorporate the wreck of *Oxford*.

Archaeologist Tsim Schneider and colleagues excavated the site of a trading post inhabited by American seaman George Thomas "Tom" Wood, who deserted his ship, married a Coast Miwok woman, and settled at the point, now known as "Toms Point," at the mouth of Tomales Bay. Wood, his wife, and other local Coast Miwok lived there, as did the Miwok working on the local ranches at Point Reyes. Schneider's excavation yielded a rich archaeological record of mixed Indigenous and manufactured North American and European goods, as well as fasteners from the ship that Wood and the Coast Miwok had salvaged from *Oxford* to build homes and other structures. I analyzed the fittings and fasteners for them. A key takeaway from Schneider et al.'s research is that the archaeology at Toms Point counters previous assertions by showing that, following Spanish-Mexican and Russian settlement, missionization and the American conquest and increased settlement that came with the Gold Rush, cultural extinction **did not** happen, and Indigenous groups survived colonization (Byram 2013; Panich, Schneider et al. 2018; Panich, DeAntoni et al. 2021).

Conclusion: Reflecting, not on the Past, but on the Future

Before the COVID-19 pandemic, a longstanding personal and professional wish to conduct a field project in the Falkland Islands happened thanks to a grant from the National Geographic Society. The focus was the hulk of the bark *Vicar of Bray*, a vessel that had sailed into San Francisco Bay in 1849 during the Gold Rush. Karl Kortum and the San Francisco Maritime Museum had sought to rescue the substantially intact, partially sunk *Vicar* from its subantarctic final mooring at Goose Green in the Falklands. *Vicar of Bray*, like a number of the ships in San Francisco Bay in 1849, had in time become a hulk in that seemingly isolated spot in the South Atlantic. Working on the now wrecked and submerged *Vicar* with Amy Borgens, Dede Marx, and Matt Lawrence, and accompanied by local diver and historian Dave Eynon and my longstanding friend George Belcher of San Francisco was the culmination of a decades-old dream. While we assessed site-formation processes and the factors behind long-term survival of wooden hulks in the islands, what also struck us all was how rapidly the factors that had preserved the hulks were now gone due to climate change. *Vicar of Bray*, like the other hulks no longer above the water as a unique museum of 19th-century wooden ships, was a canary in a coal mine (Delgado, Borgens et al. 2021).

The lesson of that was ever present as we wrote our report and prepared to publish. The publication lagged, caught up in COVID times and also because George Belcher died not long after the project. George, a San Francisco art dealer, had

A PERSONAL PERSPECTIVE

followed maritime archaeology and sponsored and led the expedition that discovered the wreck of the U.S. Navy brig *Somers* off Veracruz, Mexico. George worked closely with the Mexican and U.S. governments to see the site documented and protected, and that is how I met him and we became friends. Thanks to George I had the opportunity as the oldest child in my family to finally get a big brother; our two families were close, traveling to projects in Vietnam, where he had served as an AID officer at Nha Trang during the war, and to Turkey when we were both involved with the Institute of Nautical Archaeology, George as a member of the board. George had been fighting Agent Orange–induced cancer, was sick on the Falklands trip, and, upon returning home, had died with his wife and daughter at his side.

George's death hit hard. Then came COVID and, in the last year, coincidentally and not due to COVID, nearly a dozen other friends and two family members have died. At 65, and still young by 21st-century standards, I am at a point personally and professionally where, now paused on the road by the pandemic, I can look back, as I have done in this essay. But I can also look forward to the future. Remaining active in the field is part of that. I recently completed a maritime-focused analysis of a San Francisco CRM excavation for my colleagues at PaleoWest. The focus was not on hardware, or features, but on larger contexts of a post–Gold Rush maritime cultural landscape, ethnic and gender diversity, and how this site fits into larger regional and global patterns. It also looks at the ethnogenesis of what would become the city's Italian-Croatian community and the first site of what is today at another site and called "Fisherman's Wharf."

The ongoing work to forensically identify and better understand the processes affecting ongoing preservation of the wreck of *Clotilda*, the last known ship to bring captives from Africa to America as part of the transatlantic slave trade, has also been a central focus for me as the principal investigator. It is, as all archaeology should be, community-focused in close cooperation with the community of Africatown and *Clotilda* descendants, with intense public and media interest. Our focus has been on working with the community, on careful, minimal-impact focused work, and on preservation options. At the same time, I have also worked closely with Michael Brennan and others on deep water wreck sites encountered during voyages of exploration and scientific study by NOAA and the Ocean Exploration Trust, with a wide range of nineteenth century, World War II, and Cold War sites.

There, and with these projects several thousand meters depth, it has not been about the "discovery," but the science, including site formation processes, biological colonization, and archaeology. Collaborative, public-facing, interdisciplinary science as part of ocean exploration is now an important part of what I get to do, and with a diverse team, many of them younger, as we "boldly go" resonates with me. It has evolved into more than individual dives to assess a wreck – we recently completed a comprehensive historical and archaeological contextual study for the nineteenth century in the Gulf of Mexico, where I delighted in pointing out the Gulf of Mexico's connections to the Panama Route and the California Gold Rush, as well as National Register of Historic Places nominations for 12 deep water Gulf wrecks. As this manuscript is being readied for publication, I also was privileged to work with my colleagues, this time 5100 meters deep, as the on-shore archaeological co-lead, to assess the wrecks of the carriers *Akagi*, *Kaga* and *Yorktown* from the turning-point battle of the Pacific War at Midway.

Looking forward from 2023, there are other sites to be found, new stories will emerge, and new adventures await. Beyond the professional excitement of that premise is that, given how brief this moment in time is, as is the span of human life, that the road forward has to be cooperative, integrated, and open-minded to accept new perspectives in interpretation, acknowledging past mistakes, and, wherever possible, seeking reconciliation where past arguments and professional jealousy get in the way of what matters most: other people. After all, that's why we're archaeologists, right?

California is not an island, nor unique, and yet it has offered to the field of maritime and underwater archaeology important and at times unique contributions. These contributions are far more than what has generally been either known or acknowledged. A nexus in the maritime world past and present, California continues to exert an ever-constant pull for me as a scholar to reconnect with that physical and intellectual birthplace. I may have "left" California physically, but never emotionally or intellectually. Powerful words were once sung by Canadian folk singer Stan Rogers, who sang about the Northwest Passage across the top of the world, and they have always held personal meaning.

Stan Rogers sang of how those who quested to traverse and know that passage, how he had also done so, and in doing that he did "find my way back home again." It seems I always do. At the same time, the thought of new finds, new perspectives, reconciling with old friends to set aside differences from long ago, and forging new friendships with younger colleagues is exciting. Informed by and learning from the past, and not yet ready to hang it up, I look to the future and all it holds. I am still that ten-year old who fell in love with archaeology.

PART II:

Touching the Frolic: Wreck Divers and Archaeologists

Introduction

⌒

Thomas N. Layton

The beginnings of underwater archaeology in California, as described by James Delgado in the previous section, began long before the wreck divers and the archaeologists whose narratives are presented here were to "touch" the *Frolic*. That story was to begin with the sport-diving community of Southern California, where the breath-holding Bottom Scratchers Diving Club of San Diego, which claimed to be the oldest organization of its kind in the country, was founded in 1933. Its primary focus was spear fishing.

But it was Jacques-Yves Cousteau and Emile Gagnan's 1943 invention and patenting of the Aqua-Lung, featuring a regulator that would automatically provide compressed air to a diver on his slightest intake of breath, that would enable divers to descend and work at depths far beyond what was possible by holding a single breath.

With the introduction of the Aqua-Lung, Southern California divers were now able to descend deep enough and long enough to reach and pillage the many local shipwrecks submerged in relatively shallow water. The Southern California Wreck Divers Club, founded in Los Angeles in 1951, would be followed by the still-active California Wreck Divers, established in 1971. During the 1950s, *Skin Diver* magazine (founded in 1951) and the Aqua-Lung were to reach the Mendocino County coast of northern California.

Louie Fratis (1940–2004), whose family owned the ranch surrounding what is now called "Frolic Cove," had always been curious about the shipwreck rumored to be there. In the late 1950s he began his subscription to *Skin Diver,* and in 1960 he discovered the wreck.

Jim Kennon (1924–2006), together with Vilho "Bill" Kosonen (1923–2011), rediscovered the wreck in 1965. Jim had been a land-and-sea survival instructor during World War II at El Toro Marine Air Station between San Diego and Los Angeles. In 1958, Jim and Bill established the underwater search-and-recovery team for the Willows (California) Sheriff Department, and they enrolled in a five-day diving course at the Scripps Institute of Oceanography, after which Jim returned to Scripps to take an industrial-diving class. Then, in 1965, while spear fishing in Frolic Cove, Jim noted unnatural shapes on the ocean floor, and he searched through his back issues of *Skin Diver* looking for images that might help him determine whether the anomaly was a wreck site.

Many of the divers who would subsequently pillage the *Frolic* were members of the Southern California diving community. During the late 1960s, Larry Pierson (1937–2015), whose narrative appears here, had managed a dive shop in Los Angeles. In 1971, Larry helped organize the California Wreck Divers and became its first president. For a wreck diver, a polished brass porthole from a named shipwreck displayed on a living-room wall was the ultimate trophy, validating years of research and scores of dives.

Following his 1975–1979 pillage of the *Frolic*, Larry came to regret the information that had been destroyed. He eventually left the California Wreck Divers and enrolled in college to study archaeology. Larry would be mentored through his University of San Diego master's degree in archaeology by Professor James R. Moriarty, who with Neil Marshall in 1964 had published "Principles of Submarine Archaeology"—among the first articles discussing that nascent discipline.

Cliff Craft (1945–1999), whose narrative appears here and who rigged the explosives to break loose the *Frolic*'s cast-iron ballast pile, was later prosecuted along with fellow members of the California Wreck Divers for pillaging the 1853 wreck of the sidewheel steamer *Winfield Scott* off Anacapa Island. Jim Delgado, whose narrative also appears here, served as one of the witnesses in the prosecution of Craft and 20 other members of the California Wreck Divers. Southern California avocational divers remained the major underwater actors on California shipwrecks for many years before trained archaeologists and historians became actively involved.

The narratives of John Foster and Jim Delgado document many of the beginnings of professional underwater archaeology in California, as do the narratives of Larry Pierson and David Buller, both of whom transformed themselves from wreck divers to become professional participants in important maritime archaeological projects. As Jim Delgado describes in his narrative, it was Buller who, in 1981, mentored him during his first maritime research on the 1853 wreck of the sidewheel steamer SS *Tennessee* just across the Golden Gate from San Francisco. And it was Buller who, through years of archival research, had assembled a database of shipwrecks along the northern California coast and who later became Delgado's coauthor of a survey of shipwrecks north of San Francisco.

It was in 1960 that George Bass (1932–2021), then a graduate student in classical archaeology at the University of Pennsylvania, took his one-and-only diving lesson in the swimming pool of the Philadelphia YMCA. Bass would go on to become the widely celebrated "Father of Underwater Archaeology." But his focus was on Mediterranean shipwrecks of classical antiquity—not the United States!

The narrators of the oral histories in this section present the less-celebrated story of what was already and independently happening in California. And, in their epilogues, they describe much of what was yet to come. They discuss the legal and ethical issues faced by professional archaeologists in seeking help from the wreck divers who had already pillaged many of the known coastal shipwrecks and had assembled

INTRODUCTION

detailed databases far exceeding anything available to professional archaeologists.

Looking back, I now see that I was sufficiently clueless about the issues relating to pillaged collections from shipwrecks that, when I encountered the *Frolic*, I was able to walk in ignorance where even angels might have feared to tread. As a terrestrial archaeologist, I was proud to have subjected a pillaged collection from Cougar Mountain Cave in eastern Oregon to obsidian-hydration measurement and to have published the resulting chronology in a peer-reviewed journal—for which I had received positive responses from my professional colleagues. But, for the *Frolic*, it was to be a different story. After securing the donations of *Frolic* artifacts from the wreck divers, I was surprised and horrified when San Jose State University forbade me from receiving that stolen property. When the California Department of Parks and Recreation and the San Francisco Maritime Museum, the most appropriate state and federal organizations, also refused the collections, I was finally able to establish what became the *Frolic* Repository at the relatively unknown Mendocino County Museum—but only after receiving promises from the relevant government agencies that they would not prosecute the wreck divers for returning their collections.

The *Frolic* wreck divers rightly recognized the hubris of the archaeological community. As Dave Buller expresses it in his narrative:

I found myself in the awkward position of being caught in the middle. My background was as a wreck diver, a background that [federal archaeologists] Larry Murphy, Dan Lenihan, and Jim Delgado found despicable—"the rapers and pillagers of wrecks." Yet it seemed clearly apparent that were it not for the information I provided, their survey would have been far less successful than it turned out to be.

It should be mentioned here that although many of the artifacts from the *Frolic* recovered by wreck divers were returned, many were not! This was not a serious problem with cargo items such as the ceramics for which many exact-duplicate items were recovered. But none of the silver coinage was returned, nor many of the fragments of gold filigree jewelry, nor the brass barrels of blunderbusses, nor many of the wooden musket stocks and pistol handles that were not properly conserved and no longer exist. Indeed, the entire collection of one of the divers, who died from alcoholism, disappeared during his decline.

In their narratives, John Foster and Jim Delgado discuss the tricky issue of cooperation with wreck divers. Foster, a California state employee working within state law, had supported Robert Marx's proposal to locate and salvage the 1595 wreck of Cermeño's *San Agustin*, sharing what might be recovered with state and federal institutions. Delgado, a federal employee with a federal perspective, fought that proposal.

The story of wreck diving in California would eventually intersect with the story of underwater archaeology when, at first, wreck divers and then archaeologists were to "touch" the *Frolic*. We turn now to that part of the story.

They All "Touched" the *Frolic*

In the summer of 1844, before the *Frolic* embarked on her maiden voyage from the Gardner Brothers' Fells Point shipyard in Baltimore to Bombay, India, she had already been "touched" by woodsmen in the yellow-pine forests of South Carolina, by Irish carpenters who assembled her white-oak frames, from chalked lines on a mold-loft floor taken from her half-model—already shipped from Baltimore to Canton, China, and back—and by African American slaves who, among many other tasks, pounded-in the locust treenails fastening her pine planking onto those oak frames and, then, to seal her hull, pounded oakum—shredded hemp soaked in pine tar—into the seams between those pine planks.

Then, from 1845 to 1849, with a crew of Malay men from Indonesia and Burma and Lascars from the west coast of India who conversed in Portuguese pidgin, she made three voyages each year from Bombay (now Mumbai) carrying thousands of chests of Indian opium to China and return trips to Bombay carrying tons of silver—the proceeds from the sale of the opium.

In 1849, after the *Frolic* was dismasted and sustained extensive damage during a typhoon, she was refurbished, receiving new rigging and a new copper bottom by Chinese workmen in John Lamont's Hong Kong shipyard.

On 10 June 1850, the *Frolic* sailed from Hong Kong with a cargo of Chinese manufactured goods destined for sale in Gold Rush San Francisco, but, on the night of 25 July, she wrecked on the rocks fronting what we now call "Frolic Cove" at Point Cabrillo in Mendocino County, California.

Within days after her crewmembers had salvaged all the supplies they could carry and had hastily departed inland, the *Frolic* was "touched" by the Mitom Pomo, who began their own salvage. Their treasures included silk shawls and porcelain jars containing candied ginger, citron, and kumquats. Then came the ranchers from the interior who salvaged camphor trunks, large ornamental jars, and lacquered wares.

After being "touched" by diverse groups of humanity from South Carolina and Baltimore to Bombay, India, to multiple ports in China, and finally in 1850 to the Mendocino coast of California, the *Frolic*'s identity and location were to be forgotten for over a century, known only in local folklore as the "Silk Ship."

Then, as scuba became available to sport divers during the 1950s, a modern generation was to "touch" the *Frolic*. The wreck site was rediscovered, first by Don Pifer, a secretive Fort Bragg disc jockey, and again in 1960 by Louie Fratis, whose father owned the ranch surrounding the cove.

The most consequential rediscovery occurred on 30 June 1965, when Jim Kennon—an undersheriff from Willows who brought his diving students to the cove for training—spotted a strange anomaly on the ocean floor. Recognizing the importance of their discovery, Jim Kennon and Bill Kosonen, his dive partner, contacted Mendel Peterson at the Smithsonian for guidance on how to map and excavate the wreck site. In 1966 they brought Peterson to the cove, but the surf was too rough for them to dive.

In the meantime, Louie Fratis had approached officials at California State Parks, staff members at the National

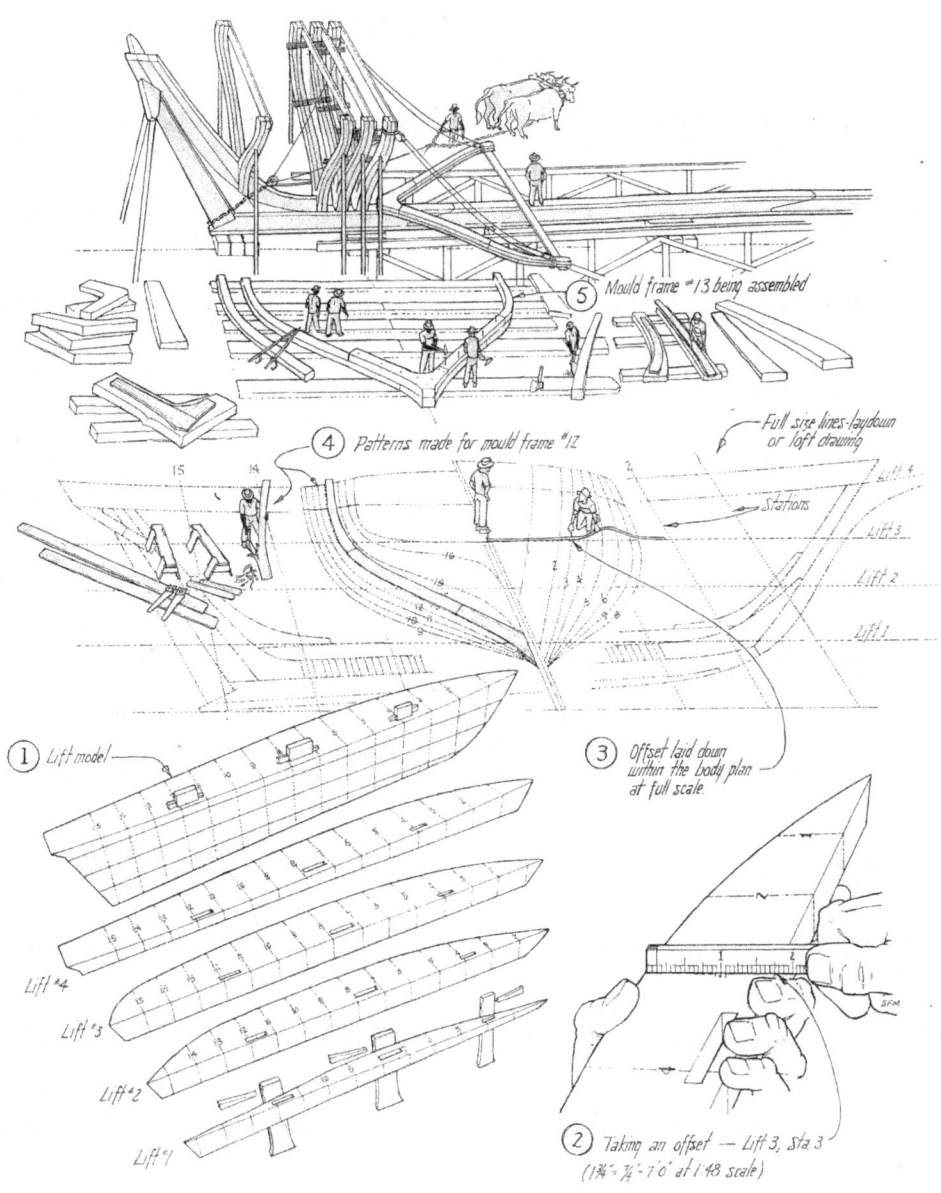

Figure 49. Building the *Frolic*: The lift model; separating the lifts; taking off-sets; laying down the plan; shaping frame moulds; and assembling frames. Original illustration by S. F. Manning.

Figure 50. Gardner Brothers' shipyard, Baltimore, Maryland, August 1844: An African American carpenter hammers in treenails fastening *Frolic's* southern yellow-pine planks to her frames. (Original illustration by S. F. Manning, 1997)

INTRODUCTION

Figure 51. Macau, China, 1845: *Frolic* offloads her first cargo of opium from India to Chinese wholesalers who will smuggle it to retailers in the interior of China. (Original illustration by S. F. Manning, 1997)

Figure 52. Point Cabrillo, California, July 1850: Members of *Frolic's* lascar crew salvage supplies before their long walk toward European American territory. (Original illustration by S. F. Manning, 2002)

Figure 53. Point Cabrillo, California, 1850: The Mitom Pomo harvest treasures from the *Frolic*. (Original illustration by S. F. Manning, 2002)

Maritime Museum in San Francisco, and, finally, Edward Von der Porten at Santa Rosa Junior College. Ed had been studying Chinese potsherds collected along the beaches of Drakes Bay. By 1970, word—probably through Ed Von der Porten—reached Robert Nash in Los Angeles, who was researching Chinese fishing junks in California coastal waters.

In 1975, Nash hired Larry Pierson and Patrick Gibson, two experienced avocational wreck divers, to travel with him to the cove and determine whether the wreck was a Chinese junk. It was not! Pierson and Gibson, together with friends, returned to dive the wreck in 1977 and 1978. In 1979 they brought Cliff Craft, who then set explosives and broke loose the cast-iron ballast pile so that they could recover the artifacts preserved below it.

Word of the wreck now spread rapidly through the wreck-diving community, reaching the three Lanham brothers (Bruce, Robert, and Rick), the Buller brothers (David and Steve), Patrick Philpott, and unknown others.

Four years later, in 1984, I and my San Jose State University archaeology students would first "touch" the *Frolic* when we excavated blue-and-white Chinese porcelain sherds from Three Chop Village, a Mitom Pomo village site located in Jackson State Forest, 15 mi. inland from Fort Bragg. Forest ranger Dana Cole would then lead me to what locals called "Pottery Cove," where Dale Hartesveldt, who lived near the cove, introduced me to several of the wreck divers, who, in turn, led me to the others, many of whom would later donate their collections from the *Frolic* wreck site to the *Frolic* Repository at the Mendocino County Museum, and whose narratives comprise an important part of this book.

Meanwhile, from 1984 to 1988, I researched the *Frolic* at Harvard Business

Figure 54. Pillaged *Frolic* artifacts displayed in a Los Angeles, California, driveway prior to division among the divers, 1979. (Photo by Larry Pierson)

INTRODUCTION

School's Baker Library, whose Augustine Heard Company Papers—over 264 shelf-feet of them—contained the story of the *Frolic* from her construction in 1844 to her loss in 1850 and even the Heard Company's insurance claims for reimbursement. During those years I carried bags of *Frolic* artifacts to archaeological conferences seeking help in their identification and then visited the Peabody-Essex Museum in Salem, Massachusetts, to view their China Trade Collection, where I could match my fragments against their pristine heirloom items.

In 1986, Jim Delgado of the National Park Service and John Foster of the California Department of Parks and Recreation met me at Frolic Cove, where each made a short dive to view the wreck. Despite getting badly battered by the surf, they concluded that the site should be professionally investigated, and in 1991 Delgado and I nominated the *Frolic* wreck site to the National Register of Historic Places. A year later I began interviewing and transcribing the narratives of the wreck divers whose collections I was studying and the archaeologists who were providing guidance to the project.

During 1989, I wrote the first draft of "Drug Runner"—eventually retitled, at the request of Stanford University Press, as *The Voyage of the* Frolic: *New England Merchants and the Opium Trade* (Layton 1997). When I passed around that first-draft manuscript for comment, several Mendocino County curators recognized that the saga of the *Frolic* provided an opportunity to tell the story of a multicultural beginning of their recorded history. In 1994, those same curators were to "touch" the *Frolic* when the Grace Hudson Museum in Ukiah, the Kelley House Museum in Mendocino, and the Mendocino County Museum in Willits collaborated to stage separate but linked exhibits, each telling a part of the story.

The prospect of three linked exhibits in 1994 inspired the actors and directors of the Ukiah Players Theatre to write a play telling the *Frolic*'s story from multiple cultural perspectives—later published as *Voices from the* Frolic, *and Beyond: A Mendocino History Play* (1998). But how to tell such a complex story? The answer came at a brainstorming session when Jim Delgado picked up a large porcelain sherd from the *Frolic*, assumed the character of the *Frolic*'s Captain Faucon, and announced: "Cheap Canton junkware—but it would have fetched us a fortune in San Francisco!"

That was the breakthrough! That very sherd would be "touched" as it was passed from actor to actor—a Pomo elder; an early Chinese immigrant to Mendocino; Mrs. Kelley, who in 1852 had traded with the Pomo for a bolt of silk; a 20th-century wreck diver; and even the archaeologist—me—each of us portrayed by one of the actors.

Linda Noel, of Koyongk'awi Maidu descent—later poet laureate of Ukiah—wrote and performed the part of the Pomo elder. Linda's personal narrative appears in this volume. In the actual performances of the play, Linda, recalling the tragic consequences of the *Frolic* shipwreck for Native Americans, and pointedly refused to touch that *Frolic* potsherd.

Already in the late 1980s, I had been struggling with how to translate the inert archaeological remains of the *Frolic* into a compelling story comprehensible to the people of Mendocino County and beyond. For that, I knew that I would need pictures, but the *Frolic*'s entire existence, from 1844 to 1850, was completed just prior to the introduction of photography. Then, serendipitously, as I began to describe the construction of the *Frolic*, I discovered a magnificently illustrated book, *Live Oaking: Southern Timber for Tall Ships* (Wood 1981), whose illustrations were drawn by master marine artist Samuel Manning. I contacted Sam and convinced him to work with me to create well researched pictures to document every stage of the *Frolic's* life—from the chalked lines for shaping her oak frames in the Gardner Bros. Baltimore shipyard, to the Pomo people harvesting China trade treasures from her wrecked remains at Point Cabrillo on the Mendocino coast of California. For me, those illustrations, presented here, comprise the most powerful lasting achievement of the *Frolic* project.

Meanwhile, during my research on the *Frolic*, I had searched for descendants of the Augustine Heard Company employees associated with the vessel. To my surprise, I discovered that the three-times great-uncle of Richard Everett, Curator of Exhibits at the San Francisco Maritime Museum, was the man who had actually assembled the *Frolic's* final cargo.

Richard was eager to join the project, and, on his way home after one of our meetings in Willits, he stopped at the Mendocino Brewing Company in Hopland for a cold one. Sitting at the bar, Richard told the story of the *Frolic's* 6,108 bottles of Edinburgh ale to the brewmaster, leading to a discussion of how to replicate that ale and ultimately to the brewing, bottling, and release of *Frolic* Shipwreck Ale just in time for the opening of the three museum exhibits and the premier performance of *Voices from the* Frolic *and Beyond*. In 1998–1999, Richard would open a major exhibit, *Found! The Wreck of the Frolic—A Gold Rush Cargo for San Francisco*, at the San Francisco Maritime Museum.

Having published the *Voyage of the Frolic* in 1997, it was now time for me to write another volume, describing the saga of her final cargo—*Gifts from the Celestial Kingdom: A Shipwrecked Cargo for Gold Rush California* (Layton 2002).

But it still remained for a nautical archaeologist to investigate the underwater remains of the *Frolic*. Thus, in 2003 and 2004, Sheli O. Smith of Napa Community College organized two summer field classes to document what remained on the sea floor at the *Frolic* wreck site, to investigate wreck-diver collections, and to prepare a digital catalogue of all the *Frolic* collections. To accomplish this, Smith partnered with Annalies Corbin at East Carolina University, Charles Beeker at Indiana University, John Foster at the California Department of Parks and Recreation, and Rob Edwards at Cabrillo College, along with students from all four institutions, all of whom would "touch" the *Frolic*. Sheli Smith published Frolic *Archaeological Survey* in 2005, replete with a detailed map of the wreck site (S. Smith 2005).

In 2014, the Advanced Laboratory for Visual Anthropology at California State University, Chico, would film *Impact of the* Frolic: *A Shipwreck that Transcends the World* (28 min.), directed by Matthew Ritenour for release on public television, with underwater footage enabling millions of viewers to feel as though they were actually "touching" the *Frolic* (Fox 2014). The film was produced by Georgia Fox (whose narrative appears here) in concert with a major exhibit featuring the *Frolic* at Chico State's Valene L. Smith Museum of Anthropology: Into the Blue: Maritime Navigation and the Archaeology of Shipwrecks.

For me, there remained one major

INTRODUCTION

task—to tell the story of the women behind the saga of the *Frolic*. These included Hu Ts'ai-shun, the Chinese wife of George Dixwell, the merchant and Heard Company partner who had ordered the *Frolic* built for the opium trade; George's aunt, Henrietta Sargent, an ardent abolitionist, who had criticized George's greed; and her own aunt, Judith Sargent Murray, the grandmother of American feminism. Begun in 2002, it took me 19 years to research and write and rewrite that book as a historical novel: *The "Other" Dixwells: Commerce and Conscience in an American Family*, which ultimately became a special publication of the Society for Historical Archaeology (Layton 2021).

Viewing the overall *Frolic* Shipwreck Project through the lens of archaeological paradigm shifts, the wreck divers were "ultra-particularists," focused entirely on the things they recovered, unconcerned with their physical contexts at the wreck site or the history they might reveal.

My own work, as a "processualist," concerned with underlying historical processes, led me first to place those thousands of things into the historical context of a particular cargo and then use them to reveal a worldwide commercial system in which Western addiction to tea from China was balanced by Anglo-American shipment of opium from India for sale to the Chinese.

The "Other" Dixwells, described above — a novel filling in the cracks between the facts to follow the lives of the women and their families behind the *Frolic* and the lasting consequences to their descendants — is clearly post processual.

The current volume joins a history of maritime archaeology in California, with the post-processual self-reflective life histories of the wreck divers, archaeologists and others who helped reveal the saga of the *Frolic*. All of the narratives presented here, except for those by me, Deborah Marx, Sheli Smith, Linda Noel, Georgia Fox, and Richard Everett, were recorded from 1992 to 1994, when memories were still fresh. Since then, five of the six wreck divers who provided narratives have passed away. Archaeologists John Foster and Jim Delgado have reviewed their personal narratives and summarized their subsequent careers in epilogues.

I had hoped to include my narrative as recorded by Annalies Corbin in 2004, but the digital was lost somewhere between East Carolina University and the Mendocino County Museum, so I have written a fresh narrative.

Now, a short explanation of how the narratives were recorded, transcribed, and edited for this volume. I asked each narrator to describe, from childhood to the present, how he or she had been drawn to shipwrecks or to archaeology, and all their experiences leading to the *Frolic* shipwreck. I recorded their interviews on cassette tapes. Over years of conducting oral histories, I had learned not to interrupt the narrators with my questions, since each question tended to send an interview in a new direction, leaving the current vignette incomplete. So I tried to minimize my prompts and jotted down questions (names, dates, facts) to ask at the end of the narrative.

I then transcribed the interviews, deleting my prompts and inserting the answers to my questions. Most of the narrators had recalled earlier events as they spoke, so I inserted those vignettes at more appropriate places in their narratives.

The narratives were to sit in an archival box for almost three decades. Then, during the social isolation of the 2020–2021

COVID-19 pandemic, I pulled them out, and, as I read them, I realized they not only told the story of pillage and research at the *Frolic* wreck site, but also provided unique personal histories of wreck diving and professional maritime research in California. This volume is the final result.

A concise listing of many of those who "touched" the *Frolic*, and when, is presented here in the *Frolic* timeline, and a full listing of related publications appears in the bibliography.

Louie D. Fratis

Louie D. Fratis was born in Fort Bragg, Mendocino County, California, in 1940 and raised on the family ranch surrounding what is now known as "Frolic Cove." As a teenager, Louie built and raced hotrods. His father raised hogs on the ranch, and Louie was expected to take over its operation, but coastal agriculture became unprofitable. Louie graduated from Mendocino High School in 1957 and took classes at Santa Rosa Junior College for a year before he dropped out. His first job was as a seasonal park aide at several local state parks. In 1960, Louie and a buddy bought "glue-it-together-yourself" wetsuits and began spearfishing and collecting abalone in the cove. Although Louie had heard stories of a shipwreck, he actually discovered it while prying an abalone off what he recognized to be a cannon. By then, in addition to his seasonal work for California State Parks, Louie had started a speed shop, selling parts to build

hotrods, and a wrecking yard, where he dismantled and sold parts from junked automobiles. About that time, Louie backed his truck, equipped with a weighted 25 ft. boom used to crush auto bodies, up to the edge of the cliff overlooking the cove and lifted the cannon.

In 1962, Louie was hired fulltime to handle maintenance at Angel Island State Park in the San Francisco Bay. He tried without success to interest his California State Parks superiors and

Figure 55. Louie Fratis at Goodies Fountain, Fort Bragg, California, 1994. (Photo by Thomas Layton)

115

then federal authorities at the National Maritime Museum in San Francisco to take an interest in the still-unidentified wreck. Louie left State Parks in 1974 to take over his father's pizza parlor in Fort Bragg, which he later converted into "Goodies Fountain." He eventually loaned the cannon to the Kelley House Museum in Mendocino, where it rusted on the lawn until 2003, when it was moved to Charles Beeker's lab at Indiana University for stabilization in preparation for display at Point Cabrillo Lighthouse. In 1994, Tom Layton taped Louie's narrative over coffee at Goodies Fountain. Louie passed away in 2004 at the age of 64.

Louie D. Fratis

9 July and 5 August 1994
Goodies Fountain
Fort Bragg, California

The Fratis family has lived here on the coast for close to 125 years, and even though we never knew the name of the vessel, it seems we've always known something about the wreck. The *Frolic* had been sunk less than 20 years when my great-grandfather, Miguel Henriques de Fratos, first settled here during the late 1860s, and I guess he learned about it from the Indians. It seems funny that my mother would be taking a historical dramatization class this spring in order to put on a play about the *Frolic* shipwreck. She was reading the *Fort Bragg Advocate* when she saw an article about auditions for a six-month workshop called "Voices of the *Frolic*," sponsored by the Ukiah Players Theatre in cooperation with the local community college. She wanted me to go, but I figured I'd already put enough time into that wreck. Still, I thought someone should give our side of the story, so she went.

I guess the story really starts with my great-grandfather Fratos. He was in his teens when he came to California from the Island of Flores in the Azores aboard a Portuguese whaling vessel. As my family tells it, he jumped ship in San Francisco and migrated up the coast to Mendocino. In 1876 he married my great-grandmother, Maria Furtador, who was also from the Azores. They bought a 20 ac. parcel at Pine Grove, the old town by the Point Cabrillo Lighthouse, where they started farming and raising sheep.

My grandfather, William Fratis, was born about 1882. In 1913, he too married a woman from Flores, Joaquina Silveria Valador, and they had three sons, my father Louie being the oldest. Over a period of years my grandfather added 300 ac. of property to the original 20, eventually surrounding the lighthouse on both sides, incorporating the entire coast from Caspar Creek down to Russian Gulch, including the cove where the wreck is located. The lighthouse went into operation in 1909; however, the community around it, called Pine Grove, was much older. There were hotels, bars, a brewery, and oxen barns for the Big River Logging Company. There was even a circular track for racing horses and, later on, Model-T Fords over on the northeast side of the lighthouse.

Grandpa Bill raised sheep and farmed and worked in the mill for the Caspar

Lumber Company. He also did ranch butchering—going out to nearby ranches and butchering cattle for them. During the early 30s he ran a butcher shop on a Model-T truck. My dad and he would go up and down the coast to the logging camps, often with my mother doing the driving, carrying a quarter of beef or half a hog, stopping at houses along the way, cutting to order, and delivering right there on the spot. My dad took up butchering as a trade and for a while ran the butcher shop for the Caspar Lumber Company. Later he sold meat at the first Purity store that was built in Fort Bragg.

Grandpa Bill could understand Portuguese, but he didn't like to speak it. He said he was an American. Grandma Joaquina never learned to speak good English. I remember she subscribed to a Portuguese language newspaper with serialized stories, like the soaps on TV, and she was always waiting for the next issue. Grandma was quite devout and was active in Portuguese social clubs, like the Isabella Club and the Holy Ghost Society. She had crosses and pictures of Jesus covering the walls of her room and her rosary beads out on the table. In honor of the Virgin Mary she had her room painted blue. She said it was "Virgin blue," but everyone else called it "Portagee blue."

We all attended Our Lady of Good Counsel Catholic Church in Fort Bragg. Every year the Portuguese community would have a big Pentecost celebration. In 1952, my sister, Dorothy Gene, was the "little queen" and carried the crown. It's said that long ago there was a famine in Portugal and Queen Isabella sold her crown jewels to feed the populace—so each year the Portuguese people honor her with a parade and a feast. The night before, they dance the "Chamarita Rosa," where they all get in a circle and yell and whoop and holler.

Next morning, with the band playing, they march some 20 blocks through town, from Pentecost Hall to the Catholic Church, with the queen and the little queen wearing white dresses with long trains, carrying the crowns to be blessed. Then they parade back to the hall, where they serve everyone a free Portuguese meal, including *sopas*: a poorman's soup of bread, cabbage, and beef, flavored with mint—just like Isabella did.

Grandpa Bill was not religious, but was willing to tolerate it, and he did have a special relationship with some of the priests. During Prohibition, people could make a limited amount of wine for home use, so the Italians and Portuguese in Fort Bragg would have grapes sent up from the Napa Valley. The Italians would make wine, and the Portuguese would make grappa and port. Of course, they all made up some extra to sell, and Grandpa Bill would let them bury the barrels on our ranch. Bootleggers who knew Grandpa was hiding wine asked if they could land whiskey down in the cove, but he refused. He figured the feds would look the other way for wine, but not for whiskey, so the smugglers used the cove down at Heritage House instead. Grandpa died in 1953, but I remember him telling how during Prohibition the Irish priest would come down to the ranch in order to get sacramental wine, and how they'd sit together out there all afternoon testing it.

I was born in Fort Bragg, 17 January, 1940. In those days, Fort Bragg was still divided into four parts. This area on Franklin Street around Goodies Fountain and immediately to the south was called "Wop Town." North of here was "Kakalavera," where the Finns lived. The Irish and the Portuguese were over by the Skunk Train, while the professionals lived in big houses around Cotton Auditorium.

At first we lived down in Pine Grove on part of the old Brinzing property, where the brewery had been. Then, when I was two, we moved into the old ranch house on my grandfather's property. Up until going to grammar school my youth was mainly spent running around the fields and helping take care of animals. We had chickens, ducks, milking cattle, sheep, goats, and hogs. During the Second World War my grandfather raised rabbits for the fur, and it was my job to help him skin them and stretch the hides over racks so they could be hung and dried. Rabbit fur wouldn't freeze, so it was used for mittens and collars on winter garments. That was a good profitable business up until just about the end of the war when they came up with synthetics. It was Grandpa Bill who first told me the story about a ship that wrecked off our property. He knew the old Indian families who were still coming out to the coast to collect shellfish and dry seaweed, and they would talk about it. Grandfather assured me that the treasure was buried somewhere on our property, but, although I searched for it as an 8-year-old, it would be 10 years before I started diving and looking for the wreck underwater.

When I was about eight I joined 4-H—the Mendocino Spartans—and I was active in that until I graduated from high school. I raised Duroc hogs and Jersey cattle, showing them at the Mendocino County Fair in Boonville and the 12th District Fair at Ukiah. At that time, my dad was raising about 400 head of hogs on the ranch.

From 1939 to 1944 he had run one of the first waste-disposal outfits in the area—hauling garbage from Mendocino and the Caspar area. In those days people had two buckets at their houses, one to put their paper and cans in, and the other in which to put the slop. My father would take the slop and dump it into the troughs to feed the hogs and then dump the rest of the stuff over the south bluff and into the cove, where I later discovered the shipwreck. I think I might have found the wreck sooner, except for that garbage introducing a note of confusion. After the war my dad would go up to Noyo Harbor and collect fish guts and heads from the fishery to feed the hogs. Then, a couple of weeks before butchering them, he'd take them off fish and put them on grain to get rid of the fish odor. We did pretty well in that business until the government said you had to cook the slop before feeding it to the hogs—and that ended that.

I started out at Caspar Grammar School in 1945. It had three rooms, but only two teachers. First through fourth grade was in one room, and fifth through eighth grade was in the other. There were about 10 students per grade and perhaps 80 kids in the entire school. When they built the new school in Mendocino about 1953 or 1954, they moved the 7th and 8th grade out of Caspar, so I went from the 7th through 12th grades in Mendocino.

When I was a kid, Caspar was a thriving community. It was a company town owned by the Caspar Lumber Company. There was a community recreation hall where we could play basketball or attend plays and community events. There was a roller-skating rink and a baseball field where we'd watch the Caspar "Lumber Jacks" play the Fort Bragg "Loggers" and the Mendocino "Colts." My father and most of the other kids' fathers worked for Caspar Lumber, either out in the woods logging or in the

LOUIE D. FRATIS

mill itself or driving trucks. As kids, a lot of our time was spent going down to the mill and pestering our parents. We'd be in and out and underneath the equipment or walking the old flume up Doyle Creek that fed water to the steam engines powering the mill.

The mill, being one of the oldest in the area, was entirely steam powered, with all the equipment run by belts from two steam engines. As kids we'd go down under the mill to look at the miles of whirling belting, some of it up to 2 ft. wide, running out to every piece of equipment. The Caspar Mill was already outmoded. It had been built to handle large trees, 6–10 ft. in diameter; however, as the timber became smaller the mill had become more expensive to operate.

The Caspar Lumber Company was originally the largest one on this section of the coast, but about 1950 they sold off to the state most of the property that is now called Jackson State Forest. The Union Lumber Company in Fort Bragg had already bought out the old Mendocino Lumber Company, so they became the largest in the area. About that time Union Lumber had a fire on their log deck out on Noyo Point, and their entire year's supply of logs was destroyed. For a while it looked as though that fire was going to put a couple of hundred people out of work.

Fortunately, however, the Caspar Lumber Company had a stack of logs in Caspar Creek that went clean across the same area where the Caspar Bridge now is—standing as high as the bridge is today. The owners of Caspar Lumber decided they would sell out to Union Lumber on condition that all of the Caspar employees would retain their jobs. Most of those Caspar employees hardly missed a day's work and finished out their years working for Union Lumber at Fort Bragg.

That was pretty much the end of Caspar because most of the town was company owned. Around 1955 they tore down the old cabins where the single millworkers lived, closed the grocery and hardware store, and sold off the larger houses to the mill executives who were occupying them. My dad helped tear down the mill.

The head rig, or headworks, that carried the lumber through the saw was sold to a mill in Flagstaff, Arizona. That fact always fascinated me because all of my learning in school told me Arizona was desert—and at 15 I couldn't understand where in the desert they got trees big enough to go through that mill. You know, in 1965 I drove out to Flagstaff just to see where the heck it was. I've been in love with Arizona ever since because I found out that there's a difference between low desert and high desert. Flagstaff, Arizona, is up about 6,000 ft., and the San Francisco Mountains go up to 12,000, and there are a lot of big pine trees up there. I saw the mill, but none of the old Caspar equipment. By then it had all been modernized.

I started driving vehicles on the ranch when I was 7, and by the time I was 14 I had my own car and was driving back and forth to school. As I got older, I got interested in automobiles and, as a lot of us did in the early 50s, got involved in car clubs. We started the "Snails," one of the first car clubs in Fort Bragg, and then another in Mendocino called the "Pacific Pacers." By 1957 and 1958 we were taking our cars down to the drag strips at Cotati, Lodi, Vacaville, Half Moon Bay, and, later, to Fremont. I had a 1939 Chevy two-door sedan with a fully loaded '57 Chevy V-8 in it. Other guys had Model-As and '40 Fords, mostly modified with bigger engines. A few of the older guys with money bought '55 or '57 Chevys when they first came out. Those were factory hotrods. Most of us, however, had what we could build ourselves. We'd find an old body somewhere, fix it up, and put in a hotter engine. At that time Mendocino was still a small community of about 500 people, but the Pacific Pacers would send as many as 45 cars to drag strips over in the Sacramento Valley or down in the Bay Area and take the team participation trophy.

Those were the days of cruising, like you see in the movie *American Graffiti*. We'd cruise back and forth from Fort Bragg to Mendocino for half the night, burning tanks of gas. The two main drive-ins were both in Fort Bragg: Stoney's, at the north end of town, and the Lone Pine Drive-In at the south end. It was a mile-and-a-half cruise, and we would drive back and forth. There wasn't much else to do except go to the movies at the State Theater on Main Street. During summers we'd go swimming at Boyle's Camp on Big River, but the rest of the time the water was too cold.

Since we lived on a ranch, my parents tried to push me towards some kind of agricultural profession. During my junior and senior year at Mendocino High School I worked part time with a local veterinarian, and I was leaning toward becoming a veterinarian or going into agricultural engineering. I graduated in 1957 and attended Santa Rosa Junior College for a year. That was long enough to decide that college wasn't for me.

During the summer of 1957 a high school buddy of mine had been working at Russian Gulch State Park, about a mile-and-a-half south of our house. He was going off to college and couldn't finish out the summer, so he asked me if I'd like to take over for him. It was a summer seasonal job, mainly picking up garbage and cleaning restrooms, and I got hired to finish out his couple of months. I liked that job, and in the spring of 1958 they contacted me, asking if I wanted to come back and work as a seasonal for the next summer. From 1957 through 1962 I worked every summer as a park aide at Van Damme Beach, Little River, and Russian Gulch State parks. During the winter months they often hired me back as a laborer, so I was eventually putting in nine months a year for them.

In 1962 I passed the state test and started working fulltime as a state park ranger. I was sent to Angel Island State Park in San Francisco Bay and worked there for five years. My job was supposed to be public contact: cleaning restrooms, picking up garbage, and maintaining the picnic areas. At that time the state was just taking over the island from the federal government, and the only way you could get equipment on and off was with a military-surplus landing craft. That was difficult, so the state brought equipment out there and left it. We had a small Caterpillar tractor, a grader, a backhoe, and other equipment of that sort so we could do our own maintenance: digging up old waterlines or grading roads as needed. Since I grew up on a ranch and knew how to operate farm equipment, I spent most of my time with the State Park Service being an equipment operator. We had a 45 ft. approach launch that I used to haul the employees back and forth to the island and the landing craft to haul fire trucks, maintenance equipment, fuel, and supplies back and forth. I was still working on Angel Island when the Indians occupied Alcatraz.

It was during the summer of 1958, while working at Van Damme Beach State Park, that I first got interested in

LOUIE D. FRATIS

diving. Most of the divers I saw there on the beach were wearing the old dry suits like the UDTs [underwater demolition teams] wore during the Second World War. Watching them go out reminded me of the old Lloyd Bridges *Sea Hunt* movies that I'd watched as a kid. Only a few of the divers at the park were wearing the new neoprene wetsuits.

Well, about this time, my cousin Mike and a friend of his from Vallejo bought wetsuits. They would come up to our place as they were learning how to dive, and they kept saying: "Why don't you learn too?" So my friend Doug Colberg and I ordered $19.00 precut "glue-it-together-yourself" wetsuits from Montgomery Ward's. They weren't lined, and once you got them on you had a heck of a time getting them back off. When we finally got our suits together, we started free diving, just snorkeling without tanks. At the time I had 8 or 10 friends from the car club, and that soon became our weekend thing. If we weren't going drag racing we'd all get together and go diving for abalone and fish.

We dove in various places along the coast trying to get really big abalone and lingcod. In 1958 my cousin and his buddy speared a lingcod down in our cove that was 46.5 in. long and weighed 39 lb. They shot it in about 20 ft. of water, and it damned near drowned them because they didn't have any air tanks. One of them would come to the surface and the other would hold onto the spear gun underneath while being dragged all over the bay. We all watched it from the bluff, laughing like heck and telling them to let it go. They finally brought it in, and after that we'd always go out trying to beat that size.

Well, ever since I was a kid, grandpa Bill told stories about a shipwreck off our property and a buried treasure. He said the Indians had told him about it. In fact, even in the early 1950s Indians were still coming out to the coast from Lake County to gather mussels and dry seaweed. Some used to stay down on Caspar Beach, and some would stay on our property. They would stick old poles up in the air and tie a rope across like a clothesline and drape seaweed over that to dry. We knew Indians had been coming for a long time because there were shell mounds along the creeks flowing through our property. I noticed the shell was mainly on the south sides of the creeks. I guess with a prevailing north wind that was a good arrangement. My cousins and I would ask my grandfather to tell us about the Indians and the wreck. Other kids' parents told how their fathers used to dig for the treasure around the old Caspar graveyard. My grandfather made up a special story for us about a big split pine tree out in a field near which the treasure was buried, and I remember going out and looking for it.

During the 1940s and 50s local people would come down to the ranch to get abalone. We controlled the coast from Caspar Creek to Russian Gulch, and my grandfather wouldn't allow anybody across the field unless they had permission. When my grandfather died in 1953, my dad continued that policy. Moreover, he decided he wouldn't allow anybody to skin dive because he thought it was an unfair advantage. He'd noticed that the divers were coming in during high tide, spending most of their time in less than 6 ft. of water, barely getting their fins wet, and taking most of the abalone that the rock pickers would have got in a minus tide.

During the mid-1950s, one exception to this rule was a diver named Don Pifer, and he used to dive in a particular cove on our property. Don was one of the original announcers on KDAC, the radio station in Fort Bragg. He used to play country and western and early rock and roll. I used to wonder why he got to dive and the others didn't. My dad told me that Don wasn't down there for the abalone. He was down there looking for old shipwrecks and taking pictures underwater. He had strobe lights and homemade Plexiglas boxes with the whole camera inside. Don had supposedly come through the war with experience in diving and had a reputation for having dove on almost every wrecked ship from Westport down to Point Arena. He had a map that showed where various lumber schooners were wrecked all along the coast. I know he dove on two or three wrecks over in Caspar Bay. I guess he mainly went down, got a few artifacts, and took some pictures to prove he'd been there.

Well, when I started diving, I decided I'd try and find the shipwreck that Don Pifer had been looking for in our cove. Of course, I didn't really know whether he'd found it or not, but I'd heard stories about the "Silk Vessel" ever since I was a kid. It's funny that for years I'd seen little pieces of pottery washed up on the beach down there, but didn't attach any importance to them. That was because during the war, when my dad had the garbage disposal contract for Mendocino, he used to dump over the bluff on the south side of the cove. So naturally I thought the dishes along there were things that local people had thrown away. Anyway, I started buying *Skin Diver* magazine and reading the articles, trying to get some idea what wrecks were supposed to look like underwater.

Well, I was fascinated by that particular cove and was always hoping I'd come across Don Pifer's shipwreck. There's a small reef about a quarter mile outside the cove, and

we'd heard that a schooner had gone down out there. My cousin and I wanted to look for it, but as we only had inner tubes and that was a long swim, so we never did. In fact, it was by pure accident that I found the wreck.

One day, about 1960, I was diving with my cousin in about 12 ft. of water when I saw an abalone on what I thought was a rock. I dove down to the bottom, pried it off, put my hand on top of the rock, and pushed off. When I got to the surface and put the "ab" into my inner-tube float, I got to thinking that it was an odd sort of rock to have a hole in the top of it, and it had had an odd sort of shape as well. I knew that urchins would erode into a rock and make pockets in it, but the hole didn't seem smooth like an urchin hole, so I dove back down to take another look. Well, the more I looked at it the more it looked like it might be in the shape of a cannon, so I knocked off a little bit of encrustation around the muzzle end with my pry bar, and that's what it was. I just left it there. I'd been working for the Park Service for a couple of summers and had begun to read their literature about local history ... so I realized the wreck might have some historical significance and didn't want anybody to mess with it.

I didn't tell anybody about it. I didn't even tell my cousin. However, I went down two more times on different days and carefully explored the area. I found some larger pieces of pottery, stacked ballast blocks, two or three anchors, and a capstan with a winch-like drum. I estimated, from the way the ballast blocks were laid out, that the vessel was approximately 80 ft. long. In about the center of the wreck area was a mound that had some lead sheathing on it, and I could see some dishes by pulling back part of the lead.

LOUIE D. FRATIS

At that time the site was pretty well undisturbed. Prior to that I don't think anybody except for Don Pifer had found it. As I recall, one of the park supervisors over at Van Damme was interested in cannons and he had cannoneer magazines lying around. I leafed through them and concluded, from the shape, that the cannon I found was probably of Chinese origin. Of course, I had been influenced by all the Chinese-looking pottery.

It was about that time I was transferred from Van Damme State Park down to Angel Island in San Francisco Bay, where I worked for the next five years. I'd come up on weekends though, and, if I went diving, I'd just look around. I didn't want to disturb the wreck too much, and I didn't know who to talk to in order to find out more about it. However, when I transferred back to Van Damme in 1966, I thought maybe it would be the right time to do something with it. By then I had become acquainted with Bob Brashears, a ranger working over at Russian Gulch. Bob wanted to learn how to dive, so I taught him. I then told him about finding the cannon. Bob was quite interested, so we worked out a plan to pull it out of the cove.

Before going down to Angel Island as a park ranger I had started a speed shop specializing in building cars for racing motors, and I had built a small building on the ranch in which two friends and I used to paint cars and do bodywork. Because we had cars lying around in various pieces, the DMV had come along and informed us that if we were selling parts from them we would need an auto-wrecking license—so we got an auto-dismantler's license, built a fence, and created a wrecking yard. Anyway, by the time Bob and I started diving, I'd acquired a truck with a 25 ft. boom

from which I'd drop a 3,000 lb. concrete block to smash old car bodies.

Well, Bob and I borrowed a 14 ft. aluminum rescue boat from Russian Gulch, got a couple of big truck inner tubes and some chain, put a tank of air on board, and took the wrecker out to the bluff on the north side of the cove. It took three tries to get the cannon out of the water. The first time we put too much air into the tubes, and when it hit the surface it went 4 ft. in the air and damn near sunk the boat. The second time the cannon broke loose from the chain, but the third time we were able to get it up and float it on the inner tubes over to the south shore of the cove, where we attached it to winch lines from the boom truck and raised it up onto the bluff. In addition to the cannon we brought up a piece of pottery bearing an inscription on its base, a heavy brass rod about 2 ft. long, and an iron ballast block about a foot long, 5 × 5 in. in diameter, with a hole going through it. Bob and I then tried to get the California State Park System interested in the wreck. My own supervisors were not interested, so I contacted the Santa Rosa office and then park headquarters in Sacramento, but we didn't get any response.

At the time, going by the cannon and the pottery, Bob and I still figured that the wreck was a Chinese junk. We'd read, either in an article or in some State Parks' literature, that seven junks had been blown across the Pacific back in the 1500s, and one had been found somewhere off Oregon, another down in the Monterey area, and a third one was supposed to have come up to this area. We figured that the so-called Mendocino Silk Ship was one of those seven junks, and, even if it had wrecked 300 years before, it might have taken that long for the story to work its way down to San Francisco. After all, nobody lived up here except for Indians, and, in 1850, when Henry Meiggs heard about it, there was no way of saying that it was a current event or an ancient one.

About that time I read something about Edward Von der Porten over in Santa Rosa, who was trying to authenticate Sir Francis Drake's arrival at Drakes Bay. I went over and met with him for two or three hours, showing him the pottery, the ballast, and photographs of the cannon. He said the pottery definitely came from the Far East, but the cannon, being cheaply made and without ornamentation, could have been on any trading vessel. He said the Chinese would probably have used rocks for ballast, and our iron blocks appeared to be more recent—possibly from some kind of trading schooner. The brass rod he thought might have been an anchoring pin to hold the ballast in place. Much later I learned that it was one of the bolts or spikes that had held the vessel together.

Mr. Von der Porten suggested I go back down and break-up some of the clumps to see if I could find some deck clips, since that was the best way to determine if the vessel was made in China. Although he wasn't interested in the wreck himself, he suggested we do some library research and see Karl Kortum over at the San Francisco Maritime Museum.

I met with Mr. Kortum, tried to explain my ideas, and basically got told I was full of shit. Mr. Kortum made it clear that he wasn't interested in some damn thing that didn't relate to the history of San Francisco. I guess our meeting was colored by the fact that Mr. Kortum and the State Parks System weren't getting along at the time. The state had opened the Hyde Street Pier area near the Maritime Museum and had the *Eureka* ferry and an

old hay scow on display. Mr. Kortum felt that they should be combined under the Maritime Museum. He knew that I had worked for the State Park System, and that might very well have turned him off—particularly since our people would sometimes have words with him when we were over on the pier.

On Mr. Von der Porten's suggestion I contacted one of the universities down in the Bay Area, and one day around 1970 several Asian students showed up wanting to see the artifacts. They couldn't give me any clues either. They were Nationalist Chinese and were unable to authenticate anything because they weren't talking to the mainlanders. They said that, if China ever opened up, they might be able to check the records there for the pottery design. By that time I'd contacted the Mendocino County Historical Society, and they weren't interested in it. I figured if the state didn't care and the National Parks didn't care either, I'd done my duty—if they weren't interested in preserving the site, I wasn't going to sit out there and watch it for them.

Although I quit diving the wreck around 1970, I'd done my best to keep its location secret. Local rumor had it that Don Pifer had found a bell, a musket, some hinges, and a lantern, so I was always leery of anybody coming around and talking to me about the wreck. They would say that Don had found this or that, "and it's supposed to be off your property somewhere." Well, we owned a mile and a half of ocean frontage, and I'd say: "It's off somewhere over there," while gesturing 400 yd. in the wrong direction.

Nevertheless, times were changing. Up to that time my father had been able to protect the cove against trespassing abalone divers, but by the mid 1960s inflatable

Zodiac boats opened up the whole coastline to access from the ocean, and my dad was no longer able to defend it. By 1964 there were skin-diving groups coming over from Ukiah and the Sacramento area. For a while they had diving instruction down there almost every weekend, and that brought even more people into the cove.

I believe that, prior to 1964, the wreck had not been much disturbed, but after that it's hard to say. Often when I'd go down to check on it the wreck would look different. It was in fairly shallow water—only 8–15 ft. deep on a minus tide—and there was a lot of sand in the area. Sometimes I'd see ballast blocks exposed on the bottom, and, other times, particularly after a storm, they would be almost covered over with sand.

For most of the 1970s I didn't think much about the wreck. I stored the cannon, the ballast block, some lead sheathing, and the pottery out in my garage. Then in 1980 a fire burned the garage and part of the house. I had 24 squares of roofing in the garage ready to go on the house, and that fire was *hot*! It melted the lead, popped the barnacles off the cannon, and I never was able to find many of the ceramics. A couple of years later, when they were putting the Kelley House Museum together down in Mendocino, Dorothy Bear stopped by and asked if they could hold on to the cannon, the ballast, and what little pottery that I had left on display for the opening of the museum. I told her "fine," but I wanted it back. Well, it's still all down there, and that's where it really belongs—on display where people can see it.

I continued working for the park system until 1974, when I took over my dad's pizza parlor here in Fort Bragg. In 1962, he started Louie's Pizza, right here in this building, where my mother and I now run

Goodies Fountain. It was built in 1870 by Sam Arthur, my mother's great-grandfather, and it's been in the family ever since. It's now the fourth-oldest building in Fort Bragg—mainly because they've tore down so many of the older buildings. I closed down the wrecking yard in 1974 and quit the body shop in 1981. My main recreation nowadays is working on this building. We've remodeled it three times over the last 10 years, and I've enjoyed doing that—adding another chunk here, tearing something out, or changing it around.

I haven't been diving since 1980. As my friends grew older it became harder and harder to find somebody that could dive at the same times I could, and one thing I learned about diving is never go in alone. Eventually, I outgrew my wetsuit, and nowadays I smoke way too much to go out there and dive. I'm no longer much interested in fast cars. I guess I've had enough of them. I still have a "loaded" '65 Ford Ranchero and a '67 Ford Van out in the garage that I keep saying I'm going to work on, but it seems like I never get around to it. The van has one of the trick paint jobs I was doing back in the 1970s—a Far Eastern Indian macramé-rope design in three colors. Back then we were customizing vans—hopping them up, redoing their interiors with paneling and couches, and painting murals on the sides. That was a good business until the car factories started doing it themselves and drove everybody else out.

During the past 40 years there have been a lot of changes here on the coast—and if you want my honest opinion, they should have locked the gates about 1955. At that time there were 400 people in Caspar, 600 in Mendocino, and maybe 4,000 in Fort Bragg—and even if you might not know each individual, you knew every house and every family. Back then you would never have referred to this place as 144 North Franklin. It was "Arthur's Corner," and the next one was Galli's, then Smith's. Today I don't know anyone.

The change started in the mid '60s when the hippies came through. They were a lot of fun, and, if you could tolerate them, it was great. But the people who moved in after—the arts-and-crafts bunch that Carmelized Carmel and gentrified Sausalito—are the ones that ruined what I knew as a kid. They bought up Mendocino and immediately decided: "Now that I'm here, I don't want anybody else!" So they brought in their restrictions.

We got that property down at Caspar in the late 1800s. First we raised sheep on it, then hogs, and later on cattle. We planted peas, potatoes, and alfalfa. If we needed a building we built it, and if we needed to tear it down we tore it down. I built my first body shop on it with some leftover lumber from the Caspar Lumber Company. Then I put a wrecking yard on it—and up to 1964 we did all of that without having to go through one damn permit

or talk to anybody. Today it's so restricted you can't build a fence without a permit, and, if I were to first discover the *Frolic* this afternoon, it would require an act of Congress to take even one little piece of evidence from it.

There are people up here with ideas, but they're so stymied by the system they can't get started. I'm sick and tired of it. It seems every year someone pops out of the woodwork saying: "You can't cut this tree!" or "You can't plow that ground!" because there may be some damn plant out there—even though you've plowed it for a hundred years and that plant is still there.

I really feel for the local people around here who're trying to make a living. Carpenters can't get work because projects are held up year after year. People complain about a chain store like K-Mart coming in, but they don't realize that most of the major businesses that have existed up here over the past 40 years were all chains. Bank of America is a chain. So is Wells Fargo and all of the filling stations. They were upset when Sprouse Reitz went out of business, but that was a chain too. Not

Figure 56. Louie Fratis with Annaliese Corbin at the public meeting reporting the 2003 *Frolic* mapping expedition results, Caspar, California. (Photo by Thomas Layton, 2003)

LOUIE D. FRATIS

only are they fighting the large department stores and new housing developments, but five motels totaling 300 rooms have been on hold for six years.

These same people are the ones who say we don't want logging or fishing and we should focus on the tourist industry. But tourists need accommodations and services. I think a lot of the hooey in support of so-called environmental causes really comes down to this: "I've got mine, and I don't want anybody else to have theirs." They don't want any more people up here. They want it kept small, and they'll use the environment to keep it that way.

LOUIE D. FRATIS

James Kennon

James Kennon was born in 1924 in Hermosa Beach, a suburb of Los Angeles, California, where he was first introduced to the ocean. The family then moved to Tennessee where, in 1943, before graduating from high school, Jim enlisted in the Marine Corps. After boot camp in San Diego, Jim trained as an aircraft mechanic before being sent to radar school and then gunnery school. He survived four airplane crashes before becoming a land-and-sea survival instructor at El Toro Marine Air Station just south of Los Angeles.

After a year at Fullerton Junior College, Jim moved, together with his parents, to the northern Sacramento Valley, where he was hired by the Tehama County Sheriff's Department, first as a jailer, then as a radio dispatcher, and finally as an investigator. About that time Jim began breath-hold spearfishing and abalone collecting along the Mendocino County Coast. In 1955, Jim transferred to the Glenn County Sheriff's Department, where, in 1958, he formed an underwater search-and-rescue team.

Figure 57. James Kennon, Fort Bragg, California, 1994. (Photo by Thomas Layton)

Although Jim had done some diving in the Marines, he had no formal training, so he and his dive partner, Vilho "Bill" Kosonen, enrolled for a five-day course at the Scripps Institute of Oceanography in La Jolla, California. Jim later returned to Scripps for a course in industrial diving. Jim and Bill began to teach skin diving at Willows public swimming pool and taking their students to the coast for ocean experience at what was later to be named "Frolic Cove."

In 1965, while spearfishing with Bill, Jim noticed an anomaly on the ocean floor and discovered the *Frolic* shipwreck. Jim and Bill sought professional advice and convinced Mendel Peterson, the underwater-archaeology specialist at the Smithsonian, to come to the coast to examine the wreck. Unfortunately, the surf was too rough for diving during Peterson's visit, but Jim and Bill shipped a large assemblage of artifacts to Peterson in hopes of identifying the wreck.

In 1978, Jim ran for election as sheriff of Glenn County and lost. By then he had reached the police-retirement age of 55. He retired to teach law-enforcement administration at Butte College into the early 1980s. In 1989, Jim received a phone call from Tom Layton and, during their subsequent meeting, showed Tom his collection from the *Frolic* and donated it for Tom's research. In 1993 the Smithsonian returned the artifacts that Jim and Bill had sent to Mendel Peterson. Those collections now reside in the *Frolic* Repository at the Mendocino County Museum in Willits, California. Jim passed away in 2006 at the age of 82.

James Kennon

28 October 1989, Willows, California
10 July and 4 August 1994, Fort Bragg, California

It was on 30 June 1965, when I actually discovered it, but I didn't know it at the time. I was scuba diving and spearfishing with three other fellows when I got this strange eerie feeling. I was about 15 ft. off the bottom, swimming slow and easy, looking for a big lingcod, and all of a sudden I had this funny feeling that something wasn't right. I did a 360° turn and surfaced to look around, and everything seemed OK, but my buddy divers had disappeared and I couldn't see their bubbles anywhere. So, I dived back down, but I still had this uncomfortable feeling that "something is wrong here," and as I swam along I began to notice that there were objects on the bottom that didn't appear to be rocks. Some of them were round or cylindrical in shape, and others were square or rectangular. Then I began to realize what the problem was—the bottom looked manmade.

At first I didn't think much about it, but when I went home I got to wondering. "Well," I thought, "it could have been a barge that dropped a bunch of garbage on the bottom of the ocean, or it could have been a house that slipped off the cliff, or maybe it was a wrecked ship?" During the next several days I kept going over it in my mind, and the more I thought about it the more I thought it might be a ship. I got out all my back issues of *Skin Diver* magazine and looked at pictures of shipwrecks underwater. I remember it was 3:30 A.M. when I finally knew it was a ship, and I told my wife: "We're going back to Fort Bragg." She thought I was crazy. Next morning I phoned Bill Kosonen, my diving buddy. "I'm pretty sure I've found an old ship," I said. "Let's go back over there, and if there's anything in it we'll go partners—fifty-fifty."

The next weekend Bill and I swam out from shore and got out to the location from dead reckoning—by lining ourselves up with objects that I'd noted on shore. We then dove down and hit right on top of the wreck site. We looked around for a little bit and saw lots of pieces of pottery and brass lying around on the bottom. There was also a chain and an anchor. Nearby we noticed what looked like a pile of rocks with a hole about 5 ft. wide going underneath—and when we stuck our heads and shoulders inside and looked up we could see the bottoms of dishes stuck to the roof. Then we spotted this pile of bricks, maybe 15 ft. long, 5 ft. wide, and 3 ft. off the bottom. They were all covered with some kind of growth and looked like they'd been there for many years. I pried one loose with my knife, chipped the encrustation off one of the corners, and it gleamed like silver. I looked at Bill and he looked at me, and boy our eyes got big. We were giving the OK sign. "We've got it!" we thought, "Oh boy, with all this stuff we've got a million dollars!"

So, up to our tubes we went, toting that brick, and we went for shore as fast as we could swim. Oh, were we excited! We jumped up and down on the beach hollering for our wives to come down from the bluff. "Look what we found!" we shouted. "And there's lots more of it out there!" We were sure it was silver, so the next day we drove down to Sacramento to have it tested. When we laid the brick on the counter the technician said: "I'll have to know exactly where you found it." Well, I may look like a hick, but I don't think like a hick. I told him it came from the Pacific Ocean and that was as close as he was going to get. The assay came out 79% white cast iron. We'd found the ballast of the ship—and there went my million dollars.

I guess I've always loved the ocean, and, as far back as I can remember, I've always been a fisherman. I was born in Hermosa Beach, California, in 1924. My father was working the oil wells over at Signal Hill, and by the time I was only a few years old he was already taking me down to the ocean. He would put me on his shoulders, wade out into the waves, give me a little push, and I'd kind of surf back. There was a big barge anchored off Palos Verdes, where you could pay to fish. My dad would take me out there and we'd fish with cane poles.

My folks had come from Tennessee, so, in 1931, when my dad lost his job, we moved back. We were the Beverly Hillbillies in reverse. We settled in Gleason, Tennessee, a small town with a population of about 900, where my father became manager of the U-Totem Grocery Store. I worked there quite a bit, but every spare moment I was down in the creek swimming or fishing.

I remember my first fishing pole and the first fish I caught with it. It was a cane rod. My mother gave me safety pins for the guides, and my father gave me twine from the grocery store for casting line. I bought a 21¢ single-action reel from Sears & Roebuck and a 19¢ Hedden "red-headed river runt" plug. I still remember walking the railroad trestle across the Obion River to a spot where a log was sticking out of the bank, and I got out on that log. Since you couldn't cast with a reel like that, I laid the line out on the log and threw the lure as far out as I could. I hooked a 10 in. bass and had to hand-line him in because my reel wouldn't turn fast enough. I remember taking that fish home and running over to the store to tell my dad. That evening, when he came home from work, I showed him my little 6 in. fillet in the frying pan. "You know son," he said, "I think that fish shrunk a little bit."

My first diving experience was almost my last. I was about 15 when I heard the government was running a free summer class in tinsmithing over in Dresden, about 6 mi. away. I enrolled and decided to make a diving helmet for my class project. The finished helmet rested on my shoulders, with ropes tied front and back running down between my legs. It had a glass faceplate and a little valve connected to an old tire pump with a rubber hose. My first dive was in a slough just off the river. It was about 8 ft. deep where I jumped in, but I couldn't get under because the helmet was full of air and wanted to float. Eventually my friends tied rocks to my feet, and I did get to the bottom. At first everything seemed to be working. Then one of the rocks started to come loose, and when I bent over to retie it my helmet filled with water. There I was at the bottom of a slough with rocks on my feet and a helmet full of water. I grabbed the air hose and barely pulled myself up to the top.

The war broke out in 1941, so early in 1943, before graduating from high school, I and four of my friends decided to enlist. Of those four, three were killed and one was crippled. I was lucky. I survived four crashes and was able to walk back. I enlisted in the Marine Corps, went to boot camp in San Diego, and was then sent to Norman, Oklahoma, to train as an aircraft mechanic. While there, they then sent me to radar school and finally to aerial-gunnery school.

I was eventually assigned to the 3rd Air Wing at Bogue Field in North Carolina,

where I survived my first crash. It was a training flight off the North Carolina coast. The pilot forgot to switch over to the second fuel tank and dove to restart the engine. It didn't start. We crash landed in a field just beyond the beach and were stopped by a ditch. I remember that for a moment the plane stood straight up with its nose wedged in the dirt before tumbling over onto its back.

I wanted to be where the real action was, so I volunteered for overseas duty, and nine days later I was there—in the Pacific, on an aircraft carrier headed southwest. My second crash was on takeoff in a torpedo dive bomber—better known as a "flying coffin." The engine conked out and we "pancaked" into an unoccupied barracks. The only injury was the lower gunner, who broke his wrist.

My third crash occurred in 1944 in a Douglas Dauntless dive-bomber, when our left wheel gave way while landing on an aircraft carrier. We whipped to the left and ended up dangling off the side of the flight deck looking down at the water 60 ft. below. Later I was in another minor crash landing without injury. I felt like the "cat with nine lives," and I was using them up awfully fast. I now feel quite lucky to have served four years without serious injury. I never wrote to my parents about the crashes because I didn't want them to worry. Even after the war was over I didn't tell them.

In 1945 I was transferred to El Toro Marine Air Station and assigned to Special Services. There I became a land-and-sea-survival instructor. We'd spend a week at Aliso Beach, south of Los Angeles, teaching pilots how to get out of their planes and come in through the surf. We'd strap them into an open cockpit on tracks and run it to the bottom of a 12 ft. pool, where

Figure 58. James Kennon (right) in Marine Corps aerial gunnery training, Norman, Oklahoma, 1943. (Photo courtesy of David Kennon)

they'd have to release themselves, surface, and inflate their Mae Wests. In another exercise we taught them how to catch a bubble of air in their helmet, shirt, or pants and use it as a flotation device. Then we'd spend a week in the Santa Ana Mountains teaching them how to survive up there.

During my last years in the military I passed the GED test for high school graduation and played halfback for the El Toro Marine Base "Flying Marines." I was 6 ft. 3 and weighed 195 lb. With seven "All-Americans," including Elroy "Crazy Legs" Hirsch, we probably had the best football team in the nation. The only loss I can remember was to "Fleet City," the Navy team. Whenever we'd scrimmage with college teams like USC or UCLA we'd just tromp them. Most of the fellows on our team later went professional.

Before I got out of the service, I wrote my folks in Tennessee that I really liked California and wanted to stay, so they moved back out and settled in Yorba Linda, a little town just southeast of Los Angeles. In 1947 I enrolled at Fullerton Junior College and began studying to become either a forester or a game warden. I wasn't able to play football there because I'd gotten my left ankle and leg torn up pretty badly with seven fractures while playing in the military. I left Fullerton College in 1948, found a job at Barton's Garage, and Mr. Barton sent me to Carter Carburetor School. By 1947 my dad had an appliance store, so in addition to working at the garage I was delivering and installing stoves, refrigerators, and televisions. As an appliance dealer, my dad had one of the first televisions in town. It was a Philco, with a 9 in. screen. In the evening he'd turn it on and shove it up against the show-window. It always attracted a crowd of people out on the sidewalk—particularly the wrestling. He sold a lot of TVs that way.

It was in 1951 that I discovered northern California. My wife, my parents, and I had come up to Woodson Bridge, near Corning, on a summer vacation, and, as I recall, it was stinking hot. We were walking along the bank of the Sacramento River, where it was a bit cooler. I was looking across at the mountains when I said: "Dad, I'm going to move to northern California." He continued looking at the water and the mountains for a moment longer and replied: "Son, so am I."

My dad moved up first and started a grocery store in Las Molinas. I came up two weeks later and found a job hand-stacking lumber at a mill about 3 mi. north of Corning. They'd bring me a big pile of fresh-cut fir or pine on a forklift, and two of us would stack it with spacers in between so air would circulate and the wood would dry. Then I got a job at Forward's Mill hand-loading boxcars. It took a lot of strength to do that kind of work and, fortunately, as it turned out, it really built up my arms.

Meanwhile, I wanted to make a bit more money, so I took a night job as a security guard. Well, in order to be guard I had to get a pistol permit, so I went down to the Tehama County Sheriff's Office in Red Bluff and gave them the required background information. About two weeks later they called me to come by because my permit was ready. When I got there the sheriff and the undersheriff were on one side of the booking counter and I was on the other—and they were looking at me sort of strangely.

The sheriff was a big man, 6 ft. 6, weighing about 260. "How would you like to work for me?" he asked. "Well, what are you paying?" I replied. "It's $221 per month, and if you can beat me arm wrestling, I'll hire you." That's when those months of stacking lumber paid off. I put my arm up on the counter and he took hold of my hand and began squeezing. I held my hand perfectly still, and, as he started getting white in the face, I knew he was pushing as hard as he could. Suddenly he let go, gave me another long stare, and told me to be at work at 8 o'clock in the morning. I guess I beat the biggest, meanest guy in town, and that's how I got started in law enforcement.

The undersheriff, Al Duncan, had come from the Berkeley Police Department, and he began my training to be a law-enforcement officer. I started as a jailer and was soon operating the radio as a dispatcher. Then, I became a deputy out in the field and eventually an investigator. Al gave me a good start. Meanwhile, I went over

to Chico State and took law-enforcement courses. There were only seven people at the sheriff's office, and we worked six days a week. There were lots of calls, long hours, lots of things to investigate, and Al taught me how to run down leads. I worked three years for Tehama County, and, in 1955, for better pay, I moved over to the Glenn County Sheriff's Office to work as an investigator.

Meanwhile, I had become involved in diving again. It started when a friend of mine asked if I'd like to go abalone diving over on the coast near Fort Bragg. "You'll need a wetsuit," he said. "No! I won't," I told him—and proceeded to describe my diving experiences in the service down at Aliso Beach in southern California. Well, I'd never been in the frigid waters of northern California. I went in for 20 min., and when I came out my legs and feet were so

Figure 59. James Kennon (right rear) served as a Tehama County, California Sheriff's Department investigator during the early 1950s. (Photo courtesy of David Kennon)

numb I couldn't stand up. The next day I bought a wetsuit. After that, I'd go over to the coast fairly regularly to fish and snorkel for abalone.

It was in 1958 that we decided to start an underwater search-and-rescue team. Up to that time I'd had no formal training in diving, so my friend Bill Kosonen and I went down to the Scripps Institute of Oceanography for a five-day crash course where we were certified by Jim Stewart, the Scripps's dive master. We had the Sacramento River on one side of us and some big canals and reservoirs on the other. People were drowning, and the sheriff's office was being called fairly regularly to find them. We were also being called to pull evidence out of rivers and canals. Thieves would steal a safe, break it open, and then dump it off a bridge. Every year, when the water would go down in the canals, we'd find all kinds of stolen property below the bridges. In fact, under one particular bridge I must have pulled up guns, safes, and other property at least a dozen times.

When I started the underwater squadron, I brought Jim Stewart, the dive master from the Scripps Institute, up to train our men in underwater search and recovery. The first recovery we did was in Black Butte Lake. A serviceman had swum out about a 100 yd. and had gone down. We anchored one end of a long line near where he was last seen, placed 10 divers at arm's lengths along the line, and began a 360° rotation around that spot. We had made about half a rotation when we found him. We made lots of recoveries after that.

As commander of the underwater squadron, I was soon receiving requests to do new tasks, often in tricky underwater situations, so several years later I decided I needed more training and returned to Scripps for a 100-hour course in industrial diving, sponsored by NAUI, the National Association of Underwater Instructors. In order to qualify for the course I had to skin dive down to 90 ft. with a snorkel and bring up a piece of the bottom. That was easy for me. In those days I could hold my breath for 5 min. In fact, I used to win bets doing that in the service. Jim Stewart and his crew taught us how to work safely in an underwater environment: to fit and repair oil-well pipes, to scrub the bottom of a ship, and how to use nitrogen-gas-powered tools. We learned to accomplish systematic surveys, laying out grid systems and running compass courses. Finally, we were trained in underwater photography and the use of television technology to aid in underwater inspections and wreck surveys.

During this time I continued to take courses in law enforcement at Butte College, Chico State, and UC Berkeley. Meanwhile, the FBI would send instructors out to provide us with specialized training. I was specializing as a crime investigator, so, in the fall of 1965 the sheriff's department sent me to the FBI Academy in Washington, D.C., for three months of training. There were 99 people in my class—officers from 38 states and 8 foreign nations—and we received the same training as regular FBI agents.

We shot all kinds of police weapons—revolvers, rifles, shotguns, and machine guns. We fired them at both moving and stationary targets, day and night, left handed, right handed, and quick draw. It was competitive, and the person with the best overall average was to receive a trophy. My best time to draw and fire a kill shot on a silhouette torso was 55/100 of a second, and my overall score for all of those weapons was 1,268 points out of a possible 1,300.

JAMES KENNON

One morning I was sitting in class when an FBI agent came in and asked to speak with me outside. "We're going to see Mr. Hoover," he said. I was thinking something bad had happened, that perhaps a family member had died; however, just before we walked into Mr. Hoover's office the agent said: "Relax, you're going to enjoy this." So, we walked in and there stood Mr. J. Edgar Hoover. He congratulated me, shook my hand, and a photographer flashed our picture as he handed me the trophy. Because of all my previous coursework, by the time I finished my training at the FBI Academy I was rated "expert" and qualified to testify in court in seven different fields of law enforcement: narcotics, blood spatters, wound sequence, crime-scene reconstruction, photography, firearms, and the interpretation of fingerprints, footprints, and tool marks.

During the year before going back to the FBI Academy I had become somewhat more involved in diving. In the spring of 1965 I was certified No. 0816 by NAUI, the National Association of Underwater Instructors, and I began teaching evening classes using the Willows High School swimming pool. By that time I was spending a lot of time over on the coast diving, fishing, and escaping the heat of the Sacramento Valley, and my diving buddy, Bill Kosonen, had got permission from Louie Fratis [Sr.] for us to dive in a little cove off his property at Caspar. In fact, early that summer I began taking my students over there to teach them how to dive safely in the ocean.

On 8 June 1965, Bill Kosonen, two other friends, and I were diving and spearing fish near the mouth of that cove when one of the guys found a 10 in. bronze spike. He showed it to me, and I noticed several pieces of old porcelain plates on the bottom nearby, but I didn't attach much importance to them.

It was two weeks later that I found the wreck. I had my tanks on and was swimming slowly, carrying an 8 ft. spear pole, carefully watching the bottom and hoping for a big lingcod to stick its head out of a hole. That's when I first noticed unnatural manmade shapes covered by sea growth all over the bottom. I surfaced, looked for my position, and continued hunting. When I returned to shore, I didn't say much about what I'd seen. Maybe it was my background in crime-scene reconstruction, but I couldn't help thinking about it, and during the next couple of days I looked at all the photos I could find showing shipwreck sites underwater. Then, when I was sure it was a shipwreck, I called my friend Bill Kosonen.

During July of 1965 Bill and I began to explore the wreck, and—after we learned that the bricks were not silver—we began to investigate other objects. One of the anchors had a shank close to 10 ft. long, and the chain had 7 in. rectangular links. We picked up dishes, pieces of dark bottle glass, and found a gun with a wooden stock and a barrel that flared out at the muzzle end. Almost everything was so encrusted in marine growth that it required a hammer and chisel to chip it out.

Bill and I decided we needed some legal assistance in claiming the ship, so we went to Jack Feeney, an attorney, and told him we'd give him a 10% split if he would handle our legal work. Jack contacted an admiralty attorney friend of his down in San Francisco and informed us that, as long as we had some artifacts and some pictures showing where we'd found the ship, it was already ours on a finders-keepers basis.

By then, Bill and I were doing a lot of

reading, and I think it was Bill who read something about Mendel L. Peterson, the curator of armed-forces history at the Smithsonian Institution, who was a specialist in underwater archaeology. That fall, when I went to the FBI Academy in Washington, D.C., I brought along some artifacts with the intention of contacting Mr. Peterson. I phoned for an appointment and met with him on 11 October 1965. We talked for quite some time, and he became very interested. I left the artifacts with him to examine, and he agreed to come out to California to dive the wreck himself and assist us in identifying it.

That winter, anticipating Mr. Peterson's arrival, Bill and I built a single hookah compressor and started looking for a larger compressor to power an airlift. Mr. Peterson arrived in California 17 March 1966, and Bill, his wife, "Pete," and I went over to Fort Bragg. We brought all our diving equipment, but for the next four days the water was too rough to dive. We took Pete out to the bluff overlooking the wreck site, but there were big swells coming into the cove, and large waves were breaking right over the wreck itself. We ended up doing a lot of talking.

We communicated with Pete quite a bit after that, and since he was willing to pay the freight, we started sending him every artifact we thought might identify the ship. We found a 5 ft. iron cannon with a 4 in. bore that had CA & CO marked on the right trunnion above the number 1773. We figured that might identify the wreck, so we towed a balsa raft out there and tried to raise it with a four-line block and tackle. The weight pulled the raft underwater, and even then I could hardly lift one end of the cannon off the ocean floor with a pry bar. We never did raise that cannon.

Pete later told us that Cyrus Alger of Boston did not start making iron cannons until 1828, and all the pieces he'd seen with Alger's imprint dated from the 1840s and 50s. Eventually we sent Pete over a 100 lb. of artifacts. These included bottles, porcelain ceramics and beads, a porthole cover, a sounding lead, cannonballs, and a blunderbuss. Smaller artifacts included a piece of gold filigree jewelry and a hinged silver locket in the shape of a seashell, with a piece of agate inside. We even sent our famous cast-iron ballast block!

Although Pete wasn't able to pin down the name of the vessel, he decided the best candidate was probably the *Susie Merrill*, which went down in 1866. Since he planned to come back out in 1968, Bill and I remodeled our air pump to have two compressors operating off the same motor to provide enough air for two divers as well as an airlift.

Meanwhile, we tried to research the wreck ourselves. We went down to the San Francisco Maritime Museum, but no one down there wanted to help us. They just weren't interested—period. They were kind of rude—as if they didn't believe us. They made me feel little—as if the wreck wasn't important and my ideas didn't amount to anything.

Apparently, someone at the museum told a diving club about my inquiry. They contacted me and said if I would tell them where the ship was, I could be one of their group. I wasn't about to tell them anything. I never even revealed how deep it was, because if you knew that you'd have a chance of finding it. Bill and I didn't want the wreck destroyed. We also contacted Ray Akers of the Drake Navigators Guild down in Palo Alto. He tried to identify the age of the vessel from some of the artifacts, like the teak winch drum we'd recovered, but no one was able to identify the vessel.

JAMES KENNON

Bill and I continued diving every chance we had during 1967 and 1968. Bill bought an underwater camera from Al Giddings down in San Francisco, and we began taking pictures—including one of the cannon trunnions with the CA & CO imprint. Eventually we sent five or six boxes of artifacts back to Peterson together with our best underwater photographs.

Generally we'd take a small boat to the site, carrying our compressor and a 4 in. airlift. Where there was sand we'd suction it away, exposing artifacts that were heavier. Most of the area was covered with a calcareous growth, almost like you'd poured cement over it. However, in one sandy area, we were able to get down 3 or 4 ft. to bedrock and found wood from the bottom of the ship with copper sheathing on it. Pete said if we could get a whole plate, they'd give us some kind of a receipt to take it off our income tax. We never found a whole plate. I don't think we ever found a whole anything out there. Unfortunately, other obligations kept Pete from ever returning to the site, and by 1970 Bill and I quit diving on it, having only scratched the surface. We kept in touch with Pete for some time after that because he still had our artifacts, but years passed and after a while we pretty much gave up on it.

I continued as undersheriff for Glenn County till 1978. During that time I worked on two cases that later ended up in detective magazines—big stories with everything blown out of proportion. One story had me out on a golf course, incognito, looking for a murderer—a figment of the writer's imagination. In 1978, when the old sheriff resigned, I automatically became sheriff and served out the last year of his term as acting sheriff-coroner. I then ran for election, against seven people, and got beat by 32 votes.

I was 55 years old and had spent 26 years in law enforcement, so I retired. Losing that election was probably the best thing that ever happened to me. Law enforcement is hard work, and somebody is always mad at you. When you catch a criminal, his family is mad at you—and if you don't, the victim is. They expect miracles from police officers, but there aren't any miracles. It's just hard work.

I taught courses in law-enforcement administration, police science, and firearms through Butte College into the early 1980s and periodically gave lectures elsewhere. It was during that time that I addressed the Second National Homicide Symposium in Los Angeles—and there was Telly Savalas, with his shaved head, out there in the audience. I like to think that I may have sharpened his technique as Kojak.

Since retirement I spend a lot of time here on the coast. In fact, I keep a trailer here year-round, and I launch my boat from the county ramp at Noyo Harbor. My wife spends about two-thirds of her time here, and my kids and grandkids are always visiting. Salmon season runs from February through June and from August into November, and I'm usually here for that. After salmon season, I hunt deer in Idaho for about three weeks and usually come back with a buck. Then I fish for bass over in Stoney Gorge, Black Butte, and East Park Lakes through the first part of April. Each spring I compete in a bass-fishing tournament sponsored by the West Side Anglers Club. This year my fishing partner and I won second place and $530 cash in that tournament with a 5 lb. 9 oz. "kicker." The guy who beat us got a 10 lber. In order to compete you have to keep your fish alive so they can be turned loose, and the only one kept is the big fish of the day.

Meanwhile, I keep a garden at my house over in Willows. In November I plant garlic, onions, radishes, and lettuce. Just before I go to the coast in the spring, I harvest the garlic and onions and plant tomatoes, squash, bell peppers, and other vegetables. We have an automatic sprinkler, so periodically my wife or I go over there, pick the vegetables, and bring them over to the coast. With electronics and vigilant neighbors, the house in Willows is well protected. While I'm here on the coast I easily catch my limit, but I like my fish fresh and usually bring home only enough for about four meals.

I take salmon either by trolling or by "mooching." For mooching you use a keel sinker, then about 6 ft. of leader out to a 4 "O" hook with the barb pinched down. You can't use barbs on salmon. I run a long needle up the anus of the bait fish and out the eye. Then I attach the leader and pull the hook back until just the tip is hanging out of the eye. I then do a half-hitch around the tail. When you're mooching you let your boat drift—if possible, through a school of bait fish—and, as you drift, the bait spins slowly. Most large salmon, 15 lb. or larger, I've taken mooching. I catch all sizes trolling.

You know, if the Department of Fish and Game would only listen to the fisherman, they wouldn't be having so many problems with their salmon. For example, right now the law is that king salmon have to be 20 in. in length to keep and you can't keep a coho at all. The first day out this year I caught and released over 20 silvers and kings. I know that a lot of those fish will die. When you damage his scales or he's bleeding, he's likely to get an infection. Of course that's if he can escape the sharks and sea lions that follow the boats picking up the fish you're dumping back. Sometimes the sea lions and sharks take them right off your line. If there's a hundred boats out there every day, each catching and releasing 20–30 fish, look at how many small fish we're killing. I think the law should be that you use a barbed hook, and you keep the first two fish you catch, regardless of size, and that's your limit. You should not be allowed to throw a salmon back. Lots of people would be happy to take a couple of 18 in. salmon home to eat, and they wouldn't have to release some 25 fish to do it. That would be a good law, and it would help the salmon population.

Well, it was in October of 1989, almost 20 years since my last dive on it, that the shipwreck at Caspar reentered my life. Then one evening, I got a phone call from Tom Layton. He identified himself and asked: "Did you find a shipwreck over at Caspar? "Yes," I replied. "Can you tell me where," he continued. "No," I told him, "I don't do business over the telephone, but if you're who you say you are, I'll talk to you about it." Tom had found me through Dr. Paul Selchau, one of my diving students. Back in the mid-1960s I'd checked out Paul for certification in a cove just north of the shipwreck, and Paul had liked the area so much he bought a lot and built a vacation house in a new subdivision directly overlooking the wreck site. At that time Paul was developing some proficiency as an underwater photographer, so I eventually told him about the wreck.

A few days after his phone call, Tom came up to my house in Willows, carrying a camera and a tape recorder, and I told him what I knew about the wreck. When I brought out the blunderbuss and the porcelain plates and showed him photos of what I'd sent to the Smithsonian, his eyes really lit up. Tom had just got back from reading the company papers at Harvard and had worked out the history of the vessel. So, 24 years after I discovered it, I finally learned it was the *Frolic,* a Baltimore clipper wrecked in the summer of 1850. I gave Tom my collection of *Frolic* artifacts to take down to San Jose State University to study, and we wrote the Smithsonian asking return of the artifacts Bill Kosonen and I had sent to them. Unfortunately, in the meantime, Mendel Peterson had retired, and the Smithsonian had lost the collection. Three years later, in January of 1993, I finally got most of the artifacts back and donated them to the *Frolic* Repository Tom was establishing at the Mendocino County Museum in Willits. We are still trying to get the Smithsonian to return the remainder of the artifacts, including a piece of gold filigree jewelry and all of our underwater photographs of the wreck.

More recently I've taken Tom out in my boat to the rock where the *Frolic* first hit. Captain Faucon wrote that when he saw breakers he put the helm to port. That means putting the back end of the ship to the left, resulting in a right turn. As he completed the turn, the stern of the vessel hit the rock, breaking off the rudder. When a wave hits that rock, the main part is blocked and bounces back, resulting in a strong current flowing around both ends of the rock towards the shore. The *Frolic* had to pass around the south side of the rock because there were other rocks to the north blocking the way. I think the *Frolic* washed around the south side of the rock and was carried by the current to her present location, on the north side of the cove, without much help from the crewmen left aboard. After all, you can't row a ship like that, and the rudder was gone.

You know, it's been almost 30 years since I discovered that shipwreck, and I'm really tickled that, after all this time, I finally know the history of the vessel—and with those exhibits in Mendocino, Willits, and Ukiah, the public knows about it too. It's just too bad that the archaeology couldn't have happened back in 1965 when I first discovered it.

Vilho "Bill" Kosonen

Bill Kosonen was born in 1923 and raised on his family's dairy farm near Willows in the northern Sacramento Valley of California. He graduated from Willows High School in 1941. During his first semester at the University of California Agricultural Branch at Davis, the war broke out.

In the spring of 1942, Bill enlisted in the Coast Guard. His initial training was at Port Angeles, Washington, and his first assignment was at Alameda in the San Francisco Bay, where he worked opening and closing the nets across the Golden Gate to prevent the entry of enemy submarines. Then he was then sent to Hemphill Diesel School in New York, where he was certified as a motor machinist and assigned to a fireboat in San Francisco Bay. There he was seriously burned while fighting a fire on the Oakland waterfront. After a long hospitalization, Bill was assigned to

Figure 60. Vilho "Bill" and Marian Kosonen, Fort Bragg, California, 1983. (Photo courtesy of Victor Kosonen)

a bar pilot near the Farallon Islands, just outside the San Francisco Bay, but was given a special-order discharge from the Coast Guard when his father was injured on the family farm.

When his father had recovered, Bill was sent to the San Diego Naval Training Station as a boot-camp instructor, receiving special training in heavy swimming, search and rescue, and survival, after which he was sent to Okinawa, where the earlier burn injuries to his feet became infected and he was given a medical discharge. Bill then resumed farming with his father, acquired more land, and converted the family ranch from dairy to rice farming.

In the early 1950s Bill began breath-hold diving for abalone along the Mendocino coast, where he received permission from the Fratis family to dive in what was eventually to be named "Frolic Cove."

In 1959, Bill helped Jim Kennon establish a volunteer search-and-rescue unit for the Glenn County Sheriff's Department. He joined Jim for underwater training at the Scripps Institute of Oceanography and began training volunteers for the search-and-rescue squad. Bill was spear fishing with Jim Kennon in the cove when Jim discovered the *Frolic* shipwreck. Bill hosted Mendel Peterson when he came from the Smithsonian to examine the wreck site.

In 1970, Bill sold his ranch and moved to the coast, where he bought a commercial salmon boat. In 1975, he began work in industrial construction, on cement plants, rice dryers, sewer plants, and installing steam turbines for generating electricity. He retired in 1984 when his knees gave out and passed away in 2011 at the age of 88.

Vilho "Bill" Kosonen

4 August 1994
Fort Bragg, California

My mother and dad came from Finland. My dad came over as a carpenter on a square rigger. I have a picture of the boat. I think it's the *Felca*. Dad arrived here around 1906. My mother came over a few years later with her sister and quite a few other ladies from Finland. They landed in New York and went through Ellis Island. My mother went to work as a maid and ended up in Philadelphia. My dad kept working on ships. I have two sisters, and that is the size of our family.

My grandfather was a shipbuilder in Finland, and my father started out as a shipbuilder: going out in the woods, getting the wood, and making boats. Eventually, my dad got the itch to get out and do something else. He wanted to go see new country, so he started sailing. He ended up on the Pacific coast and got a visa to work aboard the coastal ships.

He would come up to Albion on a steam schooner and get lumber out of there and Fort Bragg. He took trips up into Alaska, down to South America, and once around the Horn. Eventually, he ended up in San Francisco as a stevedore, operating a winch, unloading ships. He did that until 1925.

I was born on 11 February 1923. My mother had a cousin that owned a piece of property up in Willows, which, at that time, was 80 ac. He was a hog farmer and was going to lose the property. He couldn't afford to keep it. He couldn't earn enough off the property to make it pay.

Dad and Mom decided they would buy the property and start farming it while Dad continued to work in the Bay Area. Mom stayed on the ranch with my two sisters for a couple of years. Then she took the train to San Francisco, and that's where I was born. When I was a few days old they brought me back to Willows, and that's where I was raised.

At that time we had no electricity. Everything was either wind-powered or with gasoline pumps for water. We got by. We raised what we needed—eggs from the chickens and beef and corn—and we had a small orchard. Then we started a little herd of dairy cows. I started milking cows when I was knee high to a grasshopper—a little kid big enough to pack a bucket. Eventually, Mom and Dad built up a registered Guernsey dairy herd. We focused on that for a good many years.

I started school in Willows—first for a year at an old stone country school and then into town for grammar school. At the time we had a Model T Ford that my sister drove. We were 5.5 mi. out in the country. It was rough going in the wintertime because there was no pavement—just dirt roads. We'd get stuck a lot of times and wouldn't get to school until two hours late. I remember that very well!

It was the Depression. I milked our cows, worked for the neighbors and any other place I could find work. I graduated from Willows High School in 1941 and enrolled at Davis. My plan was to go on into the dairy industry. My first semester at Davis the war broke out.

I joined the Coast Guard in March of 1942 and went through boot camp in Fort Townsend, Washington. It was a tough course because it was still the old way of doing things. We pulled oars on lifeboats. That's where my sea life started. I did a little PBY flying in Port Angeles. PBYs were sea planes used for submarine observation. I was there about three months and was transferred to Government Island in Alameda.

At first I was out in the San Francisco Bay aboard picket boats, pulling the nets in and out across the Golden Gate. When the ships went out we'd pull the nets in, and after they were out we'd close the gates. The nets were for Japanese subs, and they were tight. I was just a regular seaman at that time.

Then, I got a chance to go to Hemphill Diesel School in New York. When I graduated, I made second-class motor machinist, which was a pretty good rate at that time for a young kid. They had us patrolling up and down the East Coast.

Then I was transferred back to Alameda and assigned to fireboat CGF 47O18F as second in command. I was aboard when the Albers Mill burnt down on the Oakland waterfront. My feet got burned pretty bad, and I was laid up in the hospital for quite a time. Jacuzzi had come out with the first small jets, so we could shoot right underneath the docks and even where there was no water at all with a small pumper aboard. The boats were 16–18 ft. long with a Chrysler eight-cylinder engine.

I was finally pulled off the fireboat and sent to a bar pilot as second in command.

Figure 61. Vilho "Bill" Kosonen (right), Future Farmers of America, 1939. (Photo courtesy of Victor Kosonen)

VILHO "BILL" KOSONEN

We'd do seven days off the Farallons. Then we'd be seven days in port. I think she was a 96- or a 98-footer—a sailboat, with an old four-cylinder Bollinger diesel direct reversible with great big pistons. You'd run all of your shifting by "air." To go forward you'd have to slow it way down and then kick it. To go into reverse, you had to catch it just right and then you'd go backwards. There were no transmissions on them in those days. The engine was from the early 1900s. When there was nothing doing out there we cleaned the bilges, kept the motors and generators cleaned up, and so forth. Whenever we got a little engine knock, we'd go into port, pour new babbitt bearings, and be ready to go for the next trip.

The duty of the bar pilot was to bring ships into the harbor. If it was nice weather we'd pull alongside the big steamers and transports, and the pilot would grab the sea ladder, go up into the boat, and command it from there, on into the harbor. This was being done by the Coast Guard because it was wartime.

That's when I got my call to come back home to the ranch. Dad's foot got crushed in a Caterpillar track, and he was laid up. He couldn't farm or do anything, so I got a special-order discharge and went home. I was home for nine months, almost to the day, when I got a call from the Selective Service. They thought that Dad was well enough and I was goofing off. So I ended up being pulled back into the service, which I didn't regret. I went into the service in San Francisco, and they threw me in the Marines.

As soon as I got there, I put in for a transfer to the Navy or the Coast Guard. I wanted to get back into what I had been doing. So they sent me to train new "boots" at the San Diego Naval Training Station—fellows that came from civilian life into the Navy. I trained two classes down there.

Then I got a chance to go out on picket patrol and ended up back in San Francisco, on a PT-13 out of "A" dock. Since they were just demolishing that unit, we stayed at Tanforan. During the time, in order to keep everybody in shape, all the petty officers and so forth were put into different training.

We went into a Bear Cub outfit. They're similar to the Green Berets. I think they were the first frogmen. The training we got was mostly heavy swimming, search and rescue, and survival—quite a course over three months. There were two of us who were second class. They gave us an allotment of officers and men. We would take them out to the beach each day and put them through a rigorous training. We'd dump them off in the ocean, with no rigging, and we'd swim to shore with them. We'd show them how to get off the ship, how to drop their gear when they got to the beach, and how to help themselves. These skills were what they would need to use in Okinawa and other places when they hit the beach.

We'd take them up into the hills at Salinas and put them on bivouac. They'd have to live off the land.

I was sent to Okinawa with PT-24, and after two or three weeks my feet started to bother me. Back in the Albers Mills fire my shoes had caught fire and burnt the soles right off. The old suits we had for firefighting were just asbestos. If you got against white-hot metal they'd disintegrate, and that is what they did.

I had a chance to go back to the States on a cruiser, which was shot up pretty bad. They needed a motor mech. When I got back I ended up in the hospital. My feet had gotten infected with fungus because of the burns. Finally, I got a medical discharge.

Back when I had been working in that Bear Cub outfit, we had some very primitive scuba gear—a breathing tank that we strapped on our sides so we could swim with it. We only used it if we had to. A lot of the fellows that started in those classes never did make it because they couldn't swim good enough. It was a rigorous course, about as tough as you could get. You'd run 20 mi. a day on a sand beach and then you'd go out and work in the woods to get your meals, and then you'd go back out in the ocean the next day. There was no rest. You'd just go, go, go. I was in good shape. I was pretty tough at that time. That was my first experience with a breathing apparatus

I got out of the Navy around 1945, went back to the farm, and returned to Davis with a dairy-industry major. A year later I transferred over to pre-med to become a veterinarian, then got tangled up with a lady. I married Marian in 1947 and never returned to school.

Back at home, I started farming with my dad—milking cows and working at the creamery in Willows. Things were pretty tough at that time. Between the two jobs I was barely making a living. So I worked for about a year in Woodland as a tractor mechanic. Then I got a chance to work at Travis Air Force Base as a line mechanic. I was pretty good at it, and the pay was good.

Finally, I had a chance to go back into farming. We were changing over from the dairy to raising rice. Dad needed me because he couldn't handle changing it over by himself. We started farming together. Little by little, I picked up a 20 ac. piece and then another 40 ac. and then another 20. So, after a while, I had about 80 ac. Eventually we farmed about 300 ac. with our own equipment: tractors, harvesters, cultivators, plows, and our own rice-drying bins. We farmed half and half. Everything was split down the middle.

We'd prepare the ground in March and try to get our crops in during April or May. We'd keep the fields flooded until September. Then we'd drain them and let them dry enough so we could get out there to harvest in October and November. If it was too wet we'd be harvesting until Christmas. Rice farmers have to burn to get rid of the heavy straw. It sours in the ground. If it was dry enough we'd burn in the fall, and, if it wasn't, we'd have to let it go until the next year. We'd have a terrible time burning after the rains.

We had a little leisure during summer and winter. Once the crop was coming up I could leave the water for three or four days. But it takes a month or two of raising and lowering the water to get things set, and then you have to bring your water up with the crop as it grows, so you have to stick around. And then you're hit with a north wind that busts your checks, and you have to go out and shovel mud to patch them to hold your water level.

We continued farming and just plugging along. Things weren't as good as they are today. Finally, the government gave us all of their restrictions. I was pretty perturbed. I couldn't afford to get any bigger, and there wasn't any land available.

Then, the government imposed quotas. You could do only so much in crops, and, if you left a piece fallow, you could get a little return on that—and sometimes you couldn't. The following year they'd cut you off 10% or 20%. They kept this up for a good many years.

It finally came to the point that you

VILHO "BILL" KOSONEN

had the property, but you weren't allowed to do much with it. To get any kind of payment you had to leave it lay fallow.

It came to the point where I had to raise safflower on parts of it and corn on other parts of it. And we had to keep on diversifying. I had to find work off the ranch—for the Forest Service and several other places.

It was around 1953 or '54 that I started diving up at Kibesillah, just south of Westport, with a bunch of Indian fellows probably out of Branscomb. All we had were cut-off Levi's, an inner tube with a couple of pieces of string across it for a gunny sack, and bailing wire to string the abs [abalones] through their holes to carry them. The Indians had a big fire on the beach, and they'd have their wives and kids with them, and, of course, they were just like I was—boisterous and young. We'd come back to the beach and have a little bourbon to keep warm. I tell you it was cold with that wind blowing! There were no steps down to that beach. You tied a rope to the bumper of your car and went down a cliff. I learned to dive with those Indians, and they taught me a lot. I dove with them for several years. Then I never did see them anymore.

I also had a diving group from Willows—like Hap Merrill and myself. We were free-diving with no suit in that cold water. The Indians didn't use them, so, hell, I didn't think I needed one either. You'd dive down, and after a while you'd learn to look. You can see underwater. As you progress along, you get used to diving a little deeper and a little deeper. We were diving down and getting 8 and 9 in. abalones. We never had any problems.

Finally, I bought a Bailey wetsuit. That was really something! You could stay in the water all day, and it became a real pleasure to go diving. I then did lots of abalone diving. Our group in Willows went to the coast and sometimes to the Feather River. We borrowed some tanks, and eventually we'd go into the deeper holes and snorkel around with a hookah.

We did a lot of diving at Westport, the same old way. We took a rope, tied it to the bumper of a car, and went over the side. We brought all of our "abs" back up that way, too. We mostly stayed at the Cleone Store. Then we began staying at Russian Gulch and Van Damme. Eventually we dove all up and down that part of the coast.

I had become acquainted with Louie Fratis, Sr., during the mid – to late 1950s. I had a friend from Princeton who knew Louie. He got us acquainted. Louie had a junkyard where he dealt in used parts, and he tended bar in a few places. He was also running a motel and had a restaurant. I got to know Louie real well. Louie gave us permission to go into the cove and take abalone. He showed us how to eat octopus. We would grab and throw them in a sack. They weren't big, but some of them had tentacles 5 or 6 ft. long. We'd bring in the octopus, skin them, chop them. He would fry them up, and we'd have a big feed.

Marian and I didn't have any property on the coast at the time. We had a little trailer that we left on some friends' property. We had a big banquet table that we used for big feeds!

It was during the late 1950s that I joined the search-and-rescue squad at Willows. Hap Merrill and I actually instigated it. Then Jim Kennon got involved because he was a deputy sheriff. Jim and I got to be pretty good friends, and we started working together. We dove for lost boats up in Black Butte Lake, or, if a car went into the river, we'd look for survivors. And, if there weren't any, we'd look for the bodies.

We started this search and rescue without any formal training. Jim, Hap Merrill, and I and a couple of the others all wanted to all get certified so we could be protected in case something did happen. Meanwhile, we started getting together a lot of our small equipment. Most of the guys glued their suits together, making hats and booties. We got our stuff from Steele's diving shop in Oakland. It was all fairly reasonable at that time.

When we got tied in with the sheriff's office, we started getting more involved. I had a Navy manual, and Jim got one, and we started reading. The Navy had gone a long way with scuba by that time. So we started working through the Navy course, studying on our own, memorizing decompression tables. I was busy farming at the time, so I didn't really have as much time to put in on it like I should have.

We finally went down to La Jolla to get certified by Jimmy Stewart, the dive master. We took a sheriff's car and stayed for three days. It was a crash course to see whether we had enough brains to do anything. Afterwards Jimmy said: "Hell, I didn't know you from the man on the moon when we started." We first dove to 60 ft., then to 90, and then we went to 100. Although we didn't quite go to 150, he certified us to 150. He said: "You're qualified enough to do it!" So he signed our cards.

Jimmy had been working with sharks, and he was scarred up pretty bad. They had been trying different types of shark repellent, and this one didn't work. Over at his house he showed us the movies. His wife wouldn't stay and watch the sharks get him.

So that was our crash course in scuba diving, and we were certified.

Once we were certified, Jim and I started training people in the Willows city

pool. I think we started out with 15 or 18 students. Jim more or less took it over. I did a lot of the handwork instructing the people. Jim made up the course—teaching the diving tables, how many minutes you could stay down, how much decompression time you needed to come up.

We also put together a specialized search-and-rescue course—not for the public—where they had to go down and retrieve their gear and had to buddy breathe. They had to swim for so many minutes, so many laps. It was a heavy course. We didn't baby them. Any man who went through it was qualified, and we weren't afraid to dive with him in the creek or the river or other dangerous areas.

After a while, Jim and I decided we should take the NAUI [National Association of Underwater Instructors] course down in San Francisco. It was quite a course, and there was a lot more book work than I wanted. I came out second or third as far as swimming. Jim came out first. I didn't take the final exam. I just figured that Jim had got enough of it. I was too busy working at the ranch. So, I helped in the training, but never got certified. The only thing I didn't pass was the book work. It was quite a test, two hours long. They had a lot of timetables there to figure. I finally said: "To hell with it! I don't need all this!" I was head of the overall search-and-rescue squad. We had the aqua squad, the horse squad, the mechanized squad, and the aero squad. We had 20-some guys certified for the aqua squad.

Then, Jim and I started diving together. We'd go to the Fratis's place with our wives and kids, have a picnic, and go diving. We couldn't use tanks for the abs, but we did a lot of spear fishing, and that is how we ran into the *Frolic*.

It was after we got home that Jim called

me. He said: "I think I found something. It's different. It looks like a shipwreck. I think we should go back, but I don't want anybody to know about it." So we drove back to the cove with a raft. Our wives were with us—just the four of us.

We went out from the beach and found quite a cluster of what looked like bricks. We started chipping at them with our diving knives and got a corner off of one. With the sun hitting, it glistened! We thought we had found a gold mine! We finally pried one loose and brought it to the beach. It was pretty heavy. The gals were excited too.

We got it into the car, hauled it home, and Jim got a hold of an assayer in Sacramento to find out how much we were worth! We drove it to Sacramento and got a report right away. "It's not silver," he said. "It's cast iron of unknown origin." He didn't know when it was made, but noted that it was quite porous. That was a big letdown!

When we got back to Willows, we started thinking about it. "If it's a ship, maybe it was used for ballast." So we started diving on it. I made up a big 8 ft. tube with a crook in it. We drove down to Steele's dive shop, bought a small compressor, and attached a Briggs and Stratton motor and a hookah system.

First we started finding plates, and then we started finding beads. The longer we worked the more we could see, as our eyes got accustomed to spotting what didn't belong there. In order not to tear anything up we tried to get the stuff that was loose and not break into anything that was whole. We found a blunderbuss and took it to Jack Feeney, an attorney in Willows, to see what we should do about it. Feeney suggested we call the Smithsonian.

When Jim went back East for training at the FBI Academy, we decided he should go to the Smithsonian and see if he could find somebody to talk to. Feeney more or less lined up the meeting. Jim didn't know who he was going to talk to. We knew what we had was historical, and we knew they did a lot of archaeological digging in the water. We wanted to know how they did it and how they laid it out.

Jim was sent to see Mendel "Pete" Peterson because he was in charge of the historic arms division. It turned out Pete was really interested in the pottery because a friend of his was doing a thesis on a pattern of pottery that was found all over the world. They wanted to find out what it was doing out here in California, and to do that he wanted to determine the name of the vessel. That's where the connection came between Pete and Jim. We never thought that Pete would consider coming out to see the wreck.

Pete flew in to San Francisco and then to Chico, where we picked him up and brought him to the coast. He stayed with us at the trailer off Sherwood Road here in Fort Bragg. The weather was supposed to lay down, and we were going to dive. We kept waiting and waiting and waiting. We waited four days for the surf to calm.

Pete was interesting to talk to. He told about the dives that he had made on Spanish galleons. He wanted us to come back East and dive with him. He said that he'd pay for the whole works. "Well, I've got to make a living here," I replied. I wish I would have been able to do it.

Pete saw where the wreck was from the beach. We walked the beach looking for stuff, all the while hoping and hoping that we could get out there to dive. There was just too much white water. You couldn't have seen a thing.

Pete told us at that if we could name

Figure 62. Marian and Vilho "Bill" Kosonen (left) with Mendel "Pete" Peterson, Noyo Harbor, Fort Bragg, California, 1966. (Photo courtesy of Vilho "Bill" Kosonen)

the vessel he would get the Smithsonian to give us a grant to back it all the way—100%. Maybe even Cousteau would come over! He had a ship that he used strictly for archaeological work, and we would bring it over there and park it right over the wreck and lay it all out so that we could pinpoint every piece that came out of there.

Pete wanted us to find something to name the vessel. He said the bell would have a name on it, or there might be a brass plate that went on the cabin. We dove and dove and kept looking and looking, without tearing things apart.

In the meantime, we went to the Maritime Museum in San Francisco and checked all the wrecks that were dated. We had some plates with us. We had the ballast and the blunderbuss, and we knew the cannons were there. We knew there were a couple of big anchors there, and we told them what size they were. They just shrugged us off. They didn't care. They didn't give a damn.

I think one of them told us to talk to Ray Akers in Sunnyvale. We went to see Ray with some of the artifacts. He told us he thought that a piece of brass was an oar lock. He said he would check it out and write to us. He wrote us a letter, and that was the last we heard from him.

I think word about the wreck leaked out because of Jim's diving class. He asked if he could bring the blunderbuss to show to his dive class, and I think that started it—and I got perturbed. We had taught Dr. Paul Selchau how to dive, and he built a vacation house on the bluff right above the wreck site. I know he's dove on it a lot.

VILHO "BILL" KOSONEN

I don't know how many artifacts he has or how many people he has taken out there.

To be honest with you—just between you and me—Jim and I don't get along like we used to. It's on tape, and I don't care. Those things from the wreck should have been left alone and kept until we could find out what it was and get the thing done right. It would have been good history, and it would have been a good layout. Your classes could have worked on that. I'll bet you that maybe in 10 years, little by little, going in there and mapping, you could have laid it all out. You could have had that whole ship laid out there at one time. So, that's my story.

I think that after we quit diving on it there were a lot of people that went in and just tore things apart. I know of several people over in Willows that Jim told about it, and they got some of it. I've got a pretty good idea who they are, but I'm not going to get in the middle of it. We were going to try to keep it quiet until we could find out its name. Of course, one tells one story, and that one tells another, and pretty soon you have everybody in the country looking at it.

This is what happened, and I wasn't happy about it. As for other collections, I can do some snooping around. Bill Collins could have something ... and a couple of others. Jim was diving with quite a troop for a while. I don't know who they all were. I think Talbert, if he has anything, would give it to me.

[Marian Kosonen interrupts: Some years later I was waiting at the Noyo Harbor public dock for my husband to come in with our boat. That's where I saw some fellows in their early 30s. They had a big Zodiac equipped with diving gear. They were in full dive suits, and they were pulling all this stuff up onto the dock.

I looked at it and said: "Gee, that stuff looks familiar." One fellow said: "Oh?" And I said: "Yeah, where'd you get that?" He said: "Oh, down there, down south a ways." I said: "I know exactly where you got it. Where are you from?" He said: "San Jose." And then he just kind of ignored me. He really didn't want to talk. I saw these glass jars with saltwater with beads and real small articles in them. They also had quite a few things that were about 2 in. long and ¾ in. square, and on the one end they had some kind of carving. I don't know what they were used for. All I could think of was to seal envelopes, when they used wax. Maybe it had an initial or a number on it. That's really all I remember them having.]

[Bill Kosonen continues:] In 1970 I got to feeling a little bit rough and got shook up over things. I had a little hypertension and one thing or another. It was getting to me. So I figured: "Doggone it! I'm gonna sell this place! Maybe we can make a living someplace else. I'll put the ranch on the market and see what we can do." We had always liked it over here in on the coast, and in 1968 we had bought this place in Fort Bragg for our retirement, but we didn't figure we'd be using it that quick. We sold the ranch [in] 1971, and the buyer wanted us to move out right away. It was practically overnight!

When we moved over here I bought a commercial salmon boat—a 32 ft. Monterey Clipper—and did a little fishing for three or four years. Then I bought another one and another one. The last one was a 40-footer, made up in Washington, that I used for albacore and salmon.

I sold it in 1975 and started to work in construction. I had a little background in engineering from Davis, so I started to work with turbines, setting them up at the Geysers in Sonoma County. Then I did work on cement plants, rice dryers, sewer plants, and bowling alleys. We'd either put the machinery together to make it run—or fix it. I worked on United Parcel buildings, setting up their conveyors. I did machinery work as a foreman here at the Georgia Pacific mill. I was working through the Union Hall out of Oakland. Eventually, in 1984, I had to quit because my knees gave out. I had abused my body. I finally had my knees replaced here a couple of years ago with Teflon and stainless steel. After that I did a lot of fishing and hunting and visiting with the kids.

Then, I got a call from Jim. He said that there was someone interested in doing a little research on the wreck. He gave us your [Tom's] name and said: "He'll be calling you." Which you did! We thought it was all forgotten, and then all at once it has just blown up like a big balloon and has started boomeranging, and all the parts went together, and all the little pieces we had went to the museums. And now I'm giving you this résumé, which isn't much, but maybe it will make a little story for somebody.

VILHO "BILL" KOSONEN

Larry Pierson

Larry Pierson was born in 1937 in Coquille, Oregon, into a dysfunctional logging family from which he ran away multiple times before he was 11 years old. At that time he was able to support himself for several years through thievery. He was released from a stint in the Oregon State Reformatory when he was 16. After another arrest he was allowed to join the Air Force, where, in Biloxi, Mississippi, he was trained as an electronics technician. On weekends he learned to dive in Pensacola, Florida. Then he was stationed for two years in Alaska, where he assaulted his supervising officer and was dishonorably discharged.

In 1959, Larry and a friend drove to Los Angeles, California, where they slept on Venice Beach until they could find jobs. In 1962, Larry was hired by a sport-diving shop to repair diving equipment and was then promoted to manage a store of his own. In 1963 he recovered his first porthole and became obsessed with wreck diving.

In about 1970, Larry resigned from the store to become a fulltime treasure hunter, robbing shipwrecks and selling what he salvaged. In 1971 he helped organize the California Wreck Divers Club and served for a year as its president. Meanwhile, he taught himself how to do library

Figure 63. Larry Pierson as a graduate student in archaeology at the University of San Diego, ca. 1976, with his advisor Professor James Moriarity. (Photo courtesy of Patrick Gibson)

research in order to find shipwrecks. From 1975 to 1978 Larry dove the *Frolic*, and by the end of that period he had become increasingly interested in discovering the history of the still-unknown vessel beyond simply recovering the artifacts.

By the late 1970s, Larry and his dive partner Patrick Gibson had assembled a massive compilation of shipwrecks and were hired by the Bureau of Land Management to share that information. Larry was then approached by the Army Corps of Engineers and the Dames & Moore consulting firm to conduct underwater surveys. When his name did not appear as an author of those reports, he decided to become a professional. He enrolled in Los Angeles Valley Junior College, from which he transferred to the University of San Diego, where, mentored by Professor James Moriarty, he completed his master's degree in 1986. From then on Larry was employed by Southern California cultural-resource management firms, where he enjoyed a successful career in the position of senior archaeologist. Larry passed away in 2015 at the age of 78.

Larry Pierson

13 January 1992
San Diego, California

It was in December 1975 that Pat Gibson and I went up to northern California with Dr. Nash. He was studying Chinese junks and had heard that one was wrecked up near Point Cabrillo. He needed some divers to check it out, and someone must have given him our telephone numbers. I had been treasure-hunting, so I wasn't working regular, and Pat was able to take a couple of days off from his job, so we all piled into Dr. Nash's brown van and drove straight through from Los Angeles to Louie Fratis's house in Caspar. I guess it must have been fairly early in the morning when we arrived, because he was still asleep, and we had to come back a couple of times before we could talk to him. I remember he showed us a cannon and some ceramics he had raised from the wreck, and I made a sketch of the cannon and photographed the rest of the stuff.

Well, it was storming, and for the next three days the wind and rain never let up. It was just as snotty and cold and miserable as you'd expect the north coast to be in December. But Pat and I were young and stubborn—you know how indestructible you are at that age—and, of course, Dr. Nash was paying for the trip, so we decided to put on our gear and dive anyway. We climbed down the bluff to the pocket beach where Fratis told us there would be small fragments of the ceramics. Then we swam out into the cove following the ceramic trail. That's how you find a shipwreck. If there are ceramics on the beach, you simply follow the trail of sherds.

I remember that the seas were heaving, and we were going up and down 10 or 15 ft. with each wave. Out at the wreck site it seemed like one moment we were nearly in contact with the bottom, and the next we were vertically so far away we could barely see it. We free dove because we didn't want to get battered against the rocks wearing our tanks.

My job was to determine whether or not this was a Chinese junk, and when I saw the three Rodger-patent anchors I knew it was not, so we really didn't need to go much further. You know, it's very unusual to see three anchors all of the same age and style on a vessel of that vintage, unless she has just come off the ways or gone through a major refit. Junks used by Chinese abalone divers during the late 19th century typically had a "junkyard" collection of whatever ground tackle they could pick up, including old anchors recovered from the bottom, and no junk would have had three brand-new Rodger-patent anchors.

Well, the diving conditions were terrible, and since I could see that it was not a Chinese junk we swam back to shore, put our gear into the van, and headed for home. We'd already checked out of the hotel. I remember that Dr. Nash was disappointed, but then there was also a certain feeling of relief. I'm sure he was glad that he wouldn't again have to travel that far to investigate that particular Chinese junk. When I got home I typed up my notes, finalized my drawings, and gave them to Dr. Nash. We never heard from him again, but although that ended his interest in the wreck, it piqued ours, and two years later Pat and I returned to explore the wreck on our own.

In retrospect, there was certainly nothing in my childhood to prepare me for a life of scholarship, but from the age of eight I've been captivated by diving. I was born in 1937 at Coquille, on the south coast of Oregon, into an uneducated Irish logging family. My parents were divorced by the time I was born, so I didn't have a stable home environment, and that probably led to my first jailing at age six for breaking

into cars. At first I lived with my mother, but eventually I became so unmanageable that I was sent to live with my father, a logger, working for Pope & Talbot up on the Molalla River. So, suddenly, there I was in the wilderness. The logging camp environment was absolutely different from what I was used to in the slums on the lower east side of Portland, and I went through a lot of trauma. My father was rather strict, a bit irrational, and a heavy drinker. He beat my stepmother. There are a lot of good and bad memories from that period.

It was in the summer of 1945 that I discovered the underwater world. I was swimming in the Molalla River when I dove down into a deep pool, opened my eyes, and found myself eyeballing a fish. I was enthralled. Then I saw a movie with Gilbert Roland playing a sponge diver, and from that time on I knew I wanted to be a diver.

I ran away from home for the fourth time when I was 11 and was able to support myself for a couple of years in Portland through thievery. Then I did time in several detention homes, followed by a year with an aunt, and finally a stiff stint in the Oregon State Reformatory. When I was released on probation at age 16, I tried to make it to Florida to be a sponge diver. Mercifully, I guess, I was returned to Oregon and not jailed.

Instead, I was allowed to join the service, so I enlisted in the Air Force and was treated to a year of concentrated electronics training at the Air Force Technical School in Biloxi, Mississippi. I did well and became a certified journeyman electronics technician, achieving a 5-level rating, which in those days was the skill level of a sergeant. They stationed me in Alaska, but after two years I got into an argument with a superior, who, I guess, didn't handle me properly. I did 25 days of a 30-day sentence in the stockade under a summary court martial for almost killing him. I learned from the experience that my temper, probably an inheritance from my father, was something I would have to deal with the rest of my life.

When I got out of the stockade, the "First Shirt"—the first sergeant of the squadron—came to me and said: "You know your life's not worth a plugged nickel around here?" "Yeah," I replied, "I understand that." The sergeant then told me: "I can have you home in three days if you'll take a dishonorable discharge." "Give it to me!" I said, "I'm gone!" I had carved out an excellent existence during my two years in Alaska. I had found wonderful things to do and was very happy, except for getting into trouble with that superior. Anyway, he *learned*, real quick!

I got home 30 June 1957 and walked in the door, without any previous warning, to the great surprise and dismay of my mother. For about two years I did menial jobs around town, that is to say, regular jobs for menial wages in factory settings. Then, in 1959, a friend of mine said: "Let's go to California." I said: "Okeydokey," and off we went. Well, we got real poor before we got jobs down here. We were sleeping on the beach at Venice, but we took care of each other. I held a number of jobs during the next three years.

I had learned to dive during my spare time back in 1955 while I was in Mississippi at the Air Force Technical School. On weekends we used to dive off Pensacola, Florida. Anyway, about 1962 a sport-diving company approached me to work for them. First they approached me to start a club in association with the company. Then I became a worker for the company, and finally I was given a store of my own. I managed the store, directed diving tours, organized classes, and repaired scuba equipment. I became the local expert, and that was fun, but after eight years it got boring. I wanted to go treasure hunting, and for a couple years I did. I robbed shipwrecks and sold the junk. Then I went into commercial diving, catching fish and lobster and selling them.

My first time on a shipwreck was in 1961. Well, I immediately fell in love with shipwrecks, and they became my all-consuming desire for the next 20 years. The wreck was the *Olympic* II, ex-*Star of France*, about 3 mi. off Pedro Light, and the things I saw were just unbelievable. She was an old sailing ship and had gone down in 1940 with virtually everything still attached. At that time her mast had been cut down and she was operating as a fishing platform over a sparse rock exposure on a sand bottom. Of course that was a haven for fish, and a shore boat would run people out for a half day or a full day of fishing. A Jap freighter had rammed her and then backed off, so she filled with water and sank immediately. The freighter should have stayed in her, at least until they got the people off. Anyway, the freighter's skipper was fined and let go, and that was the end of the *Star of France*.

It was in 1963 that a friend of mine, Edwin J. Summers, Jr., took me out to the *Star of Scotland*, about 2 mi. off the Santa Monica pier. They used to call Ed the "Little Dipper" because he held the microphone boom for movies at Universal Studios. Ed helped me get my first brass porthole. Oh boy! That was a gas! Wreck diving soon became almost an obsession with me.

Ed Summers had a little 16 ft. Chris-Craft, made for fishing on lakes, and with two divers and four sets of double tanks aboard, it only had about 2 in. of freeboard. We would discover wrecks, dive on them, and pick up all of the really obvious, easy-to-get artifacts. I soon discovered that I could supplement my income and establish a modicum of primacy amongst divers by restoring these objects to their "better than original" condition. I displayed them and marketed them, keeping the best ones for myself. Well, that was a lot of fun, so I became involved with a couple of dive clubs. I organized the Aqua Venturers and served as president of the Greater Los Angeles Council of Diving Clubs. Later I helped organize the California Wreck Divers Club and served for a year as their president.

Well, in order to be a treasure hunter you have to be able to find wrecks, and I was a successful treasure hunter. I got two out of the three wrecks I looked for, which is not bad, and I made monetary gain on both of them. But first I had to learn how to do research, and you have to understand that I was a high school dropout with most of my formal education coming from the Oregon State Reformatory. I was, however, reasonably literate and could use a dictionary, though I had never used a library.

Anyway, about the time I got interested in treasure hunting someone told me that the Los Angeles Central Library was a "neat place," and they had "good stuff" in there. Well, I thought I would see just how "neat" they were! I went to the California Room and to Special Collections and found a veritable wealth of information on old shipwrecks. I soon discovered that I was able to evaluate the authors and determine what was good data and what was trash. I bought a dictionary, began to take notes, and became fascinated with

learning. The library had significant holdings of maritime materials—color lithographs, contemporary documents about Gold Rush steamers, and other wonderful things. My girlfriend, Linda, kept encouraging me to go to school, but I still had an attitude: "College boys!"—"There's nothing to learnin'!"—"They don't know a God-damned thing anyway!" I was anti-intellectual, militantly uneducated, and determined to stay that way.

By the start of the 1970s I had accumulated a lot of data on shipwrecks, and my friend Pat Gibson and I began to put together the first comprehensive, searchable, computerized listing of shipwrecks. Pat had been a student at the dive shop. In fact, he and his wife met in a class taught there, fell in love, and got married. Anyway, Pat and I became close friends and began going treasure hunting together. Pat was a computer programmer and had access to a trailer where he worked that housed a huge mainframe computer with big vertical tape drives. At that time the

Figure 64. Larry Pierson, ca. 1966–1968, as manager of the United Aqua Shop in Van Nuys, California. (Photo courtesy of Patrick Gibson)

new method of storing information was stacked disks. Pat and I used keypunched cards to create our first listing. After that we upgraded it regularly based on our research. It was, at first, a compilation of wreck lists from all published sources, but very quickly I found that was not adequate. There were too many inconsistencies and inaccuracies, so I began to correct them through ship-specific research.

Well, during the early 1970s something happened in Washington, and off-shore leasing for oil and gas exploration started in California. Suddenly there was a new term called "cultural resources," and the federal government heard about Pat and me and our computer listing of shipwrecks. The Pacific Outer Continental Shelf Office of the Bureau of Land Management approached us to assist them in compiling a list of shipwrecks and shipwreck locations in their zone of interest.

So, there we were assisting the government, and since we were making noise in the right circles, good things began happening to us. I was approached by the Army Corps of Engineers and by Dames & Moore, a consulting firm, to run the first underwater archaeological surveys on this coast. I was chosen because I was a hands-on diver and knew shipwrecks and underwater search techniques. I did a survey and a test for the Corps of Engineers prior to the development of the harbor at Port San Luis. I wrote the history portion of the report, and they published my dive-master's log. However, even though I had been called on to do the nuts-and-bolts work, someone else's name went on the report, and that galled me.

Next, I designed and carried out an eyeball underwater archaeological survey of a 180 ac. site for the proposed liquid natural-gas terminal site at Point Conception.

Even though it was in the wintertime, it was successful. We found diving gear that oceanographers had lost in previous years and all kinds of other stuff. We even discovered an underwater paleontological deposit. Well, by this time I was asking questions: "Why does someone else's name go on my work?" and "What steps do I have to take to be the boss?" Well, I found out that you need academic degrees, and that meant you had to go to college. "Oh no! Not that!"

Well, I enrolled at Los Angeles Valley Junior College and I took two classes, one in geology and one in the history of Asia. I soon found that when it came to the Spanish colonial period in the Philippines, my Harvard-educated professor didn't know what he was talking about. He said that agriculture was the economic base for the Spanish occupation of the Philippines. Well, you have to understand my background. I was a roughneck and not well versed in tact. I stood up in the middle of the class and said: "You dumb son of a bitch. What you know about Southeast Asian history you can put in a fucking thimble!" I got into a little trouble for that. I only got into trouble twice more with professors, once at that school and once down here at the University of San Diego, but they were small incidents. In both cases professors were trying to cover an area of intellectual weakness with bullshit, and I was able to see through the bullshit.

Well, at that point I made a pact with myself. "OK Larry," I said, "you're going to play this game. You're going to play it by the established rules, and you're going to beat the bastards!" So I did. I took 60 units of coursework, focusing on anthropology, history, and earth science, and, in 1979, when I was offered an academic scholarship at the University of San Diego, I jumped at it. I sold everything and moved to San Diego. After that first semester at junior college, I had become a fulltime student. The least number of units I carried was 15. The most they let me take was 23. From then on I went to school every semester, every intersession, and every summer.

At the University of San Diego, in addition to my academic scholarship, I had work-study support. I was assigned to a professor as his private researcher. The school gave me to him, and I was his "fair haired boy." My work-study assignment was to read every page of every California newspaper from 1847 to 1885, and to spot read certain major papers up to 1915. I took advantage of the opportunity and privately contracted with three other professors to copy information relating to their areas of interest. I soon had five stacks of newspaper articles next to the microfilm printer, and one of those piles was mine. I became a permanent fixture in the library. I pressed the copy button whenever I found something one of those guys was interested in or that I was interested in. I found a lot of information on shipwrecks in that fashion. With work study, grants, and scholarships, I did OK, and double majored in history and anthropology for my B.A.

As I approached graduation, I discovered a program through which I could get a master's degree at the University of San Diego in about four years if I really busted my ass. I didn't have to take any entrance tests; I simply walked into the program, and although it took me longer than four years it turned out to be the best move I ever made. They had assembled a group of 10 already-practicing historians and archaeologists as graduate students, and they custom designed a set of classes specifically for us. They also gave us part-time work. It was wonderful. The fellow that ran the National Archives and Records Branch at Laguna, Niguel, came down and taught a four-unit archives class, and we did hands-on field work right there at the records center. My term project was to create a finding aid for all the materials at the records center pertaining to Spanish and Mexican ranchos in Southern California.

For part-time employment we worked on private contracts that Dr. Brandes, the graduate school dean, and Dr. Moriarty had with the Center City Development Corporation, the agency in charge of the redevelopment of downtown San Diego. That part of town was, of course, the locus of the first expansion of the American period. On weekends, together with our professors, we did surveys and test excavations, all the while learning about cultural-resource management. So, from 1979 to 1986, I got a significant portion of my education outside the classroom, but every classroom moment in that graduate program was golden because it was custom designed specifically for us. We had research classes and thesis-writing classes, and we went out to city and county agencies and discovered every data repository and what it held. Most of the government officials in charge of those records didn't even know they had them, so we put together a source manual for San Diego—published, unfortunately, in nine copies. At any rate, we got a really first-class education.

My education in historic archaeology came from excavating at the San Diego Mission and at Old Town, where our archaeological work and archival research was to be the basis for reconstructing the old houses. My field training in prehistoric archaeology was at Ramona, where I worked for almost a year on a major village site under the supervision of Dr. Moriarty. I have a two-volume report on the noninvasive intensive study that we completed. We cut 30 ac. into 100 ft. squares and triangulated and drew every rock, artifact, feature, petroglyph, and plant in the entire tract. We produced a series of maps 7 ft. tall. It was a beautiful piece of work, and I'm very proud of it. The prehistoric work was new and challenging, but my historical work came pretty naturally because I had already been doing historical research for shipwrecks. Turning the corner to historic houses was no difficult feat. I simply learned where the official records were and where the township plats were—and ever since then I've been in heaven!

I graduated with a M.A. in historic-sites archaeology in 1986, having maintained a grade point average of 4.0 in graduate school. By then I had been studying archaeology and doing archaeology for 10 years, and during the course of my education my archaeological ethics underwent a major change. I can't pin down what day it happened. It was a gradual process, and I'm sure it wasn't until after I got into graduate school that I began to think seriously about the conflict between what I had been doing on shipwrecks and what I was learning to do in school. Today that change is so thorough and complete that I have no problem packing up every last artifact I own from the *Frolic* shipwreck and sending them off to the *Frolic* Repository. I could never have done that in the old days.

Unfortunately, that change had not yet occurred back in 1975, when Pat Gibson and I were approached by Dr. Robert Nash to identify a shipwreck he had located on the north coast of California.

Dr. Nash lived in Sierra Madre, a small foothill community east of Pasadena, and he simply saw us as divers who knew a little bit about shipwrecks. I'm not sure how he got our names and phone numbers, but I remember he quizzed us a little on our qualifications over the telephone before we met with him and made the pact to go to northern California.

Dr. Nash was quite interested in the Chinese and had been excavating what he described as "Chinese camps." We had no idea when or where he had received his Ph.D. We simply presumed he was a Ph.D. of long standing, perhaps in semiretirement. He didn't seem to have a lot of money. I saw his house and met his wife, and he was living a pretty austere existence. Still, he was willing to spend the money to find out what this shipwreck was, and he wanted it to be a Chinese junk, and I clearly remember his disappointment when we found the Rodger-patent anchors and knew right away that it wasn't.

Well, when we got back to Los Angeles I typed up my notes and sent them to him, and we never again heard from him. I guess since it wasn't a junk he was no longer interested. So two years passed. Meanwhile, Pat and I were getting bored diving the local wrecks around Los Angeles. We had begun taking vacations in Guaymas, Mexico, where we would shoot fish and collect shells, but that had become boring too. So we decided it might be fun to dive the wreck up at Caspar during better conditions and see what might be there. We ultimately made three extended visits to the wreck site, returning there in 1977, 1978, and 1979.

On our first trip we tried beach diving. Pat and I piled our equipment into a van, drove to northern California, and

LARRY PIERSON

stayed in a motel. That was fun and a great adventure because we were on vacation, but it was less than satisfactory from a wreck-diver's point of view.

For our second foray up there, Bud Hazen joined us, and we towed his Zodiac inflatable boat. We tried to launch the Zodiac at Caspar Creek across a very wide sand spit, but even with our two British Land Rovers—one with a winch—we got stuck. I remember that Bud took a lot of pictures, and I think that was the year I got the porthole, but that trip wasn't very productive either.

By the third trip we had learned our lessons, and we were substantially more successful. We had spent considerable time on the first two trips learning about the area, the facilities, the people, and the various methods that we could use to approach the shipwreck, and by 1979 we had that baby scoped out! One feature of the wreck site was a large pile of cast-iron ballast bars, and we knew we would have a lot of trouble moving them by hand because they had corroded, swollen up, and solidified into a single mass. Not only were they almost impossible to separate from one another, but they were quite heavy. Therefore we brought explosives supplied by our friend Cliff Craft. We set the explosives at strategic points and caused a small but sudden shock. We killed two or three fish, but we succeeded in jarring the ballast pile just enough to separate the bars from one another. The object was not to blow up the vessel, but simply to nudge it just a little.

That was the year we launched at Noyo Harbor. We had a hard boat with a hookah rig, a davit winch, airbags, and explosives. We had the "whole ball of wax," and the four of us—me, Pat Gibson, Bud Hazen, and Vic LaFountaine—spent five full days diving, generally taking turns with two people down and two people on top sorting.

Everything went just as smooth as glass on that trip. The crew worked together beautifully, and we had absolutely no squabbles. It was a wonderful therapeutic vacation. We were doing something we really enjoyed that had nothing to do with work. We camped at Russian Gulch in Van Damme State Park. I remember we had skunks going through our camp, so Bud Hazen cut some fresh onions and spread them around the camp, and we didn't have skunks anymore. Then we met a couple of ladies, biology graduate students from Humboldt State. They were counting fish guts on the pier at Noyo. We took them back to camp and they decided to stay with us. We had a lot of fun on that trip, both day and night. Pat Gibson, of course, was so pure that he wouldn't engage in that sort of thing.

That year we were equipped with bow and stern anchors so we could maintain position directly above the wreck. First we moved all the ballast bars, one by one. Many artifacts were cemented to the ballast bars or laying between them. I remember Gibson was with me underwater and Vic was onboard when we pulled away a ballast bar and, suddenly, we saw a golden hand. Oh my God! At first I thought we'd found a whole gold statue. I picked up that hand like you'd pick up a treasure—a Greek urn—and, instead of putting it in the bag with the rest of the stuff, swam to the surface and pounded on the boat hull to get someone's attention. When Vic looked over I served up that hand and his eyes got big as saucers. I thought old Vic was going to have a fit. It turned out to be a hinged paper holder made of hammered brass, and it tarnished right away, but we sure talked about that for a long time afterwards.

When we finally got to the bottom of the ballast pile, there was only a small amount of loose material lying on the bedrock. That loose material contained beads and all kinds of small items. We bagged all that sediment, took it up to the boat, spread it out on the deck, and went through it, picking out the obvious artifacts and throwing the rest overboard. At the end of five days we had a substantial quantity of artifacts, including pistols, muskets, swords, coins, gold filigree jewelry, and beads. We brought it all back to Los Angeles and laid it out on Vic's driveway, arranging it into piles for division. There was a consensus among us. We knew that each of us had a particular thing that we were rather fond of, so we made sure that person got that pile. It was a very amicable distribution.

It's funny, but looking back on that division of artifacts I can see that I had already undergone a change of interest. I was almost ready to graduate with a B.A. in anthropology and history, and suddenly I was interested in the kinds of things that would tell me something about the wreck. I was interested in the pottery, the bottle necks, and the bottle bottoms, and I also had a strong interest in the wood and leather objects because I wanted to soak them in polyethylene glycol to see if it would actually replace the natural moisture so they wouldn't shrink and crack.

Consequently, everybody with wooden objects in their pile loaned them to me so I could soak them. You know, I never got around to returning any of those artifacts. I really wound up with the lion's share of objects by sheer mass, mainly because I was interested in technology and commerce and wanted all the miscellaneous little stuff that had no visual value to the rest of the guys. Nevertheless, I got some beautiful items, too, including the captain's cruet. In any event, as a beginning archaeologist the artifacts I asked for meant something very different to me than they did to the other guys. They were excited by the coins, but I would have gladly given up all the coins in exchange for the ceramics and glass, even though it was all broken.

There were two objects that we left on the vessel that I've always regretted leaving. One was a whole shoe, and the other was a large spool of heavy twine [both later recovered by David Buller]. Moreover, there were tiny artifacts throughout the sediment, like percussion caps for the cap-and-ball guns, that would have taken a lot of effort to recover. We did get them up on the deck in the bags of sediment, but our sorting process was not like an archaeological sort where everything is saved. We simply saved those things that caught our eye and dumped the remaining sediments right back onto the wreck. We dumped a lot of glass fragments, but diagnostic things like the bottle necks and bottoms I kept.

The guys all thought it was strange of me to do that, but it's clear to me, in retrospect, that my life was undergoing a major change. Previously I would have conspired to get all the really nifty looking stuff, the really showy things, like the parts to the navigational equipment. Of course I did get the binnacle and the compass gimbals, but for the most part I was already interested in preserving, examining, and studying kinds of things that previously would have had no interest for me at all. The *Frolic* was to be the last wreck that I pillaged, and from that time on I was to have an entirely different relationship with shipwrecks.

LARRY PIERSON

In any event, I was beginning to think like an archaeologist. I had collected some fragments of wood on the 1977 trip, and I sent them to the Forest Products Laboratory for identification. They turned out to be white oak and Spanish cedar, and this led me to the conclusion that the vessel had been British built. During the mid-19th century, the white oak could have come from British Canada and the Spanish cedar from British Honduras. By that time the English had already logged their country flat, and they were importing all of their shipbuilding woods. Of course there was no reason why it couldn't have been built somewhere else, but, at the time, Britain seemed to me the most obvious choice, based on the little bit of data I had.

The three anchors I'd seen on the wreck appeared to be Rodger-style anchors, patented in the United States in 1851, but used in England prior to that date. So, with three Rodger-patent anchors or their British predecessors, white oak, and Spanish cedar, I concluded that the vessel was British-built, and, based on the size of the anchors, I estimated that she was a 100–120 ft. long. The cast-iron ballast was more difficult for me to reason out. Iron ballast was expensive and rarely used on ordinary merchant vessels, so I concluded that it was part of the cargo, bound for iron-poor California.

The Spanish cedar still throws me. Perhaps it wasn't part of a structural member, but rather a piece of cargo or packing material or dunnage. The few fragments of wood we recovered had been miraculously preserved, sandwiched between ballast bars. We didn't find the keel or any ribs. We looked for remnants of the helm—pintles and gudgeons for mounting and operating the rudder—but found nothing.

It's possible that we didn't actually find the real stern of that vessel. Yet we did find the binnacle, and that's right next to the wheel. The binnacle was under the ballast, so the vessel must have rolled over on itself. Over the years I've watched vessels break apart in rough weather on rocky coasts, and they tend to climb up on themselves, but after about five years they are pretty much in place, and that's where they are going to be forever.

After our last visit to the wreck in 1979, we were through with it. We'd done what we'd come to do, and our tastes were changing. Pat was getting into resort diving in the Caribbean for his vacations and perhaps hoping to find a new wreck that hadn't been gone over. Cliff Craft, the Buller brothers [Dave and Steve], and others were to work the wreck after Pat and I were finished. Meanwhile, I was enrolled at the University of San Diego, where I was becoming removed from the wreck-diving community and undergoing a profound professional and ethical transition. You know, I haven't removed an artifact from a shipwreck since 1979. Education has just played havoc with my life!

Still, during that period of transition I had to sell some of my artifacts in order to survive. Fortunately I was able to keep most of my collection from the *Frolic* intact. The only *Frolic* artifact I sold was a silver eight-real Mexican dollar from the 1820s. Unfortunately, however, I did sell some of my treasures from other wrecks. One was a $20 gold piece from the *Winfield Scott*, a sidewheel steamer wrecked off Anacapa Island in 1853. It was the commissioning coin, placed beneath the main mast. I also had to sell most of my California gold coins.

I even sold two Carlos and Johanna four-real pieces from the Padre Island wreck, given to me by Robert Marx as payment for a report I wrote for him. The vessel was heading back to Spain about 1555 when it wrecked. Those two coins, some of the first minted in the New World, were almost perfect, made specifically to show the king and queen of Spain that a New World mint was capable of producing quality coinage. They were among the very few known examples, and I sold them. Oh well, I sold a lot of stuff that I regret!

In 1979 when we divided up the artifacts from our last dive on the *Frolic*, I photographed all of the coins and gold filigree jewelry on a red velveteen background. To a wreck diver, the coins and the gold were the real valuables, so I made sure we photographed them. All you have to do is divide the stuff in that photograph by four to see what the other guys got.

As for Bud Hazen's share, he was always having trouble with money, and when his wife finally got tired of supporting him he just went from girlfriend to girlfriend, selling the stuff as he went. He would call me late at night and at odd times, and then he committed suicide. Vic LaFountaine later fell in love and moved somewhere in Southeast Asia where he lost everything, including his collection from the *Frolic*. Pat Gibson was able to keep most of his collection intact.

Looking back over what we and others did to the *Frolic*, there are some lessons to be learned. First, there has to be some middle ground between sport divers and archaeologists. You have to share the resource, and there are half a dozen very successful programs for lay involvement in archaeology that could be used as models. The one thing you don't want to do is to hunt the wreck divers down and prosecute them. You want to encourage them to open up to you rather than driving them underground.

The prosecution of the California Wreck Divers Club members during the late 1980s for collecting off the *Winfield Scott* served to drive most of their activities underground. There's a lot of wreck diving going on right now that will never be revealed because of that action. That prosecution probably did more harm in public relations with wreck divers than any other single event in our history on this coast. It's rather like "off-roading" in the desert. If you really want to change destructive behavior you have to think creatively and find positive ways to modify that behavior so that it better fits what we, as resource managers, regard as acceptable.

At the same time, you have to recognize that there is always going to be an outlaw element that's going to do whatever they want to do whenever and wherever they want to do it, and they clearly think that's their right as Americans, as free human beings. I realize that I am in the resource-management camp and that my views are resource-management oriented. But, having been a wreck diver and trying to look at both sides objectively, I can see that while I would like to save all the archaeology for the archaeologists, that is a selfish and one-sided point of view. Somehow we need to rank wreck sites by degrees of importance so that we can identify certain shipwrecks for the hardcore wreck divers to dive. At the same time, there are always going to be the bandits, so we must find ways of guarding the most important sites because it's precisely those sites that are going to attract the most aggressive bandits and the pirates.

Some shipwrecks can be protected because they are so conspicuous and obvious, for example, those up at Carmel

LARRY PIERSON

Figure 65. Larry Pierson, ca. 1966–1968, holding the 1894 Mackie & Thomson engine plate he recovered and restored from the *Aggi* (1894–1915) shipwreck at Santa Rosa Island, off the coast of Santa Barbara, California. Behind Larry is one of several display frames of artifacts he recovered from the *Winfield Scott* (1850–1863) at Anacapa Island. (Photo courtesy of Patrick Gibson)

along Seventeen Mile Drive. Of course the weather up there cooperates a lot too. But it's my contention that the government should do more to preserve those shipwrecks that in a realistic sense are preservable—for example, the *Yankee Blade*.

A couple of years ago I was hired by the group that had dredged the *Yankee Blade*, a sidewheel steamer wrecked off Point Arguello in 1854. They flew me to Las Vegas, paid me my consultant's rate for a day, and quizzed me on the potential of that wreck. Well, they had dived it and dredged it, but they hadn't got down to the wreck itself. They were working in 15 ft. of overburden and they'd only removed 12 ft. I saw the pictures and talked to the guys that were in the water and working the dredges, and do you know where they were operating from? They operated from the adjacent Air Force base. The Air Force was allowing them to use the base as a staging area for operations on the *Yankee Blade*!

Now there has to be some sort of legal consistency in government, don't you think? My goodness, here we have the United States Air Force supporting the dredging of a wreck that had been pristine because, for God's sake, it was buried in sediment! That wreck probably still has preserved structural elements, and here one arm of the United States government is aiding and abetting a Goddamn salvage operation on this Goddamn wreck, while another arm of the government is trying to prosecute some Goddamn redneck working stiffs for diving the *Winfield Scott*, which has been so Goddamn molested through time that it's not even recognizable as a shipwreck any more. For Christ sake!

There are clearly some inconsistencies there, and as an archaeologist I look at this with my 56 years of wisdom, shrug my shoulders, and say: "Well, that's government, and if the government didn't provide jobs for those Goddamned idiots, they'd be collecting welfare!" So I suppose we should be thankful. It has been my experience in working with the government that they're by and large a pretty inept bunch. While one does find the occasional competent individual, he is usually ostracized because he makes everyone else look bad. It's a pretty sad situation, but it has operated successfully for a couple of hundred years, so I suppose it can't be all that bad. But, in any event, when it comes down to preservation of specific vessels, the present approach is not adequate.

In order to have a successful preservation program you simply have to look at what motivates wreck divers. Why are they wreck diving? Because it's exciting! It's neat! They can go home and tell their girlfriends at the bar: "Man I was out there wrestling them sharks!" Finally, they get these nifty trinkets.

Well, all you have to do is play into that. With professional supervision you organize them to go out and survey and test a wreck. You let them pick up a few restorable objects, and you show them how to pick them up, properly recording their position. Then you let them take the object home and provide them with supplementary publications on restoration. You let them do the restoration work on the object and bring it back to the museum completed. Then, finally, you put their Goddamn name on it in the museum! And, you know, you'll be giving them damn near what they're getting now, but you're also giving them a sense of civic pride. I think you'll have to let them participate in all of that, otherwise they're going to do it on their own, behind your back.

You'll be giving them a lot of trust, respect, and recognition by allowing them to take that object home, restore it, and bring it back. And you'll be tapping into some real expertise, because these guys include some of the most incredible restoration technicians I've ever seen. Employing the techniques that I learned from some of those fellows, I was able to restore the engine-room telegraph out of a side wheeler. When I got it it was all wadded up in a little ball and, of course, all the iron parts were missing. Well, when I traded it back to the guy, in exchange for a new dry suit, it was a fully operating engine-room telegraph, complete with a bell, with painted numerals, and all the needles, arrows, and hands stopping at all the stops, all mounted on a piece of cherry wood. I'm sure these guys get as much of a kick out of doing that as they do in actually diving the wreck and recovering the piece. In fact, they probably have considerably more fun in the restoration and display.

It would seem to me that you could simply involve them and then guide them. That means you don't want to change their behavior, you simply want to modify it a little bit and still allow them all of the joys and fulfillment that they get out of wreck diving illegally. I think that would work for many hardcore wreck divers. It's not going to work on every single one of them, but it's sure going to catch the majority. And, boy, you're going to have crowded museums, because the guys who restore those parts are going to bring all their friends and relatives in to see that sucker and show them that their name is on it!

You know, there's a group down here called the Railroad Historical Society, and they decided they wanted to go out and record this old whistle-stop station out in the desert. Boy, they were really up for

that! They were all going to bring picnic lunches, and not one of them had a clue about what kinds of information to write down. They hadn't the faintest idea, but they were going to go do it because it was fun. I simply provided them with the State Historic Resource Form and the instructions for filling it out.

Jesus Christ! Those guys had even more fun because now they knew how to do it, and it was a successful trip in more ways than one. First, that station will now be a registered site with the proper data recorded. You didn't change what those guys were going to do, and you certainly didn't diminish the fun they got out of it. If anything, you actually enhanced it. But what you've really done is to modify their behavior so that it worked for both of you. It seems to me that's a valid approach—not the only valid approach—but that's how I would handle it. You have to realize that you are never going to get a hundred percent of anything. That's reality, because there are always going to be some that enjoy breaking the law. But, if we allow the interested public to become involved in meaningful ways, we'll do much better than we're doing now.

Looking back on the *Frolic,* I know a lot of harm was done and a lot of information lost. Objects were lost or discarded—like the shoe and the ball of string—and because of our crude approach and hurried manner we lost the provenience information. Perishable objects and those that didn't attract the attention or the fancy of the divers were simply cast aside, and many of those would have been informative objects. Provenience information, of course, helps us understand the relationship between artifacts and how the wreck broke up. Unfortunately, there's a lot of site information that's just plain gone. It's not a point for discussion, it's simply a fact. Archaeologists have proven that over and over again.

But I think we archaeologists need to come to grips with another fact: that we are just another special-interest group that believes it should all belong to us. I really do feel it should belong to us, because we are the custodians for the public trust, but our archeological track record is not all that great. Most of us do not publish, and the museums are full of artifacts collected under not much better circumstances than we used on the *Frolic* in 1979. As a result, I find it hard to justify the ivory-tower view that it should all belong to us, the archaeologists, and no one else should touch it. We must recognize that people are touching it every day, and they are touching far more of it than we are because we don't have the wherewithal to secure the sites. Clearly, if we want to save what's left, we have to get the wreck divers on our side.

As a former wreck diver, now a card-carrying archaeologist, I'm periodically confronted with the contradictions of my career. Several years ago, when some of my old friends in the California Wreck Divers Club were prosecuted for removing artifacts from the *Winfield Scott*, I was called to appear as an expert witness for the defense. That was a time of real conflict for me. Years earlier I had collected artifacts from the "*Winnie*" myself, but now I was looking at the wreck divers and the ship and the event as an archaeologist. Consequently, I found my feelings, and my testimony, to be in sharp contrast with the beliefs of the wreck divers, who continue to believe what I used to believe.

You know, looking back on my 18 years of wreck diving there are a lot of things I feel badly about. But perhaps what's most demonstrative of the change in my whole attitude towards wrecks and history is the fact that I now feel at least as badly about the shoe and the ball of twine that I left exposed on the *Frolic* as I do about the coins that I sold ... and probably worse!

[Editor's note: The shoe and spool of twine were later recovered by David Buller. He donated the shoe to the Kelley House Museum in Mendocino and the spool of twine to the Frolic repository at the Mendocino County Museum in Willits.]

LARRY PIERSON

Clifton B. "Cliff" Craft

Clifton "Cliff" Craft was born in 1945 and raised in the comfortable "small town" residential community of Whittier, a few miles east of Los Angeles, California. The local newspaper reported his ninth-birthday surprise party in 1954 and the names of all of those who attended, as well as his 1955 YMCA trip to visit the Navajo Reservation. However, by his late teenage years, Cliff was troubled. As Cliff expressed it in his narrative, he spent a number of years trying to "figure out what it was all about, and, as a result of that, became involved in drugs and alcohol. Eventually, he was prosecuted and convicted for armed robbery and for smuggling narcotics."

After serving a five-year sentence, Cliff learned to dive and found work on Florida shrimp trawlers that also engaged in the underwater salvaging of lost nautical equipment and materials from shipwrecks. On his return to California he joined the California Wreck Divers Club and began to collect artifacts from local shipwrecks. Eventually, he became a self-trained, self-employed structural-steel and welding inspector, doing underwater recovery for insurance companies.

Cliff was close friends with members of the California Wreck Divers Club who were collecting from the *Frolic* and provided them with underwater

Figure 66. Clifton "Cliff" Craft, ca. 1970–1975. (Photo courtesy of Larry Pierson)

explosives to break loose the fused iron ballast. When they were finished he made several trips to salvage what was left.

In 1988 Cliff was prosecuted for collecting artifacts from the *Winfield Scott* off Anacapa Island in California. That same year he was arrested a few miles south of Singapore by Indonesian authorities on suspicion of collecting from the 1752 *Geldermalsen* shipwreck, but the charges were later dropped. Until a few years before his death in 1999, however, he remained an investor and part-time participant in other commercial salvage operations on ships believed to have carried valuable cargoes. Cliff passed away in 1999 at the age of 54.

Cliff Craft

12 January 1992
Whittier, CA

My interest in the *Frolic* shipwreck developed out of its location being given to two associates of mine—Patrick Gibson and Larry Pierson. They had already been diving the vessel for several years when, in 1979, they asked my help in devising a way for them to work its ballast pile. As I recall, it was Pat Gibson who approached me. As he described it, the wreck was in very shallow water and included a pile of pig-iron bars lying at right angles to one another, each weighing 100 to 400 lb. and all aggregated together.

I suggested using small charges of explosives. Since water is non-compressible, the end result of a well-placed charge would be to send a shock wave through the bars, freeing them from one another. Afterwards they could be moved individually and relocated so that whatever lay amongst and beneath them could be investigated. I supplied high-velocity explosives, primer cord, and dynamite. They tested out my ideas and went along with what I recommended. As a consequence, during a five-day period in December of 1979, using the explosives that I supplied together with other advanced techniques,

Larry Pierson, Pat Gibson, Vic LaFountaine, and Bud Hazen were able to recover the largest collection that I know of from the *Frolic*. The fused mass of ballast bars would have taken many hours to separate manually—by wedging, chiseling, and hammering—but the explosive charges rendered the pile into individual pieces so they could be separated, lifted, and relocated to a site about 20 ft. seaward to the wreck. Approximately 50% of the ballast pile was moved at that time. Most of the remainder, including the mound of chain, was moved about a month later when I and others began to work the site.

I first dove the *Frolic* in the spring of 1980, about a month after Pat Gibson told me that he and Larry were finished with the vessel. At that time the wreck site appeared much like it had been described to me, and everything was consistent with the details in their sketches. I could see where the ballast bars had been removed and that the area beneath them had been worked. There were three anchors, a cannon, a windlass, and one piece of exposed structural wood, which, I believe, was the keel.

Well, all of my life I've been interested in history, reptiles, and Indian artifacts, and by my teens I was already spending time out in the desert digging for arrowheads. I was born in 1945 and grew up here in Whittier, California, during the 50s and 60s. That time period had a negative impact on my life. I spent a number of years trying to "figure out what it was all about" and, as a result of that, became involved in drugs and alcohol. Eventually I was prosecuted and convicted for armed robbery and for smuggling narcotics—offenses that went along with living that lifestyle. When I finally survived that bout with drugs, alcohol, and prison, I resumed my interests in treasure hunting, metal detecting, and desert exploring—particularly old mineshafts and abandoned mining communities where I dug for bottles and other antiquities.

I learned to dive about that time and became interested in wreck diving shortly thereafter. I was traveling around the country, taking odd jobs, and had the opportunity to work on shrimp trawlers out of Fort Meyers, Florida. One of the skippers was a highly motivated wreck diver, and during the trawls for shrimp he would look for wreck signatures on his fathometer. When he picked up such a signature, we would shut down shrimping operations and investigate shipwrecks. Since I was the only crew member with diving experience, I had the opportunity to dive on a lot of Gulf shipwrecks between the Dry Tortugas and Mexico. The skipper's primary goal was finding shipwrecks that had salvageable equipment. This helped supplement his income in an industry that had highs and lows. Consequently, most of the wrecks that we dove had sonar signatures indicating that they could not have been submerged for more than 20 or 30 years.

When I returned to Whittier, I began sport diving the breakwaters and coves along the southern California coast, spearfishing, and collecting abalone. However, largely as a result of my experience with the skipper on the shrimp trawler, I had become interested in wreck diving. Among the first California wrecks I dove on was the *Dominator*, a converted Liberty ship lost in 1962 along the Palos Verdes Peninsula. Subsequently, through research, I learned of other wrecks along the southern California coast and in the surrounding islands. These included the *Valiant*—a luxury yacht built in 1926, which burned and sank off Catalina Island—and the *Olympic II* [which sank in 1940 off San Pedro], or "*Fourteen Minute*" [*Johanna Smith*], off Long Beach, which during the 1930s had served as a fishing platform by day and a gambling barge by night.

As I became more interested, I read all the books I could find describing shipwrecks. Then I began researching old newspaper accounts. Meanwhile, I joined the California Wreck Divers Club and vigorously developed contacts made there. I found it challenging to survey an underwater site, locate an object for salvage, and then come up with a feasible way to salvage it. I custom-built harnesses, flotation equipment, and specialized tools that could be used underwater. These included hydraulic cutting tools, burning bars, explosives, dredges, and airlifts.

During the late 1960s, before getting into wreck diving, I had spent a lot of time in the "Mother Lode" area of the Sierras, river dredging and crevicing for gold using the stock-manufactured equipment then available. However, when I started wreck diving, I began to modify that equipment to work in the deep marine environment. Fortunately, I had the necessary technical skills—a background in air conditioning/refrigeration, sheet metal, welding, and hydraulics fabrication and design—and I soon progressed from dredging gold nuggets out of the Yuba, American, and Trinity rivers to retrieving gold nuggets, coins, and relics from Gold Rush–era shipwrecks. I particularly remember diving three steamships, all of which wrecked in 1853: the *Independence*, which went down on the Pacific side of Baja California; the *Winfield Scott* off Anacapa Island; and the *Samuel S. Lewis*, just north of San Francisco.

During this period I was not only diving shipwrecks, but I was becoming involved in commercial diving, including commercial harvesting of abalone, and eventually I was building decompression chambers for the Navy. Today I'm a self-trained and self-employed structural-steel welding inspector. I also do underwater casualty–related work for insurance companies. This includes locating boats and airplanes for positive identification and recovery of items lost by shipping companies, such as anchors and gangways.

It was in the spring of 1980, about a month after Pat Gibson told me that he and Larry were finished diving the so-called silk ship up at Caspar, that I made my first dive together with several others on the wreck site. My interpretation of the site was that the vessel floated into the cove bow first, to the northeast, and lodged in the rocks near shore in that position. Then, exposed to the prevailing wind and sea, the vessel rotated counterclockwise into the position in which it broke up. The ship probably remained vertical for only a short time before heeling over on its starboard beam, at which time the ballast rolled shoreward, trapping some of the cargo and other artifacts. Lying on her starboard beam would

have left the keel exposed to seaward long enough for most of the intermediate framing members to break loose during subsequent storms—after which the keel would have settled beneath the seabed with no evidence of cross members.

Our initial focus was on the remainder of the ballast pile, and in those areas where we completely removed the bars. We found no structural elements lying beneath. What we did recover included muskets, pistols, and lead shot, as well as coins, trade beads, and other ship's fittings. We used airlift bags to relocate the ballast bars and then dredged the shallow deposit lying beneath them down to bedrock. Finally, we worked any crevices in the bedrock that showed signs of cabin material. I thought the crevices would be where metal items of sufficient specific gravity would ultimately work themselves, and, if pieces of a lesser metal like iron or steel had worked their way down into those crevices, their corrosion would have protected artifacts made of higher metals—like silver, pewter, or brass—from electrolysis, thus preserving them.

When I first dove the *Frolic,* there was an area, referred to as "the cave," where there appeared to be stacked plates of porcelain. This cave turned out to be a mound of anchor chain which had remained suspended in the vessel's anchor locker long enough to corrode into a solid mass and become unmovable as chain. Then, when the wood of the anchor locker had been eaten away, there remained a hollow cavity underneath this mound. It seemed clear to me that the chain was still stowed in the anchor locker, in that position, when the ship finally came to rest. There was no evidence that the stacked porcelain in the cave area had been crated to protect it from chipping or breakage, and, upon

CLIFTON B. "CLIFF" CRAFT

further investigation, none of the stacked pieces turned out to be intact vessels.

Elsewhere we found trade beads, round lead shot, porcelain sherds, brass cup weights, buttons, razors, toothbrushes, furniture hardware, ship's fittings, a blunderbuss, muskets, pistols, fine ornate pieces of gold, silver flatware, and canned goods. The cans were made of base metal—perhaps tin, pewter, or copper—with leaded seams on their bottoms and sides. There were also carved seals for making personal impressions in wax, ivory gaming pieces, and abundant parts of what we took to be wine bottles. There may have been some nuts and fruits aboard, as evidenced by their seeds and pits, but they were just in the area, and whether they were, in fact, really aboard the ship when it sank would be pure speculation. I did see some bone fragments, and there were leather goods in the form of shoes and luggage.

I remember the brass latches, tacks, and buckles for strapped luggage, as well as the leather seams of the luggage itself. Shoes were represented by brass eyelets and both brass and silver buckles. Among the navigational instruments recovered were three octants. There were also some white-and-brown porcelain doorknobs, some padlocks, keys, and a variety of door hinges, stops, and various ship's hardware. There was enough furniture hardware to indicate that either furniture hardware or the furniture itself had been a part of the cargo. There were also earthenware bowls, made thicker and from a different material than the fired porcelain.

As for the portholes, I believe, by the shape of the glass and the design of the rectangular opening scuttles, that they could have been used as deck lights and for below-deck ventilation. They are a flush mount, and they're inconsistent in their design with what would have been incorporated into the superstructure [the cabin] of a vessel of that time period. My opinion is that they were designed to ventilate and light the below – or between-deck area.

They are unique in that they open, so they would have served both as lighting and ventilation. They would have opened down, beneath the deck, and closed flush to the deck. Depending on the location of the galley they could have been significant for dissipation of heat from the galley area as well as lighting. There were, of course, a number of fixed and gimbal-mounted kerosene lighting fixtures recovered from the wreck, but my opinion of the square "portholes," based on their design, is that they were flush mounted to the deck.

All of the items we recovered were initially kept in saltwater, then placed in freshwater to remove the salts. The wooden items, like gunstocks, were subsequently treated with polyethylene glycol to stabilize them. We used reverse electrolysis, an electrolytic-reduction process, on some of the silver coins to stabilize the silver oxides.

My second trip to the wreck and several subsequent trips were with Dave and Steve Buller. Then, when Bruce and Bob Lanham became familiar with the location of the site, they began to dive on it. The Lanham brothers and the Buller brothers worked independently of each. I would estimate that after Larry Pierson and Pat Gibson finished working the *Frolic* there was a total of 50 working diving days at the wreck site among the rest of us—including me, Dave and Steve Buller, and the Lanhams. We shared information from these various trips amongst ourselves, so we were all pretty much aware of the ongoing trips and what the recoveries were. We stayed in close communication with one another by sharing trips to other wreck sites in northern and southern California and in Mexico.

All of the items that were recovered by Larry Pierson, Pat Gibson, Dave and Steve Buller, Bruce and Bob Lanham, and myself are accounted for. And, based on the condition of the site each time I returned, recoveries by others could not have been substantial. I believe that I probably acquired the largest collection of artifacts from the *Frolic*. The cannon was later removed by the Lanham brothers after the cascabel was broken by persons unknown. I believe that earlier recoveries of artifacts, made by others, were from outside the perimeter of the ballast pile, while Larry Pierson, Pat Gibson, and my circle of divers were able to recover most of the artifacts that had been trapped in the shifting of the vessel's ballast and her anchor chain.

To the best of my knowledge there is still one section of the ballast pile that has not been moved, and it should be productive because it is right adjacent to the area where most of the galley utensils, firearms, and coins were located. The galley utensils included ivory knife handles and silver flatware, some of which was of American manufacture. The unmoved and unworked portion of the ballast that remains probably amounts to an area of 2 × 2 yd. and probably represents about 10% of the area of the original ballast pile. In my opinion, that unworked portion of the ballast could at present only be identified by someone who participated in working the original ballast pile. In most instances the ballast bars have probably now fused back together, so it will require a person who was present on the early trips to identify what was moved and what wasn't.

As for how the *Frolic* arrived at its present orientation in the cove, in my opinion the vessel floated into the cove bow first to the northeast, and its bow lodged in the rocks near shore in that position. Then I believe the vessel rotated or was turned counterclockwise until its bow ultimately faced the northwest side of the cove and its stern faced to the southeast, with its keel exposed to prevailing wind and sea. In other words, it was heeled over on its starboard beam. I believe that the vessel remained vertical for only a very short period of time, and the swell quickly aligned the ship into the position in which it ultimately broke up.

My conclusions regarding the orientation of the vessel are based on the positions of the anchors and the ballast, but I'm not absolutely certain that these were their original positions at the time the ship broke up. Earlier trips there by other salvagers could have resulted in the some of those items being moved, but I do believe that she went in bow first, and I believe there is a very strong possibility that a substantial portion of the stern section of the vessel could still be out in the deeper sand towards the middle of the cove. The design of that type of vessel suggests that there is a fair portion of the ship that extends beyond the ballast point of the hull in the stern area. In other words, the ballast doesn't extend all the way to the stern of the ship. I suspect that the ballast could have held the central portion of the vessel intact while the stern might have broken off and washed away. That scenario might account for some of the vessel's trade goods being easily accessible to Indians and other persons that were there at the time the ship was breaking up. If this is true, some of the heavier objects would now be buried below the seabed further out in the cove where the overburden might be 10–15

CLIFTON B. "CLIFF" CRAFT

ft. deep. One might determine if there is something there by gridding the area and excavating square-meter test holes at predetermined locations in suspect areas. In my opinion, there would be too much background disturbance from the primary ballast pile to use sensing gear that would be capable of locating individual items buried to a depth of 10 ft. Buried out there in the cove you might find many artifacts from the stern of the vessel. For example, you might possibly find anchor chains, anchor, rudder trunion, and a variety of hull fittings associated with the rudder and steering mechanism.

If you conduct any further underwater investigation of the *Frolic*, my recommendation would be to work the remaining 10% of the ballast pile and to run a series of test holes down to bedrock in suspect locations towards the center of the cove. Given the length of the vessel and the limited length of the ballast pile, there is sufficient evidence to indicate that there should be cultural resources beneath the seabed that weren't driven ashore.

When you take all of the evidence together, my conclusion is that the *Frolic* came into the cove bow on, and the stern was then turned into the prevailing swell coming in. But the position of the anchors as I first saw them in relation to the anchor chain mound is not consistent with where they would have been stowed on that type of vessel. In my opinion, they should have been closer to the mound of anchor chain. Perhaps when the *Frolic* was washed into the cove the anchors were still lashed to the side of the vessel and hanging their catheads. The broad width of the bow at cathead to cathead could account for the distance between the two primary [larger] anchors. They could have separated themselves from the bow before the ship turned

on her beam end because otherwise they would be on top of one another. Of course, those anchors could have been moved prior to the beginning of modern wreck diving. They would have had commercial value for a good number of years while that part of the coast was being settled.

As I recall, one of the cannons was actually resting right on top of the mound of anchor chain. There are a number of conclusions that you can draw from that. One conclusion is that the cannon had been raised from a lower elevation and set at a higher elevation for an easier removal. It may have been purposefully set there awaiting a boat for a quick recovery. Although it could have settled there naturally, it was cradled in and amongst the anchor chain at a right angle to the chain. The anchor chain was principally elongated, but the cannon was at a right angle to the elongated mound. To me it's highly suspect that it could have occurred naturally in that way. It has all the earmarks of an attempt to salvage it, set up high for easy identification upon a return trip.

When the Lanham's removed that cannon they used lift bags to float it to the surface and then towed it into Fort Bragg, where they removed it at Noyo Harbor. Initially that cannon was so overgrown with marine growth that it was not even recognizable as a cannon. Only a trained person could have seen that there was a shape or pattern that was somewhat inconsistent with its being natural. But, eventually, enough of the marine growth and kelp holdfasts were removed that even an amateur diver could instantly recognize it as a cannon. Then the cascabel was broken off by someone. We know about when it happened, but we don't know who did it. At that time the decision was made that it would be best to remove the cannon and submerge it in freshwater.

As for the future work on the *Frolic*, I think it would be a good idea to investigate the wreck site for items that would be unique to that time period and could perhaps provide some more information about the wreck. I think that the original wreck and the subsequent salvage work should be well documented, including the early removal of artifacts which were subsequently found in Indian sites. This information should be made available to the general public. Moreover, I feel the remainder of the wreck site should be fully excavated by people that are familiar with the site. There is a strong possibility that significant items associated with the *Frolic* may still remain in that cove. In any event, to this day there is no evidence that they exist anywhere else. For example, perhaps the ship's name was attached in bronze letters to the stern. There are a number of other missing items that could enhance the work that's already been done. Notably, only one ship's bell has been recovered, and, in my opinion, it was nothing more than a small repeater bell. The main ship's bell, if my theory is correct, would be more out toward the center of the cove, along with the sundial, compass, lights and fittings, and the steering mechanism, all of which are associated with the stern. I believe that it's in the interest of the community and the public that the people who've worked on the *Frolic* previously be involved in any future work. They have the firsthand knowledge that would be most helpful in obtaining this additional information if it's there.

Since my last work on the *Frolic*, I've been involved with a number of commercial operations focusing on shipwrecks in other parts of the world. I'm now interested

in the South China Sea because of the trade routes passing through there and the numerous wrecks dating from ancient times right up through World War II. In my opinion, the academic community has neither the interest nor the resources to save these things and to salvage them. It'll be done by the private community or not at all. Even in Southeast Asia the local governments are investing nothing at all in the salvage operations. The salvager bears the expense of everything, plus liability

I've worked on some VOC [Dutch East India Company] wrecks in the South China Sea, most notably the *Geldermalsen*, which went down in 1752. I've also been involved with the *Ontario* and several other China-trade vessels located on offshore reefs and atolls in the South China Sea, in and around Malaysia, Indonesia, and the islands off Sumatra.

My work on the *Geldermalsen* began after Michael Hatcher completed primary salvage. Hatcher recovered approximately 150,000 pieces of Chinese export porcelain that were eventually auctioned off by Christie's in Amsterdam for $16.5 million. They also recovered the ship's bell and a number of other significant artifacts that they did not auction. Along with the porcelain were ingots of gold, cast in the typical ingot configuration for that area, referred to as "shoes," as well as hourglass-shaped rectangular bars of a few pounds in size. Our group recovered 10,000 pieces of porcelain. Based on the original manifest, we estimate there are still 40,000 salvageable pieces of porcelain remaining, and that's discounting 60,000 pieces for breakage.

On that venture I provided my skills. I'm now considering a venture in that area where I'll provide both skills and some capital investment. This is a project to

CLIFTON B. "CLIFF" CRAFT

locate the *Ontario*, which wrecked in 1801 [ca. 1798, off Borneo] en route from Canton to New York. My involvement in the project will be limited to financial support and in coming up with some ideas for surveying the site—pending the Indonesian government dropping all civil and criminal charges against me from an incident in 1988, when they arrested me and my associates on the high seas, at gunpoint, for conducting scientific survey in their "exclusive economic zone." Our survey was limited to shipwrecks, and at that time the Indonesian government's international claim to natural resources included fisheries, oil, natural gas and minerals—and not shipwrecks. So we were in no way violating any of the laws of Indonesia's exclusive economic zone.

After our arrest we were taken to Tanjung Pinang Naval Base on Bintan Island where we were held for four months. The State Department, the U.S. Embassy, and several congressmen and senators throughout the United States protested—with no positive results—that we were, in fact, violating no laws or statutes at the time. It will be interesting to see what the Indonesian government's position will be upon our location of the *Ontario*—whether they will, in fact, live up to the contractual agreements we now have with them for salvage rights at our two lease sites within their exclusive economic zone. One lease site is 130 sq. mi., while the other is a little over 100 sq. mi., and both include major reefs in the shipping lanes of the ancient trade routes.

In return for leasing salvage rights to us, the Indonesian government expects to have two of their officials on board and to receive 50% of the gross. Another 5% goes to "unidentified" government agencies or officials, giving the government a total of 55% of the gross. The salvage company has to pay all expenses. We expect to recover export-trade goods from Canton, particularly porcelain. Export porcelain from that time was manufactured primarily for the European market. In other words, the pieces are not traditional in design to the culture area in which they were produced. We also hope to recover the gold and silver that was generally carried aboard a trade vessel in order to pay for cargo, supplies, tariffs, and ship repairs.

The academic community may not like it, but I'm happy to have had the opportunity to dive on the *Atocha*, a Spanish treasure galleon wrecked off Florida. For almost 20 years it was Mel Fisher's quest to locate this wreck. About 1986/87 I had the opportunity to spend a week on the wreck, helping to relocate the ballast stones and participating in the ongoing effort to locate artifacts from both the *Santa Margarita* and the *Atocha*. I was there only a few months after the "mother lode" was located, and I remember that, after my week on the *Atocha*, I was presented with a certificate by Duncan Mathewson, the project archaeologist, qualifying me as a "junior archaeologist" [*chuckle*].

I was quite impressed with the management and persistence of that operation, particularly given the fact that there had been loss of life. Moreover, there had been many disappointed people along the way who had invested money. But, there were, additionally, those who believed in the dream and stuck it out with Mel. I have nothing but admiration and respect for those people who believed in a man who was committed to a dream, and who, in spite of many legal battles and great personal cost to his family and to his company, saw it through to the end.

Not only did Mel Fisher face assaults

by the legal community, principally funded by other wreck divers, but there were confrontations with the academic community. It seems clear to me that the academic community has developed a possessive attitude toward virtually all wreck sites, in spite of the fact that wreck sites are so numerous that the academics couldn't complete a survey of them, much less work them, in 10,000 years. They argue that wrecks are "time capsules." Well, every time I hear some academic or government official use the word "time capsule," I'm outraged. Time capsules are placed with specific intent in mind and, of course, to protect the contents from the environment. But, when a ship sinks, it is unintentional, and there are numerous metal items on shipwrecks that will stay preserved only so long as there is a host metal to protect them. Moreover, the porcelain, earthenware, glass, and marble items at many wreck sites are all subject to destruction by commercial development, such as dredging and harbor development. Many wreck sites in the United States and elsewhere have been completely lost to mankind because they were in the way of commercial projects.

In my opinion time is always of the essence with shipwrecks because most metal items don't have host-sacrificial material close enough to them to preserve them. As a result, the quantity of preserved metal artifacts on ancient shipwrecks is much less than on more recent vessels of similar tonnage. For example, I have a brass capstan cover from the *Aggi*, an iron-hulled sailing ship that sank off Santa Rosa Island in the early 1900s [1915]. This cover is stabilized now, but only partially readable. Had it been left to decompose underwater for another 60 years it would be totally unrecognizable today.

Cooperation between the wreck-diving community and the academic community is, of course, the ideal, but I think it's unlikely that any worthwhile cooperative effort could be carried out in the United States in the present political climate—mainly because the academic community's influence with government officials is sufficient to forbid sport divers from recovering any artifacts at all. This country was founded on freedom and the pursuit of happiness, but a small group of academic people in the archaeological community that are well connected with government officials have managed to close off most areas and prohibit the removal of what they term "cultural resources" from all shipwrecks that they determine are historic. In many cases complete plans or blueprints are available for these so-called historic cultural resources.

In my opinion the academics are hiding behind a cloud of dishonesty and self-righteousness in order to foster their own personal advancement by protecting these sites and limiting access to themselves. They capitalize on the work they do at the public's expense, gaining prestige and publications in their own names. In my opinion, preserving the rights of the academic community is not in the best interest of the wrecks. Furthermore, what they are doing, individually and collectively, defies the very basis upon which this country was founded. These shipwrecks are as much ours as they are theirs.

A classic example of the problem is their declaration of the side-wheel steamer *Winfield Scott*, off Anacapa Island, to be "off limits." I'm being prosecuted by the Park Service for allegedly removing and destroying cultural resources in a federal marine sanctuary during a diving trip with our club, the California Wreck Divers.

CLIFTON B. "CLIFF" CRAFT

The whole purpose of our club is for the research, recovery, restoration, and display of nautical artifacts from shipwrecks. We have lectured at trade shows. We have shared information with the public, and we have donated restored pieces to many museums. Yet we are given little or no credit at all for our work. The fact is that the majority of the sites that are now "off limits" to the private wreck-diving community were originally located by the private wreck-diving community. The professional community has clearly benefited from the efforts of the wreck-diving community, but we're given no credit by them. They accuse us of raping and pillaging. Meanwhile, because of their connections, they are above the law.

To have an academic community of so few controlling so much is a disaster to the potential information that could be collected. They term wreck divers "trophy hunters"—people who collect things for their mantels. Well, yes, there are sport divers that find pieces, and, yes, they do display them. But if you look at donor tags in the museums across this country, you'll find that the majority of the artifacts on display came from the private community, not the academic community. The academic community is interfering with my rights as a free citizen of the United States, protected by the Constitution and the Bill of Rights. They didn't buy those ships that they have on display in their museums. They were donated for tax credits by individuals and companies for inflated amounts of money. Meanwhile, the items we wreck divers have donated to museums are now untraceable.

We've donated artifacts to the Los Angeles Maritime Museum that were from local shipwrecks and clearly a part of Los Angeles maritime history, but it's impossible to find out what they did with them. The museum community operates with very little, if any, outside control. For example, when they audited museums for the moon-rock samples that were recovered by the *Apollo* project, they found that much of that material can no longer be accounted for—and it's the same for collections of maritime artifacts.

Regarding the *Winfield Scott*, I'm taking my case to the highest court of the land because, for one, I am not guilty of what I am charged with. It was a three-day trip, and there were 40 people on that boat, 2 of whom were National Park Service undercover rangers posing as a husband

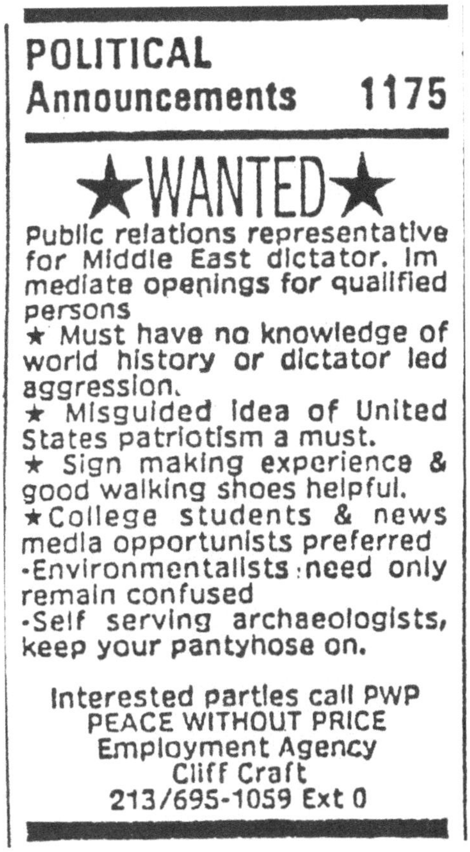
POLITICAL
Announcements 1175

★WANTED★

Public relations representative for Middle East dictator. Im mediate openings for qualified persons
★ Must have no knowledge of world history or dictator led aggression.
★ Misguided idea of United States patriotism a must.
★ Sign making experience & good walking shoes helpful.
★College students & news media opportunists preferred
•Environmentalists need only remain confused
•Self serving archaeologists, keep your pantyhose on.

Interested parties call PWP
PEACE WITHOUT PRICE
Employment Agency
Cliff Craft
213/695-1059 Ext 0

Figure 67. In 1988, Cliff was prosecuted for collecting artifacts from the *Winfield Scott* off Anacapa Island, California. His anger is best expressed in this classified ad he placed in the Los Angeles Times, circa. 1988. (Courtesy Clifford Craft)

and wife. They, allegedly, took four rolls of pictures, which they couldn't account for. It was a sting operation, and they targeted our club. It had never been done before, and it has never been done since. And regardless of what they allege, I believe that my name was specifically targeted simply because of my reputation. My constitutional rights were violated no less than six times during that operation.

The interesting thing is that the intention of the trip was well established on the first day, and we didn't dive the *Winfield Scott* until the third day. The undercover rangers participated in fanning and sifting through the sand for debris, and they did their fair share of "ooh-ing and aah-ing" over items that people brought up, which primarily consisted of copper sheathing, nails, a few hull spikes, a few pieces of wood, and some pieces of coal. That was their entire physical evidence—and then they claimed that those few pieces of coal were going to unfold some big mystery about the coal industry and Gold Rush steamers. It was ludicrous!

As for the *Frolic* Shipwreck Project, I think its success is the result of a joint effort between the academic community and cooperating private wreck-diving enthusiasts. I'm pleased with the results, and I've freely donated my collection of *Frolic* artifacts to the *Frolic* Repository. Nevertheless, I see an erosion of freedom in this country, and the problem is one of special interest groups with sufficient capital and clout that our politicians can hardly accommodate all of their demands. I believe that the foundation is being laid for a complete and total breakdown of the free-enterprise system in this country.

Today you have people voting on issues that don't pertain to them, and the only access to information they have is through the media. It's ridiculous. For example, consider the motorcycle-helmet law. If, indeed, the laws of the land are by and for the people, doesn't it seem logical that the motorcycle community—the people that actually ride motorcycles—should be the ones to decide, collectively, if this should be a law and not the entire population? Why should motorcyclists be governed by people that don't ride motorcycles?

In similar fashion, I believe that there is an effort going on—basically a "10-year plan" orchestrated by a very few people—to completely eliminate the private community from shipwreck salvage and recovery. Whenever there is a recovery, like the *Atocha*, the media describe it as a $400 million shipwreck, and that gets the attention of the government—and the academic community is, of course, always appalled at a salvage that is oriented on profit. Wouldn't it be nice if we could all be on the public payroll! I've got hundreds of books here with statements that are ludicrous. Some of the people that holler the loudest, like Cousteau and Ballard, are, in my mind, some of the biggest pirates that ever lived. How nice it is to be funded by the public to travel the seas of the world with the latest of everything. What a scam! What kind of world are we living in? Somebody somewhere has got to wake up. I think that the people need to wake up to the fact that they're being duped by the few who are controlling the many.

As for the *Frolic* items that I have in my possession, these artifacts are in a sense infinite, and they are only in my possession as I'm passing through my time here on Earth. They were here long before I was here, and they will be here in somebody's custody long after I am gone. As a person I am moving through time, but these artifacts are not. As I see it, I have items that are in my custody, and I am only a caretaker of them. They are not mine, but they are here.

CLIFTON B. "CLIFF" CRAFT

David Buller

Dave Buller's first experience with the ocean was in grade school, body surfing on Coronado Beach across from San Diego. Later, in high school, Dave and his brother Steve became active surfers off the beaches near Santa Cruz.

Dave graduated from the University of California, Berkeley in 1970 with a B.S. in vertebrate zoology, and that same year he took a scuba class. Soon Dave and Steve were entering competitions to harvest the largest abalone. Then, after meeting the Lanham brothers and seeing their collection of artifacts from local shipwrecks, Dave and Steve became wreck divers.

For 15 years Dave was employed as an instructional developer at the Lawrence Hall of Science. His first part-time commercial diving job was servicing the pumping plant at Lake Merritt in Oakland, California, after which he formed the Marine Inspection and Recovery Company.

Meanwhile, word was spreading among wreck divers of an early shipwreck in a cove near Caspar on the Mendocino coast. That was enough to

Figure 68. David Buller wearing his "Journey of the Frolic" T-shirt, Rodeo, California, 1994. (Photo by Thomas Layton)

enable Dave, equipped with a proton magnetometer, to locate the *Frolic's* iron ballast pile. Dave and Steve Buller made over five visits to the *Frolic* wreck site, dredging the sediment surrounding the wreck.

Tom Layton secured Dave Buller's name from one of the families whose homes overlooked the wreck site, and Dave introduced Tom to other *Frolic* divers, including Larry Pierson and Cliff Craft, whose narratives appear in this volume. Dave and Steve were the first of the wreck divers to return their collections from the *Frolic*.

Dave assisted Daniel Lenihan, Larry Murphy, and James Delgado in their 1981, 1982, 1983 Drakes Bay Survey, where his compilation of wrecks along the coast provided information for their final report (Murphy1983), for which Dave and James Delgado received credits as a coauthors of their chapter.

In 1986, Dave resigned from the university to become a fulltime commercial diver and changed the name of his company to Coastal Diving and Construction. His first large contract, for repairs to the California Aqueduct, was followed by many others from the California Department of Water Resources, Pacific Gas & Electric, and barge companies. After a successful career, Dave closed Coastal Diving and retired when it became apparent to him that the underwater work had become too physically challenging for a man entering his 70s.

David Buller

21 January 1994
Rodeo, California

I was born in Oakland, California, in 1948, but as a Navy brat I didn't stay much longer than three years in any location. For several periods we lived on the East Coast—at Brunswick, Georgia; Long Island, New York; and, for a while, near Chicago. At other times we lived here in the West, in Alameda, San Diego, across the bay from San Diego at Coronado, and finally back in northern California in Fremont and Alamo. I trace my love of the sea to my happy experiences exploring the coastal swamps near our home in Georgia, fishing, and body surfing at the beach in Coronado, and surfing in the Santa Cruz area.

I completed seventh and eighth grades and my first year of high school at Coronado. I was a beach bum. At every opportunity my brother Steve and I would go down to the beach, where we would fish and body surf all day. We didn't bring food, just a bottle of water. We would dig clams with our toes, crack them open on the rocks, and eat them raw. That was our food. I don't know if that was the healthiest thing to do. We did make a point of not eating them during red tides when the beaches were piled with dead fish, but, otherwise, that was our normal routine.

We then moved back up to the San Francisco Bay area, where I attended Washington High School in Fremont. I was still in love with the sea, and my brother and I got involved in surfing. Our most popular surfing spot was Cowell Beach, just north of the Santa Cruz pier. We also surfed at Pleasure Point and the Hook, a few miles to the south. As Santa Cruz surfers we were used to cold water and wore wetsuits, but we had never done any diving. Nevertheless, while we were waiting for wave sets, if the water was clear I would try to see what was below us. Still, at that point I'd never even thought about diving.

I entered the University of California at Berkeley in 1966 and completed my four years there with a major in zoology. At the time my main interest was vertebrate zoology, not invertebrate, so I didn't learn much about marine biology, even though it was to become a real love of mine.

My college years at Berkeley, 1966 through 1970, were during the very active political period on campus—the Free Speech Movement, the Vietnam War, the Cambodia crisis, and the People's Park conflict. I was at Sproul Plaza when they tear gassed us from helicopters. I was participating as a medic because by that time I had become disillusioned by both sides— the university authorities and the police and the political activists and students opposing them. Still, I wanted to contribute something, so I figured the least I could do was help people that got injured. I had a gas mask, a regular first-aid kit for treating cuts and bruises, and a mild solution of boric acid and water to wash people's eyes to reduce the stinging. While at Berkeley I didn't have much interest in history. In fact, I had the impression that, prior to the 20th century, technology and science were backwards, so I didn't have much of an interest in that period at all.

When I graduated from Berkeley I got a job working for the Stauffer Chemical Company in Richmond. It was there that I got involved with a girl who had recently been certified by Lloyd Austin, the UC Berkeley diving officer, and she needed a diving partner. At the time my girlfriend and I were renting a house two blocks away from the El Cerrito Community Center and she saw a notice in the local paper that they were starting a "skin and scuba" course. She talked me into taking the course and I was certified as a scuba diver in the fall of 1970.

For me, being in the water and diving felt so natural, it was as if I had always been doing it. It was like putting on a pair of shoes for the first time and finding they fit perfectly—that they weren't stiff, but already broken in and comfortable. In fact, I soon discovered that I was more comfortable in and under the water than I was above it. I found great comfort getting away from the stresses, the hustle, and the bustle of life above water. I took to diving like a fish to water.

After working for a year at Stauffer Chemical Company, I was switched to a new project. I found out the goal of the project was to develop a herbicide to defoliate forests in Vietnam, so I quit my job at Stauffer out of an aversion to being associated with anything that supported that war.

Fortunately, I was able to get a part-time job as a tour guide at the University of California Botanical Gardens. Since I was only working part time, mainly on the weekends, whenever I could scrounge up a partner I dove. Consequently, in the period of about a year and a half, I accumulated about as much diving experience as most sports divers do in 10 years. I was considered an expert within a year and a half of becoming a diver.

Meanwhile, I'd become friends with Frank Reneau, the instructor who had trained me, and I started assisting him right after completing the course. In the spring of 1971 I recruited my brother to take that course, and it was in that course that I met my first wife. We dove together and fell in love.

In the fall of 1973, Frank Reneau decided to retire, and I took over as the scuba instructor for the cities of Richmond and El Cerrito. More recently I've been teaching at Contra Costa Community College and the Lakeridge Athletic Club in El Sobrante. I've now been teaching skin and scuba courses for over 20 years, and my brother has been assisting me all along as an assistant instructor.

People often ask Steve and me why we do it, and the simple answer is that we've always felt we've owed a lot to diving and we want to give something back to it. One of the things that has always bothered us is seeing unprepared, poorly trained divers on the northern California coast, where the waters can be treacherous. We've always thought that the very least we can do is to train people to safely enjoy the sport of skin and scuba diving and encourage them to help preserve the underwater resources that we are lucky enough to have off our coast. But, you know, if it weren't for that girlfriend, I might not be in diving today.

My part-time job as a tour guide at the University of California Botanical Gardens eventually turned into a full-time job when the director at the gardens was appointed director of the Lawrence Hall of Science. He had been impressed with my ability to work with young people, and they received a grant from the National Science Foundation for an innovative science-curriculum project called Outdoor Biology Instructional Strategies (OBIS). They wanted to develop a supplemental

biology curriculum that would place emphasis on learning through discovery rather than reading, hearing, or watching movies. They wanted students to experience scientific discovery by facing a challenge, coming up with possible solutions, conducting experiments, and learning self-initiated decision-making skills in the process.

I started out as a curriculum developer at the Lawrence Hall of Science on a three-year soft-money job, and it lasted nearly 15 years. I worked on several major science-curriculum projects there and authored many of the activities. These included the Outdoor Biology Instructional Strategies, or OBIS project; the HAP, or Health Activities Project, from kindergarten through 12th-grade level; and the GEMS Project, Great Explorations in Math and Science. Many of the curriculum projects I worked on are now widely used in the U.S., and some have been translated into foreign languages for use around the world.

I finally outgrew that. As in most jobs, you get to a certain level and they expect you to become an administrator. But my real love was in being creative as a developer of activities that young people would find exciting and challenging. I was particularly interested in creating activities that introduced young people to the fascinating life forms that live in freshwater and saltwater habitats. When they moved me from that to being the administrator of the program, I lost interest. I left the Lawrence Hall of Science in the fall of 1986 after being there almost 15 years, but I have no regrets in that regard, other than missing some of my old friends there.

When I started losing my motivation at the Lawrence Hall of Science, I began looking around, and, coincidentally, one

DAVID BULLER

of my friends had a friend who worked for Alameda County Flood Control. This man, among other things, was in charge of a project analyzing water quality at Lake Merritt. To study what kinds of organisms populated the lake, rows of 4 in. squares of different substrates—plastics, aluminum, wood, glass, and brick—were submerged at different locations around the lake. They planned to recover one of each kind of substrate square from each location every month of the year and identify the kinds and numbers of organisms that had colonized it. The biggest water quality problem at Lake Merritt was a spring bloom of widgeon grass, which during a very short and rapid growing period depleted the water of oxygen. Then the plants would die, and their decomposition would deplete the water of even more oxygen. The result was that Lake Merritt would annually turn into a stinking body of water, and local businesses and residents would complain about it.

Since Alameda County Flood Control needed a diver to collect the substrate plates and quadrate samples just once a month, my friend asked me if I might be interested in the job. The idea of being paid for something that I loved to do seemed almost too good to be true, so starting in 1980/81 I began collecting bottom samples and substrate plates! Lake Merritt diving left a little to be desired from the viewpoint of aesthetics and health, but armed with bimonthly gamma-globulin shots I was able to meet the challenge.

That was my first commercial diving job, and they soon had me performing inspection and maintenance on the Lake Merritt pumping plant. As a result of this I began getting other commercial clients. Since I was still working at UC Berkeley I did the work on a part-time basis, mainly on weekends and before and after work. That work eased my way from UC Berkeley into commercial diving, and at the end of 1986 I cut the umbilical to the university and went into commercial diving full time.

I established my first partnership, Marine Inspection and Recovery, in 1983, when I was still with the university. It was very small, just my brother and one other individual. After leaving the university I saw the need for more partners and a company that had more capabilities, so in 1988 I recruited three additional people, for a total of 6 partners. We changed our name to Coastal Diving and Construction and started bidding on state and municipal contracts. Our first contract was with the Department of Water Resources, who managed the California Aqueduct—the state water-delivery system. The first two or three years were tough, but we continued to grow, and finally in 1992 we formed a new partnership with nine partners and shortened our name to Coastal Diving. Today we're working actively with clients such as the Department of Water Resources, the Central Marin Sanitation Agency, PG&E [Pacific Gas and Electric], and several local barge and dredging companies.

At present, our main responsibility with the Department of Water Resources is searching for breaks or leaks in the lining of the first 60 mi. of the California Aqueduct. That's the concrete canal that one sees flowing south along Interstate 5. We patch those leaks by drilling holes through the cement scour liners down to the actual waterproof membrane, which is a very deep clay layer immediately beneath the cement panels. After we drill through the cement panels we pressure grout the voids and spaces underneath. Under high pressure the grout is forced into the softened or eroded spaces in the clay substrate, where it hardens and seals the whole area. Just last season we did a similar job on the old Federal Canal for the Delta Mendota and San Luis Water Authority. This 300 mi. canal runs roughly parallel to the California Aqueduct.

Right now we're working for the Central Marin Sanitation Agency. They have a 7 ft. diameter underwater outfall that emerges from the Marin County shore into San Rafael Bay just north of the Richmond-San Rafael Bridge. Although it was built only 10 years ago, more than half of the outer end of the outfall is now clogged with sludge from their water-treatment plant. The outfall has 176 diffusers, or standpipes, spaced along its length that are supposed to gradually release the treated water. However, since the outer half is clogged, they are now reduced to discharging through only half of them.

We're now dredging through sediments 5–6 ft. deep, getting down to the base of these diffusers, disconnecting them, and then cleaning them out with a 4 in. diameter suction hose. It's a very difficult job because the openings through which we are dredging are only 6 in. in diameter. It will probably take two or three months of work to complete that job.

Some of our work is pretty straightforward, for example, removing debris from PG&E stop locks, the gigantic valves controlling water flow through channels. We also do work for barge and dredging companies, especially when they've lost something. If they lose a mooring anchor or a pile-driving head, they call us in to locate it because we're the only diving company in the Bay Area that has a stable of magnetometers amongst their equipment. So, when something magnetic is lost, a steel or

iron object, we're called out. Actually, that provides a link to my wreck-diving period, because magnetometers are a very useful tool for finding shipwrecks.

You know, with regard to our commercial diving work, none of us ever went to a commercial diving school. We are totally self-taught. After working almost 15 years at the university I was used to researching answers to questions in the library or by contacting experts, and that was how I approached commercial diving. When we needed information, I would find it, learn it, and apply it. That's how I approached shipwreck diving as well. Now, after 13 years of commercial diving, we're considered to be experts in several specialized areas, particularly in remote sensing to find lost objects, and, surprisingly, in the application of underwater epoxies to inhibit or repair corrosion and to seal leaks.

So that's how I became a commercial diver. But, let me backtrack a bit to describe how I began to dive shipwrecks. I became certified as a diver in the fall of 1970, and when my brother Steve was certified six months later, we became very tight diving buddies. Whenever one of us dove, the other one was usually there, and, like brothers everywhere, we were always looking for challenges and trying to outdo one another.

Initially, our outlet for that competition was sport diving for trophy-size California red abalone. A trophy "ab" is considered to be one in excess of 10 in. You're not permitted to use tanks when going for abalone in northern California. You have to free dive—it's all breath-hold diving. Steve and I got to the point where we would carry 10 in. calipers with us, and an ab had to be in excess of 10 in. before we would even take it. We developed some notoriety in that field and won a lot of

DAVID BULLER

abalone contests sponsored by local sporting-goods and diving stores. The largest ab that I took was 11.09 in. Steve's largest was 10.89 in.

Well, once I got that mythical 11 in. abalone, my interest in the sport of trophy-abalone diving began to wane, and I started looking for new challenges. Steve was pretty much the same way. For a while we thought we might set a new abalone world's record, but unfortunately that did not happen. Still, as a result of our trophy abs we had become pretty well known in the diving community, and we heard about two brothers who, like Steve and me, were very active divers, but, instead of game diving, their main focus turned out to be diving on shipwrecks. Now this was something we had never really thought much about before. Steve and I had both dove on the *Pomona*, a steamer lost off Fort Ross up in Sonoma County, and we had enjoyed that, but it wasn't an experience leading us to refocus our efforts.

Well, Steve and I got wind that these two Lanham brothers, who happened to be twins, had recently discovered the wreck site of a Gold Rush–era steamer a little bit north of the Golden Gate, and that did capture my imagination. I suspect that was, in part, because Steve and I had recently purchased metal detectors. When it was too rough to dive we would walk along local beaches with our detectors searching for coins and other metal objects. It was finding old coins and other metal items on the beach, using a metal detector, that triggered my first interest in the past. Being able to touch something that might be several decades or even a hundred years old and trying to imagine what people handled it and how it ended up on the beach piqued my curiosity about things of history.

So, one day, around 1980, while I was still working at the university, I decided to give the Lanhams a call. I got their number from Original Steel's, a dive shop in Oakland, and I phoned Bruce Lanham. Bruce had already heard of Steve and me because of our abalone diving exploits. I told him that we'd heard a lot of fascinating things about the wreck diving he and his brother were doing and, in particular, about their exciting discovery of a shipwreck outside the "Gate."

As you might imagine, Bruce was rather hesitant to share much information, and certainly no information about shipwreck locations. But I was able to get out of him an idea of the basic equipment that they used for shipwreck diving, particularly the way they used surface supplied air, or "hookah" diving systems, to allow them to spend extended bottom time on a wreck site and also give them the added security of a line directly back up to their boat on the surface. Bruce and I seemed to hit it off pretty well, and he invited us to come over and visit them sometime.

A week later I called and told him up we were interested in coming over. He said: "How about tonight?" So, Steve and I jumped in the car and drove out to Pleasant Hill, where the two boys, still in their early 20s, were living at their parents' home. After going through the courtesies of introductions and meeting their mother, we walked into their bedroom and were stunned to see what looked like a small nautical museum. In every nook and cranny they had artifacts from dozens of shipwrecks from up and down the northern California coast. There were oil-pressure gauges, builder's plates, portholes, bells, bottles, brass spikes—just everything that you might imagine coming off of an

Figure 69. David Buller and Bruce Lanham, Fairfield, California, 2022. (Photo courtesy of Bruce Lanham)

old vessel. They had tiered bookshelves, and every shelf was crowded with artifacts.

What really impressed us was that they actually identified the collection of artifacts. Smaller items from a given shipwreck were mounted together on a large picture frame with a velvet backing, with a label identifying the ship, when it was made, when it sank, and, often, in the center, an actual photograph of the vessel when it was in active service. Steve and I were enthralled as they regaled us with tales of shipwreck diving.

For some reason, what particularly caught my fancy was Bob's description—he was the main researcher—of how he would go about picking up the trail of a vessel, maybe a hundred-plus years after it had been lost, tracking it down, locating a general search area, and then going out and finding it. They were already using underwater depth sounders and a small,

portable, hand-held magnetometer to locate ferrous metals.

A magnetometer simply measures the earth's magnetic field, and if you have an object that is large enough in its magnetic properties to cause a fluctuation in the general magnetic readings associated with a given latitude on the planet, then you get a spike or a drop in magnetism compared to the normal background readings you've been picking up. So, if you suddenly get a drop or a rise of several 10s or, in some cases, several 100s in your gamma count, you know you just passed over something of high-intensity magnetic activity, and you can throw down an anchor, go into a circular search pattern, and find out what that object is—if it's not buried beneath the sediments.

Well, the Lanhams had used this technique, coupled with historic research in local libraries, such as the Bancroft at

UC Berkeley and the National Maritime Museum in San Francisco, and they had located dozens of shipwrecks that, in many cases, had never been located before. I was enthralled with the idea of being able to do that myself. Steve and I got together with the Lanhams on a couple of other informal occasions. They had questions for us about our abalone-diving exploits, and, as I recall, I told them that if there was ever an opportunity to dive with them on a local shipwreck, we'd be very interested. That made them kind of draw back a little bit. They said that they would have to talk about that. So, Steve and I didn't know where we stood with them, but we knew we wanted to start finding shipwrecks and to be the first to discover them.

We were ready for a new challenge. We had done just about everything you could do free diving for abalone and fish, and we were looking for new frontiers. We were considered expert divers, and we thought we had enough experience to get involved in shipwreck diving. Then, several months later, Bruce Lanham called me at the spur of the moment because his brother, Bob, was unable to dive with him that day. Also in my favor was that I happened to have a 17 ft. Boston Whaler. Bruce was interested in going to a Gold Rush–period steamer outside the Golden Gate, and since the ocean was a little choppy, he preferred not to run out there alone in his inflatable. Bruce said he'd bring the hookah gear and the airhose if I'd supply the boat—and Steve was welcome to come along too.

So, Steve and I both played hooky. We both called in sick at our jobs and met Bruce early the next morning. There was one other complication. I'd just had a vasectomy two days before and had been told not to get in the water for at least week to two. I explained the situation to Bruce,

and his response was "No problem, I'll bring a dry suit for you." I had never been in a dry suit before, so I just said, "Great." I didn't want to miss this opportunity, and I certainly didn't want to act like I was going to wink out on him and not take him up on what might be his only invitation. So, on the morning of 15 December 1979, we headed out through the Gate and headed north. Bruce pulled out their portable magnetometer, for which they had custom made a plexiglass case as a splash housing. Then he took his bearings. He had sketched prominent landmarks on the shore. His procedure was to head straight in on one bearing, and when we hit the intersection where the other bearing lined up he would start using the magnetometer. When he got his reading we tossed the anchor. Bruce was the first in the water. He verified we were on the wreck site and moved the anchor a few feet to get it into a secure location.

Bruce then commenced to suit me up in a Viking dry suit. This was a suit with no zippers in it, and you had to get into it through the neck seal. This seal had to be tight enough that it would not admit water, and yet you had to stretch it far enough apart to get your whole body inside, feet first. Well, I'm taller than the Lanham brothers, but not as heavy in the torso, so there was a lot of loose material around the waist once I'd finally struggled into the suit. "Bruce, is this the way it's supposed to fit?" I asked. "No," he said, "let me pull that up for you." And before I could stop him, he came behind me, grabbed the suit at my waist and pulled up very sharply. Well, I almost jumped out of the boat in pain because he made a direct hit on that most tender spot of my vasectomy. When I finally calmed down and saw the light of day again we commenced our dive.

It was fascinating. The *Lewis*, lost in April 1853, was a steamer carrying 350 passengers from Nicaragua to San Francisco, and among its passengers was a Captain Sherman, who, later, during the Civil War, became famous as General Sherman of Sherman's March. In 1853 he had taken a leave of absence from the Army and was coming out to San Francisco to investigate the prospects for opening a branch of the St. Louis Bank.

My friend, Richard Tooker, later wrote an article about this, in which he argues that Sherman may have been the first person to do freediving on the California coast, because, after the ship sunk, he made a couple of little dives down into the ships' pantry to recover some crackers and some tins of sardines. Sherman actually experienced two shipwrecks in one day because, when he came ashore in Bolinas, he negotiated with the owner of a small sailing scowl to take him to San Francisco, and that vessel sank too.

The *Lewis* wrecked because they ran short of coal. As a consequence, they had to break-up the ship's spars and other spare wooden things to burn as fuel. Apparently, when they switched to wood it provided more heat and thus more steam than the inferior coal they had been using, and, running faster, the captain actually missed the turn to San Francisco, which was socked in with fog. They just shot past the entrance to San Francisco Bay and ended up 14 or 15 mi. too far north. That was where the lookout on the bow suddenly reported breakers ahead, and before they could reverse her the *Lewis* was in on the rocks.

The *Lewis* was an interesting vessel. It was screw driven as opposed to a paddle wheeler. It had been originally equipped with a unique propeller built by Richard Loper in Philadelphia in 1851. Unfortunately, that propeller was damaged during its maiden voyage across the Atlantic and replaced in Liverpool with a standard English propeller. Consequently, the propeller at the wreck site was not the original Loper propeller. When it was my turn to dive down I couldn't, at first, see very much, but because of my experience diving for abalone in poor visibility, nearly "black water," I was able to locate the main propeller shaft and follow that up to the engine. I was amazed at the size of the engine. It was probably 8 ft. across, close to 8 ft. high, and maybe 15 ft. long. Within an iron, grid-like structure I could see the large flat flywheel and the lignum vitae [ironwood] gears coming off to engage the driveshaft. It was just fascinating. That was my introduction to shipwreck diving, and I was as much enthralled by the history as I was by the wrecked remains.

That was where Steve and I caught the bug for diving on shipwrecks. It also started the long relationship with the Lanham brothers that we still maintain today. Bruce and Bob are no longer as active as they used to be. At one time they used literally every spare opportunity researching, locating, or diving on shipwrecks. These days, although Bruce and Bob still dive shipwrecks, they've both settled down with families and no longer have a lot of time to devote to it. More recently, Bruce has started collecting nautical books, in particular those describing the early days of diving, and he has quite a collection. We've remained friends, and I probably still talk with those guys once a month.

So, Steve and I decided we wanted to become wreck divers. We purchased a magnetometer, put together a hookah system, and assembled all the gear commonly used to locate and dive on shipwrecks.

DAVID BULLER

You might say the Lanham brothers introduced us to it and were our initial teachers. Then Steve and I went on from there.

When we first met the Lanhams, their goal was to cover their equipment costs by salvaging metals, mainly copper and brass, off the vessels they found. To a certain extent, in our very early days of diving with them, Steve and I did the same thing. We would look for drift pins, large copper spikes used for fastening the main timbers on a wooden vessel. We'd also look for copper and brass valves and lead piping. Steve and I soon lost interest in that. After delivering our first load of scrap metal to Schnitzer Steel in Oakland, we found that the return was almost nothing for all the effort spent in retrieving heavy objects from the bottom of the ocean, floating them to the surface with lift bags, hauling them into your boat, carrying them over a sandy or gravely beach to your van, then finally delivering them to the recycling plant.

It just wasn't worth it. Moreover, I already realized, at that early date, that the people who came after us would never see those particular pieces of metal because we'd stripped them off the wreck. Steve and I were more interested in locating and exploring new sites than in hauling pieces away. As a consequence we quickly changed our focus from picking up scrap metals to researching and attempting to rediscover the locations of forgotten shipwrecks. Our interest had shifted to making new discoveries with the hope of bringing the awareness of those discoveries to other people.

The Lanhams interest in shipwrecks was so all-consuming that they had contacted various groups and individuals around the country that were expert in various realms of maritime history. They were in contact with maritime historians on the East Coast in order to get more information about some of the vessels that ultimately wrecked on the north coast of California. They also made contact with the California Wreck Divers, a club very active in Southern California, and it was through that contact that they met Cliff Craft. Cliff was a self-taught wreck diver who, prior to becoming a structural-steel building inspector, had for quite a few years worked as both a commercial abalone diver and as a commercial diver doing underwater inspection and maintenance for groups such as the Edison Power Company.

At that time I was still working at UC Berkeley, and it was quite common for me to fly around the country presenting seminars to groups of teachers and educators on the curriculum materials we were developing. One day I happened to mention to the Lanhams that I was going down to Long Beach State to give a presentation to schoolteachers. "Well," they said, "while you're down there why don't you stop in and visit Cliff." So that's how I met Cliff Craft.

Not long after Steve and I dove on the *Lewis* with the Lanhams, I began developing my own list of lost wrecks that I would like to locate. One of those wrecks, that to my knowledge still has not been located, was called the *Prince Alfred*. It was lost a little bit north of the Golden Gate, off Tennessee Cove. Being an employee at the University of California, I had access to the Bancroft Library Archives and a stack pass at the main library, so I literally immersed myself in research on shipwrecks. I developed a list of vessels I wanted to find, and as I worked and learned more I added more ships to it. I started by researching vessels like the *Prince Alfred* and the *Los Angeles*.

We were also interested in the *Natalie*, a sailing vessel lost in Monterey Bay in 1837. At that time there was a rumor, now disproved, that the *Natalie* had transported Napoleon to his final imprisonment. Well, by early 1981, when I went on that business trip to Long Beach and met with Cliff Craft, I had already accumulated a lot of research on wrecks and on the *Prince Alfred* in particular.

I met Cliff at his home, and it turned out the *Prince Alfred* was one of his pet vessels to try to locate. Cliff had been diving on ships in the Southern California area for over 10 years, and if I was impressed with the Lanham's nautical bedroom, I was even more impressed with Cliff's study. Cliff particularly liked portholes, and he appeared to have 50 of them on display in a room that wasn't much bigger than a small bedroom. In his garage and backyard he had piles of other objects recovered from shipwrecks. When Cliff discovered I had an interest in the *Prince Alfred* and that I'd found information he hadn't seen, he was, of course, very anxious to see it. So, Cliff and I started sharing information, and that's how I established my friendship with him. Cliff, like the Lanhams, is a very resourceful individual and a strong diver. But the unique thing about all these individuals was that nobody taught any of them, and maybe that's why there developed a kind of kinship among us.

It was shortly after I met Cliff that Bob and Bruce Lanham decided to buy a 37 ft. trimaran, provision it, and rework it to cruise the Caribbean looking for Spanish shipwrecks. On their way south to the Panama Canal they planned to pull in off of Baja, at Magdalena Bay, to attempt to locate the wreck site of the *Independence*, a Gold Rush–era vessel lost in February of 1853. There was a tremendous loss of life

on the *Independence*, the tragic story of a vessel burning to the water line, with passengers having to decide whether to burn or hurl themselves overboard.

A group of us, including Cliff, agreed to rendezvous with the Lanhams from shore, and their vessel would be our floating hotel. The Lanhams planned to moor just inside of Punta Tosca in Magdalena Bay near Santa Margarita Island. In that location we could dive not only on the *Independence*, but also on the *Indiana* and, perhaps most exciting to our group, the *Colombia*, which was lost during the 1920s with a load of gold and silver bars. Of course after it sank the gold and silver was salvaged, but there were one or two gold bars missing, and this excited everybody.

Not long after Bob and Bruce sailed for Baja, I flew down to LA, where Cliff picked me up, and, together with Paul Sheppard and one other person who worked for Scubapro, we drove south to meet the Lanhams. I brought my metal detector. I was able to break it down to fit into a 5 gal. bucket with a lid. I thought I might be able to locate metal objects that had washed up on Independence Beach. Paul and Cliff were more interested in retrieving portholes from the *Colombia*.

We were down there for about 10 days. They had previously verified, by aerial surveillance, the most likely beach. There were two possibilities. I think Cliff may have made a previous trip down there and had actually located skeletal remains exposed on one of the beaches. The narratives of the survivors of the *Independence* stated that they buried many of the dead in makeshift graves high up on the sandy beach.

That trip to Baja really inspired me to get seriously involved in wreck diving. It was just like paradise to be able to dive all

DAVID BULLER

day long, either for game or on the wrecks, and we had a choice of three different wrecks. At night we all ate the fresh lobster and fish we had captured that day and then talked about shipwrecks until we went to bed.

We each had theories explaining why there wasn't any physical evidence of the *Independence*. One theory was that it had come aground so close to shore that it was totally sanded out and buried. In fact, we found brass spikes and other debris from the wreck concreted like a conglomerate onto rocks exposed at low tide. In our minds that verified that the remains were probably in the surf zone and would, as a result, probably never be effectively dove. That was a disappointment, but we at least felt we solved the mystery of where the *Independence* was.

After we all got home to our respective locations, the Lanhams continued to locate new wrecks, and Steve and I took the initiative to do the same. Our goal was to dive all of the major Gold Rush vessels on our list. These included the *Lewis*; the *Tennessee*; the *Independence*; the *Winfield Scott*, off of Anacapa Island; the *Yankee Blade*, lost in 1854 a little bit north of Point Arguello; and finally, the most exciting of all, the *Brother Jonathan* off of Crescent City. We did locate two vessels south of Fort Ross. One was a small steamer, the *Whitelaw*, owned by Captain Whitelaw, who from 1875 through the 1920s gained renown as an underwater salvager of lost wrecks along the Pacific coast.

I was interested in the history of diving, and the *Whitelaw* was a diving salvage vessel on which they had reported the loss of one complete diving dress. I imagined there being a hard hat and a suit down there, and I wanted to find it. With my newly purchased magnetometer I was able

to locate the *Whitelaw* and, in fact, found one sole of a diver's dress along with a few other things. I had also learned that the *Whitelaw* was lost while she was in the process of salvaging the *Joseph Spinney*, a large sailing vessel bound from New York to San Francisco carrying general merchandise.

As a consequence, Steve and I were able to track down and locate the *Joseph Spinney* as well. That vessel had an amazing assortment of cargo items on board: hardware for Victorian houses, including ornate doorknobs and window fasteners; marbles; grinding wheels; bottles of English ale and champagne; and bottles of Carter's ink that still had ink in them.

During this time, while I was developing the expertise for locating shipwrecks using my magnetometer, I didn't realize that I was developing an expertise to locate virtually anything magnetic under water—that is, if it was large enough and the water wasn't too deep. It was my skill with the magnetometer that hastened my involvement in commercial diving.

About that time, Dutra Construction, the largest barge and dredging company in northern California, wanted to locate some moorings they had lost in a part of the Sacramento River delta known as False River. These were large iron anchors that had been moored with heavy wire cable to steel mooring balls floating on the surface. Apparently, some local kids with high-powered rifles shot the mooring balls full of holes, and they sank. Dutra wanted to recover their property. They had been unsuccessful dragging for them and were ready to try some other method. Well, when the Lanhams got wind of this, they told Dutra to contact me. So Steve and I came out with our portable magnetometer. We had bought it from the Lanhams, so they didn't have one in house or they would have done the work themselves.

We successfully located Dutra's mooring anchors, so, a year or two later, when a dike broke and Bradford Island flooded, Dutra contacted us to locate and help recover the farmer's equipment. Over about a week we were able to locate most of the major pieces of machinery, rig them with pulling harnesses, and with a big crank barge we pulled up all of the submerged items. When we finished, it was hilarious. It looked like a used car lot of farm equipment on a floating barge. We recovered about a dozen different items, including harrows, generators, Caterpillar tractors, and a diesel pickup truck.

We also had a couple of harrowing experiences diving in that black water. There was a pickup truck down there from which a father and son narrowly escaped when the dike broke. As the wall of water had rushed in, it knocked the truck off the raised road into a ditch. The father had some of his most valuable possessions in that truck. He had been a champion rodeo rider, and he wanted us to find his silver-adorned prize saddle and his favorite silver spurs. I was able to locate all 10 pairs of his spurs, the saddle blanket, his toolbox, his outboard engine, and just about everything else, except that saddle. I suppose it was buoyant enough that it just floated out into the delta.

Well, when the pick-up truck was washed off the road, it had taken out a barbed wire fence, and the wire was all tangled up around the truck. They, of course, hadn't mentioned this to the guy at Dutra Construction with whom I was dealing. The deeply submerged truck was still standing like a lean-to against the side of the ditch, and there was space underneath. I swam underneath looking for the saddle and got trapped in the barbed wire. It took me nearly half an hour before I freed myself. The job at Bradford Island was a big one, and it formally established the relevance of the magnetometer skills I had developed as a wreck diver to contract work in the commercial-diving trade.

About this time I was contacted by Jim Normandie ("Jimmie Sierra") of White's Electronics. Jimmy was involved in metal detecting and had been contacted by a reporter from the *Chronicle* who wanted to do an article on the top 10 treasures in northern California. I gave him some information on the *Lewis*, the *Rio de Janeiro*, and some steamers that were supposed to have been carrying some wealth aboard when they were lost.

It was through that article that Jimmy and I were contacted by the owner of one of those treasures. This was the famous treasure box lost at a gold-mining community in the central California foothills outside of Merced. For years and years this landowner had heard stories about this treasure box, and she wanted to lay the rumors to rest because she periodically had problems with people vandalizing her property trying to find it. So she contracted with Jimmy and me to locate it.

We went out to the site and interviewed Vern Johnson, the last individual still alive who actually had his hands on the box. As he told it, around 1940 he had been working on a giant electric-powered gold dredger, and somehow it picked up this huge iron box which apparently came down from the hopper with such an impact that it shook the whole dredge. They were using the hopper to separate the fines and the associated gold from the large scrap rock that was then passed onto a conveyor belt to be dumped at the rear of the dredge, leaving long furrows of gravel

DAVID BULLER

tailings behind. Well, Vern had grabbed hold of the box and tried to lift it off the conveyor belt. He was a 6 ft. Swede with a tremendous amount of strength, and when he couldn't budge it he knew it was loaded with something very heavy. Meanwhile, the conveyor dumped it off the dredge.

They finally stopped the dredge and attempted to relocate the box with a hook used to get large boulders off the belt. They eventually hooked the box, but when they tried to pull it up it straightened the hook. They left the hook in the water to mark the location, but the next day the foreman came on the job and said: "We can't be bothered with this sort of thing, just keep working."

So, the iron box was buried over, and that's when they got the story that during the Gold Rush period there had been a Chinese community outside of this gold-mine town with a Chinese money man in residence. He had a large iron box or safe, and the Chinese workers would bring their money to him to hold until they had enough to send back to China. Well, he was accumulating this money, and some gringos in town heard about it and went to rob him. They tortured the guy, but he refused to tell where the box was hidden, so they killed him, the box disappeared, and no one was ever able to find it. Well, the dredgers decided that was the box that they had had their hands on, so about 1948 they put together an expedition to find it. Vern Johnson, together with the foreman and a number of partners spent the phenomenal sum of $5,000 to bring in a dragline crane with a huge bucket designed to dig down and bury itself when dragged. They had some of the old charts showing where they'd dredged back in 1940, and, with the help of Vern and the foreman, the crew pinpointed the likely spot, but they used up all their money without finding the box. So the rumor was started, and, of course, it was embellished over the years until Jimmy and I were approached to find it.

This project became almost a one-year ordeal. The proton magnetometer was not sufficient to do the job because there was so much interference from other metal objects. Moreover, the site was now surrounded by electrical wires, and we were forever digging up objects that we were not interested in. I contacted Geometrics in Sunnyvale, who manufactured the "mag," and learned that they just developed a new instrument called a "Memory-Mag." It had its own microprocessor to record all the readings along with the time that they were taken. It was set up with what they called a vertical gradiometer option—two sensors stacked in a vertical axis separated by 4–6 ft. When the mag is triggered, two readings, first the bottom sensor and then the top sensor, are taken about a second apart. Since both sensors are mounted on the same vertical staff, any lateral magnetic interference affects the two sensors about the same. You then subtract the reading of one sensor from the other, thereby negating all of the lateral magnetic interference, thus emphasizing the reading directly below the sensors. We rented that instrument for a month and were able to systematically survey the quarter-mile-square area pinpointed by Vern.

It proved to be the wrong area. At first it was a carnival. People would come and watch. They had hotdog vendors there, but after months and months at this the locals lost interest and we were left alone. After reanalyzing the old daily-dredge progress charts and some aerial photographs of the dredge tailings, Jimmy decided to shift the search to a new location, where we finally got a signal that had the right parameters. At that point we brought back the guy who was donating his heavy equipment to do the excavation work. There were only three of us, and we recovered the box.

It was an old Wells Fargo strongbox. But, unfortunately, as soon as we brought it up we could see that there was a real problem. It had apparently been hit by the drag bucket in 1948. We could see marks where the teeth had penetrated through the lid, and the force of the bucket had completely flattened the box, blowing out the sides. In the lock-mechanism of the box we found a gold nugget. There were also fragments of glass, some silver coins, and a few Chinese coins of brass that we were able to metal detect in the gravel and sand that came up with the box. We concluded that the gold dust and the nuggets had been in glass jars. We then pulled up several buckets of gravel from that spot, but didn't find anything else of value. Clearly, back in 1948 the drag crane had grabbed the strongbox and pulled it some distance, and we were faced with having to literally dig up the entire area to pinpoint the spot. It was not logical to do that, so that was the end of the project. At that point some of the locals decided that we should be called the "Legend Busters." We had taken this wonderful legend and deflated it with reality. But we had at least solved the mystery.

From that experience, not only did I get more involved in shipwreck diving, but through Jimmy, who is a clearinghouse for people all over the world who want to try to locate things lost underwater, I've become involved in some rather exotic hunts.

For Walter Kurilchyk, an aviation buff in Southern California, I've searched for a Russian four-engine airplane off of the North Slope of Alaska. For a woman at Seal Beach I've made two expeditions to Papua New Guinea trying to find the B-26 in which her uncle was lost during World War II. I've been involved in the search for Montezuma's horde in Mexico, Japanese treasure from World War II in the Philippines, and in the last two-and-a-half years I've been involved with a nonprofit group called Pacific Interspace Ventures.

Employing one of my magnetometers for that group last August, we were able to locate the Japanese trawler that George Bush is credited with sinking during World War II. In fact, we already have a trip scheduled this summer [1994] to return to Palau in order to locate the TBM [a single-engine bomber] in which George Bush's wing commander was lost and to locate two B-24's and a U.S. destroyer also lost in the area. The idea is to produce documentaries on these discoveries that might be sold to a public-television network in order to help finance more expeditions in the future.

That gives you an idea of the changes that have occurred in my career from when I initially got involved in diving local wrecks with the Lanham brothers and what that has ultimately led me to today. I'm now one of the few individuals in this country called in to do magnetometer searches for underwater targets.

Even before making the expedition to Baja with the Lanhams and Cliff Craft, they were already talking about a wreck site up in the Mendocino area that had been visited by members of the Southern California Wreck Divers Club. It was a sailing vessel from the Gold Rush period with some interesting things on board. We were told it had cannons, cannonballs, and evidence of small firearms. Moreover, it had a lot of ceramics on board, particularly traditional blue-on-white Chinese

DAVID BULLER

porcelain, and lots of glass beads. Steve and I became quite interested in that wreck. We were already going up that way for abalone diving, and we hadn't yet dove on any shipwrecks in the Mendocino area.

Well, the Lanhams told us they couldn't divulge the exact location of the wreck because they had a trust arrangement with the Southern California Wreck Divers and had agreed not to turn anyone else on to the site. "All we can tell you," they said, "is that they launch out of Caspar Cove and it's located in one of the first coves to the south."

As I recall, it was during a Labor Day weekend that we made our first trip to the *Frolic* wreck site. It was a tradition for our dive club to schedule a Labor Day outing during which we would all stay at Van Damme State Park and head out from there to various destinations for recreational game diving. Steve and I dove with the club on Saturday, and on Sunday morning, equipped with a magnetometer, we headed out on our own to try and locate the site of the *Frolic*. We went first to the local saloon, the Caspar Inn, which we figured would be a good source of information. We talked to some of the locals there, and they confirmed there was a wreck in a cove just south of Caspar anchorage that the locals referred to as the "pottery wreck." When one fellow said "pottery" I asked if they knew anything else about it. "No," he said, "there's just a lot of pottery pieces on it." "You mean things like plates?" I asked. "Yeah, I guess so," he said.

So, the next day, Steve and I headed south out of Caspar Cove. For a short distance we saw absolutely nothing you could mistake for a cove or indentation. Then we came to a point where we started seeing private homes, and just beyond there was an indentation. Although it was a

rather rough day, we decided to enter the cove, and as soon as we got on the lee side of some outer rocks I turned on my magnetometer. We went well into the center of the cove and started searching along the southern wall, zigzagging back and forth, but we got no readings. "Well, this is strange," I thought. "With the prevailing winds out of the northwest and these wave patterns and currents this is where you'd expect the wreck to be."

Well, after a bit, I said to Steve: "Just for the heck of it, let's try the north side." It wasn't long after we went over there that I started getting some minor activity. I made a couple of free dives over the side and found what appeared to be a few pieces of scrap iron. As we proceeded closer to the north side, I started picking up big pieces of pottery. It was almost like following a bread trail someone had left to bring you into a site. If you went in the right direction you encountered more pieces of bread, while if you went in the wrong direction, they thinned out and you saw less and less of them.

So, by crisscrossing and free diving over the area and following the pottery, we were able to hone right in over the main wreckage, where there were literally hundreds of broken pieces of ceramics littering the bottom. Then we saw the main ballast pile, and there was no way you could mistake that iron ballast for anything else. Even though it was encrusted with a thin layer of purple coralline algae, it was obviously manmade, and when we tried to move a piece, it was obvious that it was metal.

The Lanhams had told us the site had been heavily dove by the Southern California Wreck Divers, and that they had recovered a lot of artifacts. They had even used small explosives to break up the ballast in order to dredge around it and toward the bow area of the vessel. They had found some Spanish dollars, which were the universal trade coin during the Gold Rush, some copper East India Company half-cents, and a few gold buttons and fragments of gold filigree jewelry. The gold was what caught our interest. And even though those fellows may have picked over the wreck, Steve and I had the impression that no one was as thorough as we were.

Having discovered the wreck's location, I immediately tried to determine the main axis of the vessel. I started moving back from the bow area, which I thought was obvious because of the anchors and the capstan, towards what I thought would be the stern. It was then that I found about an inch of small-link brass chain protruding from a crevice. I started pulling out the chain while fanning the crevice, and that's when I discovered a tiny ornate serpent head in gold filigree. It looked like a dragon, and the first thing that flashed through my mind was the movie, *The Deep*, which at that time [1980–81] was still fresh in my mind. In that film there's a great scene where they find a dragon pendant that had belonged to the "Queen," thus verifying the identity of the vessel. Well, when I found this little dragon, I came up out of the water just like he did in the movie and yelled at Steve, not realizing that he wasn't on the surface. I had to pull on his hose to bring him to up. It was at that point we realized that all of the things of interest had not already been picked up.

Steve and I got so fired up after our success on that first trip that we returned two or three times within the course of a month. Sometimes it was only a day trip, which was truly crazy. We both worked in the Bay Area, and it would take us close to three hours to drive up there. Moreover, when we finally got to Caspar Cove it was a physically demanding task to unload all the dive gear and walk it a hundred yards across the beach through soft sand to the water. Then we had to unload, set up, and inflate the rubber boat, drag it to the water, and carry the outboard engine on our shoulders. By the time we got to the wreck site we could only dive it for a few hours before coming back to the beach and repeating the whole process in order to drive home. We were so fired up that we actually did that a number of times.

Our impression, from talking with the Lanhams, who were relaying what they had learned about the site from Cliff Craft and Larry Pierson of the California Wreck Divers Club, was that the site had been extensively worked. Consequently we really didn't have high expectations for finding anything on it. Moreover, when we talked with the fellows at the saloon and discovered it had been dove since the 1960s, we really expected very little to be left. So, when we first located the site, we were quite impressed with the items that were still there, like the vertical capstan in the bow area and the congealed mound of anchor chain. Although you couldn't distinguish many individual iron links, that mound still stood a good 2 or 3 ft. off the bottom and was a good 6 or 7 ft. across. It was, however, positioned over a flat table-like rock that made it appear larger than it really was.

I also recall the massive pile of cast-iron ballast blocks. Most of it was still congealed together, but there were quite a few individual pieces that had been disturbed with their coralline algae coating relatively recently broken, and we could actually see some active iron oxide in those areas. Those iron bars were so massively heavy that initially we were unable to budge even a short piece. Later on we moved some of

DAVID BULLER

them using large crowbars and float lift bags in order to determine if there was anything of interest underneath them.

The Lanhams had told me the vessel was about a hundred feet long. So, measuring from the vertical capstan I tried to retrace the main axis of the vessel hoping to identify where the rudder would have been. As I worked my way back from the capstan I started finding things. There were hundreds of pieces of ceramic shards and miscellaneous bits and pieces of metal. It was then that I saw the small brass chain protruding from a crevice and found the gold dragon's head.

When we began to go through the ballast bars one of our first major discoveries was part of a leather shoe protruding from a mass of concreted iron oxide. For us it was just phenomenal to find something organic preserved in perfect condition. The shoe turned out to be almost as stiff as the iron concretion surrounding it. Lying amongst the iron ballast blocks we also found a tightly coiled roll of quarter-inch hemp rope perfectly preserved in a heavy coating of iron oxide.

We were rather surprised that there was still so much to be found. We were also surprised that the iron ballast bars had not been disturbed more. Moving toward the stern, we encountered an area we assumed to be the central portion of the vessel, including the kitchen and eating area for the men. This was the area where the California Wreck Divers had found some silverware, coins, and many firearms. We could tell that some of this area had been worked very heavily because we could see depressions where they had dredged right down to solid rock substrate, while only a short distance away areas would be filled to the top with loose sediments from their dredging. Right next to these dredged

areas were places where the surface was still hard and all congealed together and obviously had not been disturbed. Although there was widespread evidence that the site had been heavily dove and picked over, there appeared to be an equally large area that had yet to be investigated.

The discovery that large portions of the wreck site had not been heavily disturbed excited Steve and me, but the defining event was finding that gold filigree dragon's head during our cursory inspection of the wreck site and realizing there were still not only large items to be found, but a lot of small items as well.

Steve and I had had equipped ourselves with a small dredge, with a hundred gallon per minute pump, driven by the same motor we used to drive the compressor for our breathing hose. So we started "high grading." We literally started going through the tailings left by the people who had dredged before. It was easy to identify those loose sediments because in other areas everything was all compacted and obviously hadn't been disturbed. So Steve and I started re-dredging, going through what the others had already gone through, and after getting down just a few inches we discovered there were many things that had passed through their dredges. The very first day on site, as we were going through those dredge tailings, we started picking up tiny pieces of gold filigree. We immediately found a heavy concentration of beads, ceramic shards, and remnants of spikes and other ship fastenings, such as eye screws and bolts. We also found pieces of lead shot, both round and flat-cylindrical in shape, rims of buckets, and large mounds of conglomerate containing white beads, dark green bottle glass, and a few pieces of a red firebrick-kind of ceramic. We picked up some of those mounds of conglomerate and put them into the boat in order to go through them at a later date.

One of the more interesting discoveries that we made early on was portions of wood-framed windows with shell panes in place of glass. Only later did we learn from Tom Layton that one of the items on board was a Chinese-manufactured prefabricated house with oyster-shell windows. We also found checkers, hundreds of ceramic beads, a carved crystal stamp for sealing envelopes with wax, flatware forks and spoons, numerous pieces of Chinese bowls and saucers, tall green glass ale bottles, and great numbers of brass latches, pulls, and hinges from the furniture and trunks that they had onboard as cargo.

As we high graded the dredge tailings of the California Wreck Divers, we'd pick up whatever items caught our fancy. The things that didn't were simply allowed to pass through and become part of our dredge tailings. After re-dredging the tailings we moved toward the vicinity of the chain mound in the forward section of the wreck. It was there, adjacent to the chain mound, that my ex-wife Noreen found a sterling-silver tinder box in almost perfect condition. It was shaped like a scallop shell, and the flint and wadding made of newsprint were still inside. We could see the individual letters of newsprint when we first opened it. It probably was exposed during some of the dredging operations by previous groups. When Noreen saw it she almost passed it up because it looked like a dead clam, completely blackened and sooty. Nevertheless, there was a glint of something that caught her eye, so she picked it up, rubbed it, and that's when the shine of the sterling silver came through. That was the only thing Noreen ever picked up from that wreck site, but what a find!

We were able to dig out the sediments beneath the chain mound and discovered that it was, in effect, an arch of congealed chain partially supported by a rock. While dredging beneath this arch we came across portions of wooden cases that the beer had been shipped in. We could still see the corners where the sides had been dovetailed together. On one piece we could still read some of the wording on the outside. It was here, in the vicinity of the chain mound, that we also found the greatest concentration of dark green beer-bottle glass.

There were times during our dredging that about the only loose sediments in front of the dredge nozzles were hundreds of little ceramic beads, as they were a little bit heavier than the iron-oxide-stained black sand in which they were lying. When using a dredge nozzle to "high grade," you never push the nozzle into the substrate. You hold it a safe distance from the area you are investigating and gently fan the deposits with your hand. In that manner the loose sediments are lifted up high enough to be caught in the current being drawn to the suction nozzle and carried away. That way there is never a chance of sucking up something you didn't see, and you can visually review everything that passes into the dredge nozzle. In the case of the beads, it got to the point that we could literally reach out and take handfuls of them.

We soon lost interest in the beads, and instead of picking them up we fanned them hard enough to set them in motion so they would be sucked into the dredge. Heavier items were usually found at the very bottom of an area we were fanning. So, when we finally fanned down to the hardened substrate, it was there at the bottom that we found gold filigree jewelry, lead shot, brass spikes, drawer pulls,

DAVID BULLER

and other furniture fittings. Those heavier items at the bottom were the reward for all the work we had done to get there.

One day, while we were dredging soft spots, Steve happened to investigate some conglomerate he found high up on a rock. When he chipped at it with the tip of his rock pick, he suddenly saw the gleam of gold. Steve continued chipping away and removed a piece of conglomerate that was about 3 in. long and a couple of inches thick, and at spots along its whole length we could see tiny glints of gold filigree. We thought he had found a mass of congealed fragments, but when he finally got it out, first by chipping and then in a muriatic-acid bath, it turned out to be a single dangling pendant, 2 in. long and exquisite in its complexity.

Some of the more interesting pieces of jewelry we found were earrings with a gold outer rim inset with a dark stone and hooked for pierced ears. Personally, I thought the dragon serpent I picked up was the most interesting piece of jewelry we recovered, but I'm sure Steve would say it was the pendant and some of the gold buttons he picked up. Unfortunately, most of the gold items we found were severely damaged. The filigree jewelry was so delicate that it took very little force to move it about and crush it. About a year or two later I made a trip to Boston on university business and took the opportunity to drive out to the Peabody Museum at Salem. I noticed that they had some fine examples of Chinese silver filigree jewelry on display, so I asked one of the curators if they had any gold filigree in their collection. He reported that they would love to have some on display, but they had none in their collection. At that point I realized that the gold filigree jewelry we had found might have some real value because of its rarity. If an institution as well known as the Peabody, with their extensive collection of artifacts from the great Age of Sail and the China trade had none, then there probably weren't too many examples on display anywhere.

At that point I thought that someday it might be worthwhile to sell some of it. In fact, I asked at the Peabody whether they might be interested in acquiring some, and they came back with a very positive response—that they would love to have some donated. When I queried them further about the possibility of their buying some of the specimens we had recovered, they replied that their collections were all donated, and the patrons who donated received handsome tax write offs. I was actually a little disappointed to hear that because I thought there might be a possibility for finally getting something of value for our shipwreck efforts. Later, when I told my brother, he said that he wasn't willing to sell—that the gold meant more to him because of our experiences acquiring it than the few dollars it might bring. I hadn't expected that from Steve, and I was kind of impressed with his response.

We continued to dive the wreck as frequently as good weather would permit, and, as it turned out, that was not all that frequent. The wreck was in a very exposed location and was at times a very treacherous site to dive. It lay on a sloping bottom at depths ranging from 15 to 25 ft. at high tide to as little as 8 to 15 ft. at lower tides. Because of its exposed location on the coast we needed almost flat calm conditions to effectively dive it. There were a number of occasions when we started out diving under flat conditions and the winds and wave action suddenly sprang up. Twice we had our inflatable boat banged around on the rocks and nearly washed ashore. Despite that we were able to dive the *Frolic* on probably six or eight separate trips. We would average two days of diving with maybe four to six hours of bottom time on each trip. We soon made the transition from working the old dredge tailings to working any spot where we could find undisturbed areas. Then, when Steve found the gold pendant embedded in conglomerate, we started looking for more conglomerate, particularly near the forward end of the ballast pile. It was at that point that Cliff Craft joined us for the first of two joint dive trips on the *Frolic*.

Cliff had previously dove on the site. I think he and Paul Shephard had first come up on one of Larry Pierson and Pat Gibson's trips. Steve and I talked with him about the problem of moving the ballast. We described trying to move it manually using rock picks, chisels, and lift bags, and working a whole day to move only one piece. Cliff suggested carefully placing primer cord and detonating it to give just enough of a jolt to create fracture planes along the edges of the individual ballast blocks. On the subsequent trip Cliff brought the primer cord, set it off, and it had the desired effect. We were able to move 8 or 10 blocks, beneath which we found some very interesting items. Cliff found the remains of a hasp-and-lock mechanism from what he was hoping would be a small box full of valuables. That didn't turn out to be the case.

I suspect that the Pierson group concentrated their explosive work in the area of the galley where they found the firearms and portholes. I believe that even today there are portions of the main ballast area that have not been disturbed and hold promise for further investigation. If extensive explosive work was indeed done by the Pierson group, enough time had passed that by the time we were on the site the ballast pile again appeared natural and undisturbed, as there was a rather thick coralline encrustation over almost all of it.

One of the most exciting moments for me was when I was working an area just above the main ballast and finally got down to the bottom of a small rock crevice, which was a continuation of the crack I had been following when I first found the brass chain and gold filigree serpent head. There, at the bottom, I found what I think was a portion of the *Frolic*'s keel or false keel. It was a large timber about 12 in. across. I only exposed about 18 in. of it and didn't see any frame members or ribs coming out from it. However, I did see a brass drift pin and some copper sheeting derived from the outside of the hull. The fact that it was still there was exciting. I left it intact, removing only a small piece of planking with some sheeting nails in it and a very small piece of the sheeting. I suspect that the large timber may prove to be either a piece of the keel or one of the main structural timbers, and I hope to investigate it as part of the fieldwork when we survey the site this spring.

In those days, whenever we did a group dive on the wreck it was a cooperative effort, and during that trip nobody was to collect anything for themselves. Everything was pooled. Then, at the end of the day or at the end of the trip, we would literally divide up the artifacts, drawing lots to see who would pick first. A given diver might pick up 50 objects during an outing, most of them very minor—beads, fragments of china and glass, and small fragments of metal. Then, at the end of the trip, each of us would glance over what the others had picked up and identify any main items to go into the group pot. After a productive trip everyone might end up

DAVID BULLER

contributing three or four items to that pot.

Everything was eligible and nothing was hidden, so if anyone took an interest in something you picked up, it went into the pot. Then lots were drawn for the first round of selections, with the order reversed for the next round. That way the person who ended up drawing last on one round would draw first in the next. That's the way it went. There was no argument allowed, no matter how much you valued that particular thing. Of course when Steve and I would go on a trip by ourselves there was no need to divvy up things. We had a pact that what we picked up individually we could possess individually, but it belonged to us jointly. So if we had something of value that might later get sold, the proceeds would be split evenly between the two of us.

After our first half-dozen trips to the *Frolic*, we were suddenly no longer finding any more gold filigree jewelry or other things of interest, and we got the impression that the most productive areas had been worked out. It was about that time that I became involved with Jim Delgado and the *Tennessee* Project. I had heard that people involved with the Golden Gate National Recreation Area were interested in locating the wreck of the *Tennessee* at Tennessee Cove. So, on my initiative, I contacted Jim Delgado, explained who I was, my background, and that as part of their work they should consider doing a magnetometer survey off the beach to determine if there were any real remains of the wreck.

It turned out that Jim had a lot of desire, but no real equipment. He had been only recently certified and was still an inexperienced diver. The day that we scheduled to do the work turned out to be quite nasty.

There was a large swell running, and it was a hazardous situation. Jim, however, had contacted the local reporters, and they were all standing there on the beach with him. Apparently, Jim was going to single-handedly swim through the surf and attempt to locate the remains of the *Tennessee*. Seeing he was going to risk his own life and possibly force me to rescue him, I jumped in from my boat with my skin-diving gear. Luckily I'd had some body-surfing background, so I was able to make it to the beach and tell Jim there was absolutely no reason to enter the water that day and we should postpone it to a better time.

Subsequently I managed to conduct a magnetometer survey for Jim, pinpointing some very large magnetic anomalies and confirming there were major portions of that wreck right off the beach. After a couple of major storms removed the soft overburden of sand, we did a rather comprehensive survey for artifacts on the beach. Unfortunately, we were never able to get the necessary funding from the National Park Service to conduct an underwater excavation. I dove the site several times for the National Park Service, but never found any evidence of the wreck protruding above the sand.

Working with Jim Delgado and the National Park Service was a turning point for me. Jim's perspective on shipwrecks was entirely different than mine. I had been brought into shipwreck diving through other wreck divers. In most cases their interests were limited to finding something they could touch from the past and in making something out of it, either by selling the scrap metal or recovering something of real value. They were not really interested in sharing their discoveries with anyone except amongst themselves, and even that they did guardedly so they wouldn't give away the locations of their secrets.

Well, here I was talking to someone who was not interested in the intrinsic value of the remains, but was instead interested in their historical value. I had, of course, been going through a similar transition ever since I started researching wrecks, spending my lunch hours and afternoons at the Bancroft Library. In fact, I'd become such a regular at the Bancroft that when they closed at 5:00 I would simply have them send the microfilm upstairs to the newspaper division and I'd come back in the evening to read it.

It was from this research that I began to get a whole different sense for history. What particularly impressed me was reading about the technology employed on steamships and sailing vessels, and my old misunderstanding about 19th-century technology being backwards and primitive was exploded. I was amazed at the complexity of the technology and came to the realization that, in many ways, they had carried the technologies known to them to their highest point of development.

Today we don't even come close to utilizing steam to the extent and with the innovations employed during the 19th century. Thus, instead of ignoring that time period as I had done as a university student, I became engrossed in learning as much as I could about the maritime history of the west coast. I wanted to better understand the ships I was finding and the ships I hoped to find in the future. Moreover, as an educator, I had a desire to share some of this information, and Jim Delgado and his associate, Robert Bennett, were my first avenue for doing that.

I volunteered a lot of time, effort, and equipment to Jim, first for the *Tennessee* Project and then for the Point Reyes Shipwreck Survey. I soon discovered that Dan Lenihan, Larry Murphy, the other members of the Point Reyes Survey team, although quite experienced in working the east coast and the Great Lakes, had very little knowledge of the west coast. As a consequence, it was basically my files, originally based on the Lanhams' research and expanded by me, that provided most of the information we had for wrecks in the Point Reyes area.

Although we located the wreck sites of the *Richfield*, the *Munleon*, the *Pomo*, and the *Hartwood* during that survey, most of them would not have been found except that I knew exactly where they were from my background research in that area. Even though I had not personally dove any of those sites, I had wreck photos showing where the vessels were lost, and I was able to pinpoint each of those wreck sites. The *Pomo* was, of course, easy for anyone to find because the engine block is still visible at low tide.

During the Point Reyes survey I tried to learn as much as I could from Larry Murphy. He was in charge of the side-scan sonar and magnetometer-survey work. He utilized such things as the Del Norte microwave locating system to pinpoint our locations within a few feet. I had never before seen that kind of dynamic positioning system, and it opened my eyes to the possibility of doing much more systematic surveys than I could ever have imagined employing pure triangulation methods. I learned a great deal from that survey, but I was a little disappointed. The main goal was supposed to have been locating the *San Augustin*, the "Black Galleon," lost by Cermeño in 1595.

However, instead of focusing on that, it soon became apparent that they were mainly interested in pinpointing recent

DAVID BULLER

wreck sites so that they could police them and keep wreck divers from diving on them. Thus I found myself in the awkward position of being caught in the middle. My background was as a wreck diver, a background that Larry Murphy, Dan Lenihan, and Jim Delgado found despicable—"the rapers and pillagers of wrecks." Yet it seemed clearly apparent that were it not for the information I provided, their survey would have been far less successful than it turned out to be.

It was in conjunction with that survey that Jim and I were asked to prepare a listing of all the wrecks that had occurred in that area. I literally spent hundreds of hours researching it out, and we ended up with over 50 wrecks. I wrote the initial summaries, which Jim then edited, and we ended up coauthoring that section of the survey report.

It was during this period that I also became acquainted with John Foster of the California Department of Parks and Recreation, who is the chief underwater archaeologist for the state of California. Unlike Delgado and Lenihan, Foster realized that wreck divers had a great deal of knowledge and skill to contribute, and he was looking for ways to set up a cooperative arrangement between professional archaeologists and wreck divers. Obviously I preferred John Foster's outlook to Jim Delgado's.

That was how I got my first experience working with professional underwater archaeologists, and although I learned some things that were intriguing and interesting, I was at the same time a little put off by their black-and-white depiction of wreck divers. On the one hand they had no use for them whatsoever, yet they were more than willing to get any information they could out of me, and I was, in fact, a

wreck diver. However, despite the negative feelings these underwater archaeologists had toward wreck divers, I discovered there was a real need for the kind of information that wreck divers like myself, the Lanhams, the Cliff Crafts, and the Pat Gibsons of the world had accumulated. I also discovered that there was a real need for people with the ability to actually select a wreck, do the research, pinpoint a search area, and find it because cultural-resource administrators were being asked to manage these historical resources without the manpower and resources to do it themselves.

When Steve and I started diving the *Frolic* in 1981 it had never really been identified. No one had recovered a bell with a name or anything else that could positively identify the vessel. There was also a lot of misinformation. Palmer's 1885 *History of Mendocino County* referred to a Chilean tea-and-silk vessel. Don Marshall, author of *California Shipwrecks* (1978), listed the *Frolic* as one of the wrecks occurring on that stretch of the Mendocino County coast, and I had always been intrigued with his short description.

Marshall wrote that the survivors made their way down to Bodega, and it was their account of the redwood forests near the wreck site that triggered Meigs to finance a search party to go up there, which, in fact, verified that such forests did exist. As a consequence, Meigs had a lumber mill dismantled on the East Coast, shipped around the Horn, and assembled at what is now the town of Mendocino. Cliff and some of the other Southern California Wreck Divers and Steve and I all came to the conclusion that this wreck was the *Frolic* by the process of elimination. The things we found on the wreck were from the Gold Rush period, and we could find no record of any other vessel from that period lost on that section of coast. So it had to be the *Frolic*.

It was through volunteering time to the Golden Gate National Recreation Area and the Point Reyes Shipwreck Survey that I became aware of a strong public interest in shipwrecks and California maritime history. I also became aware that there was very little from California shipwrecks on public display, even in places like the Maritime Museum in San Francisco. When I first contacted Richard Tooker, he was a volunteer at the Maritime Museum and a source of expert information on dog-hole ports up and down the coast. I was interested in the shipping activity at these dogholes because they were frequently the sites of shipwrecks. These treacherous ports, frequented by lumber schooners, included such places on that section of the Mendocino coast as Caspar Cove, Russian Gulch, Big River, Little River, and on and on and on. It was the Lanhams who told me about Richard Tooker, and although we hadn't met in person, we would have these incredibly long phone conversations.

Richard apparently has a photographic memory about things that he's interested in. He was like an encyclopedia. He could recite song and verse for all of his dog holes, how he researched them, and what he had discovered. Richard told me that, in addition to doing volunteer work at the San Francisco Maritime Museum, he was a member of the Kelley House Historical Society in Mendocino. When I told Richard that we had been diving on a vessel that I thought was the *Frolic*—and, if so, it was the vessel that opened up Mendocino County to white settlement—he got quite excited. "Boy, if any place should have some evidence from that wreck," he said, "it should be the Kelley House!"

Well, after volunteering some time helping underwater archaeologists, I had begun to realize that there was really no point in collecting artifacts if they weren't studied further—and having them sitting in a bucket of water in my garage was not the way to do that. So I gave Richard some ceramics and a shoe from the *Frolic* and asked him to transfer them anonymously to the Kelley House. I didn't want my name revealed because I was helping the underwater archaeologists with the Point Reyes survey, and Jim Delgado was a bit fanatic about where he stood in regard to wreck diving and archaeology.

In order to protect that new relationship, I certainly didn't want to reveal myself as someone who collected artifacts, so I asked to remain anonymous, and Richard made the donation to the Kelley House. I guess it was a year or two later that Tom Layton, in his efforts to learn more about this mysterious wreck, went to the Kelley House, and Dorothy Bear told him about the anonymous donation by a sport diver. That lead Tom to Richard Tooker, who, after he asked my permission, lead Tom to me.

When Tom telephoned in the fall of 1984 I was still working at the Lawrence Hall of Science at UC Berkeley. By that time Steve and I had completed our six or eight expeditions up to the *Frolic* and had quite a collection of artifacts. I invited Tom to come to my office and see some of the things I had picked up. Tom was quite surprised at how delicate some of the items were that had survived. Among other things, I remember showing him a portion of a parasol with a wooden handle on which the brass apparatus for expanding the umbrella was still in very good condition. Tom's interest in the *Frolic* grew rather rapidly after that.

I think if Tom had phoned me two

DAVID BULLER

years before I would have been very leery, because that was a time period of increasing friction between the wreck divers with whom I was familiar and the community of archaeologists involved in the academic world. The Lanhams' younger brother, Richard, had recently been busted for removing scrap metal from the *Ohio* in the vicinity of the Cliff House off San Francisco. If Tom had called any earlier I would have been rather tentative about showing him anything.

But, by that time, after having worked with Jim Delgado, Larry Murphy, Dan Lenihan, and John Foster, and having spoken with Richard Tooker and a number of other historians, I was just about bursting to share the wealth of information and the artifacts that I had accumulated with other people. I wanted to do it in such a way that it would benefit the public's understanding and enjoyment of the tremendous underwater cultural resource lying off our coast. Looking at it from a selfish standpoint, perhaps I thought that an increased public awareness would result in greater utilization of my skills and resources to make new underwater discoveries.

So, when Tom called me, I was pretty positive about meeting with him and willing to talk openly about it. And Tom set me at ease. He made it clear that he was not a go-between and wasn't trying to nail anybody for illegally removing artifacts. You know, to be quite honest, when I got involved in wreck diving I wasn't even aware that there were any laws regarding this. I thought I was a pioneer looking out upon a new frontier that one could shape or modify to the extent that his resources allowed. I assumed that if you were the first to locate a wreck your reward should be what you picked up, just like a gold prospector. And a prospector wouldn't

be punished. If anything, he would be lauded—or so I thought.

When Tom came along I was making the transition from being a pure wreck diver to being a wreck historian, and I wanted the Feds over at the Golden Gate National Recreation Area to be aware of the resources I had for displays—not just for the Maritime Museum, but for other museums that might start giving ample space and consideration to our maritime heritage. If you look at any California history book there is that one great Gold Rush photo of the San Francisco Bay clogged with abandoned vessels, and that's about all there is. If you are lucky enough you may have read *Two Years Before the Mast* sometime during your high-school years, but short of that there is almost no consideration given to California maritime history in high school or university curricula.

The emphasis is totally on the land and not on what happened at sea—ignoring the fact that most of the early people and equipment did not come overland, but by way of the water. By the time Tom contacted me I was so taken with California's maritime history that I was ready to share and even assist him in learning more about the wreck.

Tom felt that in order to do an adequate study of the *Frolic* he would have to examine all of the collections, and to do that he would have to meet the other wreck divers. The problem was that these fellows were very nervous about public exposure and would probably be very guarded if Tom, an academic archaeologist, contacted them without prior introduction. Moreover, Tom had received some research assistance from Jim Delgado, and I knew that if Tom approached them as a friend of Jim's he would receive no cooperation at all.

Tom was unaware that Delgado had been the key man involved in busting Richard Lanham, and since that was known throughout the wreck-diving community nobody would want to cooperate with Jim. Moreover, Jim had made statements to the press that were very negative toward wreck divers and hadn't given any credit at all for the positive things that wreck divers had contributed to his projects, particularly the Point Reyes survey.

Following the bust of Richard Lanham, there had been a much larger bust of the California Wreck Diving Club. They had chartered a boat and were on a weekend outing to dive some wrecks around the Channel Islands. No one knew that there were two undercover National Park Service people on board documenting who was diving, and just before they arrived in port they were all arrested for illegal diving on protected wrecks. That, of course, polarized the wreck-diving community in Southern California against federal archaeologists.

Among those who had earlier dove the *Frolic*, Cliff Craft and Pat Gibson were arrested. Pat copped a plea because he couldn't afford the legal costs of fighting it, but I've always admired Cliff for the fact that he did fight it. Cliff confided in me that he fought it for two reasons. First, he thought it was really dirty pool to slip in two people, pose them as a married couple, and have them sleeping in the same bunk. He thought there was something immoral about that.

Second, on that particular trip he did not do any artifact collecting. He hadn't felt well, and he didn't do much diving. Yet, although he did not personally pick up a single artifact, he was "eye witnessed" by one of those two undercover agents as having removed something. Cliff knew for

a fact that he hadn't, and "how in hell can you identify one black-suited diver from another in limited visibility?" So Cliff took it on as a personal vendetta because he was being falsely accused of something. That's just the way Cliff is. If he's falsely accused of something, he will fight it even if it takes his last dime. But, by the same token, if he has done something wrong, he'll own up to it. He's probably spent $60,000–$70,000 in legal fees by now, and the case is still being contested.

I had kept in good close contact with Cliff Craft, and, in my mind, he was the key to contacting Pat Gibson, Larry Pierson, Pat Philpott, and the others from Southern California who had dove the *Frolic*. Cliff and I, by then, had grown quite close, and we trusted one another fully. In my efforts to get started in commercial diving I had relied very heavily on Cliff's extensive knowledge in that field, and whenever I had a problem I couldn't solve I'd call Cliff and we'd talk it out. So, when I decided that Tom could be trusted, that his main interest was not to blame anybody, but rather to try to put together the story of the *Frolic*, I called Cliff and asked him to clear the way for Tom to meet the others.

I should add that John Foster, an underwater archaeologist working for the California Department of Parks and Recreation, had had a very positive influence on me because he was a strong proponent of setting up some kind of a cooperative relationship between wreck divers and the state. John had often spoke of the cooperative relationship between wreck divers in England and various academic institutions there—often citing the *Mary Rose* project, where, lacking the money to hire commercial divers, virtually all of the work, from planning through diving, was done by volunteers.

In England they literally offer monetary rewards to wreck divers that share their discoveries with the government and with the academics. It may not be the fairest situation, as the rewards are quite modest, but the fact is that there is at least some monetary return if the diver desires it. But, more importantly, the wreck divers get credit where credit is due for being researchers and historians in their own right and successfully solving the mystery of locating where wrecks are. John always hoped that something similar might be set up in the state of California, where wreck divers would be encouraged to carry out their work within a professional framework, share their discoveries, and somehow be rewarded, or at least credited, for their work. I think John is still a strong proponent of that, but as yet there is no system for doing that. I still hope someday there will be.

Well, by this time the Southern California wreck-diving community had a strong mistrust of professional archaeologists, and Tom Layton clearly needed an introduction if he was to get any cooperation at all. So I telephoned Cliff. "Look, Cliff," I said, "you're certainly not going to believe this after your experiences with the authorities, but I have recently met an individual at San Jose State that has a pure interest in learning more about the *Frolic* wreck site, and, furthermore, he is willing to credit wreck divers for their contributions in furthering the knowledge of this wreck." I told Cliff I had showed Tom my collection of artifacts, that I personally trusted the guy and felt certain he was not going to finger anybody.

Since all the Southern California divers trusted Cliff, I asked him to clear the

way for Tom to talk with them. "Cliff," I said, "you guys are like a wreck-diving family. Why don't you talk to them? I know there are going to be some that won't talk to Tom, but why don't you feel them out?"

Cliff was dubious, so I suggested he meet with Tom just to chat and to get a sense of where Tom was coming from. Cliff eventually asked each of the divers whether they would mind if I disclosed their identity to Tom. Some of them said yes and some of them said no. I gave Tom the names of the ones that said yes, and that's how it all began. Tom was persistent in a very gentle diplomatic way furthering these contacts.

I've known Tom for 10 years now. He has given credit where credit was due, and my experience with him has been a good one. But my more general experience with professional underwater archaeologists is that they only say bad things about wreck divers. You very rarely hear any credit given, and when it is given it's given grudgingly. Wreck divers, on the other hand, feel that underwater archaeologists want to have sites remain totally untouched until they happen to get the time to do the work themselves. The archaeologists keep referring to the wreck sites as time capsules, as if no deterioration is occurring. But the simple fact is that most of our wreck sites along the California coast are not deepwater sites and are not covered with a protective overburden. Most of them are in very shallow water where they get disturbed every season by wave action. I can show you hundreds of items that have come off local wrecks that are so eaten away you can't even identify them anymore. Certainly those items are fast disappearing. There has to be some common ground. I think that people like John Foster, the underwater archaeologist at the State

Parks and Recreation Department should be encouraged to implement his ideas for developing a framework for cooperation between wreck divers and archaeologists.

Over the years, as Tom has developed the *Frolic* Shipwreck Project, the thing that's caught my interest is its potential for educating the public. Maybe it's because of my background as a curriculum developer for elementary and junior high school students. I'm pleased there will be a permanent exhibit at the Mendocino County Museum, and I hope there will be portable exhibits for schools that can travel up and down the state. I like the idea of supplementing elementary through high school students' knowledge of California maritime history by using the *Frolic* wreck site as an example. Students need to be able to actually touch and feel the artifacts from the *Frolic*.

You know, I'm much more excited by that possibility than I am by the permanent museum exhibit up at Willits. A traveling exhibit can have a far greater impact than a permanent exhibit, particularly if it is accompanied by a short videotape giving the students a sense of the historical background surrounding the wreck and its location. It should include some underwater video of what the wreck looks like today, as well as coverage of the permanent collection to give students a sense of its size and diversity. It also needs to emphasize that this is a collection of trade goods being transported from China to Gold Rush San Francisco, and how important sailing vessels like the *Frolic* were in the early commerce of this state. It's about time that some maritime history is included in the history books. I'll bet there's probably only 1 book published on maritime history for every 10 on railroading! Even logging gets more coverage than does the history of shipping on this coast.

I'll be returning to the *Frolic* this spring under an interagency agreement negotiated by Tom Layton between the California Department of Parks and Recreation and San Jose State University. We'll undertake what is termed a "preliminary mapping and survey." The initial step will be to go to the site and determine how much of it is readily visible, and how it may have changed since I was last on it during the early 1980s. My recollection of the site is that during the spring it should be relatively visible because much of the kelp will have broken loose during winter storms. If we are forced to postpone the work until summer the site gets very heavily grown with kelp, and before we can do any mapping and photographic documentation of the wreck we may have to clear some of the kelp away.

Assuming that we can clear that up, I propose to run a line that would recreate the keel line of the vessel. We know the approximate bow position from the capstan and the anchor-chain mound and the location where the cannon used to lie. Back in the early 1980s I think I uncovered a portion of the keel just ahead of the ballast pile and to the stern of the galley area. If I can run a straight line from the capstan to that exposure of keel, I think I'll be able to project the keel line to the stern. Once we've done that, we'll photograph all the large visible wreck objects, such as the ballast pile, the chain mound, the anchors, and the capstan. Then we'll do some 1 m test excavations to locate and evaluate areas that may still be undisturbed and hold promise for future archaeological investigation.

We've been given permission to do some fanning and some suction dredging

DAVID BULLER

in order to investigate these areas. It's quite possible that, despite the amount of diving activity this site has received, there may still be relatively undisturbed areas that hold promise for new discoveries. If so, I hope additional funding can be found to support a more detailed investigation of the site.

I've been asked to collect vulnerable artifacts, things like ceramic shards that are relatively small and lying on the surface where they are likely to be picked up by sport divers. We'll map these items in relationship to the keel line. In order to hold down costs we plan to use about a half-a-dozen volunteers, many of whom have some experience in underwater archaeology. Tom wants us to get this work done before the *Frolic* exhibits open this summer at the museums in Willits, Ukiah, and Mendocino. Hopefully some of our underwater maps and photographs will be used in those exhibits.

[Editor Thomas Layton: It turned out that the surf was too rough to dive or to make a map. Sheli O. Smith would direct the Frolic Mapping Project in 2003–2004, as described in her narrative in this volume.]

Richard O. Everett

Richard O. Everett is former Curator of Exhibits at San Francisco Maritime National Historical Park. He was born 1954 in New York City to a father who worked in the stock exchange and an English mother who'd crossed the Atlantic twice during wartime. Raised in upstate New York, he attended St. Mark's School in Southborough, Massachusetts, and then State University of New York (SUNY) in Purchase, New York, for two years as an art student. In 1975, he and two friends bicycled across the United States, from New York to San Francisco. In 1978 he completed a B.A. in environmental science at Antioch College in Yellow Springs, Ohio. While at Antioch he completed two internships with the National Park Service in Harpers Ferry, West Virginia, building exhibits for various visitor centers before settling in San Francisco in 1979.

From 1980 to 2017, Richard worked for the National Park Service at the San Francisco Maritime Museum, where he built and produced over 40 exhibits on a wide range of subjects related to maritime history. Among other awards, his long-term exhibits: "Cargo is King!" (2009), installed onboard ship *Balclutha*, and The Waterfront-Sailors Called it Frisco (2014), for a National Park Service visitor center, were each awarded Best Interior

Figure 70. Richard Everett at the helm of San Francisco Maritime Park's scow schooner Alma on the Sacramento River in 1986. (Photo courtesy of Richard Everett)

Exhibit by the National Association of Interpretation. In 1997–98, as part of California's Gold Rush sesquicentennial celebration, he led production of an exhibit focusing on Gold Rush commerce with China, featuring the shipwrecked *Frolic* and her cargo.

Richard produced or assisted in the production of 20 films and published articles on maritime history, including the entry for Richard Henry Dana in the *Oxford Encyclopedia of American Literature*.

Since his retirement on the final day of 2017, he has volunteered at the San Francisco Maritime Museum and the San Francisco Historical Society and enjoys sailing his 16 ft. sailboat *Frolic* on San Francisco Bay and Tomales Bay.

Richard O. Everett

8 September 2022
San Francisco, California

My mother came from an English family with artistic and theatrical roots. A teacher for over four decades, she loved creating unusual learning experiences and recounted them in detail nightly over dinner. When I was 14 years old, rather than drive me, she encouraged me to take a bus to the paleontology office at the New York State Museum in Albany, New York, lugging a 20 lb. Devonian fossil I had found. The geologic and prehistoric exhibits there were stunning. I vividly remember a giant dragonfly perched on a branch near the diorama rail.

My mother also encouraged me to take a summer session at the Helderberg Workshop with the archaeologist Paul Huey. Paul was leading an archaeology project at Schuyler Flats—the site of a 1643 Dutch homestead belonging to the founder of Schenectady, New York. I was 15 that sweltering summer as we learned archaeological methodology (how to work in extreme heat) and how to classify the many types of Dutch smoking-pipe stems. We worked all summer with hand trowels and calling out whenever we found an artifact. The work was interesting and fun, but at that time I was more interested in photography. My mother had urged me to try developing my own film, and I found the process fascinating. I built a darkroom in the basement of our house, and photography became my favorite activity.

My favorite teacher in high school was John A. Carey, who taught manual arts. John taught a class called "Art Expression," and it was from him that I learned how to turn my photographs into colorful silkscreen prints, how to turn wood on lathes, and how to use all manner of shop tools. Those skills would later serve me very well in the field of exhibits.

Our last six weeks of high school were structured as an independent study project. I located a silkscreen artists' co-op studio in Boston and traveled from school into the city every day. Robert Moore, the head of the painting department at Massachusetts College of the Arts, had started this cooperative, known as "The Graphic Workshop." The artists were all highly experienced, and I learned many special techniques from them as we silkscreened posters for the MIT theater and the Boston Public Library. David Cypress, one of the artists with whom I worked, ultimately became a prolific *New Yorker* cartoonist.

I submitted my photography and print portfolio to the fine arts program at the State University of New York at Purchase and was accepted. Shortly after I arrived, they asked me to create a silkscreen studio, where I taught other students the techniques I had mastered. John Cohen was my college advisor. He was renowned as photographer, musician, and filmmaker. He'd made the first short movie of Bob Dylan and had cofounded the New Lost City Ramblers—one of the earliest traditional and influential folk-music bands in NYC. To help pay for college, I took on a job preparing gallery walls, hanging shows, and installing sculptures in the Neuberger Museum located on campus.

After two years of art classes, I realized I could not draw, and my skills in photography and printmaking were not going to pay the rent after college. Instead, I began planning a bicycle trip to California with two classmates. The trip would provide a needed break, but it was linked to an exciting goal. Together with John Cohen, I had studied 1930s Farm Security Administration (FSA) photographers, like Dorothea Lange, Walker Evans, and Arthur Rothstein, who had documented American people and landscapes during the Great Depression. At John's suggestion I could—while cycling across the country—revisit some of the same landscapes that those FSA photographers had and document what had changed over the past 40 years. And, if successful, my project would qualify for course credit.

For the three of us, our cycle trip across the country to San Francisco was the most fun and exciting adventure in our young lives. Not wanting the adventure to end, I would return to the East Coast with my camera mostly by hopping freight trains—but that's another story. I then spent a summer living in Albany, New York, working in a bike shop, thus adding mechanical skills to my repertoire, and decided not to return to art school, but instead to finish college in a new field somewhere else.

I chose Antioch College in Yellow Springs, Ohio. Antioch stood out from the others by virtue of its internship program. It may have been the first college in the U.S. to formalize internships as part of a five-year program. Nearly half the faculty was employed to find internships all over the country and to fill those positions with Antioch students.

I transferred to Antioch in 1976 and soon accepted an internship at the Interpretive Design Center of the National Park Service (NPS) in Harper's Ferry, West Virginia. This center was charged with designing and fabricating exhibits for park visitor centers all over the United States. I liked it so much that, between stays at Antioch to complete classes, I worked in three NPS divisions totaling over a year and a half. I worked in dioramas, in the woodshop, silk-screening, mount-making, model-making, and metalwork. I hand painted animals and plants for a large mural headed to the Everglades.

I loved working on all manner of exhibitry, but I also felt I needed to explore another option before settling on any one thing. Upon graduating from Antioch, I decided to live with my uncle in Norwich, England. He had a successful picture-framing shop and was willing to teach his skills to me, the idea being I could open my own framing shop back in the U.S. I stayed with him for several months, helping to manage the business while he went on vacation. I liked the work, but decided that opening my own frame shop back in the U.S. was not for me. Instead, I found myself living with my parents for the winter. This would *not* do, so I formed a plan to drive my VW bug out to San Francisco.

In San Francisco I found my skills in high demand. I took a job at San Francisco Exhibits—a company which produced tradeshow displays, but I was laid off when work diminished during the winter. Tired of the commercial aspects of this work, I cast about, first working at a silkscreen company printing tattoo designs and then at a picture-frame shop. It was at this picture-frame shop on Polk Street, located between Suckers Liquors and Hard-On Leathers, that I had a pivotal experience that would land me a job in my desired field: museum exhibits.

I was in the basement dry mounting large prints (for the Academy of Sciences), when the only other employee called me upstairs. He was having trouble with a customer who looked deeply disturbed. Before I could help, the customer grabbed her artwork and stormed out. I returned to the basement, but he called me back up again. He was staggering around the shop before lying down in the middle of the sales floor. I called for an ambulance. I did not know it, but he had overdosed on quaaludes. A forged prescription was later found in his pocket.

I called the owner, and, when she arrived, I was handed the red leash to her toy poodle with a rhinestone collar. She asked me to take the poodle for a walk. I did, but just as far as the payphone on the corner. There, I looked up *M*, for "museums," in the Yellow Pages, and with one call to the San Francisco Maritime Museum lined up a job interview with curator Harlan Soeten, who would become my supervisor.

In February 1980, a month after I began working as an exhibit preparator, I was directed to create a presentable working space in the museum basement. This was not an easy task, as nearly all the artifact collections, including most of the library, were hanging from wires or crammed together and piled on top of each other to the ceiling. The precipitating reason was to create a presentable space because a local news station wanted to do a story on the still-corked champagne bottle that had been recovered from the buried ship *Niantic*, where Jim Delgado was one of the participants. With great ceremony, the 1840s cork was pulled and champagne poured for each person. Judging from their wry expressions, it was awful—tasting of mud, char, and seawater. That was how I became friends with Jim Delgado.

Soon after, Jim and I worked together on Shipwrecks of the Golden Gate. It was to be the museum's first temporary exhibit, together with a book. It included the wreck of the *Tennessee*, which missed the Golden Gate and wrecked on a beach just north of the entrance to San Francisco Bay. *Tennessee* was Jim's first maritime archaeological project—where he excavated part of its huge steam engine and recovered numerous other artifacts.

The Maritime Museum's director, Karl Kortum, was a little reticent about temporary exhibits. He was more interested in building out permanent long-lasting exhibits in the museum. More than once he'd correctly noted that temporary exhibits take up everyone's time at the expense of building long-term ones. Down one wall of our museum gallery was a long display case filled with brass valves from the *Ohioan*. Delgado had played an important

RICHARD O. EVERETT

Figure 71. In the mid-1970s a mammoth project to build a sewer from North Point to Islais Creek began. The trench for it exposed the remains of the whale ship *Lydia* on King Street near today's ballpark. (Photo courtesy of the National Park Service, 1978)

part in retrieving them from an illegal diving operation near San Francisco's Cliff House a few months prior, and their heavily twisted shapes wordlessly told the story not only of great loss and danger, but of powerful underwater forces. This exhibit was the first to reveal to us the great interest the public had in shipwrecks and their archaeology, and it would be essentially the first of more than 20 temporary exhibits to follow.

Multiple fires and the filling in of the bay to extend the city out into deep water had caused over 40 ships to be buried in what would become the downtown of San Francisco. A construction project in 1901, exposing part of the *Apollo*, was the first, but the number of buried ships encountered and brought to light greatly increased in the late 1970s. Roger Olmsted (curator at the Maritime Museum) and his wife Nancy were contracted by the city to research the proposed waterfront route that a new city sewer would take. They were aided by the museum's "Buried Ships Map" put together by Al Harmon, our librarian, in 1963. This well-researched map, based largely on contemporary newspaper accounts, would become one of the museum's most reproduced documents. The sewer trench exposed the remains of the whale ship *Lydia* on King Street near today's San Francisco ballpark.

Lydia was a whaler and the first of several ships to be dug up in close succession. *Niantic* in 1978, and *William Gray* in 1980 were similarly unearthed in the course of construction. Archaeologists and Maritime Museum staff (which included librarians as well as volunteers) were often hastily assembled to retrieve artifacts and record details. The financial pressures of construction conflicted greatly with those who wanted more time

to study and retrieve artifacts. It was at the dig site of *William Gray*, still reeking with the bitter odor of the fire that had burned San Francisco in 1852, that a young Jim Delgado walked on her deck and decided that he wanted to tell the stories of the lost ships beneath San Francisco.

Sometime later, having just witnessed an anchor and chain being scraped up and dropped rattling into a dumpster beneath their windows, the employees of a downtown high-rise called the museum. Harlan Soeten and I drove to the scene to recover whatever information we could, but we were unable to secure the attention of the workers to be allowed to look into the dumpster. Developers and contractors feared the costs that finding ships could entail. Meanwhile, parts of other ships and artifacts came to the museum for me to brush off and vacuum before transporting them to storage at lower Fort Mason.

In 1985, wanting extra money for a parcel of land I wanted to buy in the foothills, I began working evenings at the Exploratorium Museum on top of working full days at Maritime. This lasted a year, building interactive science exhibits full of metal and electronics till midnight. The result was Seeing the Light with the Exploratorium, two exhibits which opened in Brooklyn, New York and Parc de la Villette, France. I learned a lot and began incorporating an interactive approach to exhibits and using technology back at the Maritime Museum.

In 1992, Steve Canright, my supervisor, left the exhibit department to become the park historian. I took his position as the exhibits curator, responsible for directing and producing the series of changing exhibits that he and I had developed over the years. At the same time I was in charge of maintaining all the existing exhibits in

RICHARD O. EVERETT

Figure 72. A portrait on thin ivory of John Hurd Everett in China while he was working for the Augustine Heard Company. ca. 1850. Everett purchased cargoes for the ships *Eveline* and *Frolic*. He purchased many paintings by the well-known Chinese artist Tinqua for export, so it is possible the same artist painted this portrait for John Everett. Note the blue and white china vase. (Image courtesy of Richard Everett)

the museum, including those aboard our seven floating ships along Hyde Street Pier. That was a lot to take care of, but my department somehow kept up with the ever-increasing paperwork and produced a new exhibit every year and a half. It was tiring but extremely rewarding work.

One day in 1992, in the midst of this, I received a call from a man who identified himself as Dr. Thomas Layton, a professor of anthropology at San Jose State University. "Did I," he asked, "know that I had a relative who sailed with Richard Henry Dana on the *Pilgrim*?" My first reaction was to concentrate on his voice and try to guess which of my high school friends was prank calling me. (Richard Henry Dana, Jr.'s book *Two Years Before the Mast*, published in 1840, is one of the most important books about coastal California.) Tom had just spoken with my aunt in Woodside, having obtained her name from my uncle in New York. He was tracking down all living descendants of John Hurd Everett (Dana's 1834 shipmate), and my aunt had told him I was working at the Maritime Museum in San Francisco.

Tom told me about a ship named *Frolic* that had wrecked on the coast up by Mendocino in 1850, captained by Edward Horacio Faucon, former master of *Pilgrim* (Dana's ship in the book). When I realized Tom was serious and that his story might be true, I was both mystified and stunned. Tom invited me to come up the next day to the Kelley House Museum in Mendocino, where, if I wanted to learn more about it, he would be giving a slide lecture on the whole affair.

Leaving work early and accompanied by my five-year-old son Carson, I drove to Mendocino. When I arrived the slide lecture had already begun, and I carried my sleeping son to a bench in the back, my

shadow obscuring the screen. Just minutes after I arrived, I sat transfixed as a color painted image of my three-times-great-uncle in China filled the screen.

My family has at least two amateur genealogists, and we had talked often enough about who was who, yet no one had ever mentioned this uncle. He had escaped all notice. Not only had he sailed with Dana, but he had also traveled by stage up and down the California coast, trading with the rancheros between San Francisco and Los Angeles during the famous hide-and-tallow days of the 1830s and 40s.

I was thrilled to realize that, suddenly, I had California "roots." John H. Everett had later moved to China to work for the American firm that owned *Frolic* and employed Edward Faucon as her captain. *Frolic* was a swift Baltimore-built opium clipper, but steamers were already taking over the India to China transport trade. Thus, in a last-ditch effort to keep her employed, *Frolic* was dispatched from China for Gold Rush San Francisco with a cargo of Chinese manufactured goods, all of which had been purchased by my ancestor, John Everett. That vessel and her cargo were lost on the night of 25 July 1850, only 2 mi. north of the Kelley House Museum, where I was sitting and listening to Tom's lecture.

That evening—rather than having to sleep in my camper bus—Tom invited me to join him at the Little River Inn, where he had decamped with several of his students. I slept on a couch with my son on the floor. Then, at 6 AM, the suite came alive as we prepared to drive farther up the coast to a high forested ridge near Westport, where Tom was conducting an archaeological field class at a Native American village site. Amazingly, the bark house

RICHARD O. EVERETT

depressions were still visible, and soon the trowels and screens were being worked. I could not stay long, as my son was proving to be a lot to handle, but, as I left for home that afternoon, I was determined to do something big with this story at the San Francisco Maritime Museum.

The following year, a large meeting of interested people in Mendocino County was called together to discuss the *Frolic* Shipwreck Project. There I met with people from the California Department of Forestry, the Mendocino County Museum, the Grace Hudson Museum, the Kelley House Museum, several Native Americans, the Ukiah Players Theatre, and Jim Delgado! A plan to design and produce exhibits at the three museums quickly emerged. Never before had I seen exhibits guided by such a large and diverse group. The theater people suggested telling the story in a historical drama, whereupon Jim Delgado captured everyone's interest and attention by holding aloft a Chinese pottery sherd and then speaking to it in multiple voices: as a Pomo Indian, as *Frolic's* captain, and as the Chinese potter who had shaped it.

We left that meeting with a plan to mount exhibits at three museums, each telling a different part of the story—and there was so much to tell. *Frolic* had been built in a Baltimore shipyard and was one of the fastest types of American sailing vessels ever built. Frederick Douglass, the abolitionist, had worked in that very shipyard as a slave. Edward Faucon, the *Frolic's* captain when it wrecked on the shore of Mendocino County, had earlier sailed the coast of California multiple times trading with the Mexican Californios for their hide and tallow. Finally, *Frolic* had been carrying a Chinese cargo to Gold Rush San Francisco. The Pomo Indians had been the first to salvage that cargo, and, serendipitously, my three-times-great-uncle had been the merchant who assembled that very cargo. Newspapers, museums, a newsletter, an education program, a historical drama, and a book would publicize this narrative—but I chanced upon another way to tell the story.

During the planning and coordination of the exhibits I found myself frequently driving Route 101 back and forth from Ukiah to San Francisco. While returning from one of those planning meetings, I stopped at the Mendocino Brewing Company's brewpub in Hopland. It was not my first time there as I loved good beer. While at the bar I started to tell the bartender the story of the *Frolic* shipwreck. *Frolic* had been carrying 6,009 bottles of beer to San Francisco. After she wrecked, the Pomo had carried beer-bottle glass inland to their villages, where they flaked the glass into arrowheads. I well knew that Mendocino Brewing Company prided itself by claiming to be the first microbrewery in California, so I finished my spiel with a bit of a flourish—that "the Frolic's cargo would have been the first beer ever drunk in Mendocino County!"

At that, the head brewer, several stools over, walked down the bar and sat with me to learn more of the story. Towards the end I suggested they ought to replicate the beer. "*Frolic* Ale" is too good a name, I thought. He liked the idea, and I brought this news to the next planning meeting. "*Frolic* Shipwreck Ale" was soon created by the brewery, and Dan Taylor, director of the Mendocino County Museum, negotiated that a dollar per bottle sold would be donated to the exhibit efforts. The beer was brewed for several years afterwards, and a new color added to the label each year on the anniversary of the wreck.

Two 6 lb. rated cannons had been retrieved from the seabed by the sport divers. One was in the lawn at the Kelley House in Mendocino, and the other was in a bathtub filled with water outside a barn nearby. It was hoped that the long water soak would draw out the harmful salts within the porous cast iron. Dan Taylor, director of the Mendocino County Museum, wanted the cannon to be treated before exhibiting it, and Maritime Museum conservator David Casebolt was willing to help. All I needed was to drive up from San Francisco to fetch it. We had all the requisite supplies, and Dan had a friend that worked in Willits that had a AAA tow truck. The truck's lifting crane would be used to lift the 800 lb. cannon onto the pallet to place it in my pickup truck. I asked Dan how much was the fee, and he replied there wasn't one. He explained he was a AAA member and that the driver had entered in the company book that he'd responded to a "dead battery." The three museums coordinated their parts of the story, each opening with well-attended exhibits one month after the other in the summer of 1994.

I had consulted closely with Tom Layton and the three museums as they crafted their exhibits, and I was relating all of the developments to Karl Kortum. He was fairly interested, but for most of the time he had been working steadily and hard on his own research projects. He had not had much time to understand my relating of the story and the exhibits up north. Tom now had a draft for his book "Drug Runner"—eventually published as *The Voyage of the Frolic: New England Merchants and the Opium Trade* (Layton 1997). This draft made it possible for the first time to bring Karl into the fray. From beginning to end the full story was presented, not as a string of astonishing facts, but as a complete manuscript. There were many nautical and seafaring aspects, including terminology, that Tom desired input on, and Karl was quite happy to be asked. I delivered the draft to Karl, and when he had finished reading and making his notes, Tom and I visited him at his home in April 1995. Karl had not been feeling well for some time, but none of that showed the afternoon we visited. He went over his notes and spent considerable time with Tom examining the wind, current, and waves present when *Frolic* wrecked, 25 July 1850. I was thrilled to have Karl onboard and to support the exhibit.

It was no secret I really wanted to bring the exhibit to the museum—thus finally delivering *Frolic*'s cargo to San Francisco. It was just too good a story, and it kept growing. Auction records kept by San Francisco merchant Jacob Leese revealed how, just the year before *Frolic*'s cargo was dispatched to California, his own cargo aboard the *Eveline* had been auctioned off on the shore of Yerba Buena Cove. Samples of that cargo had been displayed in a Chinese prefabricated house which was itself part of the cargo. *Frolic* had also carried such a house, and a window mullion with oyster-shell glazing had magically survived to be collected by a sport diver.

Eveline's auction records indicated that Chinese lanterns had been employed to light the auction items, and sawhorses and boards rented to display them and to provide champagne and crackers for the serious bidders. The elements of this unique and detailed scene fascinated me. Had *Frolic* reached San Francisco, this is exactly how her cargo would have been auctioned. I realized that this was how San Francisco Maritime Museum's exhibit should look. I attended meetings of the California

RICHARD O. EVERETT

Figure 73. Dan Taylor, director of the Mendocino County Museum (left), and Richard Everett (right) successfully approached the ship *Pride of Baltimore II* with the idea of delivering a few cases of Frolic Ale to San Francisco in 1996. The publicity action was symbolic, as *Frolic* would have delivered 6,108 bottles of this Edinburgh ale to San Francisco had she completed her voyage in 1850. Frolic Shipwreck Ale was featured at San Francisco Maritime Park's annual Festival of the Sea that year, and the Pride of Baltimore II was present. (Photo courtesy of Richard Everett, 1996)

Sesquicentennial Commission in Monterey led by California state librarian Kevin Starr and officially registered our potential exhibit. This would enable it to receive all kinds of publicity.

But first I needed my own institution's permission because my staff and I would be working on this for four months straight and it would cost money—at least $50,000, not counting staff time! I needed to convince the Chief of Interpretation, Marc Hayman, who luckily liked the project and advocated for me with the park superintendent, Bill Thomas. To build necessary staff support I took a vanload of colleagues for a visit to the brewery in Hopland, the Three Chop Ridge Pomo Village site, and the Point Cabrillo beach where *Frolic*'s pottery sherds still washed ashore.

Meanwhile, I realized I needed a reference, an authentic record of what an 1850 Chinese prefabricated house would look like. I phoned Tom Layton, who told me he'd learned that the remains of a Chinese prefabricated house still stood three hours away at Double Springs in the Sierra foothills. Because I was totally submerged in planning our exhibit, I sent an intern who returned with out-of-focus photos. I sent him back, and this time the photos, though still blurry, indicated that the house might serve as a template and was worth a visit. The only person who could verify it was Tom Layton, so together with his father, my intern, and two of my staff, we drove to Double Springs. The house turned out to be exactly what we were looking for. It had Chinese inscriptions at all the joints, was designed to be assembled without nails, and its dimensions closely matched those of the prefab house listed on *Frolic*'s manifest. It even had a door with a glass window, but with mullions exactly the same

size as *Frolic*'s. We were ecstatic and spent the day photographing, measuring, and drawing every aspect. We had an authentic reference for a Chinese Gold Rush auction house! And soon we had a title for the exhibit: FOUND!—The Wreck of the *Frolic* A Gold Rush Cargo for San Francisco.

With the aid of two hired carpenters and a mount-maker we set to work. Mary Lou Herlihy, my graphic designer, designed and created a beautiful model of the exhibit. Her husband Mark created three ambient sound pieces: mosquitos and Pomo voices for the bark house; sounds of the auction for the Chinese prefab; and, next to a 19 ft. long photo panorama of the cove where *Frolic* had wrecked, background sounds of the seagulls, the ocean, and shipwrecked pieces of rigging groaning and bumping amongst the rocks. Ghraydon Wallick, exhibit fabricator, constructed a theater with a Chinese-styled roof (suggestive of the cargo's origin in Whampoa). A recently produced History Channel film about *Frolic* (Lindahl and Martenez 2003) was installed on a continuous loop in the theater.

I displayed gold filigree earrings, actually recovered from the *Frolic* wreck, in a sealed Lexan box able to resist bullets, its outside bristling with auto alarm sensors. Thankfully, it never went off! A recreation of Captain Faucon's desk aboard the *Frolic* had an actual *Frolic* porthole placed over it and a historical image of Hong Kong placed on the other side of it to show the view ashore. On the desk were actual *Frolic* artifacts: a pocket watch and parallel rules used with charts in navigation. The largest thing in the exhibit was a partial replica of the Chinese prefab house reconstructed at full scale according to the drawings we made of the Double Springs prefab.

RICHARD O. EVERETT

Figure 74a. The exhibit research team in front of the Double Springs Chinese prefabricated house in 1997. The building was recorded and later replicated for the exhibit. Left to right: Property owner, Tom Layton, Laurence L. Layton, Danny Darr, Mary Lou Herlihy, Richard Everett, and Ghraydon Wallick. (Photo courtesy of Richard Everett)

Figure 74b. The prefabricated building was constructed of Chinese camphor wood. The panels that made up the walls can be seen here. (Photo by Richard Everett, 1997)

Figure 74c. An architectural drawing of the Double Springs Chinese prefabricated house by Peter Gallagher, 1997. (Photo courtesy of the San Francisco Maritime NHP)

RICHARD O. EVERETT

Visitors could step inside the house to view the many types of China-trade items found on *Frolic*'s manifest: crates of beer, vases, camphor trunks, silks, furniture—even peacock feathers! Leaving the exhibit, visitors passed by modern Chinese items purchased from currently operating Chinese stores in Chinatown: a camphor trunk, a disposable film camera, silk shirts, and pottery, all evidence of still-ongoing Chinese trade. A color photo of a steel-hulled cargo ship named *China* was displayed passing under the Golden Gate Bridge into San Francisco Bay.

Earlier, while the Chinese prefab was taking shape, I attempted to contact Philip Choy, San Francisco's most prominent Chinese historian and president of the Chinese Historical Society of America. I encountered difficulty reaching him. My emails had gone unanswered. Phil later told me the reason: he simply could not believe that a Chinese prefabricated house from the Gold Rush period could have survived. Phil, together with Thomas Chin, had taught a Chinese history class at San Francisco State University. He was also by profession an architect and had written about Chinese architecture in San Francisco. I finally reached Phil by phone and offered to drop off on his doorstep (he lived just up the hill from the museum) information that I promised would convince him. The packet of documents was 5 in. thick when I was done xeroxing—and convince him it did! He called me the next morning wanting to come down to the exhibit shop and learn more.

By this time we had already constructed cedar-wood replicas of the wall panels of the Double Springs house, and they lined the hallway. Phil became gleeful as we walked through them to the office, and we soon had a wonderful, learned voice to add to our exhibit. As Phil became more familiar with the *Frolic* story and the house in Double Springs (that we were replicating), he called it the most important surviving evidence of the earliest China trade with California. Phil loaned our museum an 1870s Chinese lamp that had once hung in San Francisco to help light *Frolic*'s cargo in the exhibit. When the replica house was finished and painted a "Chinese red," the same color as the original Double Springs house, it was Tom's idea to ask Phil to paint Chinese characters on the rafters in the same places as those first observed at Double Springs.

The exhibit opened with a large reception on 6 March 1998. Michael Oakes, the actor who had played Captain Faucon in "Voices of the Frolic" four years earlier, addressed the crowd. Michael and his wife, also an actor, would soon create a Chautauqua-styled presentation of the *Frolic* story that they performed onboard the park's ship *Balclutha* throughout the summer months. San Francisco's Chinese TV station KTSF Channel 26 filmed a news segment on the new exhibit in both Mandarin and Cantonese, which helped to bring in visitors from the local Chinese community. When the major exhibit ended that year, a *Frolic* ship model, the replica auction house display, together with refreshed exhibits and the theater remained on display in the museum until 2006, when the building closed for renovation.

The *Frolic* project and exhibit helped my career and opened new opportunities for the museum. Shortly after it was completed, Kathy Lohan, director of the Park's Association, invited me to lead Ken Richardson through the *Frolic* exhibit. Ken, the former president of Hughes Aircraft in Southern California, wanted to fund an exhibit on radio as a tribute to

Figure 75. Left to right: Phillip Choy, Tom Layton, and Richard Everett discuss building features at the site of the Chinese prefabricated house at Double Springs. (Photo courtesy of Richard Everett, 1997)

Figure 76a. The exhibit featured a replicated portion of the Chinese prefabricated house in Double Springs. (Photo by Richard Everett, 1997)

RICHARD O. EVERETT

Figure 76b. Inside the replicated house were placed examples of *Eveline's* and *Frolic's* cargo for auction purposes. *Frolic's* manifest listed all the antique items seen here: stoneware plates, ginger jars, lacquerware fan boxes, ivory gaming pieces, and stacked leather-covered trunks. These were designed to be shipped one inside the other to save space aboard ship. (Photo by Richard Everett, 1997)

Figure 77. Phillip Choy is seen here pointing to one of a hundred or more inscriptions found on the timbers of the Chinese prefabricated house. Inscriptions paired with Arabic numerals helped guide reassembly, while some translated as "long life" and "good luck." (Photo by Richard Everett, 1997)

Figure 78. Opening night of Found! The Wreck of the *Frolic*—A Gold Rush Cargo for San Francisco, 26 March 1998. Actor Michael Oakes, in character as Captain Faucon, speaks to the crowd in the lobby of the Maritime Museum. (Photo courtesy of San Francisco Maritime NHP)

RICHARD O. EVERETT

his father, a former marine radioman. Ken was greatly impressed. We had lunch, and subsequently he donated $250,000 to the Museum Association for us to create what would become the award-winning exhibit Sparks, Waves and Wizards—The History of Marine Communication at Sea. It was the largest donation the association had ever received up to that point and for many years afterwards.

The California Sesquicentennial, led by Ken Starr, celebrated the discovery of gold in 1848, which led to the Gold Rush of 1849 and statehood in 1850. The Oakland Museum had decided to do a major Gold Rush exhibit. Early in its planning, Thomas Frye, their history curator, phoned me. He had toured the Maritime Museum's storage facility in Alameda and thought he had seen the bow of a clipper ship that he wanted to display in his exhibit. It was actually the stern of the *Niantic* with its rudder removed. Clearly, *Niantic* would make a fabulous artifact to educate visitors about the Gold Rush, and it was a ship we knew a great deal about. Tom Frye decided to use it and ordered a beautiful rolling aluminum mount that would enable it to be easily transported. With its rudder rehung back on its gudgeons and with its beautiful copper sheathing intact, it made for quite a sight. Today, in 2022, it is still on display in the large lobby of the San Francisco Maritime Museum.

I later decided to apply for funds to have a diorama made with *Niantic* appearing as it once had, hauled up onto the San Francisco shoreline, propped up by its own yards, and surrounded by the city's encroaching wharves. I found Tom and Joan Snyder, a diorama-building team in Oregon who, guided by the boxes of documents I had given to them, were able to create a fabulous diorama of the whole *Niantic* scene. They even set up a model shop aboard the park's *Eureka* ferryboat during the park's annual Festival of the Sea celebration, where the public could watch them complete the final touches before delivering the diorama to the museum.

Between 2000 and 2009 we produced both small and large long-term exhibits for the front of the Park Visitor Center and aboard *Balclutha*. Meanwhile, in September of 2001, a wonderful archaeological event began to unfold. Archaeologist Allen Pastron was excavating the site of the ship *General Harrison* at Clay and Battery streets in downtown San Francisco. *General Harrison* had been tied to the same wharf as *Niantic* when the fire of 4 May 1851 reduced both ships to their waterlines. Allen phoned to let me know about the dig and asked me to invite our staff down to see it. Not being a ship expert myself, he asked me if I could find someone to advise him. I suggested our historian Steve Canright, but added that he really ought to contact Jim Delgado.

Jim Delgado and Allen Pastron had actually worked together on waterfront archaeology years earlier, notably the Hoff Store and Harbormaster's Office, as well as the Hills Plaza project in 1988. "Of course!" said Allan, and the next day he had put Jim up in a downtown hotel to assist with the dig. Almost immediately the New York City 9/11 terrorist attack closed the dig for two days over fears that other buildings might be struck. The dig was in the shadow of the Transamerica Building. When work resumed, John Muir (the museum's small craft curator) brought his archaeological expertise to the site and helped string up a huge grid. Our park photographers helped document the project, and their best overview photograph was eventually selected by the

Figure 79. Exhibit diorama of the *Niantic*, built by Moments in Time, was based on information learned from the excavation of the ship on San Francisco's waterfront and much research. It is seen here being photographed by a team filming a television episode for National Geographic's Drain the Oceans. (Photo by Richard Everett, 2018)

Smithsonian to use in one of their exhibits. I was able to bring Harlan Soeten, the man who had hired me years earlier when he was the museum curator, to provide onsite advice. As Harlan descended the ladder into the pit to have a look around, it was for both Jim Delgado and me a deeply meaningful and sentimental moment.

Parts of the ship's cargoes, not fully consumed by the 1852 firestorm, lay about. Surprisingly, a great deal had been preserved by the water and anaerobic mud—even bolts of cloth. So much was collected that Jim would spend months in Pastron's lab analyzing and researching it. It would become an important data set for Jim's doctoral dissertation and his book, *Gold Rush Port: The Maritime Archaeology of San Francisco's Waterfront* (Delgado 2009).

What came next for me was 14 years of attempting to procure the *General Harrison* collection for San Francisco Maritime Park. Allen Pastron had offered it to us, but still needed a few years to be sure it was fully processed and to clarify his rights to the collection. As it stood, the

Masterworks Development Corporation owned all the artifacts. Not wanting to wait forever, we asked for two artifacts: a trestletree and a ship's door. Masterworks wanted perfect replicas in return. Luckily, our exhibit specialist, Ghraydon Wallick, was a wizard when it came to faux creative projects. This work would be especially challenging, as the artifacts would end up side by side for approval by Masterworks before being formally donated. In the end, they were virtually indistinguishable, and the artifacts were released to us. The *General Harrison* collection was particularly important to the National Park Service.

Up to that time, of all the buried ships unearthed, it was the only one that had benefited from good archaeology. Acquiring the rest of the collection would require a major effort on my part. Eventually, Allen Pastron was able to work things out with Masterworks Development such that he had rights to the artifacts. Rhonda Robichaud, who worked for Allen and had been the field supervisor on the *General Harrison* dig, proved to be an essential and helpful ally when negotiating with both

RICHARD O. EVERETT

Pastron and Masterworks. However, internally at San Francisco Maritime Historical Park there were still bureaucratic hurdles. Although I had the support of Robbyn Jackson, Chief of Cultural Resources, it was still a long slog. In the end the Park Service acquired all of the photo and film documentation of the dig as well as all of the artifacts.

For me, exhibit design and production continued for the front half of the park's visitor center, which opened in 2003. At its center we installed the 14 ft. tall first-order Farallon light lens that I had procured for the museum in the 1980s. Some of the best *Niantic* artifacts were chosen to be installed there for long-term exhibit as well

Figure 80. For two days following the 9/11 attacks, the *General Harrison* archaeology site was closed because it was so close to the Transamerica Building. The building was thought to be a potential target. (Photo by Richard Everett 2001)

as a section of the buried *Apollo* ship's stem with its copper fastenings sticking out. We researched and created a large interactive map indicating the changing shorelines of the city waterfront to be placed alongside.

Design work in collaboration with Academy Studios for a much larger exhibit in the back of the visitor center was completed at this time. It was to include an area on the buried ships, but there wasn't enough money to fabricate it. Instead, the exhibit department turned to producing "Cargo is King", an exhibit of cargoes presented onboard the ship *Balclutha*, together with three films, tells the story of the ship's three careers. That exhibit would win the John Wesley Powell History Award and Best Interior Exhibit Award from the National Association of Interpretation in 2009.

In 2009, money to complete the Visitor Center exhibits arrived, and we revisited and overhauled the original 2004 design. I selected exhibit specialists who would take three years to build the exhibit now named "The Waterfront - Sailors called it Frisco". Conceived as a walk along the shore, in the buried-ships area of the exhibit, we added a recently discovered 12-footlong section of rabbited keel from the Charles Hare ship-breaking yard. Three archaeology digs over 27 years had successively revealed Hare's yard at Folsom and Spear Streets, and produced a wide range of artifacts. First, the 1988 Hills Plaza excavation by Delgado and Pastron~ then, Jim Allan's 2005 dig that turned up the *Candace*; and his 2013 dig that turned up a virtually complete lighter. The story of the Charles Hare ship-breaking yard was rich. Chinese from a nearby shrimp camp on the south side of Rincon Point worked for Hare dismantling ships for salvage. The exhibit included

Figure 81. The hull of the *General Harrison* burned to the waterline in the 4 May 1851 fire along with much of the waterfront. Allen Pastron's company Archeo-tec is seen here recording features. At the stern in the foreground, pilings from some of the early San Francisco wharves can be seen as well as the exposed sandy shoreline, five blocks inland from today's shoreline. (Photo courtesy of the San Francisco Maritime NHP, 2001)

RICHARD O. EVERETT

Figure 82. A remnant of one of San Francisco's oldest wharves at Thompson's Cove, near Broadway and Front streets. The cove was named for Alpheus B. Thompson, who operated a hide house there in the 1830s. It is thought that the first evidence of the hide-and-tallow trade in San Francisco was found here. (Photo by Cyler Conrad, 2013)

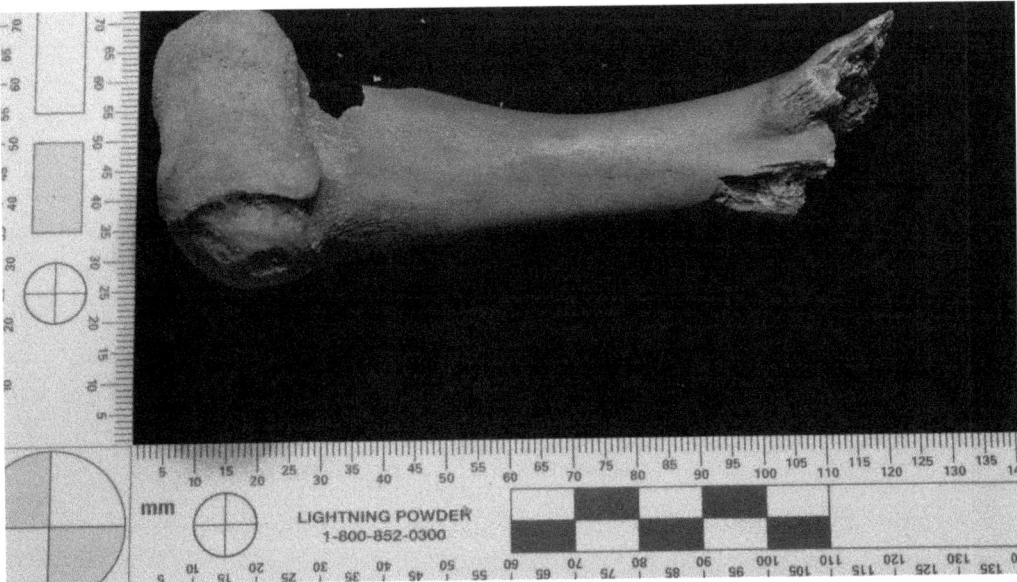

Figure 83. A Galapagos tortoise bone found at Thompsons Cove, San Francisco. Tortoises and green turtles were captured for feeding both crews and passengers on Gold Rush ships sailing up to San Francisco. Other ships set out from San Francisco during the Gold Rush to procure hundreds more and bring them back. The meat fetched a high price and was served as a delicacy in many San Francisco restaurants. (Photo by Cyler Conrad, 2013)

Figure 84. Entrance to San Francisco Maritime National Historical Park's Visitor Center exhibit "The Waterfront – Sailors called it Frisco." (Photo courtesy of Vance Lear, 2012)

a glass covered "dig-zone" and beneath the visitors' feet we placed artifacts recovered from various digs over the years.

This buried-ships immersive environment was crafted to simulate a downtown financial-district archaeology dig. In addition to the large keel placed against the wall was the ubiquitous chain-link fence that surrounded almost every dig. We installed an anchor and chain from the *Rome*, encountered while boring a tunnel for the MUNI subway, and a time-lapse looped video depicting the original Yerba Buena Cove full of ships and then how it was filled in up to the present.

Just as the visitor center was completed, I found myself at a poetry reading at Dave Eggers's 826 Valencia writing lab in San Francisco. Two educators had created a workshop for children who, in turn, wrote poems about each of their favorite buried ships. Poems by Don Menn and Sarah Wisby—respectively *General Harrison* and the *Rome*—were so impressive that I added them to the buried-ships exhibit together with the artifacts from those vessels.

The map of San Francisco's buried ships created by Al Harmon in 1963 was long outdated when the visitor-center exhibits neared completion in 2012. We needed an updated map to serve as a large wall graphic in the buried-ships area. I decided it was time to update the 1963 map—which had passed uncredited into the public domain—and thus secure credit for the Maritime Museum along with all those who had an important hand in its creation. Amy Hosa, graphic designer, created a new version of this map indicating not just the ships' locations, but also the original shoreline and wharves. Added to it was a Google satellite map overlay. We worked on updating all the ship information with James Delgado, James Allan, Allen Pastron, and Rhonda Robichaud. After a few tweaks, all signed off on this magnificent new map and the exhibit was finished.

But, no sooner had the map been updated than new discoveries occurred. A dig led by Allen Pastron began at the site of Thompson's Cove at Clarks Point— roughly along Broadway between Front

RICHARD O. EVERETT

Figure 85. Lighters were flat-bottomed workboats required for shallow waters, such as Yerba Buena Cove. Every day, dozens of these transported cargo and passengers ashore, and this is the only one ever found in San Francisco. It was constructed of imported Chilean beech, *Nothofagus Dombeyi*, during the Gold Rush period. (Photo courtesy of the National Park Service, 2013)

Figure 86. The "Buried Ships of Yerba Buena Cove Map" produced in 2017 by the San Francisco Maritime National Historical Park. Red ships represent those that have been dug up and some archaeology performed. A proof was submitted to all the archaeologists for their approval before printing. (Image courtesy of the San Francisco Maritime NHP)

and Battery streets. Alpheus B. Thompson, for whom the cove was named, had operated a hide house there during the 1830s. Our first solid evidence of this hide-and-tallow trade was found here thanks to Allen Pastron and his team, who encountered the bedrock of Telegraph Hill that had once been the shore of the old Clark's Point waterfront. Now hundreds of yards inland, this rock bore the marks of wave erosion along with part of an old wharf, together with many butchered cow bones documenting the pre–Gold Rush hide-and-tallow trade .

This location was the only deep water to be found along the shore in Yerba Buena Cove. It made sense that the earliest dock would have been located here. Cyler Conrad, working for Allen Pastron, was an expert on the flora and fauna of the Gold Rush. He had previously researched consumables from oysters to rabbits to cows. Curiously enough, in addition to cow bones, some mysterious bones were recovered, which Cyler ultimately identified as Galapagos tortoise. The reasonable explanation was that the tortoises had been brought to San Francisco aboard a ship and were intended to be used as food for either the crew or passengers. Cyler subsequently discovered that hundreds of tortoises were imported during the Gold Rush as food for San Francisco restaurants. He researched the restaurant names, addresses, their menus, as well as stories of the many ships that had set sail for the Galapagos in order to capture and bring back tortoises.

Still more information was uncovered in August of 2013 with the discovery of the lighter at Rincon Point. A lighter is a flat-bottomed boat used for transporting passengers and cargo to shore. The lighter was oddly affixed to a small custom deck on which were found salvage materials. Rhonda Robichaud had worked for Dr. James Allan and William Self Associates on the lighter dig at Folsom and Spear, and, based upon the distribution of artifacts, she had concluded that the lighter was being used by Hare's neighbor John Houseman. That the two businesses collaborated in some ways is probable, and the salvaged materials from one yard would likely have been used in the other.

The lighter was removed from the site by Tishman Speyer, the developer, who generously transported it to the National Park Service storage facility in San Leandro to be conserved by David Casebolt and Eloise Warren of the San Francisco Maritime Museum. The wood was determined to be from a Chilean beech tree. Valparaiso, Chile, was known to be a frequent stop and supply center for ships coming to California by way of the Horn. This lighter might have been shipped assembled aboard a ship, but more probably it was built from imported Chilean lumber in San Francisco.

It was now clear that our updated buried-ships map would need further updating. During my last year at the Maritime Museum, together with graphic artist Michael Warner, we added in the lighter, Hare's yard boundaries, and the old wharf at Clark's Point where the Galapagos tortoise bones were found. We also added artistic elements. The final map came to the attention of both *National Geographic* and KQED television, each of which did a story on it and featured it on their Websites.

In 2016, I was contacted by Jim Delgado and invited to participate in a survey of Sonoma Coast doghole ports. These were the numerous "ports" for loading lumber and supplies aboard coastal

RICHARD O. EVERETT

schooners for transport to San Francisco. The "doghole" name has more than one explanation. One was that it was a hole so small even a dog couldn't turn around in it. More generally it implied that there was no real port and that the schooners had to anchor in the lee of some offshore point. Anchors being insufficient because the swells were so large and offshore the rocks so close by, ships had to be tied into numerous "iron eyes" drilled and set into the coastal rocks. The lumber was loaded down by wire cable or a wooden chute suspended by trestles and wires.

With the announced expansion of the Gulf of the Farallones and Cordell Bank National Marine Sanctuaries to more than twice their original size, it was Jim Delgado's vision as Director of Maritime Heritage at NOAA to survey the Sonoma coast both on land and by sea. Jim established a partnership between NOAA and California State Parks, represented by Richard Fitzgerald, to document this vast cultural landscape and nominate it to the National Register of Historic places.

I joined the terrestrial crew for an initial week during which we surveyed more than half of the doghole ports as we worked our way northward along the Sonoma coast. We completed our survey the following year. This intense process involved flagging every possible feature observed—usually a piece of iron or timber. A colored flag would be placed there and a GPS location recorded. At Stewart's Point, in one of the outbuildings, were discovered many salvaged items from the steamer *Klamath*. These included life preservers and two huge stout baskets that were used to transport passengers and supplies from ship to shore. The baskets were designed to hang from overhead pulleys on a wire and were reportedly constructed by local Pomo Indians.

We camped out at the Fort Ross "Arky Camp," a small clearing down a rural road near Fort Ross. I brought my kayak and was able to flag several iron eyes along the rocks, which were too difficult to reach otherwise. At night, around the campfire, we could view the cloud of GPS tags concentrated around each site on a project computer. It was productive work, and the campfire stories were extremely entertaining. It seems that archaeologists love to tell stories, and each tries to outdo the others.

When I retired on the last day of 2017, I realized how lucky I had been to have a front-row seat to nearly all the buried ships of San Francisco found over 40 years. I knew all the archaeologists and had amassed hundreds of photographs throughout that time. I thought it would be fun to share this with others, so I put together a slide lecture. In the ensuing years up to the present, I've presented this illustrated lecture at many venues, including the San Francisco Maritime Museum, the San Francisco History Association, the Exploratorium, the Mechanics Institute Library, and the San Francisco Historical Society.

After retiring I was contacted by Susan Schwartzenberg, who managed the Exploratorium Science Museum's Observation Gallery. The Observation Gallery is a large glass box at the end of Pier 17 with a panoramic view of the bay from one side to the other. The gallery was planned to interpret the setting from an historical perspective, thus the Exploratorium was very interested in all kinds of local history and particularly the buried ships so close to their location. Interspersed among their science exhibits are wooden barrels and ships' timbers—an astounding collection

Figure 87. A basket and an overhead wire were used to transport people and supplies between ship and shore. This one is believed to have been salvaged from the steam schooner *Klamath* along with many other items and was likely woven by Native American Pomo on the coast. (Photo by Richard Everett; courtesy of California State Parks, 2017)

RICHARD O. EVERETT

of all manner of things, including a map table with a hundred or more indestructible historic maps (printed on Tyvek).

Years earlier I had collaborated with Christina Larsen, one of their staffers who was developing history displays in advance of the gallery's opening. Susan now wanted to develop even more ways to talk about the waterfront ships, and she created a symposium, inviting a large number of us in the "history field" to come with ideas to share. Jim Delgado, then director of NOAA's Maritime Heritage Program, brought John Cloud, a librarian with NOAA. I brought the latest "Buried Ships Map." Allison Vanderslice, who had been involved with past archaeological projects for the city planning office, came, as well as community members, such as Joel Pomeranz, who had researched the historic groundwater systems of San Francisco. After the symposium, the Exploratorium decided to create an online "buried ships" tour. This online site, created by Rob Rothfarb, contains many deep layers of information, photographs, as well as recorded sound passages, and it required several years to complete. That exhibit portal now resides in the Exploratorium History Gallery, and the public can access it by smartphone while exploring the various sites on the map of the waterfront. It is an astounding piece of work, and many people, including Jim Delgado, helped with it.

I have enjoyed helping to bring many of these fascinating stories to the public, and I look forward to the inevitable discoveries along San Francisco's waterfront yet to come. Such discoveries will add even more to the larger story of San Francisco and those who helped create it. This larger story is a tantalizing puzzle that lies not far beneath the city's surface. It is drowned regularly by the tidewaters of San Francisco Bay, which still rise and fall unseen within the wet sands below.

Linda Noel

Linda Noel is a California Native of the Koyonghkawi people from the northern Sierra. She was born in Willits, California, in 1957 to hard-working parents, the seventh of eight children. She graduated from Willits High School in 1975 and attended Mendocino College, where she enrolled in a variety of diverse classes and where she was offered her first fulltime job in the employment and training field. She continued working in the field of human services, serving as social-services director for a Mendocino tribe for 10 years, community educator for an Indian health-service clinic for 5 years, and career-development coordinator for a Lake Country tribe, while engaging in her longtime love of poetry.

She considers herself to be "self-taught," while attributing encouragement from Ruth Rockefeller of Willits High School, who taught journalism, as fueling her writing abilities. Their relationship continued long after high school, as her former teacher would attend poetry readings and, at times, defend the poet when her work was publicly challenged. In turn, Linda attended Rockefeller's public-speaking events in support. Linda's first publication was a chapbook entitled *Where You First Saw the Eyes of Coyote*, published by Strawberry Press in 1982.

Linda was recruited to the *Frolic* Shipwreck Project by Kate Babcock McGruder, director of the Ukiah Players Theatre, who was framing *Voices of the* Frolic *and Beyond: A Mendocino History Play*, for which Linda

Figure 88. Linda Noel, 2021. (Photo courtesy of Linda Noel)

agreed to write and perform the part of the Pomo elder (Ukiah Players Theatre 1998).

Linda is poet laureate emerita of the city of Ukiah (Mendocino County) and is known for having coordinated many well-received public poetry events. She has a poem included in the permanent exhibit at the Autry Museum of the American West, and a piece has been adapted to music for the Pasadena Choir.

Linda's work has been included in many anthologies, with the last being *When the Light of the World Was Subdued, Our Songs Came Through*, (W. W. Norton & Company, 2020).

Mountain People

I come from mountain people—high-country terrain. A people who dwelled in what was once one of the most pristine, wild, and rich-in-bounty regions; a people who were inundated with the coming of the white man, first with disease and then followed by perhaps the most devastating influx of people in world history—the California Gold Rush. We were high-country people who traveled from the foothills to the valley floor during the cold, brutal, winter months of the High Sierra. My tribal name, Koyongk'awi, more commonly known as Konkow, can be interpreted as "People of the Meadow," having occupied timber lands enclosing circles of virgin meadows.

Though I was raised 35 mi. inland and have lived all my years in this vicinity, mountain blood is where I come from and

Figure 89. Linda Noel, and her father, Willits, California, 1982. (Photo courtesy of Linda Noel)

LINDA NOEL

what I am. I come from mountain people. My blood is that of mountain veins, mountain streams and rivers.

I regret never asking my parents about the first time they ever saw the Pacific Ocean, and almost as important in my contemporary curiosity is wondering if there was ever talk among the old people about the ocean—or even speculation. I never asked either of them, though there are photos of my older siblings, uncles, and relatives I'd never met at beachside. Having lived "only" 35 mi. from the shore, we visited rarely. My father said that it was always cold and miserable when he visited the coast. The drive there, between Willits and Fort Bragg, is up and over redwood ridges and down into ravines, and eventually follows a small creek all shadowed in thick redwood timber, eventually opening up to short brush and then the sea. As a child, the ride was always dark. You could not look through the timber across to the other ridge—so thick it was, unlike today.

Redwood timber was what brought my father to leave his homeland of pine, fir, and cedar. The logging industry offered employment to many men, Native and not. My father would become known as an expert Cat operator, blading the skidding roads to and through the timber and creating the flat landings where logs would be pulled by chokers set by tough men and loaded onto the log trucks to be hauled to not-so-nearby mills. This was in the northern Sierra country of Plumas, Yuba, and Butte counties of northern California in the 1940s. These were tough men making a tough living, working seasonally, then toughing out the winter months.

As the story went, word of the riches of the West Coast, based on giant trees and the promise of prosperity, was abuzz in the mountains. Many families took the risk and made the trek across the valley floor to redwood country. My father did, and eventually brought his family to Willits. Other relatives and families from the homeland also came, but all returned home. My mother told me of her desire to return, she said, to the familiar, to what she knew. My father won out on that one, so my younger brother and I were born at Howard Hospital, delivered by Dr. Babcock in Willits, far from our homeland and 35 mi. from the Pacific. We equaled out our family of four boys and four girls.

I was never one for science; it did nothing for me and seemed overcomplicated. I did, however, always like books, though I wasn't considered an avid reader. Both my parents were curious, inventive, innovative thinkers. They had to be, having come from those who raised them. My mother's mother died when she was 10, her father when she was 13. My father lost his mother at six and was abandoned by his Irish father, leaving him to be raised by his full-blood grandmother. Both of my parents were raised by those who were Native-language speakers first, with English being their second language.

I bring this up now because it is the same quest for knowledge I inherited that brought me to and gave me the propulsion to stick with the *Frolic* Project at times when I was uncertain of myself within the project. Now, all these years later, revisiting writings and articles of Tom Layton's work, I find myself ever curious and wishing I could have shared some aspects of the story with my parents—such as the Native women wearing silk, the connection which I will elaborate on later, and of the village site and my father and brothers gathering essential firewood and target practicing, sighting their hunting rifles right near that site and never having any idea of the village or shipwreck salvage there in the state forest, on Three Chop Ridge, where, eventually, the shipwreck of the *Frolic* would lead.

What a different experience it must have been—salvaging finished goods/products, acquiring such items, premade and ready for use, by those whose entire existence depended upon the work they performed to supply themselves with the essentials to survive. I imagine them—those who were accustomed to weaving vessels from materials they had gathered from the wild—turning the porcelain bowls in their hands. Though retrieving materials from the ocean would be no easy feat and transporting them inland took effort, I can picture the Native women adorning themselves in the colorful silks. Tom is quoted as calling the *Frolic* "a floating Cost Plus." What a contrast to the efforts required in every aspect of Native survival: gathering, hunting, weaving, carving, etc.

While working at Mendocino College as the Native American outreach worker, a position long fought for through the bureaucracy of a community-college hierarchy, I was approached by Kate MacGruder about a project she was working on, called "The Wreck of the *Frolic*." She conveyed how the project was in the developing stages and that further input was needed, especially when it came to compiling the role/script of the Pomo woman they were asking me to portray. That word, "portray," that sentence, that invitation almost made me uneasy. Portray: to represent dramatically, as on the stage. Something I had never done and, additionally, for most all my adult life had avoided as pretense. Right behind that thought was "Pomo woman"; I was not Pomo, in case she didn't know that. Additionally, to be a representative of a tribe from whom I did not originate was, in my view,

disrespectful. I asked if there wasn't a local Pomo woman they could approach. Kate relayed that a local female tribal leader, whom I knew fairly well, had been slated for the project. However, for reasons I don't recall, the team, which consisted of several individuals I knew and had been acquainted with through community, had thrown in my name after having seen me read my poetry publicly.

I was apprehensive and asked for time to think this over and discuss it with my then-husband, himself a local Pomo. Having been incorrectly referred to in the past as Pomo, I was sensitive to the notion of Native people identifying themselves correctly out of respect for each individual community. Part of this misperception sprang from the fact that I was with a Pomo man and had lived and grown up in Pomo country. Beyond those thoughts and sprouting confusions, questions arose about "acting." I told Kate I had never had any aspirations of being an actor by any measure. A lost and drowned clipper ship? Why would I care about that? I really had no interest in the historical significance or depiction or reenactment of such. Then the word "archaeologist." That was a siren not only ringing out loud, but banging against the inside of my best sense inside my cranial activity.

Archaeologists were not friends to Natives. They were referred to as "grave robbers"—and rightfully so—an archaeologist being a person "who studies human history and prehistory through the excavation of sites and the analysis of artifacts and other physical remains."

I was skeptical, though it was certainly an opportunity to confront misgivings based on real experiences that I did not seize on.

Natives are also very much aware

LINDA NOEL

of anthropologists—those who study what makes us human, who take a broad approach to understanding the many different aspects of the human experience. They consider the past, through archaeology, to see how human groups lived hundreds or thousands of years ago and what was important to them.

I knew of Kroeber, his wife Theodora, and that sad story of Ishi. I had read Heizer's book, *The Destruction of California Indians*. I knew we were a studied group. I knew we were more than back dirt.

This all needed to be taken into consideration when deciding to take on the role. This also made the role of the Native definitely unique to the rest of the cast.

As Kate's invitation was taking hold of me, obviously, I started immediately thinking too much. Still, I didn't feel I knew enough about the project to determine my participation or not. Kate was kind, and both of us found ourselves talking and talking, not only about the project, but also about college stuff, artistic stuff, and drama stuff that I knew nothing about and was somewhat skeptical of. A ship, a professor archaeologist, a sea captain, the Antiquities Act, the Chinese temple, artifacts, and a tribe surviving. What was my role? Would I, should I, could I contribute to what Kate was trying to accomplish? Did I care enough about silk and broken pieces of porcelain china to commit to a long project that would involve some sort of acting role of tribal people of whom I didn't come from that involved an archaeologist, and I was not an actor. I would eventually always preface my appearance with somehow stating that I was not an actor by any means, and that I was simply a poet who read her work.

I come from mountain people. My grandparents spoke English as a second language, their native tongue of Koyongk'awi being their first language. Somehow my grandparents emerged out of the dark days, years, and times of the California Gold Rush. When I speak of this publicly, I am often asked why surviving the aftermath of one of the most horrific, murderous times in California history is significant, a question I have no need to ask assistance from an anthropologist or archaeologist to answer or understand. I will speak on this later. I am the descendent of a people who lost an estimated 70%–80% of their population in a period of a half century, only 120 years ago. My grandparents were born in the 1870s and 80s. How their grandparents survived, first the diseases sweeping through the lands prior to the Gold Rush and then the onslaught that the nuggets brought, amazes me still. Brutality in every form and, of course, displacement when Koyongk'awi and other tribes of the northern central valley were driven over the mountain range into the Round Valley Reservation where descendants reside today. I bring this to light now when speaking publicly because it almost seems miraculous that they did survive that time, that I am here able to speak of it and honor them.

Because they were of the old way, my parents learned, experienced, and lived the customs of the old traditions. My mother's mother was doctored by Indian doctors who were paid with baskets, and they were with her when she departed. My father would say Indian doctors accomplished "stuff you could never believe unless you saw it." These topics were rarely discussed out of respect and reverence for their significance, power, and place.

This might be considered an intersection, where science meets sacred beliefs. This came into play during the rehearsal of a scene in which the piece of a porcelain saucer, a small, stained and battered, triangular-shaped piece, was being passed around to the cast. It was fingered, handled, examined, admired, questioned, and discussed. I did not care to touch the object, having been taught to be cautious of handling objects that might or could hold the lasting shadow of whence it came, especially if it had been involved/handled by the deceased, of which we knew no origin. This is not spoken of lightly or often. I need not handle it anyway. What would it accomplish? Would it make me feel something? Closer to its origin, closer to the story it told? Would I receive some deeper understanding of what this project was trying to accomplish? Would I regret touching it? Possibilities existed, so I did not touch the object, just as I would not touch an arrowhead, a piece of gambling bone. Even if I desire to touch a living person's basket, I would not do so without first asking. This is deep, serious respect in a way that is not often voiced.

A non-Native friend was once very anxious to show and hand me a tooth derived from a mountain lion. I can't recall the story of the cat's death or any of that, but I recall his enthusiasm to share the tooth— how he rolled it in his long fingers and offered it with pride, as if I couldn't help but be as excited as he was for me to see it. I kindly declined, to his disappointed amazement and his wanting to know why. I didn't explain, though I did say it was Indian law, that's all. I wasn't about to try to explain that I didn't want that mountain lion haunting my day – or night dreams, seeking me out from the taste of me in the space that tooth occupied. This is where my parent's knowledge/experience of the old way meets the theories of the scientific. The idea of an experiment

to provide proof, one way or the other, of the validity of these practices in my view is absurd. There would be no evidence to dissect or examine in the dissipating smoke accompanying these practices.

I felt somewhat pressured in deciding to take on a place in the project. I had come to terms with representing a Pomo after discussing it with my husband and several close friends and relatives. Early in my career as a poet and being with a Pomo man, I was often mistakenly named as a Pomo, which in Native country can be a big deal. People who you are purported to belong to do not want people who do not legitimately belong to be assumed to belong, and individuals who do not belong to a certain community do not care to be referred to as such, but as a representative of their own community, both with pride, respectfully. Of course, there are always exceptions. Having been considered part of the community because of my mate, I was known by many, including his relatives, and didn't risk being castigated for taking on the role. Yet my main concern was to pull it off respectfully.

When Kate gave me a brief look at the tentative schedule, I was somewhat surprised. I hadn't realized the depth which would require a significant time commitment in simply framing up the script. I wasn't a scriptwriter! Could some of my poems be incorporated into the script? Sure, as long as it isn't exploited. And what did I mean by that? Only that I wasn't there to fill in the blanks needed from a Native person's view or perspective. Or was I?

How would I feel about working with someone portraying an archaeologist? Could I "dig" it, so to speak? I was uncertain. I didn't want to be the patronized character in the cast; I would not feed

LINDA NOEL

into any romantic or demeaning version of Native portrayal.

I knew nothing of the theater. I had been amazed in high school when a rural music department on a hair-string budget produced the first musical, of which name I can't recall. I knew nothing of production, direction, stage presence, or segue, and never had any desire to find out about any of it.

I was pleasantly surprised to learn certain aspects of theater that otherwise would have never crossed my mind for any reason.

Scriptwriting wasn't my thing either, yet I felt the need to have the character be believable, genuine to the role, and neither inflated nor marionette-like. It must be genuine and real. The importance of that became paramount to the point where I couldn't quite make out the forest for the single tree. And, after all, I was a writer.

It would take time for me to understand the comprehensive story as a whole. Okay, sailing from Canton to San Francisco, wrecked for lack of proper navigating, and discovered by and utilized by Native Pomos at Three Chop Ridge, where my father and brothers chopped essential wood for our fireplace and, just as importantly, sighted their hunting rifles. This was a common outing; much time was spent there in the forest, simply referred to in our house as Three Chop. No one had an inkling of its history or the village. Had my father known that, he would have, I'm sure, viewed the area differently and, in turn, considered his activities there more carefully.

This could be an interesting story, even though the main catalyst was an archaeologist; even though I was no actor; even though I was not a Pomo woman, but a Koyongk'awi woman married into the Pomo community; even though I was not a scriptwriter; even though I cared not to learn about props, costumes, and cues.

The north coast Pacific Ocean of California is not a gentle lady. Although she can be that, along with being a brutal beast knocking on the rocky edge of this continent.

I would learn of the vast abundance, the bounty that came with the beauty of landscape in which native Pomos enjoyed living. And, like any people facing adversity, they survived by means of adapting to the coming of the non-Native and all the changes that would ensue.

After the upheaval of gold fever had subsided, many Natives in that exploited region took to surviving as they could. For my mother's father that meant continuing to mine the leftovers on their ravaged homeland. It is the same concept as the Pomo salvaging from the *Frolic* in the simple quest to survive, to continue in the face of overwhelming destruction, though the Pomo were yet to experience the brutality to come.

Hesitant or reluctant that I was to get on this "ship," I had no idea what kind of journey it would become and how my thought process or view of the world might evolve as the ship sailed through performance after performance, up and down the north coast, from San Francisco's Hyde Street Pier to the Eureka Inn in Humboldt County.

Could I be referred to as a grain of gold dust having survived disease followed by the invasion of the gold rush?

Oh rush, rush, rush, head for the hills. Little did they know the mountains they would encounter and all the natural elements and challenges that high country habitation requires. Yet they tore up the land at every attempt to find any dust and glowing piece. Am I simply a remnant of those times of over-rated romantic golden glow bliss or horrific blood red dislocation blown down through the seasons of history?

Contemporary Natives and certainly most common citizens might not recognize the term "proof of habitation." But, aren't we all, after all, each one of us, proof of ancestral survival? Blood down the river, literally. I was determined to exhibit that we are certainly proof of more than habitation by our mere presence in modern-day America, as proof of habitation infers that we are of the past. That we *once* existed in a certain area, yet we are still here, all over America. I know that, scientifically defined, that might not hold water like our baskets did.

Can archaeologists bring us out of the shadow of history, or does even that notion perpetuate the myth of us being only something of the past, simply history, as opposed to us being living contemporary people/Natives?

All this surfaced, came bubbling up when I was asked to write a narrative of my experience in the *Frolic* Project in Mendocino County.

At the time I thought of parallels. Okay, when the *Frolic* was being built in Baltimore, what was going on in California territory? When the ship crashed near Casper, what was historically happening with the local Pomo peoples, and, of course, what was happening in my homelands of the northern Sierra?

Some of these parallels have already been pointed out: Pomos surviving on shipwrecked products. My people surviving for a century later, living on leftover gold tailings. The *Frolic* shipwreck led to the discovery of valued redwood trees. And those redwood trees are what brought my family to Mendocino County and up to Three Chop, where my family resourced essential firewood to warm our home. Meanwhile, the Chinese were brought to the high country as laborers for mining and then for building the railroad.

I wouldn't name my consideration of working/collaborating/interacting/learning from an archaeologist as an internal conflict, yet it sort of was, though not a battle or competition. But there certainly were times when I would ask myself what I was doing in the middle of this project that I had no inclination or imagining of my ever doing. Still, I abandoned any stubborn pre-perceived views and knew that there was knowledge I could gain and would benefit me as a thinker and writer. Sometimes, though, the rigorous sitting and sifting through script possibilities, comprehending the context while keeping in mind what was to be accomplished, wore on me. Had I been presented with a script to read and the opportunity for editing, it would have been easier and more appealing. Yet I was a writer. I was entrenched in the Pomo community, and though thoughts of backlash in representing a Pomo woman when I was not Pomo were always present, I did feel that I could offer a contemporary view from a Native woman looking back on the history of the ship and its eventual role in a local community.

After all, I did come of age following the tail of the 1960s, aware of the evolving Native movement, of the Alcatraz BIA building seize, Wounded Knee occupation, and the emerging Native writers at the time. I read *Custer Died for Your Sins* by Vine Deloria, Jr., in which he discussed the roles, mainly of the anthropologist, the relative of archaeologist. And what Deloria said not only represented the Native

LINDA NOEL

sentiment at the time, but what was playing out in my own personal life.

I mean this literally. Though the exact date has escaped our collective family memory, the incident is clearly enshrined in our contemporary memory. Our family has buried our people on the eastern slope of the northern Sierra on land that has become privately owned for decades. Landowners had not interfered or questioned our doing so until the early 70s, which is another story. My relationship with archaeology began when told by my parents and sisters that, upon visiting our burial grounds, they encountered a professor, an archeologist, with students from Chico State University digging at the graves of my grandparents, aunts, uncles, and siblings. Needless to say, this was very upsetting. At the time I was a new teenager and knew little of the family history surrounding our burial grounds or any inkling as to what archaeology was. But I knew the reactions of my parents and the pain and discomfort just the re-telling caused them, imprinted in my psyche the contempt, distrust, and hatred of those who would disrespect our dead in such a way.

Over the years I became more aware of the field of archaeology as siblings were taking college courses, which included cultural anthropology, and these professionals were crawling the hills leading to the Sierras, seeking out Natives willing to discuss history in terms benefiting their studies.

So when I heard about Tom Layton and the *Frolic* and this production I wasn't as easily impressed, which seemed to dismay many involved, all who were giddy and so impressed with the potential of the project.

The thought of working/collaborating with an archaeological project and archaeologist coupled with portraying a Pomo woman, writing script to be inserted into a presentation about clipper ships connected to the Gold Rush and trying to memorize my role was not appealing to me, to say the least.

I have been unable to recall the first meeting with the group that was putting together the program—composing the script and cast, determining roles, props, and costumes. But I do recall many meetings in which enthusiasm and rigor for accuracy prevailed. I was taken by the zeal shown by crew and cast, which caused me to feel oddly about my lack of such in learning about the ship's history, including the different ships, their riggings, and seafaring abilities, much of which I had held little interest in. To watch the delight of Michael Oakes in understanding some specific operation of a clipper ship was somewhat amusing, but also intellectually stimulating. He really did immerse himself in being Captain Faucon and portraying him truthfully. Never being around actors, I soon witnessed what was meant in submerging oneself in one's role. Unfortunately, although I was impressed with the enthusiasm and dedication of the other cast members, I never became submerged in my role. The *Frolic* became a learning experience as a writer and as someone who performs/reads her work publicly.

As for maritime history, I once took a ride on the Red & White Ferry Fleet on San Francisco Bay and never again had any inclination or desire to go out on the sea aboard any-sized boat. I knew little of tides and even less about ships and seafaring. Most of what I did know I learned from my then-husband, himself a Pomo, who told me tales he'd heard over the years about his uncles, cousins, etc., lowering themselves down the coastal cliff to reach the prized abalone. He taught me to identify plants, their slang tribal names, and how his people traveled annually to the sea for sustenance and ceremony.

I'd also, of course, learned things about myself during the preparation, production, and even years later while contemplating this narrative. I certainly gained a deeper appreciation for much that I had little knowledge of or exposure to, such as drama and maritime history, notably: The *Frolic*, the ship. The *Frolic*, the location. The *Frolic*, the wreck. The *Frolic*, the contents. The *Frolic*, the salvage. The *Frolic*, the Natives. The *Frolic*, the reverberations. The *Frolic*, Three Chop Ridge. The *Frolic*, the coolies. The *Frolic*, the divers. The *Frolic*, the archaeologist. The *Frolic*, the story. The *Frolic*, the learning.

Nevertheless, I was haunted by the thought of speaking for a group of local Natives of which I was not—though I had been warmly welcomed into the communities when attached to a Pomo man whose grandmother was well respected and remembered by some contemporaries. Was that my credence? Would I have "cred"? How would I feel having been in the converse situation of someone speaking/representing my community when their relatives weren't mine? It never came up, at least not to my knowledge, and I would have easily deferred to anyone who would replace me.

I couldn't imagine memorizing my words, though I attempted several times. Yet I felt out of place holding the script in my hand and reading directly from it while everyone was a real actor. I took to announcing, sometime during the show or right after, that I was merely a poet who read her work and not an actor. In doing so, I wanted to let the audience be aware of my different presentation than the actors, and to also ask for understanding or patience in some way. I never really felt pressure from the directors or fellow cast, but was always aware of that difference, though the cast was tolerant and kind.

To simply complete the script was somewhat menacing. In developing the script I called upon my poetry at times when I felt I was foundering. The lines from the Pomo traveling to the coast was an older poem originating from a story my ex had told, which had been told to him by his maternal grandmother. I felt it fit and aided me in a time of spinning my wheels.

The sessions of composing were not always pleasant for me. I never really thought of it much until writing this piece. The sessions seemed longer for me than they really were, perhaps because my enthusiasm lacked at times. I was not intellectually stimulated, which I believe had more to do with personal goings on in my life rather than the project. This would come to light as the production ended and as I end this piece. At the same time, as a writer, I had an internal drive to rise to the occasion, along with respect for the value of one's word.

I had stepped onto this ship. I had made a commitment. There was no way I could, figuratively speaking, step off the ship. I was aboard, a needed cast/crew member. And having taken that step, I felt I must stick with it, no matter the gales nor my own undulating doubts/insecurities as part of a drama. I never felt unwelcome in the composing/developing sessions. I did, however, feel odd in a way I was aware of at the time, while being unable to define it.

As a Native who is known for reading her work in public, it is sometimes assumed that, because I am Native, that I do or should have knowledge of all things Native. Even then I was well aware of this

LINDA NOEL

dynamic. After a reading followed by a Q&A session, one might be asked anything from giving their opinion on Mayan sacrifices to what was the name of my horse, for surely, being Native, I certainly must have had a horse. Though I knew some of the crew/committee coordinating the project, I was new to meeting most of the cast and some supporting members. I did not want to become the go-to expert on all Native aspects of living, of history, though this was a history project.

By introduction, I became aware that most of the crew had had little if any contact with Native people in their lives. This is always interesting to me because Natives are everywhere. Logic dictates this. Though no one may know there is an Indian in his or her small, quiet, Midwestern town, there certainly are. How could there not be? We inhabited this entire continent, and, try as they might, with vicious intent, the powers of America from the beginning to this day were unable to vanquish us to the past, a product of yesterday to be remembered, to be excavated and studied by archaeologist and anthropologist.

I was determined to defy that notion yet unwilling to instruct a brief Native 101 mini-lesson every time something interesting to an individual for individual reasons arose.

To acquiesce is to condone or accept, and at times I felt too tired of explaining some aspect of some obscure stereotypical ceremonial gem waiting to be unearthed.

Don't get me wrong. There are individuals who relish in doing so, providing long-sought-after answers about visions and trauma and sweat lodges and dreamcatchers. I'm not one of them. In fact, my efforts as a writer and Native are to dispel the notion that we exist only in pretty past images made into posters or the grunting portrayals of Hollywood.

So this was an internal route/avenue within the workings of this sailing ship and my cranial activity. That phenomenon was not prevalent in the working sessions, but I was always aware of it when questions arose and the whole room turned to me. And there were times when I was willing to explain/discuss/shed light on certain things, while at the same time knowing the complexities involved when you discuss Native culture, history, etc. Surely archaeologists are aware of this.

Many Americans know something of or have heard of Custer, Chief Joseph, Sitting Bull, even if it is from Hollywood. But few know of Bloody Run or Bloody Island. Many have heard of the Trail of Tears, but very few know of the Nome Cult Walk, so I did and still do feel that, as a writer of that ancestry, it is my duty, especially as a poet, to tell of it from the truth of that ancestry as well as I know. However, there is a thick, dense code of federal regulations—titled *Indians*! Even the learned professor is limited to certain/specific disciplines and is not an expert of all-encompassing knowledge.

This was often in my cranial activity during the working sessions and lingered throughout, especially after performances. Even if there was no Q&A, I was approached and asked questions that sometimes troubled me. I tried not to let my face betray me and answered the questions as honestly as possible, even though sometimes I wanted to snap sarcastically at such an inquiry. One example was being asked why the reservations are so filthy these days when Indians were supposed to love nature so much. My response surprised me, as I simply said that he, the inquirer, must not be aware of the poverty there and why it exists, and that reservations were a sad segment of American history that he might want to learn more about. I additionally went on to tell him of several distinct groups of Pomo people who had worked diligently to purchase pieces of property for their peoples without assistance from the federal government, and, at the time, it certainly was a proud accomplishment.

In retrospect, hindsight being what it is, I take pause at how timid the Native script seems to me now. I select that word purposefully. I attribute it to what I reference many times prior, my reluctance, my uncertainty, my inexperience in theater and scriptwriting, and the fact that I had committed to a project that I had felt was ill-defined in my own mind from the start. All this was influenced by my personal life situation of a deteriorating relationship.

As the project developed I was able to come to terms with my role as I had allowed it to play out during the creative process. I can't imagine me, now, not being much more stern/deliberate in the interactions with the archaeologist.

I recall a practice run in which I was to confront the archaeologist and wasn't feeling it, and it was obvious. I recall Kate and maybe another crewmember emphatically saying that I needed to display contempt or anger or some kind of disturbed reaction as cued. I almost wanted to remind everyone that I wasn't an actor and let him or her know I wasn't certain what I was doing there. I didn't. I took a deep breath, and in exaggerated actor style took a stance in the width between my feet, swung my arm, and looked at Gary/Tom, and said: "Okay, so f—k you!" All in jest, of course, and the cast erupted in laughter, except Gary, who hesitated for a minute before I laughingly told him I was kidding.

It was an interesting moment. Everyone knew it was shtick and enjoyed it except, it seemed, the archaeologist. Moving on, I managed to summon some sort of faux contempt in the scene of passing around the pottery piece. It was safe and easy at the time. These days I would have plenty more to say.

Another exchange that stood out at the time was between Michael (Captain Faucon) and myself during either a planning session or a rehearsal. I don't recall the topic I was speaking of before being abruptly interrupted by Michael who was so excited over discovering some maritime detail that had bothered him until he, right then as I was speaking, discovered and confirmed his inquisitiveness. As he spoke, I said: "Excuse me." To which he raised his hand to wave me off with an "I know, but I just have to ... this is important (to me)." I have experienced this all my life with men, most always white men, who, by virtue of who they are and who I am, should and would be heard over me, even if it is an abrupt, rude interruption. As Michael gleefully told his tidbit and all listened, I took a deep breath. Somewhere in there I encouraged Michael to continue speaking, as what he had to say was, obviously, so much more significant than me or what I had to say. The room paused for a moment. Michael's face turned red. No one said anything until I repeated my comment.

Michael apologized, I found and reestablished my thought, and the room moved forward in a slower more cautious way. It didn't become a negative thing. It became a lesson for all, myself included. It was a moment presented to the collective group that could have evolved into a lasting shadow of misunderstanding that might have lingered and haunted the production.

256

I say this because it is something that occurs often in the coming together of polar dynamics: a Native and an archaeologist, a white man and an Indian woman, and Natives will voice to this day that there is always a white man who knows what is best for the Native, knows how the Native should progress, knows how to teach the Native to think and be in their society, notice: *theirs* not ours. Though very slight, this was an example of that dynamic which could have turned negative and didn't. I think it fostered an awareness and seeded understanding and respect. It was a living example of conflict that can be overcome by communication, and that, perhaps, the archaeologist and Native can converse and not have to argue, though arguing has its place.

I came to respect each cast member as a talented individual who was willing to learn. This applied to myself as well. I knew that part of the project was to increase awareness, portray history in a real way. I, too, learned from cast and crewmembers not only about acting, but parts of their own stories of being on the north coast and how they came here.

I was most taken by their acting, having not been around the theater scene. I'll always recall with a smile Kathy O'Grady (pioneer, Eliza Kelly) talking of "what a boon it was," the voice she conjured, and Holly Tannen (music-hall singer) singing away from one character to the next. Carter Sears (translator for the 1851 Army expedition) was special for me in that he offered calmness and humor when I needed it. Gary (the archaeologist) and Michael (Captain Faucon) were made for their roles: Michael, with his booming, dictating captain's voice and drive; Gary with his methodical, almost quiet way of examination. And me, uncertain in my capacity, which is reflective in the almost placid portrayal.

As things progressed, the pace increased. I recall being told by Kate that the photographer, a very well-known local, would meet with us to take group photos of the cast and then individual photos. I did not look forward to this, as I knew my appearance was reflecting an unsettled time in my life, though the magnitude would not become clear for a few more miles down the road. I felt that because, again, I wasn't a local Native woman and having my photo out there, cast as that, would or could become a negative. In hindsight I realize most of this was my own creation based on my own uncertainties brewing.

I tried to summon enthusiasm and met the photographer. He gave me some tips, like lower your chin and look up at the camera, realize you are looking into/at something. His efforts to help me be comfortable were commendable. But he couldn't do miracles! Then the photos came out. I remember Kate's look when I saw them. My face obviously spoke and hers did the same. Silently, I saw her disappointment in witnessing mine. The photo was a reflection of my life at the time, though I was ignorant (the word derived from "ignore") of the state of my 20-year relationship/marriage, which would play out just after the end of the project.

The photo was chosen to be the centerpiece of the project's poster, which was the paramount means of publicity at that time. I was surprised when some relatives and friends assured me that the photo wasn't as bad as I perceived it to be.

As was often the case, I took a deep breath and told myself: Onward!

Other publicity photo shoots turned out to be fun, and the photos served their

Figure 90. Linda Noel wrote and acted her part in the Ukiah Players Theatre 1994 production of *Voices from the* Frolic *and Beyond* (Published by Ukiah Players Theatre,1998), but she chose not to touch the *Frolic* potsherd. (Photo by Evan Johnson; courtesy of the Mendocino County Museum)

purpose, especially in the compilation of the accompanying booklet, *Voices from the* Frolic *and Beyond: A Mendocino History Play.*

The maiden presentation was nerve wracking, almost to the point of spawning an apathetic approach to the whole production. This went against my natural inclination to accomplishing tasks or challenges with sufficient respect and class to spawn positive results.

I wondered what I should wear. I'm a Native woman speaking from a perspective from before the white man came. Other cast members would be, of course, dressed as the characters they were portraying. I can't recall any real discussion about a costume or what attire my character would don. The thought of constructing what would be called "traditional" clothing—actually depicting the time of

my character—didn't enthrall me. It somewhat puzzles me now, looking back, that there wasn't much discussion of what the traditional clothing of Natives would have been at that time.

I don't recall opposing the notion of traditional clothing or what it would be, as I knew it to be minimal and made from surrounding natural resources. This, I believe, derives from my efforts as I became an adult and continue to this day to combat Native stereotypes, although it was a play, a depiction, a period in time replicated for this presentation. Of course, in hindsight, this did not add to the production and perhaps did not lend to the cred I had aspired to earn, in spite of my misgivings regarding my portrayal.

I wore navy-blue trousers and a white blouse with thin red stripes to the first production. I was uncomfortable. I was sure

LINDA NOEL

the lines on the pages of script I held were shaking with the paper, within my hands. I felt out of place in that I was out of character because I lacked acting experience and, thus, wanted no costume, felt I needed no costume. Yet I was part of and amidst a play in which characters are portrayed through costume. I was uncertain of what traditional clothing would be. My understanding was that most Native women wore no top coverings and grass, tule, or other natural material skirt-type bottoms. I never considered wearing bright silk shawls, which would have been acceptable, appropriate. I wouldn't have gone barefoot; I know that for sure.

Looking back on it, the cast was not— or did not appear to be—conflicted with my exception in portraying as I did it. They were actors, they were into it, and they wanted their characters to be portrayed as closely to the truth as possible. Their zeal and that of Director Kate were inspiring to me, though at the time my lack of theater experience hindered me from feeling secure in seeking out further acting lessons.

I actually thought that, as each performance concluded, I would become more at ease with my role and perhaps maybe even begin to memorize parts of my script. I did to an extent. But as each performance ensued, I was becoming more aware of what more the character might have included in her portrayal.

I so admire both Kathy O'Grady and Holly Tannen for their acting experience and theater savvy. Their ability to portray multiple characters, switching voices, tones, and expressions with acute affect sticks in my memory all these years later. Kathy, with her bonnet, her carrying of voice, made her characters real. The multiple-character aspect applies to Holly Tannen as well, with the addition of her singing. I'd never experienced such multitalents exposed in one setting from one person before. And, as with Kathy, Holly presented honest portrayals of a variety of characters while singing segments of the script with gusto and sincerity. The same holds true for Carter Sears, whom I came to feel a connection with that sticks with me today. Being a lawyer and then acting in this play, along with his smile and wit, impressed me. He was always willing to listen in a comfortable manner that put me at ease.

Michael Oakes was meant to be captain. His enthusiasm was sometimes imposing as he wished to hone and improve on his character's portrayal at every point. His gaining of knowledge and the need to share it was admirable, though sometimes ill-timed. Michael and I seemed to have developed an unspoken regard for each other. Always greeting each other with knowledge, somehow, of our differences and that it didn't have to be explained, our smiles spoke it in some respectful way.

Driving with Kate through San Francisco to get to the Hyde Street Pier, where we would present on the ship *Balclutha*, was fun and harrowing at the same time. The experience on the ship was one that stands out. To board the ship and check out all it had to offer was very interesting. I thought of my father and what he would think of the craftsmanship, the labor, the engineering, especially during that time period, lent to my fascination on just being aboard the ship. I can't imagine any other reason over my lifetime that I would board a ship such as the *Balclutha*, its sails flapping in the breeze through the Golden Gate, the smell of old wet wood and the sound of the tide licking at its curved edges. While this turned out to be one of the most memorable of performances, it also harkened me back to the whole concept of California's history, the bay clogged with clipper ships, a forest of masts after the discovery of gold, and what that meant to my mountain ancestors.

Each place we performed, the audience was different. Being on the ship lent to a mariner's atmosphere. The crowd was different. There were half-barrels filled with ice and bottles of beer. The ropes swayed. It was a satisfying performance enhanced by the coming on of all the lights lining the piers and Ghirardelli Square.

We were treated very well, and the cast and crew seemed happy and invigorated by the seashore atmosphere, along with the pulse of the city. Richard Everett, Curator of Exhibits at the Maritime Museum, lent us his place on Dolores to spend the night after a very pleasant evening.

I would later learn that, outside of the museum, there at the marina, a small tented kiosk, as it was described to me, was erected to showcase parts of the Voices from the *Frolic* Project that included a picture of me or some sort of audio or video piece of me. I was pleasantly surprised when a colleague told me of it and how she came upon it with friends and was able to tell them she knew me. I never learned anything more of that "exhibit" than that and can't be certain what it actually consisted of.

The closing performance was to be held in Eureka, up the coast. It would be staged at the 29th Annual Meeting of Society for California Archaeology. Additionally, I was asked to participate beyond the play and be included on a session of the meeting slated as "Symposium 15, The Frolic Shipwreck Project: Getting Archeology Back to the Community." The session would include an introduction of Captain Faucon, of course played by Michael, a talk

by Tom, Mark Rawitsch, Daniel Taylor, Lorraine Hee-Chorley, and Victoria Patterson. My segment was titled: "The Frolic Dig: Education vs Exploitation."

As I write this, I can't imagine having had such an opportunity to discuss that topic and not doing so—not rising to the occasion, which is what actually occurred.

Overall, the trip up the coast, the hotel setting, the sea wind, it being the closing performance, all appeared onboard. What sticks out in my mind about that trip, other than my lacking performance at the conference, was Tom's dad. Myself and my husband were able to spend time with him and thoroughly enjoyed his company. Such a pleasant man, who shared with us and was inquisitive about our lives.

I've made reference earlier in this piece about the comportment of my personal life during this entire project. From my initial invitation to that last performance, I was somewhat reluctantly aware of the state of my 20-year-old relationship. In hindsight, it was in tatters in Eureka and continued to unravel quickly afterwards, though at the time I was in proverbial denial. This, of course, impacted my presentation in every way, not just while performing.

The night before I was to speak to the group was tense and uncomfortable personally. I didn't prepare as I could have. I was somewhat apathetic, as were many aspects of my life at the time, though I didn't realize to what degree.

Standing at the lectern could have been an ideal time to voice and illustrate, bring to light the skepticism I had about archaeologists, my own personal experience of their imposition on my dead relatives, and other aspects of the dynamic existing between science and Native practices/customs. But I did not. I was more than hesitant. I was almost frightened, and I was intimidated. I was adrift in my personal life, and it showed in many ways. I was weak at the lectern and, while standing there, knew I was disappointing people, including myself. What an opportunity not taken. I didn't have the internal strength at that time and didn't know it. As of this writing, I hold some regret in that experience, while at the same time having grown and learned so much since then.

After my marriage dissolved, I ran into Mark Rawitsch (of Mendocino College), who, upon hearing that news, quickly asked me if that was occurring while we were in Eureka. I found his question interesting; it was obviously evident that I was somewhere in my cranial activity that did not lend to my addressing the archaeologists that day.

I found it interesting, at long last, when reading Mark's quote in the booklet: "I took a view from my perspective of local, regional, national, international history." And, to that, I would add my personal history at that time and all these years since.

I could use this closing to name all the things I did learn during the project, such as mariner terms, acting and stage terms, more archaeological terms, history—and the glaring face of all that wasn't learned by myself about the Mitom and the connection to contemporary Sherwood Valley tribal people who reside on the reservation in Willits, and much more.

I do not make light of what was learned, which is too much to scribe here. However, learning of the Chinese temple and its continuance was significant for many reasons. A lasting tribute to the contributions of the Chinese, though few are aware of this. Interesting in that the temple marks their existence and time in the region, and yet it took until this century for the local Natives to be acknowledged by the creation of Pomo Bluffs Park at the south end of Fort Bragg. Though I realize that the temple endured due to the efforts of the Chinese descendants of those times, I didn't ask at the time and am still ignorant of where the Pomo "Temple," a ceremonial round house, existed. Still, I know that its location would not be something talked of as common knowledge.

I will use this closing to discuss what I did not discuss during the development and program production that I now know contributed to my using the term "timid" to describe the script's speaking parts of the Native woman I portrayed.

Natives are a unique people of America, in that this is our homeland. We stand on this as no other peoples in America can and in spite of scholarly theories touting the opposite. Archaeologists uphold the theory that we Indigenous people actually migrated during the Ice Age. Ask a Native person where they come from and you might hear as many different answers as there are tribes: we were created from the mud under turtle's claws when he emerged from the deep; we came out of a hole in a log; and many other versions that can and are disputed by scientists.

Our view of the world is born out of belief taught down through the centuries, sometimes in convoluted notions based on historical distrust, which is difficult to dismiss when considering past factors such as bounties, servitude, Indian schools, to name a few.

Though the crew and cast and most all peripheral participants were respectful, I rarely shook the feeling of being and remaining on the margins. This was partially self-imposed out of insecurities mentioned earlier and very much a real dynamic that I wrestle with in certain instances still.

My distance from the cast and crew comes from cultural differences that continue to go unspoken. How would I relay the unique worldview that Natives considered archaeologists grave robbers?

I've spoken about conflict with archaeologists and personal experiences. Yet I did not consider sharing these concerns with the cast or crew. I did not tell them of the experience with our own burial ground, though it is contemporary. I did not tell them of my parents' endeavors, endurance, and witnessing of the old ways. I did not tell them because many aspects/beliefs are not to be discussed in the presence of strangers. Would they understand? Were they worthy of such knowledge? Would what I said be misunderstood, exploited, or mocked? Would they understand what "invasion" meant from my view?

I did not share my personal experience of our burial ground as evidence of destruction by archaeologists nor refer to what they sought as "grave goods," being obviously what they were digging for. I did state emphatically that I was not Pomo and that my origins were of the northern Sierra, while not saying that we as a people believe in this more than mere "provenience."

I did not share the devastation that Natives—and, in this case, California Natives—faced and survived, including the Mitom of Three Chop Ridge, as part of the "formation process."

And, finally, I think my presence and contribution, though flawed, certainly conveyed that we are not "back dirt."

I don't recall any goodbyes.

James P. Delgado

April 9, 1994
Vancouver, BC

I was born in early 1958, in San Jose, California. My parents were divorced when I was two and my mother didn't remarry until I was five. During that period, I bounced around quite a bit. Although I lived with my mother for brief periods in that time, I was largely raised by my grandparents. My grandfather was an airline mechanic for United Airlines, so that period included a one-year stint living on Puget Sound, in Federal Way, Washington. My grandparents were very important to me, and they form an integral part of my earliest memories. One thing that I see now in my sixties is that at an early, formative age, many of my values were passed to me by an older generation. Throughout my life, I have found myself occasionally out of step with my own generation and have had more friends and associates who are from ten to twenty years older. My grandmother took me to my first day of school. She had already taught me to read and write, and my introduction to school was being disciplined for not wanting to start over again and writing in an "old fashioned" way.

My mom was always insisting that I go to college. No one in her family had ever been to college, and she hadn't even finished grade school. My dad only had a year or two of college. Still, it was assumed that I was going to college, and I was going to work hard. I had channeled anger into hard work. Anyone who knew me in my younger years would say that I was always hard working, focused, very serious, and bookish. I learned the hard work from my dad. He had been married before and had other children, one of whom, my brother Dan, lived with us. My dad had to pay alimony to his wife and child support for his other kids, so he had to work two jobs to support two families. He never complained. As a fireman he would work a 24-hour shift and then be off for a day. He worked a second job on his days off.

To give you an indication of what kind of a man my dad is – the second job he took to make ends meet for our family, was at an auto body shop. He hated it, but he did it for his family. He did it because he was a man of honor and a man who understood the meaning of commitment. What better role model could a boy have than a man like him? Needless to say, we grew up without a lot of money in the household. I can't say we were poor, but there was

Figure 91. James Delgado and Deborah Marx in the Falkland Islands on the *Vicar of Bray* mission (Photo by Matthew Lawrence, 2017)

never any money for extras. Bag-of-Burgers was a favorite place we'd go to eat out. You could get a bag of burgers for a dollar. We'd go to the drive-in movies every once in a while. We bought our bread at the day-old bakery outlet. As dad's career progressed, with him studying at home in the evenings when not at his second job, he passed the various exams to advance in the Fire Department; he retired as the #2 officer, the Deputy Chief. My Dad was, and is, one of my heroes. He always taught by example.

At an early age I became interested in the past and in history. That interest was encouraged by my parents, not in a big way, but it was allowed. Looking back now, it was more than allowed. It was fostered. My Dad drove me to the museum every weekend. He also took me to the Public Library. As for the Rosicrucian Museum, I was fascinated by Egypt. I begged my parents and finally got taken to the Rosicrucian Egyptian Museum in San Jose. I haunted that place. Every opportunity I'd

get, I'd go there, thanks to Dad. I would walk through the halls and stare for hours at the mummies and the artifacts. The exhibit that impressed me the most – and I think that's where I got my desire to be an archaeologist – was a full-scale recreation of a rock-cut tomb from the Valley of the Kings.

Whenever we had extra money, I begged my parents for books, and they bought and I bought every imaginable book I could get on Egypt. I loved to read. Apparently, I started to read when I was three. My grandmother encouraged it. My mother would brag that she'd come over to her parents' house and find me reading the newspaper at four years of age. I had a library of thirty or forty books on Egypt by the time I was ten, and I didn't just have the kids' books. I'd get the older books and work through them. I remember getting a book on hieroglyphics and learning to write them. I decided I was going to be an Egyptologist, and I begged my parents to send me to Egypt. I wanted to go into the

JAMES P. DELGADO

Great Pyramid and the Valley of the Kings, ride on a camel, see the Hall of Mummies and meet Ramses II, face to face.

By the 5th grade, I began to be encouraged more by teachers. Mr. Pat Franklin, my 6th grade teacher, allowed me to build a cardboard replica of Tutankhamen's tomb and his grave goods as a class project. As I presented it to the class and explained the nuances of Egyptian rock-cut tombs, and the significance of the Tutankhamen discovery, I found that I really liked telling other people about the past and sharing what I'd learned.

It was in 1971 or 1972, when I was in the 7th grade, that my dad's cousin, Gil Resindez, told me about a new housing project where they had come across an old Indian burial ground. He'd been out there because he worked for PG&E, and he told me how he'd picked up an Indian skeleton. He said he had it in the garage. I really wanted to see it, so he took me out to the garage and opened this brown paper bag, and there it was, the first human skeleton I'd ever seen.

I was hooked. I begged him to show me where he'd found it. He said it was off Bernal Road and maybe he'd take me out there sometime. Well, he had piqued my interest from mummies to burial grounds, and I was almost frantic to get out there. I begged my parents to drive me, but they were not eager to visit a construction site. "We'll just get in the way," they said. Well, I was 14 years old, and I was feeling independent. I had started my own paper route, and had my bike, and I was determined that I could go out and find that burial ground on my own. So, one morning I got on my bike and I rode the five or six miles out to the construction site. It was back up against the foothills, and they were building hundreds of homes. They were scraping streets and digging trenches, and there in the dirt I could see broken stone mortars and crushed bones virtually everywhere.

It was a known archaeological site, but at the time there was no real protection for it. The California Environmental Quality Act [CEQA] had just passed, but no one was really thinking much about prehistoric archaeology. It was a contentious time. Local archaeologists were often out there trying to do salvage work before the bulldozers came through, but they were equally often confined to the side lines wringing their hands while the sites were being destroyed. I didn't realize that a San Jose State University archaeology crew, under Karen Bruhns, had started working on the site but had pulled out. Karen and team had been confronted by a site seemingly destroyed, and their decision at the time as I look back made perfect sense; I did not at that stage have enough life experience to come to that realization those decades ago.

I was appalled. A bulldozer would go past and you'd hear a crunch and see the top of a skull come off, or a skeleton ground-up, or a stone mortar crushed. I knew this was wrong. I went home, scraped up some money and bought a book by Maurice Robbins called *The Amateur Archaeologist's Handbook,* and I studied it. It told how to survey and plot sites, how to record data, and how to take field notes, so I bought a notebook, created my own forms and got some tools out of my parents' gardening kit, put them in my pack and started being an archaeologist all on my own. I actually went up to the construction trailer and announced that I was an archaeologist who'd come to study this site.

Here I was, at 14 going on 15, asking

for a set of the blueprints showing the street lines and where the grading was, and they gave them to me. I carried around that tube of drawings and wherever I found something, I'd mark it. I found a mortar here, a grave there, and I numbered the finds. I carefully excavated those that were half-exposed, drew them as best I could, bagged them and took them home. Fifty years later, we archaeologists can look back at horror at the entire situation; I naively, not even knowing the actual cultural context of these long-ago people, or that they had descendants, responded in my youthful ignorance and passion to protect and preserve. It's not who it is done now, but back then, it was the only way I knew as a young teen to do the "right thing."

One day, in the middle of all of this, I came across a test pit where somebody else was digging in the PG&E easement that ran right through the middle of the site. Somebody else was trespassing on my turf. I came back that weekend and there they were, three San Jose State University students, Chuck Cecil, Bill Wallace, and Sue Grant. I sauntered up with my pack and my finds, announced who I was and told them I was working the site. They had been students of Karen Bruhns, and when her field class had ended, they decided to come back and finish off their work. They told me the site was called SCL-57. It is now known as CA-SCL-125, and the finds I saved, less the human remains that were repatriated and buried, are in the collections of San Jose State. Elizabeth-Anne Mabie did a comprehensive review of the site and the various finds from Karen Bruhns and other archaeological collections as an M.A. thesis at San Jose State in April 2015.

They were excavating a house pit, and they gently explained what they were doing. I pulled the *Amateur Archaeologist's Handbook* out of my pack and showed it to them. "All I've got is this book and I've been trying really hard to learn," I said, showing them my notes. "Will you teach me how to be an archaeologist – can I work with you?" I asked. "Sure, kid," they said. So, I worked with them. They showed me how to use a trowel and carefully scrape off a millimeter at a time, but we finally came to a parting of the ways because I couldn't understand why they weren't out there doing as I'd been doing. I had been trying to salvage everything I could in the midst of all of that destruction, whereas they were content to methodically dig that house pit. I didn't fully understand that they were doing research. I was trying to save the past from being destroyed, and at the time that seemed nobler. So, I continued working on my own, salvaging the stuff as best I could. Nevertheless, it was through that interaction that I began to meet real archaeologists. The students invited me over to San Jose State University to visit their lab in the basement of an old apartment house where the professors had their offices. I'd ride my bike over there and help them wash and catalogue the things they found.

This was at a time when the Edenvale area of San Jose was really starting to boom, and our family moved into one of the first new subdivisions. Archaeological sites were showing up everywhere, so I decided to start a survey to record them. It was through this effort that I met Rob Edwards from Cabrillo College. He was doing survey work and he hired me as his assistant. It was Rob who taught me how to walk a plowed field and do a systematic survey. Working for Rob, I began to shift from just doing the archaeology to doing history. I started going out to the

JAMES P. DELGADO

old ranches where I'd interview the old timers, and they started giving me pictures and telling me about the past. In support of this work, I started doing research in the San Jose Public Library and in the old records at the Historical Museum. Looking back now, I think the fact that I had been raised in part by my grandparents, and knew, respected and liked older people that I was allowed into the homes of the older people. The children and grandchildren of the folks who had come out to farm, and ranch on the Rancho Santa Teresa as it was subdivided and sold off in the 19th century. They shared their stories, they shared family photos, and they gave me a glimpse into a California, a Santa Clara Valley, and a San Jose that was just then on the brink of vanishing.

It was about this time that I met Chester and Linda King. Linda had just started teaching archaeology at West Valley College and Chester was working as a contract archaeologist. They had just formed something called BAAC, the Bay Area Archaeological Consortium. I joined BAAC, and through Chester and Linda I was introduced to a whole new world. They took me seriously and treated me like an adult. I would ride my bike over to their house in Willow Glen and we'd go out and do things like site surveys and meeting with other archaeologists. I went out on surveys and digs with them.

The swath of destruction at SCL-57 that introduced me to archaeological activism as graves were desecrated and crushed by construction equipment and meeting the Ohlone descendants had instilled in me a sense of the sacred nature of such places, and that archaeology was less about things than it was about people. And yet that site proved impossible to "save." That instilled some radicalism in me. Nobody was interested in saving the site, which had been systematically bulldozed, trenched and graded, so I started getting more into history, working more on the Bernals, the history of their Spanish (Mexican) Rancho, and other locals too. I kept notebooks and amassed all sorts of files. I went everywhere I could go interviewing aged people, meeting Bernal descendants, and collecting artifacts, all of which I ultimately gave to the California Room at the San Jose Public Library. I would borrow their original photographs and copy them. It took all the money I was making from Rob Edwards. I'm glad I did because those negatives and the prints have survived, while in most cases the originals are gone.

By this time, I was clearly getting out of prehistoric archaeology. In fact, one of the last prehistoric projects I worked on was at the Holiday Inn in downtown San Jose in 1975. They were excavating for a new parking garage and found human remains. I went down there with Chester and Linda King and the West Valley College crew and helped with the excavation. I had gone from being a Youth Commission liaison to the Landmarks Commission to being a full member of the San Jose Bicentennial Commission in 1974, where I served for two years. Meanwhile I was hired for a while by the Redevelopment Agency to give walking tours of downtown San Jose.

Through all of this I was going to high school, and I was being supported and helped by my teachers. My English teacher, Bill Sheehy, insisted that I take every possible course, and I ended up taking English every semester. I took Comparative Literature, Creative Writing, Speech, and Drama – everything I could to learn more about the language, how to use it, and how to write. As a junior, I took historiography from Warren Brown, and for my senior

Figure 92a. Among the first archaeological mentors who made a difference were Linda and Chester King, shown here in 1975 in San Jose during the archaeological investigations of the Peralta Adobe.

JAMES P. DELGADO

Figure 92b. Seventeen-year-old James Delgado bagging rock samples at the Peralta Adobe investigations, 1975. (Photos courtesy of the Sourisseau Academy for State and Local History, San Jose State University.)

year he put me in a special studies course. "Get out of here," he said. "Don't stay around the school. Go to the Bancroft. Do a book review. Read this book and tell me what you think about it. Go out and visit historic sites."

With a friend's car, I toured up and down Central California visiting sites and digs. I went over to Pleasanton where I met some of the Bernal family descendants, and visited Agustin Bernal's adobe home, which was then owned by Walter S. Johnson, a very wealthy elderly gentleman who had been one of the big forces behind the American Box Company. Walter was the man who had restored the Palace of Fine Arts for the City of San Francisco. He and his housekeeper, Mary Benetti, allowed me to carefully examine the house. As a result, in 1976, I published a pamphlet on the Agustin Bernal adobe, co-authored by Greta Kleiner. I did the drawings myself. Greta and I analyzed the house and how it had changed through time. I remember crawling through the attic and finding a wall stub that hadn't been repainted, with a fragment of the original wallpaper still in place. I dug up Walter's garden and found the original mill stones. We titled the pamphlet *Sombras de la Noche: The Agustin Bernal Adobe Its Inhabitants and & Heritage* (1976).

Well, the time had come to go to college. I graduated from high school, and I was really fretting. My parents had decided we didn't have enough money for me to go to a university, so I was going to San Jose City College. They said that after a couple of years there, if my grades were good enough, I could go to the University. I remember moaning about this to Lynn Vermillion at the San Jose Public Library. Lynn was on the Board of the Sourisseau Academy over at San Jose State,

so she talked to Ted Hinckley, a professor in the History Department, and gave him my home phone number. Ted called my mother and talked with her. Then he came over and talked to both my parents and convinced them to send me to the University.

In the Fall of 1976, I started attending classes at San Jose State University. Largely because Ted had encouraged me – and because I felt that archaeology wasn't going to work out, I enrolled as a history major. I was bound and determined to write a book on the Bernals, but I never got around to it. Still, before I left San Jose State two years later, I did two things. First, I wrote a very detailed paper on Juan Pablo Bernal – a much extended version of one of my high school papers. Dr. Ben Gilbert, from whom I was taking California history, liked it and helped me polish it up for submission to *The Pacific Historian*. It was to be my first professional publication. I then applied for a Sourisseau Academy grant through the history department and started researching a paper on one of the Bernals' relatives, Antonio Maria Suñol. Much to my delight, the Sourisseau Academy published this paper under their own imprint.

I was introduced to John Bruzzone, a local businessman who owned Pied Piper Exterminators. Mr. Bruzzone had just restored the Roberto Adobe on Lincoln Avenue in Willow Glen and needed somebody to organize tours and help run it, so at the age of 18, I was hired to be the curator. I thought that was a big step up in the world. I had gone from assistant curator at the New Almaden Museum to curator of the Roberto Adobe. I organized a group of volunteers to give tours of the house, and I'd bake bread. I would buy a little loaf of Pillsbury pre-made dough that rose on its

JAMES P. DELGADO

own, build a fire in the stone oven, rake the coals, bake the bread, and give people samples.

I also turned again to publishing – a booklet illustrated (not so well by me) and written together with Chris Wade, a young advertising executive from PRX, the firm handling the adobe for Mr. Bruzzone. Chris became a great friend, and Leonard McKay printed it – *How California Adobes Were Built in the 1830s: A Simple Guide to a Lost Art*. Chris and I drove to every historical site, every historic adobe, and every California mission to sell the book. If we ever calculated the time and the gas, I know it would have been a loss, but we were both proud to have told the story and to make a small profit.

I enjoyed running my own museum, and when it closed I didn't at first quite know what to do. Finally, I swallowed my pride – after all I had been a curator of my own institution – and was hired as a guide at the Winchester Mystery House. Meanwhile, I was still working at Taco Bell, and I took a third job at the Century 21 Theaters, replacing seat covers, scraping gum off the floors, fixing light bulbs, cleaning the carpets, selling tickets, and being an usher. I worked all three jobs until I was hired as a student assistant in the History Department over at San Jose State. I worked for the two secretaries; I was their clerk typist. There were three desks, and mine was out in front, right where people walked through the door into the History office. There I was, in my suit and tie, greeting people, sorting mail, doing my research, and helping Charles Burdick, the Chairman.

Dr. Burdick was a wonderful man, and he taught by example. He is one of the most modest self-effacing persons I knew, and although it took time for the lesson to sink in, he taught me that sometimes it's better to just stand back and let others take the praise. I enjoyed San Jose State, but things were starting to go bad at home and my parents were heading for a divorce, and I wanted to be on my own. I was 20 and in my sophomore year when I heard about a Federal Government program, the Cooperative Education Program, where they'd take kids who were in their second or third year at the university and give them government jobs. It was called career conditional employment, and you'd work for a government agency full-time for a semester, go back to school for a semester, and then come back to work for a semester. Although the program would extend your time in school for a couple of years, you were guaranteed permanent employment in the Federal Government upon graduation.

The program announcement had been mailed to the History Department, and I saw it while I was sorting the mail. One of the jobs they listed was as an assistant archivist at the National Archives Branch in San Bruno. I sent in my resume and appeared for the interview, only to find that the National Archives people hadn't shown up. Sitting there instead was Rich Harned, head of the personnel department for the western region of the National Park Service. I sat down, and he said, "Well, all I've got is a job as a personnel clerk in San Francisco, a GS 4 for $8,902 a year." That seemed like a fortune. Only recently I had visited a friend from the Roberto Adobe who was now working for an advertising agency in San Francisco. "What a city," I had thought. "This is life!"

Suddenly my opportunity had come, so I went home and told my parents that I was going to take the job. They argued with me as to whether they would let me. I submitted that I could do as I wished, and they replied, "Well, if you go, we won't pay your tuition." I thought that was a back-handed threat because they said their biggest fear was that I would never go back to school. "You guys don't know me," I said. "I promise you I will finish college." Finally, my parents had another long talk lasting into the night and my father convinced my mother that they couldn't stand in the way.

I moved to San Francisco in May of 1978, found an apartment, and on June 2, I entered the employment of the National Park Service – but not as a personnel clerk. Rich Harned felt that given all my love of history it would be a waste for me to be a personnel clerk, so he talked to Tom Mulhern, the Chief of Historic Preservation for the Western Region, and Gordon Chappell, the Regional Historian, and I was hired as student assistant to the Regional Historian for the National Park Service. Meanwhile, archaeologists had begun working on the just discovered buried Gold Rush ship *Niantic*. I remember watching television in my parents' living room just before moving to San Francisco and seeing a clip about the discovery of a buried Gold Rush ship called *Niantic* lying downtown at the corner of Clay and Sansome Streets. That had fascinated me, and when I got to San Francisco I actually saw them doing the dig. Then, after the dig was done, I watched the bulldozers come in and smash it all to pieces. The San Francisco Maritime Museum which had supervised the work on *Niantic* was just coming into the Park System, so I watched pieces of the vessel being delivered to the museum building at Fort Mason. I was fascinated, and when I mentioned my interest to Tom Mulhern and Gordon Chappell, they assigned me to work on it. I went through all of the *Niantic* material, accessioned it, and did the research to write up a National Register nomination.

The *Niantic* experience led me to become captivated by the Gold Rush in a way I'd never thought possible. I got so carried away doing research on the *Niantic* material that I ended up writing a detailed National Register nomination that went far beyond what was required. Then, with the blessing of the Park Service, I turned it into an article for the *California Historical Quarterly* – "No Longer a Buoyant Ship: Unearthing the Gold Rush Store Ship *Niantic*." That was my second professional article. My colleagues were pleased with the article, and as a result, began to take me more seriously, and I quickly realized that I could be a real historian if I actually got out there and published. That experience showed me a path to success, and it imbued me with the drive to publish – to write until my hands got tired. I got the publishing bug in a big way, and I never stopped publishing after that.

Meanwhile, I was still working on my B.A. It wasn't easy. I had to convince the Park Service not to put me on limited hours when I went back to school. Thus, after my first semester, I continued to work full-time for the Park Service while going to school full-time at San Francisco State. I continued to major in history, but by the time I graduated in 1981 I had almost enough hours to graduate as an anthropology major. I took courses in archaeological method and theory, and a historical archaeology class from Marley Brown. I took prehistoric archaeology from Gary Pahl and helped him dig a site up in Marin County. That site, on Silva Island at the edge of Richardson Bay, CA-MRN-17, was excavated with care and precision; three units ended up being 22-foot-deep

JAMES P. DELGADO

shafts that reached down to c. 5000 years ago, based on C14 and obsidian hydration. It was fascinating, and I loved the work, but the siren song of history and especially the Gold Rush had taken a firm hold of my imagination and professional interest. I kept at my studies, working hard to finish and move on to the next step. During my last two semesters at San Francisco State, I took 18 units, and then 21 units.

I had probably learned more in the Regional Office of the Park Service than I did in school, but eventually they could no longer keep me, because they ran out of money. Fortunately, they talked with Rich Harned and he got me a new job and a promotion. As a uniformed and uninformed ranger who had much to learn I was assigned to the Historic Ships at the Hyde Street Pier. That's where I really began to learn about ships, and it's where an important part of my maritime career really took off. Harry Dring, a retired seafarer, was in charge of ship restoration, and he took both me and Steve Hastings, the Chief Ranger, under his wing. Dring's office was in the wheelhouse of the tugboat *Eureka* which was tied up there at the pier. I would go up to his office on cold foggy San Francisco mornings and we'd drink black coffee and Harry would tell me about ships. From there, I moved to the Golden Gate National Recreation Area as the acting park historian, a job that in time became a permanent one, working for another mentor, Doug Nadeau, the Chief of Resource Management and Planning for the GGNRA. Working for the GGNRA was a wonderful experience. When I started, it was a 35,000-acre park, but it quickly grew to 70,000 acres and 2,000 historical buildings – more than any other national park in the Western United States. It included Alcatraz, Angel Island, the Marin Headlands, three separate forts, the Tennessee Valley, the Olema Valley, Point Reyes, Tomales Bay, the San Francisco Bay Discovery Site, Sutro Heights, the Cliff House, all of Ocean Beach, Land's End, Lincoln Park, the Marina Green, and the entire Presidio.

The way that the National Park System works is that you have National Parks, which are the cream of the crop. Then, with lower status, you have National Cemeteries and National Historical Parks, and finally at the bottom, you have the National Recreation Areas, designed as playgrounds for the public. "Parks for the People" had been the big rallying cry during the 1970s, and they had created two big National Recreation Areas: Gateway in New York and Golden Gate in San Francisco.

The idea was to mass together Federal, State, and municipal resources to create a big national park accessible to urban people, and the GGNRA was created because of the outstanding natural, cultural, scenic, and recreational resources that were combined to make it. But, in the process, history got shorted. Even though it was only a National Recreation Area, they clearly needed a historian, and I was the only historian on the scene. Thus, my position quickly shifted from being historian in my division, to being the Park Historian for one of the largest parks in the Western United States, comprising virtually the entire San Francisco Bay Area, and because of my position I quickly became a frequently heard voice for historic preservation in the San Francisco Bay Area. Largely because of Doug Nadeau, my supervisor, I had the authority to define my work, and much of my style today comes from being managed by Doug.

It was in February 1979, that they found another buried ship downtown

– the *William Grey* near Telegraph Hill. I was invited to help excavate the vessel by archaeologist Allen Pastron. As a result, I became more interested in Gold Rush ships and decided that I would try to research all the buried ships in San Francisco. Thus, on my own, over the next few years, I amassed thick files from all sorts of archival sources on every known buried ship in the city. When the Federal Reserve Bank of San Francisco was ready to move from their old building into their new headquarters, I was able to get them to donate artifacts and a set of original logs kept by the supercargo of *Apollo*, a buried vessel found in the 1920s when they built the original bank building.

Because of their interest in *Apollo*, the bank directors had located and purchased the original logbooks, and I got them donated to the Maritime Museum in a big public ceremony. Over the next few years, on my own time, I edited and annotated the log of *Apollo*, wrote a chapter on the Gold Rush and all the buried ships, a chapter on the archaeology of *Apollo*, and then an inventory of all of the artifacts. In 1985 I submitted the finished manuscript to the *Book Club of California*, and it was published in 1986. That volume, *The Log of Apollo: Joseph Perkins Beach's Journal of the Voyage of the Ship Apollo from New York to San Francisco, 1849*, was my first scholarly book, and of all the things I've written it's the one of which I am most proud.

In addition to Harry Dring, there were three men who spent a lot of time teaching me about 19th Century vessels: Karl Kortum, Ray Aker and Harlan Soeten. Karl Kortum was the Director of the Maritime Museum and he hated everybody in the Park Service. Karl had founded the Museum, and when it came into the Park Service, he lost a lot of his say. Indeed,

Karl felt he'd made a mistake in agreeing to join. He didn't like the bureaucrats and was always railing against us. Although we didn't always get along, Karl took the time to help me and educate me. Ray Aker, a retired mariner and naval architect, taught me how ships are built, and Harlan Soeten gave me encouragement and advice as I pursued my study of the Gold Rush.

One day in 1979, Harlan told me something that was to bring about the next stage of my career – as an underwater archaeologist. Harlan knew I was researching Gold Rush vessels. "You might be interested," he said, "that back in 1965, over at Tennessee Cove, some Boy Scouts found part of a buried engine, probably from the Gold Rush steamer *Tennessee* that wrecked over there. You should go over and take a look." So, Marty Mayer and I went over to Tennessee Beach, and sure enough we found the tips of a piece of machinery sticking out of the sand. We excavated around it and found the cross-tail of the engine of *SS Tennessee*. The *Tennessee* Project was to be an entirely volunteer effort because the Park Service didn't have the money, and Marty and I made it happen on our own hook.

I really didn't know much about marine archaeology then, so once again I did what I'd done as a kid. I went out and bought a book: *Maritime Archaeology* by Keith Muckelroy. That book became my bible, just like Robbins' *The Amateur Archaeologist* had been when I was 14. I studied it through and through. With the book and frankly with Marty's years of experience as an archaeologist and my own youthful projects, we were able to learn how the ship had torn apart and how the heavier stuff had stayed in one area while the lighter had moved down the beach. We recovered torn pieces of copper sheeting, sheathing

JAMES P. DELGADO

nails, spikes, bottle fragments, fragments of machinery, a big section of boiler plate, a silver coin, and many other artifacts.

In order to do the work, Robert Bennett, a local wreck diver named Dave Buller, Marty Mayer and I created a non-profit society incorporated as *S.S. Tennessee* Archaeological Project. About this time, Marty and I realized that if we were going to continue to work on this project, we needed to learn to dive. We talked to Doug Nadeau, and he gave us enough time to go over to the Presidio where we learned how to dive with the U.S. Army. It was not an easy course. Moreover, it was expensive, and we had to buy our own gear. We learned how to dive in the San Francisco Bay area and did our open water check out down at Monterey. I remember buying my first wet suit and not being able to afford all of the necessary equipment.

Going to diving school was only part of the learning. What had to follow was experience, and I was woefully short on that. Fortunately there was Dave Buller, a seasoned diver, who would play a strong, mentoring role for me and help *S.S. Tennessee* project and others immeasurably.

Dave had a couple of things we didn't have in addition to experience. First, he had a hand-held magnetometer that could find metal artifacts, and second, he had solid information about the underwater remains of the *Tennessee*. Dave told us that some wreck diving friends of his had found *S.S. Tennessee* and had been diving it. Apparently, a Florida-based wreck diver they all knew claimed he had even recovered the builder's name plate from the engines. "Oh, gosh that's wonderful," I thought. I didn't exactly blurt out, "Well, let's have it back for the Park!" but I did ask Dave if it would be possible to get it. One of the first things that angered me about wreck divers was my belief that they went in and took things, split the stuff up, and often sold a lot of it for scrap. That name plate was an important artifact, and it would have been a wonderful object to put on display at the Maritime Museum, but it had been taken to Florida. We worked quietly on Dave, but *S.S. Tennessee* name plate never came back. As it turned out, the name plate story may have been just a story, or a convoluted one, as Dave's wreck diving friends, the Lanham Brothers, had found the builder's plate from the engine of the Gold Rush steamer *Samuel S. Lewis;* today it is on display in the visitor's center of San Francisco Maritime National Historical Park thanks to Bruce Lanham, who donated it.

The thought that some folks might be stripping wrecks was annoying, and it reopened the old wound, and anger over what I'd seen in San Jose as workers laughed as they crushed burials. It helped to solidify in my mind that, while working with volunteers was pretty good, there were some people out there who really didn't care about history. They were greedy and wanted it for themselves. To my mind they were no different than some of the construction workers I'd battled as a kid, who in absolute ignorance and joy would tear up a burial so they could have a skull to put on their mantlepiece at home, while only a few feet away, working in the easement, San Jose State archaeologists were trying their best to preserve some history and reconstruct the prehistoric record of the valley.

I saw the parallel, and it made me angry. I thought that while preservation law and sensitivity to indigenous sites was rising, there seemed to be no sense of interest in underwater archaeology in California. To do more work in California, as it turned out, meant going elsewhere for some projects and returning home to participate in the projects that were starting to happen. In 1981, while we were working on *S.S. Tennessee*, Dan Lenihan, Chief of the Park Service's Submerged Cultural Resources Unit, came out for a visit. His unit had been established some years earlier to study the effects of reservoir inundation on previously dry Indian sites in the Southwest. The reservoir project had ended, but in the meantime he and Larry Murphy had become the Park Service's underwater experts. I had written to Dan and sent him the research design for *S.S. Tennessee*. Dan was interested and very supportive, and both he and Larry Murphy became close personal friends. They were responsible for my becoming an underwater archaeologist as opposed to a half historian/half land-digging archaeologist.

One day during the *Tennessee* Project, Dave Buller and I were looking at one of the brass drift pins recovered from *S.S. Tennessee*, and I was remarking on its size and shape, when Dave said, "Well, I've got one that looks just like this from a Gold Rush wreck I'm working up on the Mendocino Coast." Dave didn't know the name of the vessel, and he wasn't willing to reveal its location either, because he had friends who were still actively pulling things off it. Dave did, however, bring the drift pin over and I photographed it. He told me there were Chinese ceramics aboard the vessel, and he showed me a little bottle of water in which he had parts of an ivory fan. I was, of course, quite interested in learning about another Gold Rush vessel, but Dave never took me up to see it. That vessel was later identified as *Frolic*.

Meanwhile, Dave was working on other wrecks. Only a month after *S.S. Tennessee* wrecked in March of 1853, the steamer *Samuel S. Lewis* had wrecked on Duxbury Reef. The Lanhams had found this wreck and had been removing brass from the valves. Dave and his brother had been diving it too and had bought some of the brass back from the Lanhams so it wouldn't be scrapped. I went out to Dave's house in Pinole, met his wife Noreen and his kids, and then went into the garage with Dave and his brother, Steve, where I saw all of this great stuff, including the valves from *Samuel S. Lewis*.

Dave also showed me some doorknobs and hardware from another vessel he'd been working on, *Joseph S. Spinney*, wrecked up off Fort Ross in 1891. It was pretty clear to me that Dave was out there raising things from a number of different wreck sites. It was also clear that he was in some sort of a transition period, from going out and diving and picking things up, to a more scholarly appreciation of the past, so I did everything I could to encourage him and to work with him. I think it was a nice two-way street, because Dave had extensive knowledge about where wrecks were. He had already done some research at the Bancroft Library.

In 1981, when Dan Lenihan invited Marty Mayer and me to join him and Larry Murphy on the Point Reyes survey, we told him about Dave Buller and got them to invite Dave to participate. All of us learned a lot about doing systematic surveys and working with different plotters from Lenihan and Murphy. During 1981, 1982, and 1983 we combed all of Drakes Bay and the tip of Point Reyes looking for every shipwreck that had ever gone down there. I worked closely with Dave. He pulled his files together, did some additional research, and wrote a preliminary report. I did additional research in the archives, tracking down more information, photos,

JAMES P. DELGADO

and finding a couple of wrecks that Dave hadn't covered, while deleting a couple of Dave's wrecks that had been pulled up by salvors. Working together we were able to amass a large file of historical information.

Dave's research was great. He had done the lion's share of the work, but it needed to be organized, so I rewrote it. We submitted a manuscript to Lenihan on which Dave was the principal author. I wanted Dave treated as a full member of the team, and I worked with him as a peer – as another budding underwater archaeologist. At the time there were no established formal programs to study underwater archaeology. They were just getting started. Virtually all the people in the field had learned by doing, and so were we.

During those years I was constantly hunting for opportunities to look at Gold Rush shipwrecks, and I managed to convince Bill Ehorn, the Superintendent at Channel Islands National Park, who was a friend of Lenihan's and a big diver, to let us come on down and look at the 1853 wreck of the steamer *Winfield Scott*. Marty Mayer and I made the first map of that wreck and pulled together a lot of research on it. I also talked to Dave Buller, who had once dug a big hole in the middle of *Winfield Scott* and asked him to donate all of the stuff he had taken. I cataloged all of it, brought it down to the Channel Islands National Park, and they proceeded to embarrass me by neglecting to acknowledge Dave. All of Dave's stuff is down there, and some of it is on display, but to this day they've never bothered to thank him. That's the harsh reality when you work for something big like the Federal Government. You can work with people, and you can make promises, but ultimately you can't make the government do anything, and sometimes it all comes

to naught. Unfortunately, that experience ended up, in my opinion, alienating Dave towards the government, as did my own anger toward wreck divers.

Although *Winfield Scott* had been worked over by wreck divers and salvagers for decades, the park still had problems managing it. I remember finding intact concreted masses of iron and timber imbedded down in the rocks and going back the following year only to find somebody had blasted it open, hacked a big hole out of it, and destroyed the original wood of a ship for which we had no plans. I got mad. I felt that no matter what we did with people like Dave who were interested in the history, there were other guys who just didn't care. I never felt that all divers were the enemy. Ninety-nine-point nine percent of them were great folks, but the one-tenth of a percent, who were outlaws, were clearly doing disproportionate damage to the resource. I saw them as the same sort of people who would tear up a wilderness area with a four-wheel drive or go to Mesa Verde and dig a hole in a 2,000-year-old adobe wall to find a pottery chip.

As a Federal employee and a preservationist, I increasingly saw myself in an adversarial position, and the more I got into it, the angrier I got. Every time we tried to do some research, I was either being thwarted by the Park Service bureaucracy on one hand, or by these people who were ripping stuff off. I really wanted to convince Dave Buller of our good intentions, and credit him and work with him on a more ambitious comparative project focusing on a whole series of Gold Rush steamers including *S.S. Lewis, S.S. Tennessee, S.S. Winfield Scott,* and *S.S. Independence*, which Dave and the two Lanham brothers had found down off Baja California.

In fact, I began doing the research and wrote a paper discussing all the Gold Rush steamer wrecks on the coast, explaining how they'd make a good study group. Dave was interested in individual ships from the Gold Rush, but I think he began to see that working with a group, representing a theme, could result in a more impressive product. At that time many people were still thinking of shipwreck work in terms of one wreck alone. You'd find a wreck, hopefully a famous wreck like *Mary Rose* or *Monitor*, and that wreck would define the parameters of your research. You wouldn't waste your resources on wrecks like *Colonel Baker*, a little schooner that went ashore at Point Reyes in the 1870s with a full load of potatoes.

Indeed, on the Point Reyes Project I tried to convince Dave that we wanted to identify all the wrecks, even the modern ones, because taken together they represented a whole slice of history – the commerce and culture of an entire region. I think he felt we were looking for the modern wrecks only because we wanted to police them. That wasn't my intent. I thought *Colonel Baker* was an important local wreck because the vessel, rather than being unique, was truly generic, so working from Dave's extensive research notes, I did additional research to put these vessels into a historic context. Dave would give me information on a lumber schooner, and I'd write a general introduction to the lumber trade, describing its growth and the types of vessels employed in it. As a result, the chapter we wrote was handled thematically in terms of specific trades and the types of ships employed in them.

During the Point Reyes Survey, Dave Buller and John Foster, the State Underwater Archaeologist, had wanted us to find *San Agustin*, and I got a fair amount of grief from the guys because of the emphasis I placed on modern vessels like the 1913 wreck of the steam schooner *Pomo*. "Why work on this ?" I figured if we could show how *Pomo* broke up and spread apart, we could start building a predictive model of the site formation process that would help us find *San Agustin*.

Meanwhile, I was going back through all of the archaeological reports from nearby Coast Miwok sites dug by Robert Heizer and others during the 1940s, looking for artifacts from this galleon. I studied the collections, talked with local collectors, and tried to work out the distributional pattern of porcelain still being picked-up along the beach. Through the work I did on *Pomo*, assisted by a geomorphologist and some other scientists, we now know how the ocean worked there, how the spit has changed, and how material from the wreck washed in. And comparing that model with materials from the vessel, recovered in the middens, we were able to plot a likely location for *San Agustin*. We were fortunate that a fellow had been collecting porcelain off the beach for 40 years and plotting where he picked it up. From this distributional study we concluded that the wreck was buried in about the same place as our magnetic anomaly.

It took some years to carry this research to a point that we knew enough to go back and work on *San Agustin*. Unfortunately, by then the Park Service had sent the Submerged Cultural Resources Unit off to Pearl Harbor to work on the wreck of the battleship *Arizona*. As a consequence, Marty and I were left to figure things out by ourselves. Then, in the midst of all this, a likable, well known international treasure hunter, Robert F. "Bob" Marx, innocuously asked to see our data. We explained to him how the shipwreck material had

JAMES P. DELGADO

come ashore and been reused by the Miwok, and described the porcelain bead blanks, bottle glass, and iron fasteners that had ended up in nearby graves and house pits. We told him about our plans for the site and naively shared our data with him. Then, to our surprise, we found out that Bob was trying to get a permit from the State to excavate the wreck.

Bob's proposal was to deflect his propeller wash downward, rev-up his engines, and blast away the 23 feet of sand covering the wreck. That's an effective technique to blast a big crater in the bottom, but it is rather uncontrolled, like taking a bulldozer and cutting a swath through an archaeological site on land and collecting artifacts as they pop out. We were horrified. Here was a wreck, partly inside the National Park boundary and partly within State-controlled waters which were part of a National Marine Sanctuary. Here was the oldest, and most significant wreck in California, and Bob Marx wanted to blast

it open and then sell his share of the artifacts in order to pay for it. An intense battle ensued. Roger Kelly, from the regional office, Dan Lenihan and a lot of local people took my side. Unfortunately, John Foster, my good friend from the California Department of Park and Recreation, took the other. John was just as frustrated as I by the fact that none of us in state or federal government could get our agencies to fund shipwreck research. He thought *San Agustin* project as proposed by Bob Marx would be a great means for galvanizing public interest in underwater archaeology.

Unfortunately, fighting Bob Marx strained my friendship with John Foster. Ultimately Bob Marx got a chance to come in and do a survey, and he was able to relocate the magnetic anomaly which the National Park "Service" had mapped earlier. Nevertheless, he immediately proclaimed to the press that he'd found the wreck. He didn't bother to survey the whole bay. He just parked within

Figure 93. James Delgado at Candlestick Cove SRA, posing for a local news magazine. (Photo courtesy of James Delgado collection, 1984)

150 yards of our position, and carefully "magged" [magnetometer] what the NPS had already found. Fortunately, we were able to prevent Marx from digging, but it was a tough and very contentious fight.

In the middle of all of Marty and I were helping other people with shipwreck discoveries. Rangers working at Año Nuevo State Park found the bow of the steam schooner *Point Arena* eroding out of the beach, and we helped them document it. Meanwhile, the Nautical Heritage Society at Dana Point was building a tall-ship replica of the Coast Guard revenue cutter *Lawrence* and needed some help with the research. They put up some money for a magnetometer survey and we were able to find the possible site of the buried remains of *Lawrence* on Ocean Beach. Meanwhile, severe winter storms during the early 1980s exposed the remains of *Neptune* and then *King Philip* on Ocean Beach, and I helped to document both vessels.

But then the siren pull of gold (as in the Gold Rush) again tugged at my archaeological heart strings. I had first become well acquainted with John Foster when he volunteered to help with the *Tennessee* Project and the Point Reyes survey. Foster was having some problems in the Sacramento River where divers were going down and recovering things. John had just busted a couple of guys for pulling out an anchor from the city's historic waterfront. John cleaned it off and saw the date 1844, so he invited Marty and me down to have a look. Since it was a relatively small kedge anchor and had stud-link chain which comes in after 1812, I concluded it probably dated to the Gold Rush and was either an isolated find or was associated with a wreck down there. John was able to locate a wreck close by that he thought might be the Gold Rush brig *Sterling*.

I traveled to the National Archives to do some research and was able to show that the vessel was indeed *Sterling*. That led to more work on the Sacramento River funded by the State. I joined John's team as historian and was able to do some diving on the wreck of *La Grange*, located nearby, which for a while had served as Sacramento's prison during the Gold Rush. In addition to John, that team included Sheli Smith, Jack Hunter, Steve James, Jim Duff, and Franklin Fisher. I also helped them on two other wrecks, *Ninus* and *Dimon*, located at the foot of "R" and "S" Streets.

At this time I also helped Allen Pastron with his excavation of Hoff's Hardware Store, a complete ships chandlery, which burned and fell into the bay mud right next to *Apollo* storeship in the same fire that burned *Apollo* in 1851. We had sluiced-out the bay mud and found barrels of hard tack, ships goods, and all sorts of Gold Rush material. I also continued to work closely with the State, mainly John Foster and Nick Del Cioppo at the State Historic Preservation Office. Nick, John, and I spent a lot of time fighting the State Lands Commission. Salvagers were trying to tear apart *Brother Jonathan* and the Gold Rush steamer *Yankee Blade*, and we had to provide good reasons why the State should not issue salvage permits allowing their destruction. John and Nick would ask for help, and I'd use every argument I could within my power as a Fed to say, "You can't do this!" At their behest I ended up nominating a lot of these vessels to the National Register, because if it wasn't historic the State Lands Commission would issue a permit for it to be salvaged.

The nominations were a means by which the larger picture of the maritime aspects of the Gold Rush came into focus for me as a scholar. Ships had borne most

JAMES P. DELGADO

of the 49ers to California. They had provided the supply lines and carried people up the rivers. All of the sites I had been documenting – the steamers that went to and from Panama, the buried ships downtown, the burned stores built out over the San Francisco waterfront that had supplied sailors and miners alike, the sunken ships that lined the banks of the Sacramento waterfront – were compelling evidence that taken together told a great story. I really wanted to tell that story, so as I helped other people with their projects, I carefully built up my files. I wanted my work to culminate in a big book melding the maritime history and the archaeology of the Gold Rush.

That's how I became involved with *Frolic*, a site that I'd first heard about from Dave Buller in 1980. Of course, back in 1980 we didn't know its name, but it was apparently a Gold Rush era wreck located up near Caspar, California on the Mendocino Coast. Dave had worked on it, as had some of his friends, but although he had shown me material from it, he had never revealed its location. Richard Tooker, a volunteer at the Maritime Museum, had also told me about it. Then I was contacted by Tom Layton. I had briefly met Tom many years earlier, when my early archaeological mentors in San Jose, Chester and Linda King split up, and after a while Linda King had a new man in her life. This fellow, who had just arrived at San Jose State University in the fall of 1978, was Tom Layton. Tom contacted me in 1984. He said he'd been working on a prehistoric site and found Chinese ceramics that the Indians had collected from a shipwreck. I was fascinated. Not only was it a Gold Rush wreck but, like *San Agustin*, there was this wonderful cultural tie to the

Indians. So, I worked with Tom as best I could.

In 1985, I went out to the site with Tom, John Foster and several other divers, and we did a dive. It was a tough day. The surf was up, but I had always been foolish that way. I told people that I really didn't care to dive if it was just to float in the water and look at fish, but I'd dive in Hell to look at a great shipwreck. It was such a bad day that nobody else wanted to get in the water. Foster went in and got out because it was too rough. I went in and got beaten up and thrown around in the surf, but swimming along the bottom I saw porcelain scattered everywhere. I saw the ballast pile of cast iron blocks, the ship's capstan and what looked like it might be a cannon. I really got knocked around by the waves. Tom told me that watching from the bluff, every once in a while, he'd see my head and then my fins. It was like being in a washing machine. I did a quick sketch and collected a few pieces of porcelain closer to shore.

I thought at first that the cast iron kentledge was a sign of either an expensive merchant vessel or a warship sold private. The British Navy had a long tradition of naming vessels *Frolic*, so I wrote to London for Tom, but couldn't match it with a British warship. I ended up traipsing around looking for information, but I can't really say I was a big influence on the whole thing. Nevertheless, occasionally, I'd find something that would help. I found a letter from *Frolic*'s captain (Edward Horatio Faucon) down at the Huntington Library and identified him as a key character in Richard Henry Dana's *Two Years Before the Mast*. I remember going to Harvard and sifting through business records but missing the collection that Tom later found telling the entire story of *Frolic*. I also did some work in the National Archives for Tom and ultimately was able to provide him with a copy of the vessel's registry from Baltimore.

I was fascinated with *Frolic* because here was another Gold Rush site, and from Tom's research, it clearly represented a link between China and San Francisco during the Gold Rush, that powerfully connected to a site adjacent to Hoff's Store that I had helped Allan Pastron and his crew excavate; it was a "Chinese Emporium" that had partially burned on the waterfront and fallen, half-charred into the bay to be immediately sealed under mud and later landfill, preserving it. That link between California and China had been there during the *maritime* fur trading days, but its continuation into the Gold Rush had largely been ignored. Most people thought in terms of Chinese coming to California as laborers without realizing that throughout the Gold Rush there was a regular trade going on with China. Ships didn't just sail in and get abandoned. They were constantly coming and going, maintaining an intense trade around the Pacific Rim and with the rest of the world. I thought that Tom's research on the *Frolic* would contribute to our understanding of the California Gold Rush as a global maritime event.

Meanwhile, the need to continue to study to be a scholar was pressing. At the SHA conference in Denver in 1984 I met Bill Still, who had just created a master's program in maritime history and underwater research at East Carolina University in Greenville, North Carolina. Just before that, while at the conference, I had asked George Bass, pioneering "father of underwater archaeology" from Texas A&M University, if I could come to his program, but he told me, with kindness, that what I

wanted to do was not real nautical archaeology, and suggested I join his program, if I wanted to work on ancient wrecks. Bill Still overheard this and came up to me (I was easy to spot as I was in uniform) and said he needed people who were actually working in the profession to come in and get a degree. I got a year's leave of absence from the Park Service and in the summer of 1984 packed up with my wife Mary and our toddler John and newborn daughter Beth and headed to North Carolina. I took more than a full academic load and took all the archaeological and historical data I'd accumulated on *Tennessee* and wrote a thesis.

I later took the first part of my thesis and boiled it down into a scholarly article on the New York and Savannah Steam Navigation Company which had owned and operated *Tennessee*. If I'd been smart, I would have done the log of *Apollo* for my thesis, but being near Atlanta, where the records of the firm that owned *Tennessee* were archived, I did that instead. I also wanted to do a project with maritime archaeology, not just history.

Just before I was ready to leave North Carolina, I got a call from Ed Bearss, the Chief Historian of the National Park Service. The Park Service had just signed an agreement with the National Oceanic and Atmospheric Administration to administer the wreck site of U.S.S. *Monitor*. Ed was calling to say that they needed a maritime historian to work on this project and he wanted me to be the guy. They would provide some money, and when I got back to San Francisco I would be appointed Official Project Historian for U.S.S. *Monitor*.

We went back to San Francisco, and I started working on *Monitor*. Ed liked what I was doing, so they started assigning me to other maritime things. At the same time, there was a big push for the federal government to take action on maritime preservation, and I got pulled more and more into that. I left my duties as Park Historian at the end of 1986, and in 1987 assumed the role of an acting Maritime Historian for the Park Service, with a small staff, and we started what would grow into the federal government's Maritime Preservation Program. The NPS decided to move the program to Washington D.C. in late 1987, and with that, I again moved east, never again to live in, but certainly to visit and still do projects in California.

As I was getting ready to leave California, I was contacted by Linda King's sister, who was a member of the California Wreck Divers. She invited me down to Los Angeles to address their club. I gave them a slide talk and told them about the work we'd done on *Winfield Scott* and the four-masted ship *Goldenhorn*. I gave them copies of the site maps, described what we'd been able to accomplish with wreck divers on other projects, and invited them to work with us to do more of that sort of thing. I also told them about Dave Buller donating his collection from *Winfield Scott* to the Park Service. It was at that meeting that I first met Pat Philpott, Pat Gibson, and Cliff Craft.

After moving to Washington, D.C. a few months later picked up a magazine called *Nautical Brass*, and there was an article by a member of the California Wreck Divers describing how they had gone out to visit the destroyers at Honda but had been blown off, so they had instead gone into the Channel Islands Park, dived and removed artifacts from *Goldenhorn* and *Winfield Scott*. They even had pictures of their finds. After explaining how much we still needed to learn about *Winfield Scott*, they had gone in with rock hammers and

chisels. I was absolutely incensed, and I flashed back to 1972 and bulldozers tearing up burials in San Jose. To make things worse, a couple of guys in the pictures were people I had talked to. The article went on to say that it was an annual outing, and they were about to go out again. So, I copied the article, and faxed it to the Regional Office in San Francisco with a note saying, "You guys should do something about this." Well, the Regional Office got together with the Channel Islands National Park staff, and they decided they were going to bust these guys. I didn't know anything about this. It was all very hush hush.

At that time there was a young married couple who had just started working at the park. They were both divers and had recently worked for Dan Lenihan at the U.S.S. *Arizona* Memorial in Hawaii. Since they had just started work at the park, nobody really knew them, and they were able to go on the California Wreck Divers outing, incognito. "Oh, we've just moved here from Hawaii," they said. They dove with the California Wreck Divers, observed everything and took notes. Apparently, when the vessel entered the Park and the Marine Sanctuary, the Captain announced it over the P.A. system. "We're in the Park Marine Sanctuary. The regulations say that you can't remove anything, and if the rangers come, we'll get busted, so if I sound the underwater alarm don't surface with anything." He hid the recovered artifacts in his cabin while the divers took air hammers, chisels, and picks to *Goldenhorn*, after which they dug big pits in the bottom throughout the *Winfield Scott* site.

When the party boat got back to Santa Barbara, the Sheriff's Department and National Marine Fisheries Service Agents were waiting for them. Depositions were taken, artifacts were confiscated, and charges were filed against the group: criminal charges because they had broken California State Law in the counties of Santa Barbara and Ventura; and Federal administrative charges under the National Marine Fisheries and Marine Sanctuary Regulations.

I attended the trial as an expert witness for the federal government. I testified on the importance of *Winfield Scott* and how I'd tried to gain the cooperation of the California Wreck Divers. Unfortunately, given my long-standing history of butting heads with salvors and pushing for ship-wreck preservation, the divers concluded that I had been in on the planning and execution of the sting, and in their eyes, I became the quintessential devil. Most of the defendants plead guilty and received much reduced sentences or nothing at all. Those who fought it received heavy fines. Most of them pled guilty to the State charges too.

The trials went on for a couple of years, and I carried a lot of personal anger to them. I had tried to work with these peo-ple. I thought we had extended a hand, and I felt personally betrayed. As for the divers, they were just guys who were interested in collecting something from the past, and they had no reason to trust the govern-ment. The most unfortunate thing about the prosecution was that it really ended my friendship with Dave Buller. Dave was caught between a rock and a hard spot. He had been my friend, and now I was the enemy of his friends. I talked with Dave once after that, but I got the feeling he really didn't want to have anything more to do with me. I still feel badly about that because Dave is a great guy. I learned a lot from him, and he probably learned a few things from me. It still troubles me that

because of my job and my beliefs I lost two close friends: Dave, because of the Chan-nel Island sting; and John Foster because of Bob Marx and *San Agustin*. Fortu-nately, John Foster and I reconnected, and our friendship has continued; I was able to work with John recently on two proj-ects in California, and we stay in touch. I remain sorry to not have reconnected with Dave Buller; I'd love to reconnect, to apol-ogize, and even if we do not pick up the friendship after all these years, for him to know what I feel in my heart about how I put him in a terrible place with my atti-tude, my push and my actions.

My career after California has spanned more than a few years and is really out of the scope for a reminiscence on my life as a California maritime type and early work there – and my ongoing love of the state's maritime history – especially the Gold Rush. It's particularly wonderful to note, though, that one California Gold Rush period shipwreck, *Frolic* has kept reappear-ing and involving me every few years from the early 1980s when Dave Buller showed me a brass drift pin and pieces of an ivory fan, right up to the present. That started again in the 1990s when I was asked to be a historical consultant to three museums in Mendocino County that were develop-ing a public display interpreting the *Frolic* story. I felt honored being selected as one of the humanities scholars to advise the process, but I accepted with some trepida-tion because I would likely meet some of the wreck divers that I'd testified against in the *Winfield Scott* case during my Park Service days. I didn't want my presence to hurt the *Frolic* project by offending the wreck divers who had donated their arti-facts to the *Frolic* Repository at the Men-docino County Museum.

I participated in a number of planning

JAMES P. DELGADO

meetings with a wonderful group of people and have enjoyed the group dynamic. I have to say that in the end the experience influenced my thinking, strengthening my resolve to tell stories employing artifacts. The concept that came out of *Frolic* discussions was the use of multiple interpretive voices – having the artifacts related through the differing perspectives of people from different cultures and different times who had used them. One of the voices that the narrative included – as it needed to – was that of the wreck divers. What Tom did with the *Frolic* wreck divers in California gave me hope.

I did not think that the future should be defined by people going out and taking whatever they want from a shipwreck, having it sit in their garage for twenty years falling apart, then giving it to an archaeologist or a museum and feeling as if they had done an absolutely wonderful thing. Those who dove on the *Frolic* did damage to the site and to the materials they recovered. Indeed, a number of things recovered from the *Frolic* no longer survive, and we're not quite sure where most of the things that were recovered came from on the wreck, thus their value to us as artifacts is much diminished. But to their credit,

most of the divers saved their artifacts and generously turned them over to Tom, allowing him to repair some of the damage and make the story accessible to the public. Moreover, Tom did the work in a way that doesn't beat up on these people. And while he did not paint them in a bad light, he drew attention to the fact that there is a right way and a wrong way to deal with a shipwreck site.

But what I find most hopeful is that Tom developed a positive working relationship with the divers, and perhaps, in the long run, that approach has been more successful than the strictly law enforcement approach we were pushing during the 1980s. Through that positive approach: by involving and crediting sport divers, by showing how much more one can learn from a well-researched shipwreck, and by generating community excitement, Tom was able to define a new paradigm for California shipwrecks that has divers and archaeologists working together mapping, studying, and excavating ships, and then putting them on display – and in doing so, imbuing the public with a sense of excitement about California's maritime history. I hope that will be the lasting contribution of the *Frolic* Shipwreck Project.

John W. Foster

John W. Foster retired from California State Parks in 2009 after a 34-year career as a field archaeologist, state underwater archaeologist, and chief of the Archaeology, History and Museums Division in Sacramento. He previously worked as an archaeologist for the National Park Service and the Museum of Northern Arizona.

As a generalist in the field, John has published on a wide variety of subjects—rock art; shell middens; mission-period archaeology; heritage-site conservation methods and philosophy; the Manila galleon, Gold Rush, and steam-powered shipwrecks; stone fish traps; and the archaeological shipwreck signature of silver smuggling. He has done fieldwork in California, the Dominican Republic, Baja California, the American Southwest, and mainland Mexico. His work has been recognized with such honors as the Olmsted Award for Leadership and Vision (California State Parks), the Mark Raymond Harrington Award for Conservation Archaeology (Society for California Archaeology), and the Governor's Historic Preservation Award (State of California). He has served as an advisor on submerged cultural resources to the National Oceanic and Atmospheric Administration (NOAA) and as member of the adjunct faculty at Indiana University. Within California State Parks and in partnership with the State Lands Commission, John has been the driving force behind bringing underwater heritage sites into the state park system. He holds degrees in anthropology from UCLA (B.A.) and California State University, Long Beach (M.A.). He did further graduate work at University of Arizona.

John was born in Burbank, California, and grew up in a rural setting with orange trees. Down the road lived "Mr. Ed," the talking horse. They both learned to speak at about the same time. John was raised in an Air Force family, and they moved every two or three years. By the time he entered high school he'd lived in eight states and Japan. That experience tended, perhaps, to promote a comfort level in meeting new people and exploring different cultures across many landscapes and time periods. John is the oldest of six Foster kids. Brother Daniel is also an archaeologist, making them one of the few sibling archaeologist pairs in the country.

John is currently a volunteer boat operator for California State Parks and an advisor to the State Park Dive Team. In his off time he enjoys camping, drone photography, visiting World Heritage Sites, and driving a vintage Volkswagen bus. He continues to assist State Parks in developing methods for conserving heritage sites in the underwater realm.

John W. Foster

25 March 1994
Ventura, California

I grew up as a military brat, and I find this to be a common experience shared by many of my colleagues in archaeology. I was born in Burbank, California, 1 September 1946, but since my father was an Air Force officer we traveled all over the country, living in eight states and in Japan. I think this wide exposure stimulates an interest in how things are in different parts of the world and how they might be in those places you haven't yet managed to see.

I picked up my interest in archaeology when I was in the sixth grade. We were living in South Carolina, just outside of a little town called Sumpter. Some of the kids going to my school were from the Air Force base, but the others came from the farms and small towns in the area. One of my best friends had an uncle who had a farm, and every time he went out and did the spring plowing Gary and I would follow behind him with our coffee cans, picking up arrowheads. I'm sorry to say that when I moved from South Carolina I left all those arrowheads with Gary. Looking back on it, I sure would like to have kept them. One day in South Carolina I had a revelation. After reading in school about the Norse explorations of Iceland, Greenland, and, finally, Vinland, I became aware I had learned something important my parents did not know. I couldn't wait to demonstrate this knowledge. My chance came at the dinner table that evening when I asked my dad, innocently: "So Dad, who was it that discovered America?" He looked at me with mild contempt: "Well, it was Christopher Columbus, the greatest mariner who ever lived. I thought you knew that." (The Fosters had been prominent in the Knights of Columbus in Queens, New York.) I had him—and quickly corrected him with facts learned only hours before regarding Leif Erikson, his father Erik the Red, and the landing in Vinland on the North American continent some 500 years prior to Columbus. He never interrupted, but sat smiling as I blathered on with my newly acquired facts. Finally, he delivered the knockout: "Well, all I know," he said with a mild scowl, "is that once Columbus discovered America, it *stayed* discovered!" Truer words were never spoken; game, set, and match!

Little did I know that my career would eventually have me tracking this Columbus fellow and trying to locate one of his ships lost in a hurricane in Bahia Isabela in 1495–96.

My father had begun his career in the Air Force, and at one time in his life he was considered to be the top U.S. pilot. That's why Howard Hughes hired him out of the

Air Force to be his private pilot in 1946. After a couple of years of that my father decided to go back into the Air Force, and that was good for me. Then, in the summer of 1963, just before my senior year of high school, my father retired from the Pentagon and we moved from Arlington, Virginia, to Southern California.

For me, that was a total disaster. I was plucked out of a very secure situation, where I had girlfriends and was on the basketball team, and I was plopped down in a California setting that I knew nothing about. I didn't know how to surf and had no way of fitting in. You know, going into your senior year you're supposed to be top dog, but in my case it was a traumatic relocation.

In any event, I began college at UC Santa Barbara in 1964 and eventually gravitated toward anthropology and archaeology as a major. I was lucky enough to take the Introduction to Archaeology course from James Deetz. It was a fascinating course, and Deetz, of course, was a fabulous teacher. I was hooked on anthropology, and after two years at Santa Barbara I transferred to UCLA. I enjoyed my anthropology at UCLA, although it wasn't quite as exciting or invigorating as it had been with Deetz at Santa Barbara.

I graduated from UCLA in 1969 and, at the age of 22, went into the Navy, where I had a somewhat brief and interrupted career. I was in the flight program at Pensacola, Florida. I had earned my commission, completed primary and secondary ground school and flight training, when the Navy decided to reduce the number of students in their training "pipeline." Fifty-three of us in my flight class were sent home with a thank you and honorable discharge. My career plan to become an airline pilot was over, just like that.

My year in the Navy was completely spent in training and groveling around. I loved the flight training and had top marks in primary and secondary flight school. Like diving, being airborne sets you free. You're weightless, you feel wonderful, and you gain a different perspective on the world. One of the most important things I did in Pensacola was to go through sea-survival school. We were dumped off the transom of a ship into Pensacola Bay, where we inflated life rafts, paddled several miles to shore, dug beach wells, and tried to survive several days. That experience was later to save my life. That's one thing for which I can thank the Navy.

When I returned to California in 1970, I enrolled at Long Beach State as a graduate student in anthropology. I took my first anthropology class there from Bill Wallace. It was during the summer of 1970, and it was his last class before retirement. Talking to Wallace opened a whole new world to me. It was Wallace who recommended that I talk to Professor Franklin Fenenga about California archaeology. Up until that time I hadn't focused on California Indians or on California archaeology, but, after my first 10 min. with Frank, that changed. Frank was a tremendous teacher and a great source of inspiration to me throughout my graduate career at Long Beach. He always made time for his students and challenged us to understand the intricacies of California prehistory.

I finished my master's degree in 1973. My thesis in cultural anthropology was a cognitive analysis of Creek Indian folktales. I then entered the Ph.D. program at the University of Arizona. I spent two years at Arizona. While there I worked part time for the National Park Service and learned the CRM [cultural-resources management] business by reviewing contract reports and carrying out small-scale surveys at what was then the Arizona Archaeological Center. During this time I became acquainted with Professor Emil Haury and Bernard "Bunny" Fontana. I was particularly inspired by Bunny Fontana, one of the foremost authorities on the Spanish colonial period in America, because he made archaeology fun and interesting by connecting it with the real world. Bunny encouraged me to do some ethnographic work on the Papago Reservation and among the Seri of the Sonora coast. He was also a California native, so we spent many hours talking about Maidu and Costanoan cultures from central California.

Well, there I was in Arizona. But, I'd had some exposure to the California coast, and, like everyone else in California, I had liked it. I liked Arizona too and would have loved to stay there, but I just wasn't a Southwestern archaeologist. You're either one of them or you're not—and if you're not one of them, you're never going to be one of them.

Well, it was clear I was never going to be one of them, so I looked around for a thesis topic closer to my research interests. I had become acquainted with several of the marine biologists at Arizona and I began to take some graduate courses in marine ecology. My main conspirator in marine science was Lloyd Findley. His father had been the president of ASA (Archaeological Survey Association of Southern California) and had dragged Lloyd along on many archaeological projects in Southern California and the Southwest. Lloyd developed a very strong interest in archaeology, although marine biology remains his primary field. Since I was the only archaeologist around that neck of the Arizona campus, Lloyd found

it kind of handy to have me along on their field trips to the Sea of Cortez to tell them about Indian use of marine resources. In return I could always get help in keying out midden shell and fish bones.

We made many trips down to the Sonora coast to sample the intertidal zone, but while the other graduate students were filling up their buckets with marine organisms at low tide, I was prowling the beaches and the dunes documenting the extensive shell-midden deposits. I was finally managing to put my two interests together, and I knew they were going to lead me in the direction of coastal-subsistence studies and ultimately to underwater studies. In 1975, I published my first article on the shell middens of Estero Morua on the Sonora coast. At that time I was still prowling the beach and snorkeling. I was not yet scuba diving.

I can remember our first trip, in 1971, to visit the territory of the Seri in the state of Sonora. Lloyd Findley, Eric Fisher, Curley Griffin, and I stuffed all our gear in an old VW van and crossed the border to seine *esteros*, collect insects, and map coastal middens. We had a terrific time exploring our way south from Puerto Libertad towards Kino Bay. One of the goals of this trip was to collect an ethno-ichthyology of the Seri. There had been only one article published on this subject, but it had many inaccuracies. We managed to escort Jose. Luís, a Seri elder then living in Punta Chueca, out to our desert camp, fed him breakfast and coffee, turned on the tape recorder, and opened a new illustrated volume on gulf fishes to document the Seri names.

Of course, the Seri had a detailed knowledge of the fishes. Their classification was in many ways more complex than the Linnaean system, emphasizing color,

JOHN W. FOSTER

size, and usefulness of the fish. At the back of one book was a chapter on whales. Jose Luís never hesitated. He rattled off the whale names, and when we turned the page he gave the Seri name for gray whale! The biologists looked at each other with astonishment. How would Jose Luís know the gray whale? The fact that some gray whales migrate around the Baja Peninsula to enter the Sea of Cortez and bear their young off the secluded coasts of Sonora and Sinaloa was not known to science at the time. We collected this information from a Seri expert who had spent years catching fish and hunting turtles from a small boat on that magnificent sea.

In 1975 the California State Department of Parks and Recreation advertised a position in Sacramento. I applied for it from Tucson. As I recall, they lost my application once or twice, but I finally got interviewed and was selected for a state archaeologist position in Sacramento as the assistant to Fritz Riddell. I replaced Bill Olsen who, some years earlier, had gone on to work for the BLM [Bureau of Land Management]. Looking back, Frank Fenenga, Bunny Fontana, and Fritz Riddell have been the most influential people in my career as an archaeologist, and, of those, the most important figure in my career has been Fritz Riddell.

Figure 94. Francis A. Riddell and John Foster, 1984. "Fritz" Riddell was John Foster's supervisor at California State Parks. He was also his mentor and friend, giving Foster the opportunity to take up underwater archaeology for the State of California in 1979. (Photo courtesy of Glenn J. Farris)

For many years, as head archaeologist for the California Department of Parks and Recreation, Fritz Riddell was in fact the state archaeologist for California, and, in many ways, Fritz invented cultural-resource management in our state. Much of what we do today to record, protect, and to manage archaeological resources is the direct result of his early efforts.

Robert Heizer, at UC Berkeley, had never shown any interest in public archaeology. He felt the university had a higher calling. Therefore it was up to Fritz to round up the funding to excavate archaeological deposits being obliterated by highway, reservoir, and park projects throughout the state. He built a program that is still in place today and is recognized as an international model for cultural-resource management. Those of us who inherited the program owe Fritz a great debt.

Between 1975 and his retirement in 1983 I worked very closely with Fritz on a wide variety of State Parks assignments. We traveled the state together, "riding herd" (as Fritz always referred to it) on California's historical and archaeological treasures. While most of my assignments did not involve underwater archaeology, Fritz always encouraged me to pursue this interest and supported my efforts to expand the park concept to underwater areas. I must say that Fritz also inspired me to build cooperative links to the wreck divers and clubs in order to locate and preserve historic shipwrecks. We were commonly doing this with prehistoric-artifact collectors at Tulare Lake and many other places, and big dividends were often the result.

From Red Van den Enden, for example, were able to gain access to large collections gathered from the shores of ancient Tulare Lake. These included more than three-dozen fluted points (including one made of quartz crystal), many crescents, and mineralized bone fragments gathered from the surface of private farmland. Red and his friends spent years walking the furrows and collecting ancient artifacts. Instead of criticizing the collectors who were pursuing their passion, Fritz organized them into TULARG (Tulare Lake Archaeological Research Group) and worked with Bill Wallace, Frank Fenenga, and others to record the data and analyze these materials. The result has been a greater understanding of the archaeology of Tulare Lake. We also dated a mineralized human skull fragment to 12,275 years [B.P.] by the uranium-thorium technique. This stands today, I believe, as the earliest dated human bone known from California.

The other important lesson Fritz Riddell taught me was to cultivate public support for our archaeological efforts. This is extremely important. We must try to give back the results of our studies to the California citizenry who support us. They crave this information. Barely a day goes by without some archaeological discovery being reported in the newspaper. There is tremendous natural interest in what we do, but many archaeologists fail to actively interact with the public or produce a popular version of their technical reports. I feel this is an important obligation, particularly for those of us in public archaeology.

In 1977 an event occurred that changed my life. It took place on a reef on a far distant shore. My father, my younger brother Dan, another friend, and I were taking my father's newly purchased 52 ft. cabin cruiser from Miami to California. We planned to pass through the Panama Canal and then head north along the Pacific coast. We did it with minimal preparation, and as I look

JOHN W. FOSTER

back on it, I would have done things differently. We thought we were beyond hurricane season and would have an easy time cruising to California.

For the first week or so, things went great. We left from Miami and sailed to Key West, Isla Mujeres, Cozumel, and Roatan in the Bay Islands. Our plotted course had us hugging the coast around Cape Gracias a Dios, down past Bluefields, and into Limon, Costa Rica. However, without warning, off the coast of Honduras, we ran into a tremendous storm. Talking later to the Coast Guard, I learned that five other vessels were lost in Honduran waters during that storm.

It was around noon on 12 November 1977 when our vessel, the *Dorris M*, ran up onto a sandbar off a remote section of Honduras near the Laguna de Caratasca. The sandbar was about a mile offshore. We had been staying in close to get some shelter, but the waves were too large for us to see the reefs, and we were unfortunate enough to end up on that sandbar. We tried for quite a while to get the boat off, but it began to take some terrible waves and became fairly full of water. The waves were 10–12 ft. high; however, since they were pushing in strongly from offshore, we felt it would be relatively easy to take the lifeboat in to the beach to get help and return to the boat the next day when the storm subsided. We set the anchor and launched the life raft.

I'm going to summarize this by saying that we spent 11 hours in the water in a swamped lifeboat that finally broke up and left us swimming. My father didn't make it; his heart gave out in the effort, but the other three of us finally managed to make it to shore just before midnight. My survival school experience was very helpful in this ordeal. Suffice it to say that, after being held captive by the Honduran military in a town called Barra de Caratasca, we were rescued through the efforts of the U.S. consul and transported out of Honduras. It was a horrible nightmare.

The relevance of this to my career is that, for about a year after this experience, I suffered from the guilt of having survived. It's called a "lifeboat complex," I believe. As a consequence, I couldn't go anywhere near the water. I couldn't go to the beach, and I got very nervous just looking at the ocean. I realized this would be a tremendous handicap if I didn't overcome it, so in 1979 I decided to face the problem head on by enrolling in a scuba-diving class. I figured that if I could take up scuba diving and become a member of the State Park Dive Team, I'd be able to overcome that fear. It worked, and I've been an avid scuba diver since 1979. I thank my father for that.

Scuba diving allowed me to further express my interest in things maritime and things old, and since the State Parks Department didn't have any other archaeologist who dove, I became, de facto, the state's underwater archaeologist. I admit that I've had no formal training in underwater archaeology, but I've taken every certification and worked very closely with others to develop my underwater skills. My real education was as a terrestrial archaeologist, but I like to think of myself as an "amphibious" archaeologist—one who has taken to the water and has managed to adapt the techniques, the theory, and, in some cases, the methods used on terrestrial sites to those underwater. When someone comes along to replace me who does have the formal training, I will happily hand over my title. As an archaeologist I'm a generalist. I know a lot about the prehistoric period, quite a bit about the historic, and I've managed to keep up fairly well in the underwater field. I've sure worked at it, and I've made an effort to participate in the discipline at a scholarly level.

When I assumed my role as the state's underwater archaeologist, I discovered a whole new constituency that I had never been exposed to as a terrestrial archaeologist—namely, the wreck divers of California. My initial contacts with some of these people were somewhat confrontational. An anchor would be hauled up by someone off the Sonoma coast, one of our park rangers would report it, and it would be my job to contact the person who had been traced by way of his license number. This scenario was particularly common in and around the Sacramento area. The Sacramento River has produced scores of anchors, some of which are in very good condition, and they decorate a number of the seafood restaurants around town.

It was my job to try to track down some of these historic artifacts, and in the course of doing this work I became aware of a network of wreck divers and diving enthusiasts that were very knowledgeable about historic and prehistoric archaeological features underwater in California. I enjoyed talking to these people because they had the extensive and varied diving experience which I did not. I had only recently learned to dive, and these people had dove all over the world, on all kinds of fabulous shipwrecks, and, in some cases, had extensive collections from these sites.

My experience as a terrestrial archaeologist had prepared me for understanding people who shared a common interest, often with intense enthusiasm, but from a different direction. After all, we terrestrial archaeologists often deal with artifact collectors who have amassed large collections, sometimes from their own land and sometimes by purchase, and these collectors often have considerable knowledge about the material culture of a given area. Indeed, some of these collectors have gone on to become professional archaeologists, and some of the most famous archaeologists in California started out just like me, collecting arrowheads in a coffee can—Robert Heizer and Fritz Riddell being two good examples. In any event, I couldn't see why wreck divers and the state couldn't work together in finding, identifying, and preserving important archaeological and historical sites underwater.

For several years I made it a practice to go around the state and speak at dive clubs. I showed them slides of underwater parks, talked to them about shipwreck sites, described why we needed to know about them, and explained how, as sport divers, they could help us. I found that this approach was well received by most of the sport divers. Of course, anybody that works for the government is always going to be resisted by some people, regardless of the context. As a result of this outreach several underwater sites were reported to me by the divers who discovered them. Typically, wreck divers keep this information secret. Those sites were recorded and are now included in the state's inventory of underwater archaeological sites.

In 1980 or 1981 I met two people who were influential in helping me develop my skills as an underwater archaeologist. One was Jim Delgado, who was then working for the National Park Service in San Francisco. The other was Jack Hunter, a maritime archaeology consultant in San Pedro. I met Jack at the Redding meeting of the Society for California Archaeology in 1980. I had recently become certified as a scuba diver and was full of enthusiasm, and here was a trained archaeologist who had

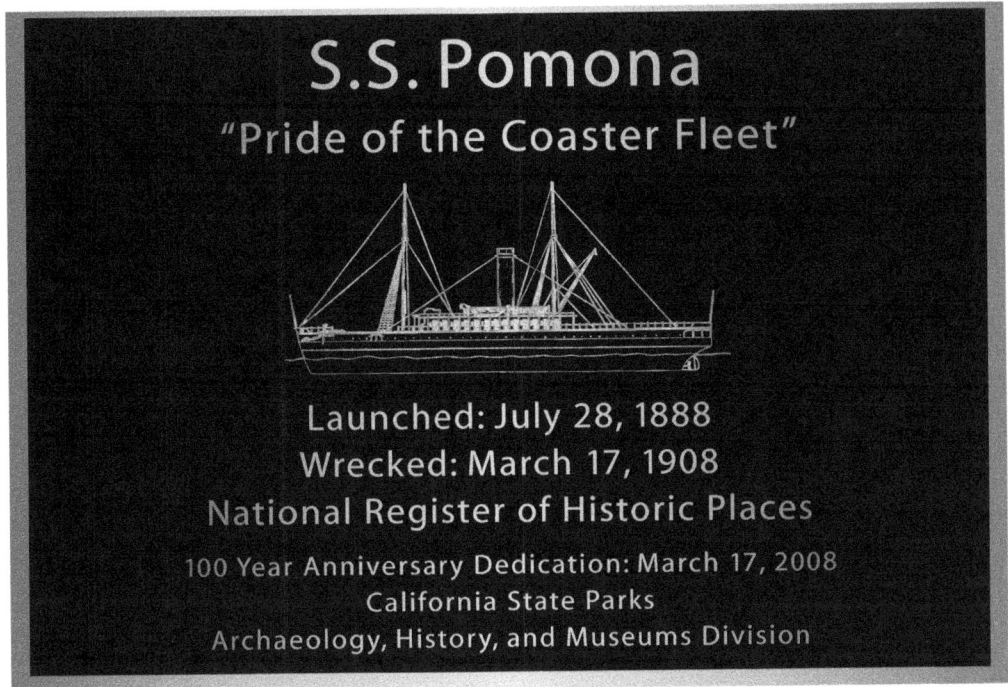

S.S. Pomona
"Pride of the Coaster Fleet"

Launched: July 28, 1888
Wrecked: March 17, 1908
National Register of Historic Places

100 Year Anniversary Dedication: March 17, 2008
California State Parks
Archaeology, History, and Museums Division

Figure 95. After documenting the wreck of the SS *Pomona* in 1981, John Foster and colleagues worked toward adding her to the National Register of Historic Places. The SS *Pomona* was listed on the National Register on 17 March 2008, the centenary date of her sinking in 1908. (Photo by John W. Foster, 2008)

actually conducted research underwater. I was fascinated. It turned out that Jack had gone to the same high school as my wife, and they had a bunch of friends in common. It was an instant connection. Jack Hunter helped me develop my underwater archaeological skills. He has a tremendous library, which I have frequently used, and he has always been an important source of information for me as I've attempted to stay current in this fast-developing field.

As a state archaeologist I've been able to work, over the years, on a number of different projects involving underwater sites. One of these was the 1981 offshore magnetometer survey at Fort Ross Cove, where we identified six anomalies. Ultimately four of those anomalous readings proved to be shipwreck sites. Although we didn't find anything from the Russian period (1812–1841), those wrecks helped to document the rich history of the

post-Russian period when Fort Ross was a busy doghole port.

The Fort Ross project proved the effectiveness of using volunteers to aid our efforts. Through Bob Taylor of Sacramento I was put in contact with the U.S. Naval Reserve Salvage Team from Treasure Island. They agreed to work on the project as part of their regular readiness training and brought up a boat, compressor, and tons of equipment for a diving expedition. We also enlisted aid from Professor René Perón of Santa Rosa Junior College as well as the local sheriff and other divers. It was a great learning experience for me and a chance to demonstrate that California's underwater areas could contain cultural – as well as natural-resource values. The major find was the *Pomona*, a 226 ft. passenger steamer sunk in 1908. We extended the underwater park boundaries as a result of these efforts, and I reported our discoveries at [the meeting of] the Conference on Underwater Archaeology.

In January of 1981, a ferocious storm struck the southern California coast. At Goleta State Beach the sand was completely washed away after days of heavy surf and high tides, exposing the sandstone bedrock. A beachcomber named Nolen Harter discovered five iron cannons concreted to the sandstone bedrock beneath a high bluff overlooking the entrance to Goleta Slough. He reported his discovery to the anthropology department at UCSB and thus began a strange odyssey to explain how the cannons could have come to rest there. I worked on the research and conservation with Jack Hunter and Jim Gilmore. We drove four of the guns, still encased in concretions, to be x-rayed by the largest machine in the world at the Naval Weapons Center at Concord. Full-sized radiographs were obtained, and that enabled the conservators to focus on areas where iron corrosion was most advanced. Key diagnostic features were also revealed.

The origin and age of the Goleta cannons, however, remains a mystery. Some local historians maintain they are 18th-century guns, others that they are much earlier, perhaps dating to the California landfall of Francis Drake in 1579. Jack Hunter and I attempted to narrow the range of possibilities by performing a magnetometer survey offshore from the discovery site, but no shipwreck evidence was found. We did locate a concentration of stone bowls—typical of the middle period in Santa Barbara channel prehistory. Six were recovered in one dive and accessioned with Travis Hudson at the Santa Barbara Museum of Natural History. I still work on aspects of this vexing mystery from time to time. The guns

themselves can be seen at the Goleta Valley Historical Society Museum.

Another project, important in my development, was the work done with Jack Hunter, Sheli Smith, and others on the Sacramento River. We surveyed a stretch of the riverbed along the city of Sacramento side, working at a depth of about 30 ft. It was miserable black-water diving. In my opinion, if you can dive there, you can dive anywhere. The visibility was typically 6 in. or less. The current was strong, and there are all kinds of nasty junk down there to run into, including barbed wire and sturgeon rigs with large hooks. Moreover, since it was numbingly cold water, we had to move very carefully because we couldn't feel ourselves getting cut or snagged.

But the payoff was really great. We found two Gold Rush–period sailing vessels and managed to do a first-rate job in documenting them. One was the bark *Sterling* at the foot of J Street. The other was the brig *LaGrange*, which served as Sacramento's first prison. Both vessels were part of the Gold Rush fleet which came around the Horn in 1849. Among the artifacts recovered was a 250 lb. "Admiralty style" anchor from deep anerobic sediments next to the *Sterling*. When cleaned with a sandblaster the inscription in the crown read: 1844. This anchor is now on exhibit at the restored B. F. Hastings Building in Old Sacramento State Historic Park.

Both the *Sterling* and *LaGrange* had been tied up on the Sacramento waterfront, where they became decrepit and eventually sank down into the mud. The city fathers tried everything on them, including explosives, to get them out of the way, but to no avail. The hulls were completely imbedded in the mud. Then, with hydraulic gold mining in the Sierra foothills, the sediment level rose in the

JOHN W. FOSTER

Figure 96. The crown of an iron anchor recovered from the Sacramento River in 1986 reveals a date of 1844. The anchor came from the site of the Gold Rush brig *Sterling* on the Sacramento waterfront. (Photo by John W. Foster, 1986)

river and completely buried these ships for a hundred years. Only in the last 30 years has the river been able to cut down through this sediment load, reexposing these two Gold Rush–period vessels.

The Sacramento River project was a fabulous experience for me and could never have been accomplished had we been forced to rely solely on professionally trained underwater archaeologists. The river bottom had to be searched literally foot by foot within a grid of ropes, and when objects were located they had to be buoyed to the surface and those areas mapped by hand. It involved a tremendous amount of labor. There were only a few of us "real archaeologists," so we invited in the U.S. Naval Reserve Salvage Team from Treasure Island. We also used a number of volunteers from the Mother Lode Dive Shop and from other dive shops in the Sacramento area. This helped us build a bridge to the sport-diving community. Of course it was made clear that any items retrieved were going to be kept by the state and used for interpretive purposes. Still, we had strong participation by sport divers. I think we were able to show them why archaeologists want to preserve sites until they can be studied for the public benefit and for the interpretive value they contain, and I think we made a number of converts.

Over the years I've been fortunate to be able to continue developing my career as an underwater archaeologist. I've documented Ahjumawi fish traps underwater at Ahjumawi Lava Springs State Park, mapped stone anchors off the Palos Verdes Peninsula, and recorded historic lumber-barge wrecks in Emerald Bay. The latter resulted in the first shipwreck park in California.

Figure 97. John Foster surveys a submerged lumber barge in Emerald Bay, 2005. The documentation of the submerged maritime landscape in Lake Tahoe enabled California State Parks to add Emerald Bay to the State Parks System. (Photo courtesy of Sheli O. Smith)

Working with Sheli Smith, Jack and Monica Hunter, Dick Swete, Margie Purser, and Charlie Beeker, we documented the site, installed an underwater interpretive panel and mooring, and invited divers to explore California's history underwater.

In August 1993, I worked with Charlie Beeker, Steve James, Barto Arnold, and Jack Hunter as part of a research team in the Dominican Republic, doing a magnetometer survey at Bahia Isabela on the north end of the island of Hispanola. We were attempting to locate one or more of the vessels lost by Columbus on his second voyage in 1494. We managed to identify 17 different magnetic anomalies, including 2 which are highly suspicious and contain the electronic signatures that would be expected from vessels of that period. We plan to return this year and hope to excavate and identify a vessel that was actually under the command of

Christopher Columbus. I consider myself extremely fortunate to have been included in this research team headed up by Indiana University.

It was through Jim Delgado on the *Tennessee* Project that I first became friends with Dave Buller, about 1983. Although Dave was an avocational wreck diver, I was fascinated and impressed at his level of knowledge and understanding of underwater wrecks and their history. I soon found that we had something else in common—a love of Baja California. For many years I had been exploring Baja California and the Sonora coast on the opposite side of the gulf. I found that Dave Buller, too, had traveled all over Baja and had dove a number of the shipwrecks on that remote peninsula. We had a lot of fun talking about that and sharing experiences. It was through Dave that I first became aware of what was then being referred to as the "Silk shipwreck" in Mendocino County.

JOHN W. FOSTER

This, of course, was the *Frolic*, wrecked in 1850.

I need to backtrack a bit here. Tom Layton, at San Jose State University, began running archaeological field schools up on the Mendocino coast about 1980, and in 1983 my younger brother Dan, who is chief archaeologist for the California Department of Forestry, tried to convince Tom to work on some interior sites. Dan took Tom to see MEN-790, a Pomo village site up on Three Chop Ridge in Jackson State Forest.

Meanwhile, by happenstance, my brother and I undertook a private consulting job for the residents of the Greenfield Ranch, a rural development near Calpella in Mendocino County. As we set out to record the archaeological sites, we were fortunate enough to meet Greenfield property owners Mark Gary and Deborah McLear, who volunteered to introduce us to the individual landowners and show us the archaeological sites. This was a fabulous experience. The Greenfield Ranch owners, many of whom were counterculture people who had retreated to Mendocino County during the 1970s, didn't have a lot of money to pay us, so they tried to make our visits there as friendly and easy as possible. They arranged for us to stay at Orr Hot Springs, a wonderful old historic resort. I remember taking my family up there one weekend in the spring of 1984. As I recall, we got in late on a Friday night, and Dan and I were off to survey at the crack of dawn the next day, leaving my wife, Kathy, and our little girls to enjoy the day in the pools there at Orr Hot Springs. That evening, when I got back, my youngest, who was only six at the time, said: "Well, dad, we all had fun, but you know what? Everyone else forgot their swimsuits." Such is life in Mendocino County.

As Dan and I recorded archaeological sites with Mark and Deborah, it was obvious to me they had the same burning interest in archaeology that I remember as a little kid picking up arrowheads in South Carolina. They just didn't know what to do with this interest. Dan and I like to think that we had a small hand in helping them channel that interest into professional careers in archaeology.

That summer Dan brought Mark and Deborah out to see Tom's excavations at Albion, and they spent the next several weeks as volunteers on Tom's crew up on Three Chop Ridge, where they participated in recovery of the porcelain sherds that would lead Tom to a small cove just north of Point Cabrillo and, ultimately, to the *Frolic* wreck site.

Dan and I then suggested to Mark and Deborah that it would be productive to have a professional archaeologist come in and conduct excavations at some of the significant sites on the Greenfield Ranch property. We knew Tom Layton wanted to expand his work into the interior of Mendocino County, so we put Tom and Mark and Deborah together into what turned out to be a very productive relationship for all involved.

In the summer of 1985, assisted by Mark and Deborah, Tom dug Nightbird's Retreat on the Greenfield Ranch. As a consequence of this, Mark and Deborah were connected to the world of professional archaeology. Subsequently, they both completed their undergraduate degrees in anthropology at Sonoma State.

By 1985 I had heard about the *Frolic* shipwreck from several different sources. The first information had come from discussions with Dave Buller about 1983, while we were participating in Jim Delgado's SS *Tennessee* Project. As I recall, at

Figure 98. In May 1986, John Foster and Jim Delgado prepare to dive and evaluate the *Frolic* wreck site. Delgado nominated the *Frolic* to the National Register, and Foster worked to create an underwater management area protected by California State Parks. Left to right: Denée Deckert, Jim Delgado, Jim Barry, and John Foster. (Photo courtesy of Thomas Layton)

that time Dave was still referring to it as the "Silk Ship." Then, by the fall of 1984, I was hearing about it from my brother Dan as a result of Tom's excavations at Three Chop Village. By this time Tom had contacted Jim Delgado for assistance in identifying the builder of the vessel in order to do a proper site record for the wreck. Jim and I both felt the site should be nominated for the National Register, so in May of 1986 Tom, Jim, several other people, and I traveled up to Mendocino County to view the wreck site. Although the water was quite rough, we did a short dive, and I was immediately impressed by both the site's research and interpretive potential.

Since 1960 the California State Department of Parks and Recreation had been designating underwater-park areas, however most of these were devoted to preserving outstanding examples of natural history—mainly environmental regions and habitat types. Only recently had we begun to consider protecting historic archaeological sites with this underwater-park designation. As I dove the *Frolic* wreck site, I became convinced that the wreck and the cove that contains it would be a fabulous underwater park—a place where people could really experience through interpretive messages what it was like in the pre–Gold Rush era in California before the state changed forever. Moreover, since the wreck of the *Frolic* opened up the north coast and in many ways marks the beginning of history in Mendocino County, what more significant site could you find in that region for preservation and interpretation? My job is as a planner as well as an archaeologist, and I placed the *Frolic* wreck site and cove high on my list of potential underwater-park sites as we expand our inventory of these sites in the future. I felt the *Frolic* wreck and the surrounding cove could be interpreted as both a historic and an ecological preserve, with a visitors' center situated on the adjacent Point Cabrillo Lighthouse property.

JOHN W. FOSTER

Over the years many wreck sites had come to my attention, but I had never seen one with more research potential than the *Frolic* site. Accordingly, I managed to put together a small amount of research money in the form of an interagency agreement with San Jose State University to help Tom Layton investigate the site and determine its historic potential to be an underwater park. Tom used some of this money to research the history of the vessel in a number of East Coast archives. Through Tom we later arranged for David Buller to handle the underwater evaluation and recordation of the site itself, but the heavy surf made it impossible to do this work, and Tom returned the money.

In retrospect, I can say that my experience in working with Mark Gary and Deborah McLear has strengthened my commitment to working cooperatively with property owners and collectors. I've become skilled in convincing people that we archaeologists are not going to take away their artifacts, nor are we going to threaten their livelihoods. Quite simply, we're interested in the ancient history of a particular place, and generally that's something that they are interested in themselves.

Of course, I work for the government, and I always carry that burden, but what usually occurs, and I've seen it dozens of times, [is that] once I've overcome the initial suspicion most people are anxious and willing to share important information with me. This is something that I learned from Fritz Riddell years ago. The people who really have the information are the old timers and longtime residents in a particular region. Anyone that thinks they can go into an area cold—no matter how hard they work at it—and expect to learn as much as the locals already know is crazy.

The same is true, of course, with the sport divers and wreck divers of California. Working with terrestrial sites and dealing with artifact collectors over the years I've come to understand the value of working with wreck divers. These people certainly don't have the same approach we archaeologists have, but they often have the same interest, and many times they have far more knowledge than we do about a particular site or a particular region. I firmly believe that, in order to successfully research the history and the archaeology of an area, whether it's terrestrial or underwater, we need to build bridges to the local experts and avocationals who really know the area.

In 1986, I was the program chair for the Conference on Underwater Archaeology, held jointly that year with the Society for Historical Archaeology in Sacramento. Leading up to that, for most of a year, I corresponded with the Advisory Council on Underwater Archaeology and became acquainted with Robert Marx. Bob Marx is a tremendous person—an absolutely incredible source of information about shipwrecks and underwater archaeology. He's a professional in every sense. He's also an underwater archaeologist and a treasure hunter. He's a combination, and, in that sense, he's very different from most of the people who hold formal positions as underwater archaeologists in academia, in museums, or in state and federal government bureaucracies.

Bob Marx influenced me a lot. Of all the people on the council he was the one who was most helpful to me, a neophyte, in setting up the 1986 conference in Sacramento. I mention this because, over the years, I've tried to expand my network beyond the people who have formal training in underwater archaeology to include a lot of other people that have a tremendous amount of knowledge about the subject and who share the interests that I have. This has allowed me to go far beyond where I would have ended up had I just limited my exposure to those with formal education and formal credentials.

In 1987 Bob Marx and his investment group approached the State of California for a permit to do some research at the site of Cermeño's *San Agustín*—wrecked 1595 in Drakes Bay in Marin County. Bob asked me to help him go through the state permit process so he could conduct an underwater survey of the area in order to determine whether anything from the *San Agustín* itself might still exist. I did my best, but I found that the state bureaucracy can be awfully inflexible and unforgiving when it comes to combining the interests of preservation, research, and private enterprise. It's an area that is fraught with all kinds of philosophical disagreement. Still, the current law of the State of California is that a person can file a salvage claim on a historic shipwreck site, and if the state grants that person a permit, the state then splits the economic take from the salvage of that site according to a formula established in law. That is the law. You may not like it, but this is the way it is.

Well, when Bob Marx applied to the state to undertake this research project he made it clear to us that he was primarily interested in historical information this site might contain regarding Spanish galleons, especially those that worked the Manila trade. I felt it was an excellent opportunity to go beyond what the National Park Service study had accomplished at Drakes Bay, which was to document a number of later-period shipwreck sites. The location of the *San Agustín*, one of the oldest shipwreck sites in the state of California, has

remained a tantalizing mystery. I felt the site could be found and would warrant all of the effort we could muster to locate, protect, and possibly excavate it. A number of my colleagues who reviewed Bob Marx's application decided that it was inappropriate for the state to enter into a partnership agreement with him.

Bob had the money that we did not have. His group was willing to put up something like six million dollars to carry out this project, and they didn't have to make a nickel. They were willing to approach the project in phases—first doing the remote-sensing work and then allowing the state to decide whether to proceed. Then they'd do the testing, and again we would decide whether to proceed. It didn't have to be an all-or-nothing deal.

Nevertheless, in spite of what I felt to be good terms, very beneficial to the State of California, a number of my colleagues in the National Park Service vigorously opposed this, and leading the charge was my friend, Jim Delgado. We looked at the proposal quite differently. He felt there was no urgent need to explore this site and no pressing reason to take up Bob and his partners' offer. He was philosophically opposed to any cooperative work with Bob Marx.

We already had some indication from a magnetometer survey that there was something present in the near-shore area where one would suspect the remains of the *San Agustín* to exist. It had the right magnetic signature—that is, a widely dispersed, low-gamma anomaly—matching what you'd expect from an early vessel that had broken up in the surf, which is, of course, what happened to the *San Agustín* in 1595. The challenge was that this wreckage lay deeply buried in the sediment. As a consequence, we still don't know

JOHN W. FOSTER

whether we're managing one of the most important wreck sites in California or just the location where a couple of old washing machines fell off some trawler. The National Park Service has put together this fabulous management plan for Drakes Bay, but the critical resource—a 1595 Manila galleon—has never been documented. With Bob Marx we had an opportunity to use private money to do that documentation—far more money than either the Park Service or the state will ever be able to come up with. We could have done the work without jeopardizing or foreclosing on any future management options regarding the site.

Unfortunately, this disagreement left me somewhat at odds with a number of my colleagues whom I greatly respect. I do understand their point of view. However, I took the other position because I felt that, as long as the state had an applicable salvage law under which Marx's proposal was clearly a legal and proper activity, then it was appropriate for us to look at all of our options in dealing with what I consider to be one of the most important underwater shipwreck sites in California. Suffice it to say that after a number of years of litigation, going back and forth, Bob and his group gave up and turned their attention elsewhere, and the *San Agustín* remains unexplored, unevaluated, and as big a mystery as it ever was.

I think we missed an opportunity. Bob has worked all around the world, and he has complied with the laws in force, whatever the jurisdiction. Laws regarding maritime antiquities vary widely from country to country, just as they vary from state to state. In the state of California, underwater sites that contain an economic value can be salvaged by an applicant in partnership with the state itself. To claim that

there was something unethical about that just doesn't make any sense to me. It is perfectly legal. In the Bob Marx case I felt we had a cooperative applicant who was willing to bend over backwards in working with us. Moreover, what we were really after was historical and archaeological information and not the Ming porcelains believed to have been on board the *San Agustín*. Whether any of those porcelains might be found, whether they would be intact, and whether they would have any commercial value, no one can say. Still, Bob Marx was willing to look for that site and explore it. Unfortunately, that opportunity has passed.

Looking to the future, it's unclear to me how we'll resolve this. Wreck divers, archaeologists, and preservationists share a common interest in things maritime and things old, but in many ways it's becoming more and more difficult for us to work with wreck divers, collectors, and avocationalists because our laws are becoming more rigid and inflexible. We tend to categorize things as good or bad—people who want to preserve the past vs. those who want to exploit it. That's not really the way the world is, but unfortunately that's the way it seems to be at times.

At this juncture I should say that one of my mentors in underwater archaeology was Jim Delgado. When I began to research the two Gold Rush sailing vessels that we discovered on the Sacramento waterfront, Jim shared with me the knowledge and experience he had gained on the *Niantic* project in downtown San Francisco. After its abandonment, *Niantic*, also a Gold Rush–period vessel, had served as a storeship on the San Francisco waterfront until it was covered over with fill during an early land-reclamation effort. Jim was able to ferret out important historical details about the various vessels that had been tied up in Sacramento during the Gold Rush, and those details were critical in ultimately enabling us to identify the two ships in question—the *LaGrange* and *Sterling*. Without Jim's knowledge and expertise I don't think we would ever have been able to pin those names to our vessels. Through Jim's work on the *Niantic* he was able to provide a lot of critically relevant references, including a number of journals and accounts written by people who came to California aboard the *Sterling*.

In researching the *LaGrange*, Monica Hunter and Sheli Smith produced a video which contained a number of vignettes about the ship and its passengers, and, on that video, I sang a song that was recorded in one of the diaries. Jim always teased me about that! He thought the video should have been subtitled "John Foster Sings the Hits of the Gold Rush." Of all of the people I've met working in California maritime history, Jim has, by far, the most encyclopedic knowledge, and I am happy to have been exposed to it.

As regards the *Frolic* shipwreck, we are now at the point where, due to the efforts of Tom Layton, we have a tremendous amount of documentary information about the ship itself and its history. He has also conducted a series of oral histories,

recording early accounts of diving, exploring, and artifact recovery from the wreck site. Soon, through the efforts of David Buller, we'll have a detailed map of the actual wreckage itself. I think the future holds great promise.

I believe the *Frolic* should be the subject of some intensive underwater archaeology. Although we've documented a lot of them—some in the mud and some in landfills—as far as I'm aware nobody has ever done a full-scale excavation of a shipwreck site in our state. I don't know that we'd be ready to fully excavate the *Frolic* site, but I do think it would be important to do a test trench to see if there are timbers and other preserved elements of the vessel itself under the big pile of iron ballast which overlays the main hull area. From what I've been told I believe there are probably timbers still preserved down there, in place. I think a good deal of important information confirming some of the construction details identified in the documentary record could be confirmed at the site itself. I think that the *Frolic* wreck site is an extremely significant historic locality in California, and I hope, in the future, we have it preserved as an underwater park, test excavated, and interpreted at a visitors' center on the adjacent Point Cabrillo Lighthouse property.

Epilogue (March 2021)

Like a bubble slowly rising from the depths, my career developed a more intensive engagement with underwater archaeology over time. With California State Parks I became the replacement for Francis A. Riddell upon his retirement. My opportunity to do land archaeology was replaced by staff and budget meetings,

but I was still the only state archaeologist certified to dive. That allowed me a useful role in making underwater parks in California and investigating submerged cultural resources. We developed the philosophy that parks' values do not stop at the water's edge—they continue offshore on a publicly owned and now submerged landscape. I took a leadership role in expanding California's underwater parks and developing the State Park Dive Team.

At the same time I received an appointment as an adjunct lecturer in anthropology at Indiana University, Bloomington. I never taught in Indiana, but I did assist in their Caribbean Studies Program in the Dominican Republic. My vacation days and off time were often spent in that fabulous country. What began as a search for a Columbus shipwreck transformed over time to a companion effort to understand the Taíno people who greeted him on the shores of the Caribbean Sea. In 1996 our Indiana team was told of a mysterious site deep within Cotubabamá National Park. It consisted of a village site with several plazas and surface features, as well as a dramatic limestone sinkhole—a passage to a watery world. Park rangers observed divers entering the hole and retrieving artifacts without permission. Our team was requested to dive and inspect the site and recommend appropriate management actions. That led to a full research effort at the site, called Manantial de la Aleta.

The diving was rigorous. It involved a rappel of 50 ft. to reach an underground lake and a dive of 115 ft. to reach the top of the underwater archaeological deposit. Bottom time was 11 min., so each dive was carefully planned and executed. Over the course of two years I made almost 50 dives in the sinkhole to recover rare and beautiful Taíno artifacts. Some organic objects were perfectly preserved in anaerobic conditions—baskets, gourds, feathers, and carved wooden objects. Taíno mastery of woodcarving was demonstrated in the bowls we recovered. These were offerings made to ensure balance between the living world and the spirit realm. Diving La Aleta was truly an incredible experience. I felt we had given the Taíno culture a chance to speak through the beautiful objects it left behind. We left most objects to be preserved in place, but recovered a sample as directed by Dominican park authorities. Our work added new information to better understand and appreciate the Taíno cultural heritage of the Dominican Republic.

It was my role in California to identify significant heritage sites that should be included as underwater parks. We identified the *Pomona* at Fort Ross and *Frolic* near Caspar, along with several Gold Rush ships in the Sacramento River. My Sacramento River contacts led me to a retired police officer who developed a passion for locating vehicles that had crashed into the river from levee roads. This would often happen at night, and the vehicle (and sometimes its occupants) would disappear without a trace.

Well, my friend would rent a magnetometer and tow it behind his boat to locate a metallic target, then dive to confirm its identity. About 20 mi. south of Sacramento he located a very well-preserved sailing-ship hull—a relic of the Gold Rush. I arranged for the best archaeological shipwreck recorder I ever met to help me document it—Dr. Sheli O. Smith. Her documentation of the *Frolic* shipwreck, the *LaGrange*, and a fleet of vernacular boats and barges in Emerald Bay were the best. Sheli knew 19th-century ship construction better than anyone and had the drafting skills to document important elements. Together we worked to record the Clarksburg wreck—the best-preserved Gold Rush vessel known from the Sacramento River.

Over time I had the opportunity to study important underwater sites that have heritage value for today. One such

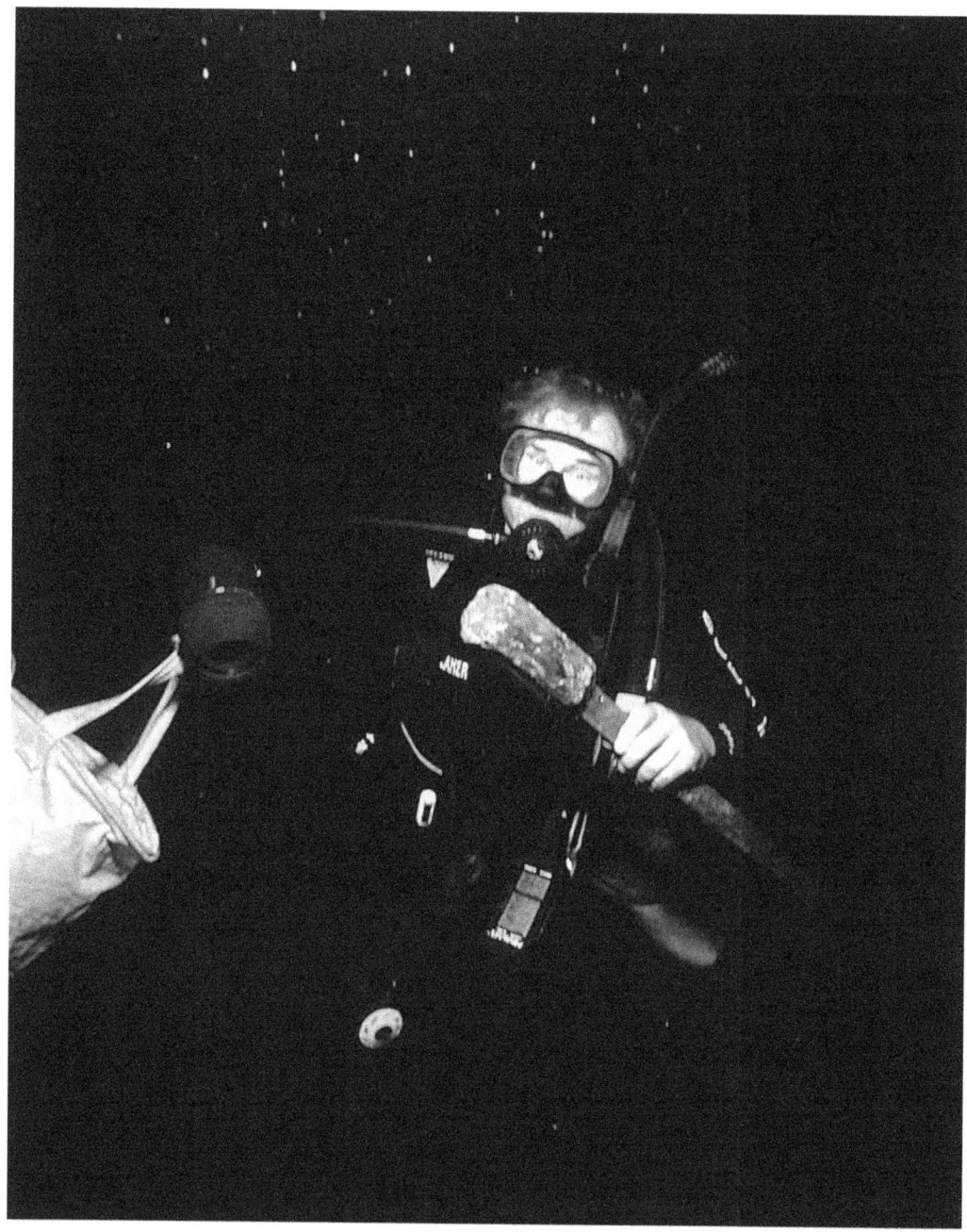

Figure 99. John Foster brings a fragile Taino war club to the surface from Manantial de la Aleta, an offering site in the Dominican Republic. This macana, described by Spanish chroniclers as the weapon most feared by Spanish conquistadors, is the only one ever recovered archaeologically. Radiocarbon analysis returned an early 15th century date. (Photo courtesy of Charles D. Beeker)

JOHN W. FOSTER

site was the *Montebello*, a 400 ft. oil tanker torpedoed by a Japanese submarine two weeks after Pearl Harbor. It lies some 6 mi. offshore from Cambria, California, at a depth of 880 ft. Diving in a two-person sub to view the rusting hulk of a casualty of World War II was a moving experience. Documenting Ahjumawi stone fish traps of the Pit River drainage was likewise important. These ancient features were constructed to harvest Sacramento suckers (*Catostomus occidentalis*) and promote their propagation as an important winter food for the Pit River people. They are still used and maintained today. The traps are an example of traditional ecological knowledge passed down from time immemorial. I worked with Native people to help protect this important cultural patrimony. In 1999, at the request of the government of Baja California, I was dispatched to assist in documenting the remains of a Manila-galleon shipwreck on a remote and forlorn Pacific beach. It probably came to grief in the 1570s. The artifacts our binational team recorded include Chinese coins and porcelains made almost 300 years prior to those aboard the *Frolic*. Both ships and cargoes ended up as heritage sites.

My parks career never provided the opportunity to focus exclusively on maritime sites and heritage. I still had to manage programs and budgets, develop policy, and oversee the cultural-heritage mission within the department. But in the time I had I do feel we made significant progress in adding maritime-heritage sites to the State Park System and building support for submerged cultural heritage as an important component of state historic preservation. The *Frolic* played a significant role in that success. The *Frolic* wreck site is now within a state underwater park; its conserved artifacts can be appreciated by the visiting public. I want to acknowledge Dr. Thomas Layton for making that possible.

Sheli O. Smith

Sheli O. Smith, Ph.D., was born in 1955 and raised in Napa, California. She learned to sail on the Napa River, and from an early age was fascinated by the Mothball Fleet of World War II and Viet Nam–era vessels anchored along the shoreline of nearby Suisun Bay. Following her graduation from Justin-Siena High School, Sheli enrolled at the University of Arizona, graduating with bachelor's degrees in anthropology and classics in 1976. Then, following her interest in nautical archaeology, Sheli enrolled at Texas A&M University, where she completed her M.S. in nautical archaeology and an M.S. in geography in 1979, after which she enrolled at the University of Pennsylvania, where she completed her doctorate in American Studies and historical archaeology in 1986.

Throughout the 1970s, 1980s, and 1990s Sheli worked in museums from Maine to California. She directed the Newport Nautical Museum in Southern California and the Fort Gibson Historic Site in Oklahoma. Her knowledge of ship construction, together with her underwater mapping and documentation skills, brought many requests from colleagues to research shipwrecks from the Falkland Islands to the Yukon. Starting in the 1980s Sheli began teaming with California State Parks on Gold Rush wrecks in the Sacramento River, on the coast, the barges and the mini-fleet scuttled in Lake Tahoe, and other California Marine Managed Areas.

In 2001, Sheli joined Dr. Annalies Corbin in the creation of the PAST Foundation, where she worked

Figure 100. Sheli Smith, 2022. (Photo courtesy of Sheli O. Smith)

until 2019. Known as "the Provocateur," she developed problem-based educational programs to engage young people in science, innovation, and technology, along with professional development to help teachers successfully deliver immersive learning. In 2003 and 2004 she directed the *Frolic* Shipwreck Mapping Project.

After 20 years with the PAST Foundation, Sheli returned to Napa, where she was appointed executive director of the Napa County Historical Society in 2021. Sheli continues to serve on the California State Parks Diving Advisory Board and the SCHUNRS (Sonoma Coast Historic Undersea Research Society) Board.

Frolic: A Reflection of Past and Present

Sheli O. Smith

I've always thought of the *Frolic* as a mirror reflecting the best and sometimes the worst of humankind in its story of mid-19th-century American history. At first it was the reflection of disparity between the archaeological context and the written record, but as I learned more about the ship, the people, the events, and rediscovery, I saw *Frolic* as a mirror of her dynamic times, changes in technology, culture clashes, and ultimately even changes in how we perceive the value of historic sites. This was not an overnight revelation, but rather lots of discussion, comparison of sites, and reevaluation of information, building toward a more holistic view. Although fascinated with the history of my home state, California, I came late to the investigation of the *Frolic*, as Tom noted in his introduction. Thus I benefited from what the salvors found and what Tom's research unveiled. Where Tom understood the context of the Pomo people and Jim Delgado the history of the Gold Rush, I brought an understanding of what the *Frolic* looked like and how she worked. My work with the *Frolic* was really among the last pieces, combining the virtue of hindsight with the events of the 1840s and the archaeological remains.

By 2002 I had already read Tom's first book on the *Frolic* and reviewed his second book. I had visited the archaeological site of Three Chop Village with Dan Foster and Tom Layton, and visited all the museums exhibits on the *Frolic* as well as enjoyed the *Frolic* play and Mendocino Brewing Company's shipwreck ale. I had even gone to the Baltimore Historical Society and done some research for Tom.

So, why didn't I get involved earlier? Simple. I spent the 1970s and 80s honing my skills in maritime archaeology outside California, primarily in the Atlantic from Labrador to the Falklands. It was in those early years that I met Jack Hunter and Jim Delgado, but never had the opportunity to work with them. Then, in the early 1980s, John Foster and Jack Hunter asked if I would return to California from my work on the East Coast and investigate the Gold Rush shipwreck *LaGrange*. I remember John being worried that as a maritime archaeologist I would not work well with sport divers interested in shipwrecks, but I think he soon learned that was not always the case. In fact, my career had already sent

Figure 101. Sheli Smith and Annalies Corbin view *Frolic* artifacts at the Mendocino County Museum. 2003. (Photo by Thomas Layton)

me in the direction of museums, where the public is key to interpretation and outreach.

The *LaGrange* investigation brought me home to California and launched lifelong friendships with John Foster, the folks at State Parks, and Jack and Monica Hunter. Through my museum and maritime-archaeology experience I had the privilege throughout the 1980s and 90s to work on several other beautifully intact California Gold Rush shipwrecks as well as the ongoing studies of Maritime Managed Areas, or MMAs.

When John approached me about the *Frolic,* I was excited to marry my love of eastern-seaboard ship construction with my interest in Pacific trade networks. Plus, I was looking for a place to run a hands-on field school for underwater archaeology. The *Frolic* fit the bill, although I remember Tom's extremely worried expression at the idea of putting young divers in the surf zone at Caspar. I assured him it could be

done and that we would all survive. Thanks to the wonderful Caspar and Mendocino communities, we not only survived, we prospered!

We ran two field seasons on the *Frolic.* I turned to my friends and colleagues for students and help with housing and equipping the investigation. Generous people came out of the woodwork. We enjoyed donated coffee from the Mendocino Roasters and desserts from chefs at the CIA (Culinary Institute of America) in Napa. Point Cabrillo Lighthouse housed us the first year, and a donated home in Mendocino housed us the second. Volunteers brought us lunch and helped haul tanks and dive gear up and down the cliff at Caspar Cove. Students from Napa Community College, Cabrillo Community College, Indiana University, East Carolina University, and Texas A&M University joined the field school, and with them came their professors, Annalies Corbin and Charles Beeker.

Because it was a field school, we focused on growing knowledge bases through experience with material culture, underwater-mapping techniques, and conservation, as well as public outreach. The students systematically photographed and recorded the artifacts recovered by the earlier sport divers and donated to the Willits Museum and Kelley House. We also advertised and opened up a weekend "American Treasure" event, inviting local residents to bring any artifacts that they had recovered from the shipwreck and nearby beach to be photographed and documented. While the objects were being recorded, we interviewed the owners, collecting their stories. Once the students had a firm understanding of the material culture associated with the shipwreck, we went underwater to record the archaeological site and document the state of the site.

Although there may have been hull remains when the shipwreck was first investigated, the exposure to oxygenated water through salvage eradicated any remaining fragile wooden structure. Thus, reconstructing how *Frolic* was built and what she looked like relied more on the historical records than the minimal archaeological artifacts. By 2003, only the more durable objects, such as the anchors, windlass, and concreted porcelains, remained, ghosting an outline of the wreckage. The artifact dispersal in the high-energy surf zone revealed where the 100 ft. brig came to rest, wedged in between two surf rocks with the bowsprit almost assuredly touching the cliff face. Over the two seasons of 2003 and 2004 the archaeological team successfully mapped the site and, with the help of the Indiana Mather's Museum conservator Judith Sylvestri, recovered and conserved a porcelain-encrusted ballast "pig" along with a baseline collection of ceramics from around the site. On her final voyage, Captain Faucon used iron bars, known as "pig," for ballast. The Indiana team, with their professor Charles Beeker, also conserved one of the small cannon recovered earlier by sport divers. Today the baseline collection is housed at the Mendocino County Museum in Willits, while the cannon and ballast pig are on display at the Point Cabrillo Lighthouse.

To better understand what *Frolic* looked like, Tom supplied my archaeology classes at Napa College with the Heard Company repair invoices for *Frolic*'s tenure in China. So, in the months between field seasons, students deconstructed the invoices, creating a searchable database in order to better understand the details of the hull and rigging, as well as the career of *Frolic*. Finally, Annalies Corbin of East Carolina University and the PAST Foundation helped me assemble the large catalog of *Frolic* artifacts that incorporated all recovered salvaged items, the "American Treasure" items, and the baseline sample recovered during the two field seasons. We jokingly called it the "Mother of All Databases." Ultimately, the database catalogued 2,729 artifacts from 33 different assemblages that had been collected between 1965 and 2004.

Under the aegis of State Parks and thanks to help from so many, both in research and community support, I was able to complete the database and write a report on the two-season survey in 2005. The research further cemented my view of *Frolic* as a mirror, starting with the men of the Heard Company who were willing and able to take advantage of any and all markets globally. All they needed were the tools and people to do so. *Frolic*, with her sharp hull and enough canvas on her two masts to make her fast, was the tool

SHELI O. SMITH

Figure 102. Sheli Smith drafts a map of the *Frolic* shipwreck, Point Cabrillo, California, August 2003. (Photo by Thomas Layton)

the Heards needed to capture some of the lucrative opium market.

Frolic was a successful opium clipper ship. Captain Edward Faucon, an experienced sea captain, was given command of *Frolic*. Based on Richard Henry Dana's accounts under Captain Faucon in *Two Years Before the Mast* and Faucon's record in the opium trades, I believe he was among the class of captains known as "drivers." Drivers were called thus because of their reputations for driving the ships and crews hard, squeezing out as much speed as possible on any transit. These men of the 19th century and its advancements in tracking time were enthralled with concepts of speed and possibly the adrenaline high of pushing the edge with some of the world's most technologically advanced equipment.

The supposition that Faucon was a driver is borne out by the number of times copper had to be repaired on the lower hull of *Frolic* during her six years in the opium trade. Faucon consistently cut in close to the reef edge as he rounded Southeast Asia through the treacherous, pirate-infested waters of St. Brendan's Straits. This tactic cut transit time, made it difficult for pirates to pursue, and increased profits. But it was hard on the ship and crew.

By 1849, *Frolic* had paid for herself numerous times over, but the Heards were not finished wringing profit from the ship. They turned their gaze to another market, the California Gold Rush. The six-year-old brig was worn and ready for replacement. So the Heards directed Captain Faucon to California, where he was instructed to sell the cargo as well as the ship in San Francisco. Even her pig-iron ballast would have fetched a handsome price in Gold Rush California. If she had made it to her destination, *Frolic* would simply be a footnote of history, but, in wrecking on California's north coast, *Frolic* took on a much bigger story in the state's history.

The rediscovery of the *Frolic* reminds us that the passage of time erases many of the details of the past. Within six months the wreckage of the *Frolic* had disappeared beneath the surf of the cove. But the wreck and subsequent trips by surveyors set in motion events that would dramatically transform the rugged north coast of California into bustling timber communities. But few would remember that it was *Frolic* that launched the lumber boom.

For over a hundred years, the story of the *Frolic* remained shelved in the archived journals of the Heard Company, the historical newspaper accounts, and insurance records. Then the 20th-century invention of scuba made it possible for adventurous young men to rediscover the shipwreck. The American attitude of "finders keepers" sanctioned their recovery efforts. In truth, without their adventurous spirit the *Frolic* might remain lost to time. Still, it took the combined events of the *Frolic* or "Silk Wreck" salvage and Tom's queries as to how Chinese porcelains turned up in a Pomo village to crack the door of history and bring the full story of *Frolic* back into the light.

Thanks to Tom's inquisitive nature, the *Frolic* story did not end with "Wow, look at that!" but made him delve deeper into the records and written histories of the people who were involved in the career and wreck of the *Frolic*. The records he compiled reflect so many aspects of the cultures and people who interacted with the *Frolic* that Tom has now written numerous books on *Frolic* looking at those various aspects. Through this retrospective we can explore the rediscovery and look at the wrecking event, achieving clearer vision with the benefit of that hindsight.

In combining the information from the rediscovery, the salvage, the underwater survey, and the records Tom collected, we can build a fairly accurate picture of the ship and thus better understand the wrecking event. For example, we know that the *Frolic* shipwrights in Baltimore had little understanding of how stifling the conditions would be below decks in the tropics. Faucon had numerous portholes added to the stern cabins over the brig's six years in India and China. The portholes allowed both air and light below decks. Those glass portholes survived into the archaeological record.

Although Faucon's accounting of wrecking and the actual disposition of the wreck do not fully jibe, we can surmise that Faucon's letters to the insurance company and the Heards have nuggets of truth. He may have surmised, by the time he reached San Francisco, that the insurance money would be more profitable to the Heard Company than the sale of the cargo and ship. By August of 1849, San Francisco was bursting with abandoned ships on the waterfront, deserted by crews headed off to the Sierras to seek their fortunes.

Whatever Faucon's reasoning, in all likelihood he tried to turn his ship when he neared the reef rocks that run south from the northern point of Caspar Cove by using the sails against the wind. He recounted that he was not successful and caught the rudder on the rocks, severely damaging the steering capabilities. At that point he only had his sails to steer the ship. From this point his account and the archaeological facts differ. He claimed that the ship sank then and there at the outer reef in deep water. However, the facts reveal that he managed to turn the ship back around and drove it into the harbor

SHELI O. SMITH

all the way to the cliffs on the northern side of the cove.

He and his white officers immediately debarked in the longboats, leaving behind his Malaysian sailors. It is clear from his accounting, once he reached San Francisco, citing the ship sank a quarter-mile offshore in deep water, that he had no intention of returning to rescue the Asian crew. His callous actions reflect his Western view of superiority. Faucon's story was almost immediately contradicted when the insurance company got word that both the Mitom Pomo and ranchers were salvaging the *Frolic*. They dispatched a team to survey the wreck, but by then storms and surf had done the damage, and the *Frolic* was a total loss. Even with the disparity of the reports, the insurance company paid out to the Heards, then hired Faucon to help them spot future fraudulent claims. Thus, even in wrecking, the *Frolic* was profitable.

The salvage of the *Frolic* reflects how frontier communities let few things go to waste and often repurposed items. Pottery, ale, glass bottles, camphor trunks, fabrics, and even the ship's stove are known to have been salvaged. In all likelihood, the rigging, tackle, and canvas were also removed and reused. Anything that could be recovered from the hold and lifted to the top of the cliff was likely salvaged in the immediate weeks after the wrecking. The Malaysian sailors may have helped in the salvage efforts, using the spars and rigging to hoist cargo from the hold up the cliffs. What happened to the sailors left behind is unknown. The remains of porcelain and ale-bottle glass repurposed into beads and arrowheads by the Pomo villagers reinforces the precious value of durable objects.

From historical knowledge of the hull and the extent of the wreckage on the seafloor, it is clear that the bow sat in about

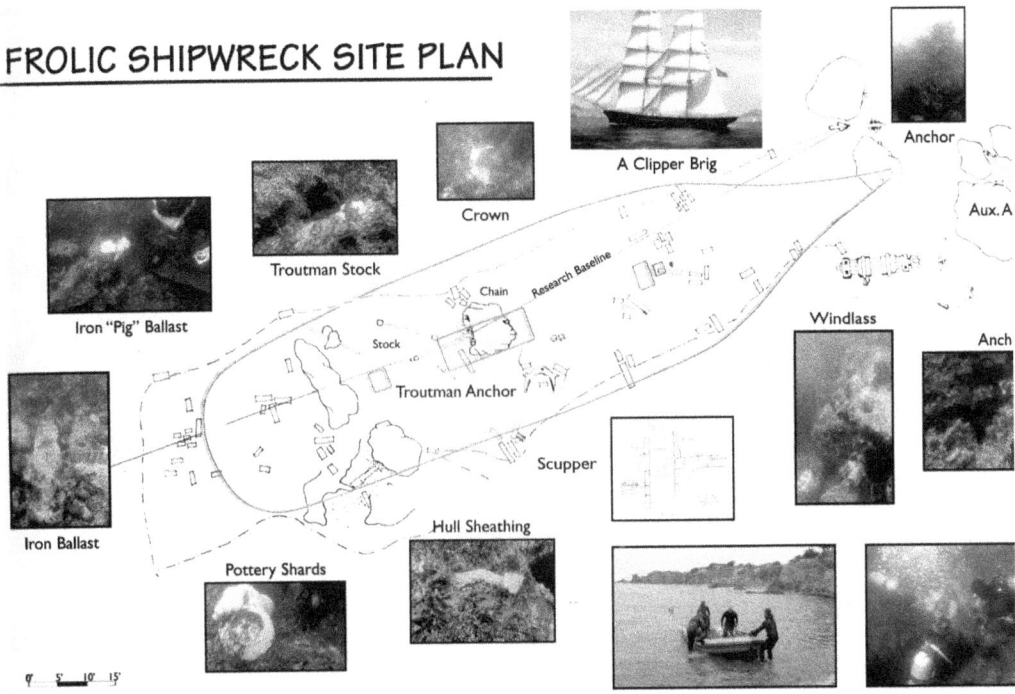

Figure 103. Completed map of the *Frolic* shipwreck site by Sheli Smith, 2003. (Photo courtesy of the California Department of Parks and Recreation)

9 ft. of water, sticking proudly out of the surf some 10–15 ft. The officers cabin located aft settled in deeper water, between 30 and 40 ft., thus completely submerging the stern of the ship. Her 100 ft. mainmast would have easily extended above the water, but would not have helped salvage some of the deep cargo and cabin goods. This may be the reason that some of the porcelains and jewelry were not salvaged immediately.

A Trotman anchor, novel for the time and stored at the bottom of the hold, was left in place, suggesting that the cargo salvage was predominantly in the upper reaches of the hold and hefting large weights up the cliff may have been a deterrent to salvaging the cannon and anchors. The fact that the galley was located forward near the foremast would also account for the salvage of the stove. Along with the cargo, the rigging and sails were most likely dismantled and salvaged. The lack of durable tackle parts among the salvaged artifacts and those now concreted to the seafloor, suggests the salvage above water and in the shallows was fairly extensive. Shipwrecks were often stripped down to the lower masts, recycling the spars, iron upper-mast couplings, tackle, line, and canvas.

Finally, we circle back to the more modern salvage of the shipwreck. It is through the sport-diver interest in the shipwreck that many of the artifacts were recovered and Tom Layton was able to connect the shipwreck to the Pomo village. We are lucky that Tom was able to connect with these men. The connection in all likelihood saved many of the salvaged items. This is not a poor reflection on the sport divers—several of them were well meaning—but all too often artifacts from both terrestrial and underwater sites end up either parceled out through sales or left in someone's garage to be thrown out at a later date. Kennon, Pierson, and the Bullers all realized that their contribution was in finding the *Frolic*, and their collections would serve a broader audience by being displayed in museums. Tom Layton's willingness to engage the divers and their willingness to donate the recovered artifacts reflects the changing attitudes of private collection and shared appreciation.

Frolic's role in history was amplified by her wrecking and subsequent salvage. The wreck of the *Frolic* was a catalyst. The Layton-led investigation set in play the various ways to look at the Heard Company, the captain, and the ship's role in 19th-century Pacific history. By bringing all of these aspects together, we enjoy a fuller understanding of the use of technology to command markets, the interactive nature of the cultures along the north coast of California at the moment of the Gold Rush, and the changing perceptions of how history is discovered, interpreted, and shared. Thanks, Tom, for including me in this investigative journey.

SHELI O. SMITH

Georgia L. Fox

Georgia Fox, Professor Emeritus at California State University Chico, served as department chair and as codirector of both the Museum Studies Program and the Valene L. Smith Museum of Anthropology. During her time at CSU Chico, from 2001 to 2021, she contributed new courses to the growing Museum Studies Program and to the expansion of the anthropology museum, as well as developing new courses for the archaeology curriculum. Her specializations in anthropology are historical archaeology, the conservation and preservation of archaeological materials, museum studies, and cultural heritage outreach. She has conducted archaeological fieldwork in the Channel Islands off the central coast of California, Israel, Turkey, Greece, the Netherlands, and the Caribbean.

Much of her archaeological work has focused on maritime and island communities and coastal sites, ancient harbors, and terrestrial sites related to maritime trade. Georgia's work focused on the late Bronze Age Eastern Mediterranean and, more recently, on the Caribbean in the early modern period. She received her B.A. degree in history from the University of California, Santa Barbara, and her M.A. and Ph.D. degrees in anthropology from Texas A&M University. She also served as the head curator of the Santa Barbara Maritime Museum. She has published two books, one monograph, numerous peer-reviewed journal articles, and has served as a reviewer for the Institute of Museum and Library Sciences and the National

Figure 104. Georgia Fox, 2009. (Photo by Jeff Teeter, 2009)

Science Foundation and serves on the editorial board of the *International Journal of Historical Archaeology*. She was the holder of the endowed David W. and Helen E. F. Lantis University Chair and was awarded an Emmy for her documentary *Impact of the* Frolic: *A Shipwreck that Transcended the World* (Fox 2014). Georgia was born in York, Pennsylvania, and moved to California with her family at age 13.

Georgia L. Fox

30 August 2022
Deep Gap, North Carolina

Growing up around a library jam-packed with history books and weekend jaunts with my parents to Gettysburg and other historical sites sparked my interest in the past. Born in York, Pennsylvania, in 1954, my first memorable experiences were formed when we lived downtown in an ethnically mixed neighborhood. In 1961, my parents built their dream house on 30 ac. of land, so I spent a childhood reading and playing in streams, roaming the forest, and being outside much of the time. Both experiences—urban and rural—converged in my later interests in history, archaeology, and travel. Key among childhood memories was our annual summer car trip to the Jersey shore. The trip always filled me with great anticipation, especially as we drew nearer to the briny marshes and lovely dunes of Stone Harbor. Other summers we also went to Maine, where my grandmother was carted over the rocky beaches in a wheelbarrow during high tide. From those days, my love for the sea was deeply ingrained.

My father, who was vice president of Fox's Bakery, which had been in my family for three generations, was an active supporter of the civil rights movement. He was devastated by the assassination of President Kennedy in 1963. His love of nature, classical music, and art was infectious, but, sadly, his early death in 1967 at age 46 did not leave him any time to enjoy these things. Soon afterwards, my mother, who was an advertising writer for WSBA radio and the local newspaper, the *York Dispatch*, packed us up, and we left Pennsylvania for the sunny climes of Santa Barbara, California. My mother, born and raised in Brooklyn, New York, was one of three children of immigrant parents. In 1965 she fell in love with Santa Barbara when she attended my brother's wedding there. The palm trees and balmy weather were alluring selling points after enduring long, cold East Coast winters.

My mother has been one of the most influential people in my life. Her wisdom, New York sense of humor and quick wit, her inner strength and cheerful outlook toward life, plus her generosity and patience were all traits to aspire to as I was growing up. She was really my best friend in many ways. My mother emphasized the practical aspects of life, but also understood and encouraged pursuing a fulfilling life's path. Often my friends from high school would seek her out for advice—I sometimes think they came to our house just to hear her golden nuggets of wisdom.

She passed away in 2003 at age 93 after a long struggle with Alzheimer's disease.

Santa Barbara was a radically different place than what I was used to, but I loved it. Blessed by both ocean and mountains with a Mediterranean climate, Santa Barbara can seem almost idyllic. Almost. In January and February of 1969, one of the worst oil spills in human history occurred off the Santa Barbara coast when Union Oil's Platform A gushed a sickening tarry slick, coating the ocean's surface and the unsuspecting pelicans, gulls, and sea mammals along with it. Although heartbreaking, this tragedy also ignited an already developing environmental movement and the beginning of Earth Day. The oil spill was followed by a strong local movement against out-of-town developers who wanted to build condominiums on any available land along the coast, but, fortunately, certain development projects were averted through public outcry and good lawyers. My French teacher gathered up her students to protest these plans, especially on land around Santa Barbara City College, which I was attending at the time. Observing local government at city council meetings and then participating in a human chain of bulldozer blockers was heady stuff for a young college student like me in the early 70s. In the case of Santa Barbara City College, some these efforts paid off when the college was granted the available land to expand. Today this is one of the best community colleges in California and the U.S.

Transferring to University of California, Santa Barbara (UCSB) in 1974, I majored in French, but soon grew bored and switched to history. The history department at UCSB thrived with great faculty, one of whom served as a mentor to me, Dr. Alexander Callow, whose upper-division seminars in American urban history were memorable and fun. He influenced us through his emphasis on the importance of good scholarship, and he could be formal in a large lecture hall, but in our smaller upper-division seminars he was warm, personable, and genuinely interested in his students. Dr. Roderick Nash was also on the faculty in those days, and his "Wilderness and Man" class was immensely popular, filling one of the largest lecture halls on campus. The class was life changing, as we learned about early settler attitudes about taming wilderness and deep notions of land ownership which clashed with Native American points of view. Many years later I would apply what I learned from Nash's class to my own courses.

Upon graduating from UCSB, I began a graduate program toward obtaining a teaching credential, but, tired of school, I moved on to my first fulltime job after college, working as a bookkeeper at a law firm. Although this was not my dream job, I learned a lot and developed skills that would be useful in subsequent employment, including how to craft a good business letter and apply legal terms appropriately. This skill came in handy when I had a shoddy landlord during my graduate school days. My next job at ABC-Clio, an academic publishing house, was really a formative experience in writing and editing, as well as developing lifelong friendships. After a few years there, however, I grew restless, not knowing what I wanted to do with my life.

Traveling and work filled the next few years as I explored options, but, during that time, 1982 and 1984 stand out as pivotal years in my personal growth. In 1982, I took a long trip with a friend to Italy, Israel, and Greece. During this trip I was intrigued with the fantastic archaeological sites of the Mediterranean. On my return I spoke with archaeologists at the university. One archaeologist discouraged me from pursuing this field, informing me that I "wouldn't get rich or famous doing archaeology," which I found amusing.

In 1984, a second life-changing event happened—I learned how to scuba dive on a bet. A good friend was keen to get certified for her upcoming honeymoon. A long time before this, in 1974, I was at a resort in Puerta Vallarta, Mexico, where for $25 you could have a tank of air strapped on your back and go for a 30 ft. dive. I remember how much I liked it, so I accepted my friend's offer to do the scuba course with her. She hated every minute of it, but I fell in love with the sport, and for the next few years I dove whenever I could—on the weekends in the kelp forests of the Channel Islands and during dive vacations such as in Roatan, Honduras. During this time I also applied for an assistant museum educator position at the Santa Barbara Museum of Art. Unfortunately, a miscommunication resulted in my not getting the position, and I was told that I had been their first choice for the job. I was deeply disappointed, but life sometimes has a way of coming around, unbeknownst to me at the time.

Moving on, I wondered how I could combine this diving hobby with a career, when, in 1986, a small advertisement in the bottom right-hand corner of *Archaeology Magazine* jumped right out at me, an ad for the Port Royal, Jamaica, Summer Underwater Archaeology Field School, which was sponsored by the Department of Anthropology and Nautical Archaeology Program at Texas A&M University. I saw the ad and told myself: "That's it. That's what I want to do with my life—be

an underwater archaeologist!" This made sense—it combined my love of history, diving, and scholarship. I applied to the field school and, when accepted, I then agonized over whether to quit my job at a magazine publishing company to apply to the master's degree program at Texas A&M. I relayed these concerns to my supervisor over a lunch of Chinese food. He encouraged me to take advantage of this opportunity, which was further reinforced by a fortune cookie that stated: "You will go to a warm and sunny place."

The Port Royal Field School, directed by Dr. Donny Hamilton, was a blast and differed from sport diving in many respects. As scientific divers, we worked long hours in the water in carefully gridded excavation units, followed by artifact cataloging and data entry, while keeping a field notebook and learning about Jamaican culture. This is exactly what I wanted—a way to combine diving with research, fieldwork, traveling, and the desire to eventually teach and research at the university level.

In the fall of 1986, I began the M.A. program at Texas A&M, focusing on four-field anthropology together with nautical and underwater archaeology. The four-field approach in anthropology requires a well-trained anthropologist to be proficient in the four major subfields of anthropology, including: physical or biological anthropology, archaeology, sociocultural anthropology, and linguistic anthropology, with a specialization in one of these areas of the discipline. I chose archaeology. Pursuing an M.A. and a Ph.D. in the social sciences is a long and often arduous process, living frugally, and being at the mercy of your mentors and advisors. Fortunately, I had great mentors, and I learned how to become a four-field anthropologist in what

GEORGIA L. FOX

I consider one of the best anthropology programs in the U.S. Teaching introductory anthropology courses as a graduate student also helped me learn the material and prepared me for the job market.

During my time at Texas A&M I had several wonderful mentors, including Donny Hamilton, a maritime and terrestrial archaeologist who directed the Port Royal field school and served as the chair of my thesis and dissertation committees. Dr. Bruce Dickson, a terrestrial archaeologist, is a superb scholar and introduced me to good teaching practices and other areas of anthropological research and served on my dissertation committee along with Dr. Sylvia Grider. Sylvia, a folklorist, taught me a greater appreciation for the cultural influences and traditions of human societies that are reflected in the material culture or things that are meaningful to them. Material culture, or the objects we create, use, and discard in the form of archaeological artifacts are often among the few things that we can rely on to interpret human behavior and the lives of those who lived before us. Artifacts help provide a window into why certain trends and styles became so important, such as Rockingham Ware, a type of ceramic that reflected middle-class values of 19th-century America.

I also served as a graduate assistant to cultural anthropologist Dr. Norbert Dannhaeuser, whose specialty, economic anthropology, would later become an interest of mine as I explored the roots of capitalism in the 17th century for my dissertation research. Several years later, I became a member of the Society for Economic Anthropology through the encouragement of Dr. Jeffrey Cohen, another faculty member at Texas A&M at the time. My faculty mentors stressed excellence in scholarship, deep research, and the importance of proficient writing. They were all taskmasters, but that is what a student needs in their educational training. Critique of one's work is ongoing, even after graduation, so getting used to this is part of lifelong learning and becoming a professional in the working world,

While at Texas A&M, I was able to fulfill another strong interest—the conservation of archaeological materials. Archaeological artifacts recovered from terrestrial and underwater sites often need to be stabilized for study, interpretation, museum exhibitions, and public outreach. Archaeological conservation, unlike invasive restoration, employs methodologies and approaches of preservation that require specialized knowledge and an understanding of how and why objects deteriorate over time as part of good stewardship of cultural heritage.

Before attending Texas A&M University, I had basic chemistry in high school and was vaguely aware of the applications of chemistry to professional careers, but I don't even remember how I became aware or even interested in conservation. I just know that, somewhere along the way, I became keenly interested in the preservation of objects as a potential career choice. Knowledge of organic and inorganic chemistry is important in conservation because the nature of deterioration processes is composed of chemical reactions between artifacts and their surroundings, whether in the ground, underwater, or even in museum exhibitions and collections storage.

Toward this interest, in the late 1970s I apprenticed in the conservation studio of Carlos Osona and Carol Kenyon, the latter who for many years was the chief conservator for the California missions. During that time, I had applied for a Rotary scholarship to study conservation at the Courtauld Institute of Art in England, but was not awarded the scholarship. Fortunately, in the graduate program at Texas A&M, there was an opportunity to gain experience from Dr. Hamilton in the conservation of archaeological materials, particularly those recovered from underwater sites. This was much better than studying at Courtauld, where the conservation of paintings was the focus. The conservation of archaeological materials poses distinct kinds of challenges, but through training and apprenticeships it allows one to add other skills to their archaeological tool kit. If a student is interested in becoming an archaeologist, I always suggest developing additional skill sets that can open doors to joining archaeological projects and in seeking gainful employment. Developing specialty areas like geographical information systems (GIS), remote sensing, human osteology (the study of human bone), and zooarchaeology (the study of animal bones from archaeological sites) are just a few of the many areas of expertise that can prepare those interested in a career in archaeology. For me, developing a specialty in archaeological conservation was a ticket to working on other projects and, later, contract projects, where I could train interested students.

For my M.A. thesis at Texas A&M I focused on the conservation of artifacts recovered from the coastal archaeological site of Tel Nami, Israel, directed by Dr. Michal Artzy. In the fall of 1986 Dr. Artzy was a guest speaker invited by George Bass, who was one of the founders of underwater archaeology and the Nautical Archaeology Program at Texas A&M. Following her presentation I approached Dr. Artzy and asked if I could participate in her excavation at the coastal site of Tel

Nami, which is just south of Haifa, Israel. She said yes, and for the next five years I participated in this project as well as an underwater site at Dokos, Greece, directed by Dr. Yannis Vichos.

Because the artifacts recovered from Tel Nami were exposed to salt and moist conditions, I asked Dr. Artzy if I could develop a program of conservation treatments for the artifacts for my M.A. thesis, and she consented. In 1989 I was awarded a Samuel Kress Foundation Grant, one of the few available for conservation projects by individual researchers. With these funds I set up a small conservation laboratory at Haifa University and spent the summer and fall of 1989 conserving the artifacts recovered from previous field seasons and then wrote up my thesis. I learned a lot from this project, including diplomacy in efforts to retrieve the artifacts that were in possession of a colleague of Dr. Artzy. I also learned how to set up a lab in a foreign country and navigate the streets, shops, and bus system of Haifa and its environs, and learned basic Hebrew at Haifa University. That lab was the first of four labs that I developed in my 35 yr. career.

Setting up a basic conservation lab takes funding and equipment, but it can be done from a shoestring budget of $5,000 all the way up to a state-of-the-art lab that can cost millions of dollars. I managed to create my labs on a shoestring budget if I had an adequate space that could accommodate decent ventilation, good natural light, tables, shelf space, and proper cabinetry to store chemicals safely. After my thesis project concluded, I also ventured into field conservation methods and consulted with Dr. David Scott at the Getty Conservation Institute for an independent study of the deterioration of bronze. I conducted these experiments at Texas A&M under Dr. Hamilton, then published my findings in *Studies in Conservation*, the journal published by the American Institute for Conservation.

In 1990, I decided to pursue a doctorate at Texas A&M, this time focusing on the clay tobacco-pipe collection recovered from 10 years of underwater excavation at Port Royal, England's foremost port in the Caribbean in the 17th century. In 1692, a devastating earthquake destroyed much of the port city, resulting in the excellent in situ preservation of the site. Along with the clay tobacco pipes, thousands of spectacular artifacts were recovered from 1981 to 1991, revealing daily life in a 17th-century Caribbean port town. Spending long hours in the lab going though bags containing 21,500 pipes and pipe fragments plus poring over 10 years of original field notes revealed more than just clay pipes. By applying world-systems theory, also known as dependency theory, I demonstrated how consumer goods, like tobacco, sugar, chocolate, and tea, spurred a preindustrial consumerism in the 17th century, where core areas like London and Bristol relied on peripheral colonies like Jamaica for raw materials to process and sell. Under this system, tobacco, then sugar, helped propel Great Britain to become a hegemonic empire that lasted well into the 20th century. My research culminated in the publication of my book, *The Archaeology of Smoking and Tobacco*, published in 2015 by the University Press of Florida.

After successfully defending my dissertation, a remarkable job opportunity came up. The new Santa Barbara Maritime Museum was seeking a head curator. It was the perfect job, and, after being offered the position, I left Texas and began the next phase of my life at the museum. Situated right on the breakwater in Santa Barbara Harbor, the museum's mission is to create "quality exhibits and educational experiences that celebrate the Santa Barbara Channel and illuminate our rich connections with the sea." The position opened a whole new vista of possibilities for me, and I was happy to be back in my hometown and to be part of a new start-up nonprofit museum where I could apply my knowledge and skills.

Being responsible for overseeing the burgeoning collection and the planning of 21 new exhibitions focused on the Central Coast and Santa Barbara maritime history was a dream job. Through this position I met so many wonderful people, including one of my heroes, Dr. Sylvia Earle, an explorer and pioneer in oceanography and deep-ocean exploration. She was a major contributor to the development of human-occupied vehicles technology used in deep-ocean research. I also met some of the great commercial dive pioneers, experts in marine biology, such as Milton Love from UC Santa Barbara, and others. I met and collaborated with NOAA staff member Robert Schwemmer and local Santa Barbara historian Neal Graffy, as well as worked with board members, visitors, volunteers, and staff, particularly the late Paul Mills, who was the former director of the Oakland Museum and who sat on the Maritime Museum's board.

While at the museum I rolled up my anthropological sleeves and delved into all the minutiae of museum collections policy and management; exhibition design, planning, and installation; numerous planning meetings; networking with community members; and working with our various development directors and volunteers. I enjoyed interacting with members of the Chumash Maritime Association, a group of local Chumash Native Americans whose involvement and input in the creation of the "Chumash Exhibit," was essential. At the time they were deeply involved in the revitalization of the great traditional sea-going plank canoe, the *Tomol*, through training members of their community to navigate this magnificent 26 ft. long vessel in the Santa Barbara Channel. Although no complete *Tomol* has been recovered archaeologically, replicas have been created through the ethnographic field notes of anthropologist J. P. Harrington and a 1912 photo of a *Tomol* built under the direction of Fernando Librado Kitsepawit. *Tomol* canoe planks were lashed together with natural cordage and caulked with local asphaltum (naturally seeping tar), but their construction was much more complex and dependent on available or traded materials. These boats were one of the great achievements among many of the Indigenous Chumash of the Central Coast.

By 2001, much of what I wanted to accomplish at the museum was completed, and the museum was well on its way, but, at the heart of my career aspirations, I missed teaching and research from my graduate-school days. Miraculously, two anthropology departments were advertising for an unusual dual specialty: a faculty member who could teach anthropology courses, specializing in archaeology, and museum studies. I interviewed at both universities, one in Southern California and the other in northern California, and was offered both positions. From an anthropological perspective, this was a good omen! On the day of my travel to Chico, due to heavy fog several of us missed our flight connection from San Francisco. I managed to hitch a ride with a rock band who rented a Lincoln town car, and we arrived in Chico

just in time for my two-day round of interviews. I was warmly received by the faculty and happily accepted the position when it was offered.

The day I moved to Chico, 6 July 2001, it was 106°. Regardless, I was excited about my new job, and now it all came together: the archaeology, a four-field anthropology department with long-held traditions, collegial colleagues, the freedom to conduct scholarly research of my own choice, and the opportunity to create and teach new courses. Other responsibilities included codirecting the Museum Studies Program and Museum of Anthropology (now the Valene L. Smith Museum of Anthropology) along with Dr. Stacy Schaefer, professor emeritus. Stacy, a cultural anthropologist, specialized in Indigenous Wixarika Huichol lifeways of Mexico. After she retired, I codirected the museum with Dr. William Nitzky, a cultural anthropologist specializing in Asian cultures, fluent in Mandarin Chinese and Japanese.

Created by Keith Johnson in 1971, the Museum Studies Program and anthropology museum were, by 2001, well established. The Museum Studies Program was well known for being one of the few hands-on museum studies programs in the U.S. and provided me a wonderful opportunity to build on this groundbreaking program. Although I had lost out on the Santa Barbara Museum of Art position all those years ago, things came full circle; I now had the opportunity not only to teach courses in archaeology and museum studies, but also to codirect the museum and take it to the next level. Keith had created a wonderful template for the future. Here, my interest in material culture, its discovery, preservation, conservation, and interpretation all came together in one place.

During my early years at Chico State,

GEORGIA L. FOX

one of my major goals was to develop a long-term archaeological project in the Caribbean. Searching the Internet, I discovered the "Seawall Project" at Nelson's Dockyard on the island of Antigua. A Website for the dockyard showed images of artifacts being recovered in the harbor during the rebuilding of the seawall. Excited by this maritime activity, I contacted the island archaeologist, Dr. Reginald Murphy, via email. In 2004 I went to Antigua to meet Dr. Murphy and identify potential projects. I returned in 2005 to conduct pedestrian surveys of potential sites, and, in 2007, after settling on the Betty's Hope Plantation, our fieldwork began in earnest.

Betty's Hope was ideal in so many respects. Although not an underwater site, it was significant in other ways. As one of the largest plantations on the island in its heyday, Betty's Hope was also supplemented by almost 300 yr. worth of documents in the form of the Codrington Papers housed in the National Archives of Antigua and Barbuda. Betty's Hope was owned and operated by the Codrington family from 1674 until 1944, an unusual situation in the region. The site was easy to access for a field school, and this would be the first sugar plantation excavated on Antigua.

Thanks to the support and generosity of Dr. Murphy, the island's chief archaeologist and UNESCO representative, and his wife Nicki from 2007 to 2017, I began 10 years of an archaeological field school and the Betty's Hope Research Project, which resulted in Chico State students, Antiguans, and students from elsewhere to participate in the field excavation of a former sugar plantation. For some students, this was their first opportunity to possess a passport, and others had never experienced swimming in the ocean before coming to Antigua. The clear blue waters and white sandy beaches, plus Nicki's cooking, all helped create a magical experience for students.

My research logically progressed from

Figure 105. Betty's Hope field school participants and principal investigator, Georgia Fox, 2012. (Photo by Georgia Fox)

Figure 106. Students working at Betty's Hope. (Photo by Georgia Fox, 2012)

GEORGIA L. FOX

tobacco to sugar and life on a sugar plantation. With an international team and all the bells and whistles that technology can offer to conduct archaeological survey and excavation, we examined the plantation's layout, its ecology, and mapped and surveyed the site extensively, as well as excavating the great house, rum distillery, and a section of the former slave quarters. Our project examined the colonial landscape from many perspectives as well as the remarkable lives of enslaved Africans and Afro-Antiguans who lived out their lives in this place and who achieved agency through their Afro-Antiguan pottery traditions. Although this project did not involve the excavation of shipwrecks, the plantation and island were caught up in historical events that profoundly impacted the world through the transatlantic slave trade, the popularity and consumption of sugar, and the postcolonial realities of former European colonies. It is also noteworthy that the Caribbean was the maritime gateway to the exploration and colonization of the Americas. Working at Betty's Hope was the logical extension of my work at Port Royal, but, instead of tobacco, here sugar was the vehicle to research and explore the tragic consequences of colonial initiatives that were chiefly maritime in nature.

During the project we also had several opportunities for Chico State museum studies graduate students to conduct their thesis projects at the Betty's Hope Visitors Center, the Museum of Antigua and Barbuda in downtown St. John, and at the Nelson's Dockyard Museum in English Harbour. Much of this has been discussed in *An Archaeology and History of a Caribbean Sugar Plantation on Antigua*, which I published through the University Press of Florida in 2020, just as the pandemic brought us into lockdown.

Back on the Chico State campus, I initially tried to develop a class in underwater archaeology, but there was little interest, so, in my archaeology courses, particularly the historical archaeology class, I tried to insert examples of underwater archaeology, which made for great case studies. More successfully, a course I proposed, Conservation of Archaeological and Ethnographic Resources, was accepted into the curriculum. This was a lab class where I could share my conservation knowledge and skills with students. We were the only university on the West Coast that offered this course at the undergraduate level to help our students prepare for the archaeology job market, especially in cultural-resource management. This was also the fourth conservation lab that I established in my career, the third one being at the Santa Barbara Maritime Museum, which was never used. Subsequently, through my contacts at the National Oceanic and Atmospheric Administration (NOAA), I received contracts to conserve objects recovered from several shipwreck sites located in NOAA national marine sanctuaries and monuments that allowed me to train interested students. My favorite project was the conservation of a ship's bell from the New Bedford whaling ship *Parker*, which met its fate in a fierce storm in 1842. The bell was recovered during the summer of 2008 by NOAA maritime archaeologists in the Papahanaumokuakea Marine National Monument in Hawaii.

Bringing underwater archaeology and shipwreck anthropology to Chico, however, finally happened on a lark. In preparing to teach the historical archaeology course in the fall of 2012, I was casting about for a new case study that

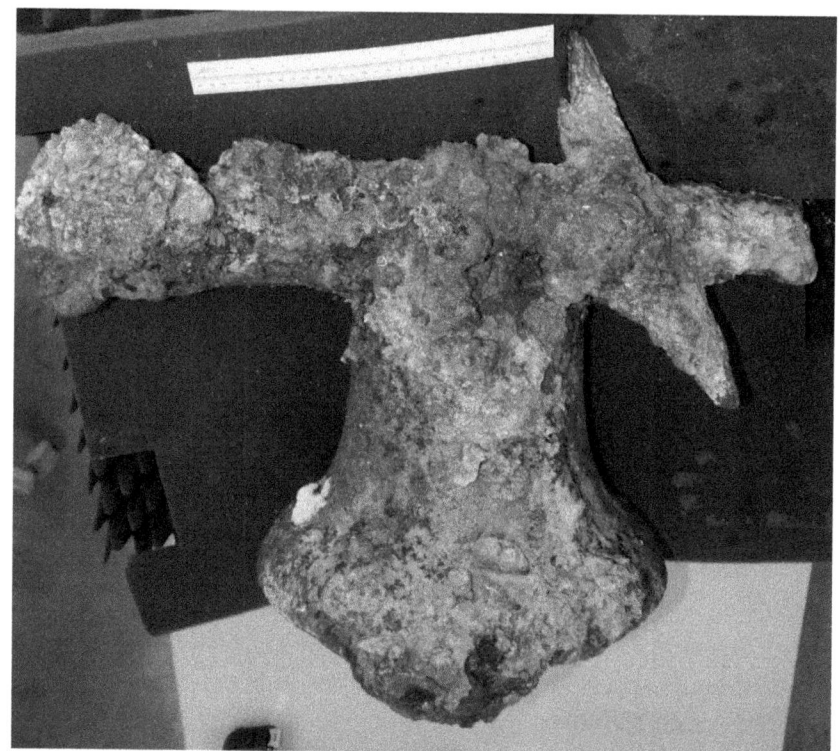

Figure 107a. The *Parker* bell before conservation. (Photo by Georgia Fox, 2008)

Figure 107b. The *Parker* bell after conservation. (Photo by Georgia Fox, 2009)

GEORGIA L. FOX

was interesting and relevant to California history and archaeology. Somehow, I stumbled upon Tom Layton's 2002 book, *Gifts from the Celestial Kingdom: A Shipwrecked Cargo for Gold Rush California*, which was required reading for the course. In the meantime, I was also thinking about exhibit topics for teaching the Exhibit Research, Design, and Installation course in 2013. The anthropology museum's benefactor, Dr. Valene Smith, happened to be married to Robert (Bob) Benner, a former U.S. Navy sailor who was an avid collector of nautical instruments, many of which were quite rare, such as a Davis quadrant dating to the 1700s in excellent condition. Suddenly, it occurred to me that we could highlight parts of Bob's collection as well as the *Frolic* shipwreck for the exhibition. I decided to contact Dr. Thomas (Tom) Layton. I had met him some years before, during a Society for Historical Archaeology conference, and was impressed by his knowledge and collegiality. I emailed Tom to find out where the *Frolic* artifacts were located, and he responded right away. The artifacts were part of the Mendocino County Museum's collection, located in Willits, California, only three hours from Chico. In the meantime, in our museum exhibits, we liked to include videos, particularly videos we could make ourselves through the Advanced Laboratory for Visual Anthropology (ALVA) that my colleague, Dr. Brian Brazeal, established in our department. It dawned on me that we should make a film about *Frolic*. I watched the 2003 documentary "Gold Rush Disaster: *Frolic* Shipwreck" aired on the History Channel (Lindahl and Martenez 2003) but found it wanting and overly dramatic.

The prospect of making a documentary about this shipwreck was immensely appealing. We just had one slight problem: we needed the funds to make this happen. Thanks to Brian's enthusiastic presentation to Bob Benner, Bob generously provided the funding, and off we went. I asked Tom if he was interested in being filmed and telling his story. Wow—was he! Once he shared with me his experience with the History Channel version, we decided Tom's input was top priority, especially in view of his painstaking scholarly decades-long research. We also felt it imperative to include local Pomo groups or individual perspectives on the *Frolic* as well as Pomo reuse of *Folic* artifacts that washed up on the beach near Three Chop Village. It is a fascinating story.

This is the beauty of the *Frolic* saga; it is deeply multifaceted, involving so many disparate events, peoples, and places, as revealed through Tom's research. Ship captains, the opium trade between China and India, the California Gold Rush, Indigenous Pomo peoples of Mendocino County, the beginning of the California lumber trade, and other fascinating facets of this one shipwreck make for an exceptional story. One thing that is less known or discussed is California's long relationship with the sea. This dates to early Indigenous lifeways and settlements along the coast, the Manilla galleons, European exploration and establishment of the California missions, the hide-and-tallow and sea-otter fur trades of the 1820s and 30s, followed by the mass migration of hopeful young men who came by sea to find gold, my great-grandfather being one of them.

Our connection with Alison Glassey, the Director of the Mendocino County Museum at that time, allowed us to borrow select *Frolic* artifacts for the exhibition. In turn, we offered one of our stellar and talented museum studies students, Kim Ornellas (now Whitfield), to thoroughly document and catalog the borrowed artifacts; it was a solution where our respective museums mutually benefited.

The exhibition, Into the Blue: Maritime Navigation and the Archaeology of Shipwrecks, opened to a packed house in late January 2014. Visitors could see Bob Benner's outstanding collection of nautical instruments, view a video about sailing around Cape Horn, learn about shipwreck archaeology, see the *Frolic* artifacts on display, and view our newly completed documentary film, *Impact of the Frolic: A Shipwreck that Transcended the World* (Fox 2014). Two of the former salvage divers that Tom had interviewed also joined us and were quite excited to see the objects they recovered in the exhibit—it was a magical night! One of our students, Arik Bord, built a special theater for the *Frolic* film that mimicked the inside of a ship. He also had worked on the documentary, filming underwater footage of the *Frolic* shipwreck site. Brian then sent the completed film to our local PBS affiliate in Sacramento, and the documentary was subsequently shown on PBS throughout the U.S. and eventually won an Emmy award in 2014. I also showed the documentary at the Society for Historical Archaeology meeting in Seattle in 2015,

and we received rave reviews and requests for copies of the film. The documentary is now required for California State Parks archaeologists to watch as part of their State Parks training

In sum, I could not have asked for a better life and career and all the experiences that contributed to it. The opportunity to have this career and to mentor several generations of students has been the most rewarding of my life's trajectory so far. I have encouraged our students, many of whom have felt overwhelmed by the myriad of career choices, to think of life's path not so much as a linear progression, but more of a path that zigzags. No matter how much we plan, life can offer delightful and unexpected surprises if we are open to opportunities and the unexpected. The *Frolic* shipwreck is a case in point. This ship and its fate reveal the meaningful threads of human interactions and historical developments that ensued from one solitary event. It reminds us that life is both unpredictable but complex, parts of it fleeting, unknowable, and unknown. That is the beauty and challenge of both historical archaeology and life: that there are mysteries to solve if we know how and where to look for them.

GEORGIA L. FOX

Figure 108. Georgia Fox and her Chico State University crew at Point Cabrillo, about to begin filming Impact of the *Frolic*: A Shipwreck that Transcends the World. Left to right: Arik Bord, sound; Matt Ritenour, camera/director; Joerg Thiele, assistant camera; and Georgia Fox, producer; with Tom Layton and his partner, Mabel Miyasaki. (Photo courtesy Thomas Layton, 2013)

Figure 109. The opening reception of the exhibit Into the Blue, 2014. (Photo by Jason Halley)

Deborah E. "Dede" Marx

Deborah E. Marx, M.A., was born and raised in California's San Francisco Bay Area. She attended Burlingame High School, participated in Semester at Sea, and graduated from the University of San Diego in 1998 with a B.A. in political science. she received her master's degree from East Carolina University's Program in Maritime Studies in 2002. Her thesis, "... With the Speed of a Stag Hound: The Steamship Winfield Scott: A Case Study in Early United States Steam Navigation," comprehensively examined a California Gold Rush steamship from its design to its demise off the Channel Islands (Marx 2002).

Between 2003 and 2018 Deborah worked in support of the National Oceanic and Atmospheric Administration's (NOAA's) Office of National Marine Sanctuaries (ONMS) in a variety of capacities. She was a maritime archaeologist for Stellwagen Bank National Marine Sanctuary and the ONMS Maritime Heritage Program, and also worked as an exhibits and communications specialist for the Communication Division. Deborah briefly worked for the cultural-resource management (CRM) firm SEARCH, Inc., between 2018 and 2019. Most recently she has been assisting California's Department of Parks and Recreation with a variety of maritime-heritage projects related to the terrestrial and submerged maritime cultural landscape of Sonoma and Mendocino, California's doghole ports, and the Redwood Coast timber industry.

Figure 110. Deborah "Dede" Marx, 2022. (Photo courtesy Deborah Marx)

Deborah has developed expertise in nominating maritime archaeological sites to the National Register of Historic Places (NRHP). She has authored or coauthored 20 individual site nominations, 2 district nominations, 3 multiple-property submissions, and 2 determinations of eligibility. Her most recent NRHP work is related to the northern California doghole ports and district nominations within several California State Parks. Since 2017 she has been living in the Florida Keys and volunteering at the Florida Keys National Marine Sanctuary. She spends her free time with her two horses and competing at shows around the southeast.

Deborah (Dede) Marx

18 October 2021
Key Largo, Florida

The *Frolic* has captured the interest of archaeologists, divers, historians, and many others who have engaged with the most recent chapters of this multifaceted story. All have played a role in revealing a window into California's Gold Rush through the wreckage of this opium clipper. I was fortunate to be a small part of that process through some of my first fieldwork and again 10 years later when *Frolic*'s connections reemerged as I researched the maritime-focused development of Mendocino and Sonoma counties.

During the summer of 2003, Dr. Sheli Smith, along with Dr. Annalies Corbin, Dr. Charles Beeker, and Dr. Thomas Layton, directed a field project I participated in as a newly graduated maritime archaeologist. As a native Californian I was delighted to join this team and dive on the site of a significant event in California history. This was the first year of a two-year project to archaeologically document the site and associated artifacts. *Frolic* came to have additional meaning for me as I investigated the remains of other California Gold Rush vessels, including the shipwreck that was the focus of my master's thesis. Since *Frolic* is located on a treacherous

part of the Mendocino shore, which very few divers have the chance to access, I was fortunate to spend a week documenting the shipwreck while staying at the Point Cabrillo Lighthouse facilities. I was joined in 2003 by six other hearty divers: three undergraduate students from Indiana University, a fellow recent graduate of East Carolina University's (ECU) Program in Maritime Studies, a Ph.D. candidate from ECU's Coastal Resource Management Program, and a local firefighter.

Following along with the project's 11-person team was a camera crew who filmed an episode of *Deep Sea Detectives*, "Gold Rush Disaster: The Frolic." The show, which aired in November 2003, was my first taste of trying to get work done while having a camera in your face—a hard and at times frustrating combination. As a recent graduate from ECU's Program in Maritime Studies, I still had much to learn and was appreciative of the opportunity to gain experience working with leaders in the field who were welcoming and generous with their time.

The archaeology community is a small tight-knit group, and the connections you make, last. I stay connected with many of

Figure 111. Dede Marx documents an anchor at the *Frolic* wreck site, Point Cabrillo, California, 2003. (Photo by Matthew Lawrence)

the colleagues from the *Frolic* 2003 field-work, and it is fun to reminisce and share stories. The coastal Sonoma and Mendocino communities are my favorite part of California, and throughout my career I have tried to remain connected to that area, as my first taste of maritime archaeology was there on another shipwreck, the steamship *Pomona* off Fort Ross State Historic Park. This narrative serves as one person's experience at the *Frolic* site early in a career and its personal impact years later when its meaning came full circle in another perspective not originally realized.

I grew up in the San Francisco Bay Area in a household connected to the sea. I am not a relative of a famous captain or naval officer, just part of a long tradition of family members who have loved being on or near the water. I was taken to maritime museums on vacations and spent summer weekends boating the Sacramento and San Joaquin Delta during high school. Days were spent exploring the expansive river

system, waterskiing, wakeboarding, and hanging out with friends.

Trips to lunch in Stockton or Locke, a once-thriving predominately Chinese community south of Walnut Grove, revealed glimpses of maritime communities outside of my suburban world. While I missed the larger picture of how this inland river system connected people both past and present, my experiences and the enjoyment I felt left their mark. I only wish that I had paid more attention to the few remaining hulks of half-sunk vessels I passed by on the way to my next adventure. San Francisco Bay offered so many interesting sights to explore for a boating family. Beyond the San Francisco waterfront, we took trips north from the Oakland Estuary to see the mothballed National Defense Reserve Fleet at Suisun Bay and to the Angel Island Immigration Station.

Trips beyond the Golden Gate Bridge to the Farallon Islands immersed me in the wild beauty of the ocean and kindled a desire to see beneath the water's surface. Fortunately, most family vacations centered around a beach, so I spent hours each trip snorkeling. When I was old enough I took scuba courses at the resorts we stayed at and ultimately got certified in 1993. Diving opened a new world of exploration, and, like many young girls, I wanted to be a marine biologist.

As I entered my senior year at the University of San Diego (USD) majoring in political science, I wondered what was I going to do after graduation. Without a clear plan I enrolled in a nautical archaeology class offered by Dr. Jerome Hall. I believe this was his first semester as a professor at USD, where he is still inspiring students. Dr. Hall's class was amazing and made me realize that I could combine my interest in diving and maritime history. Following my graduation from USD, Dr. Hall connected me with Dr. Charles Beeker at Indiana University, who was working with California State Parks to document cultural resources in several parks.

In August 1998, I joined the team at Fort Ross State Historic Park for my first maritime archaeological project. The fieldwork focused on mapping the steamship *Pomona*'s remains. Lost in 1908, the kelp-covered fragmented wreck was a challenging dive for me, having only recently learned how to dive with a dry suit. The project exposed me to the techniques needed to document a shipwreck and my role holding the tape measure's clip end with limited responsibility. Sitting around the campfire at Arky Camp after a day of diving, I listened to the entertaining stories and hard-won life experiences from Dr. Beeker, California State Parks archaeologist John Foster, and Dr. Sheli Smith,

all of whom I would intersect with on many future projects, including *Frolic*.

Inspired by the professional archaeologists that I had met and the fun I had working with them, but with no formal training in anthropology or archaeology, I applied to graduate school at ECU. After a semester off to take the GRE and to confirm that a job in the consumer-retail sector was not for me, I made the cross-county drive to Greenville, North Carolina. Over the next three-and-a-half years, between 1999 and 2002, ECU was the center of my academic and social world. In addition to the classwork, ECU expanded my diving capabilities through the AAUS (American Academy of Underwater Sciences) Scientific Diving Program and allowed me to participate in several field schools and fieldwork on student-thesis projects. My cohort was an enterprising bunch whose thesis research interests allowed me to join their field projects beyond the faculty-organized field schools. Their engagement with other professionals in the field and their collaborative spirit allowed all of us to learn and support each other with free labor. Similarly, living on the East Coast opened access to many of the nation's premier maritime museums, where fellow students and I pored over artifacts, maritime infrastructure, and museum vessels to gain a better understanding of the material culture of the maritime world.

When it came to picking a thesis project, I knew I wanted to do something in California. With the help of two ECU students and staff archeologist Frank Cantelas, we undertook a weeklong mission to continue the investigation of the Panama Route Gold Rush steamship *Winfield Scott* in the Channel Islands National Marine Sanctuary in California. The project was only possible with my parents' help and their willingness to use the family boat for day trips from Ventura Harbor out to Anacapa Island. Support from and generous assistance by sanctuary and Channel Islands National Park staff rounded out the collaborative team. National Park Service archaeologists had mapped the site 10 years earlier, but it needed a fresh look and a dedicated historical and archaeological assessment to assist with the site's management and monitoring.

Winfield Scott is the oldest identified shipwreck in the sanctuary and the only one listed on the National Register of Historic Places. It sank en route to Panama after leaving San Francisco in 1853 with a full complement of homeward-bound passengers, a cargo of gold specie, and mail. The lure of treasure made the vessel a target for looters, and it was the focus of an undercover operation to catch and prosecute divers and a dive charter that were destroying the site. *Winfield Scott* was a jumping-off point to connect with Dr. James Delgado and become exposed to additional Gold Rush shipwrecks, increasing my knowledge of and interest in the topic. The connection with this fellow Californian in the field also began a friendship, which has led to adventures around the world connected to the Gold Rush vessels and early steam navigation.

After graduating from ECU, the *Frolic* project continued my maritime archaeological education. Working again with Charles Beeker, John Foster, Sheli Smith, and now with Thomas Layton, I learned important lessons about community engagement. Working directly with the staff of the Point Cabrillo Lighthouse Museum allowed for dialogue about the collection of artifacts from the shipwreck in their care. Equally important for me were larger community interactions and

an evening presentation that gave people a better sense of their local heritage. The fieldwork at the *Frolic* site was equally instructive, challenging, and rewarding. Simply accessing the fieldwork day camp involved a hike down a narrow path that ended in a strenuous climb down the coastal cliff to the beach. Scuba gear and tanks had to be brought on our backs to the beach each day. I learned quickly how important it was to have a low air-consumption rate, because when your tank needed to be changed it was a long hike back to the car for a full one. Dr. Layton organized a trip upland to the Mitom Pomo Three Chop Village site, 15 mi. inland from *Frolic*, where he discovered repurposed shipwreck artifacts.

This was an important experience for me, as it emphasized the cross-cultural aspects of the *Frolic* shipwreck. It was not an isolated event taking place in a wilderness, but an interconnected aspect of the Indigenous cultures in the area and their interaction with a changing maritime cultural landscape. Following *Frolic*'s wrecking, the resulting Euro-American recognition of the economically valuable redwood and tan-oak forests would fundamentally change the area. It would be this topic that would reconnect me with the *Frolic* story years later, as I focused on the use of doghole ports for the extraction of timber and ranching products during the late 19th and early 20th centuries.

After leaving California behind to pursue employment opportunities, I was thrilled to join a new collaborative project between California State Parks and NOAA's Office of National Marine Sanctuaries that began in 2015. The project sought to document the remains of 14 doghole ports within Sonoma County. Dr. James Delgado, at that time director of the ONMS's Maritime Heritage Program, and Leslie Hartzell, chief of the Cultural Resources Division at California State Parks, saw an opportunity to combine forces for Redwood Coast field investigations in 2016 and 2017. I and other researchers examined the submerged and terrestrial remains of timber-landing sites by using the maritime cultural-landscape approach to connect those locations to the broader cultural environment within the areas of the California State Parks and Greater Farallones National Marine Sanctuary. While working for the ONMS Maritime Heritage Program I was extensively involved with project planning, fieldwork, historical research, and the resulting publication of results in both a technical report and a California State Parks publication (Delgado et al., 2018 and Delgado et al., 2021).

Remnants of the doghole ports' infrastructure, including lumber chutes, mooring hardware and anchors, buildings, and railroad/road grades, were found at 12 sites on land and 2 underwater. Additionally, team members investigated 10 reported shipwreck locations associated with the lumber trade or the area's larger maritime context. Eight of these locations contained shipwreck remains. Project results have assisted with site management and interpretation efforts to convey to the public the extensive maritime network and infrastructure required to move materials to and from the Redwood Coast.

While working in Sonoma County, the team began to reveal the larger Redwood Coast timber-industry story, its related coastal communities and their industries, and the way in which *Frolic*'s wreck was part of the genesis of interest in the Redwood Coast. In 2019 California State Parks revived the doghole-ports work with

support for the development of a Northern California Doghole Ports Maritime Cultural Landscape Multiple Property Submission (MPS) along with associated district nominations for Salt Point Landing and Fort Ross Landing. Working with California State Parks colleagues, particularly Denise Jaffke, I developed the MPS context document and drafted the Salt Point District nomination.

The cultural-landscape approach explored through the MPS chronicled the history of the timber industry and community development in Sonoma and Mendocino counties using the doghole ports as the connecting geographic loci of maritime activity. The California Historic Commission is currently reviewing the MPS and Salt Point nomination for submission to the National Park Service. The efforts are ongoing, with historical and archaeological work focused on doghole ports at Little River Landing and Bear Harbor Landing on the Mendocino coast.

Frolic's wrecking was a pivotal turning point for northern California development and natural-resource extraction that coincided with the migration of people into the state during the Gold Rush. After *Frolic*'s wrecking in 1850, Henry Meiggs of San Francisco financed a salvage party that traversed the coastline from Bodega Bay to Point Cabrillo, seeking to profit from the ship's spilled cargo. Their passage brought them through stands of massive trees abutting the shoreline and readily accessible to the lumbering techniques of the day.

While by no means the first Europeans or Americans to sight the forests, Meiggs and his associates recognized the opportunity to generate wealth from the forest and acted on it. Two years later, Meiggs set up a sawmill at Big River near Mendocino, originally named Meiggsville, and began lumbering operations, marking the start of the timber industry and American development of the Sonoma and Mendocino coastline focused on the export of Redwood and tan-oak timber products, including lumber, railroad ties, tan bark, fence posts, shingles, shakes, laths, stave bolts, grape stakes, and pickets, to San Francisco markets. Eventually, a system of 57 doghole ports along the coastline sprang up, with most operating into the 1920s—a system that relied on coastal schooners, steam schooners, and steamships as their transportation link.

The region was transformed, after Meiggs's first sawmill, into an industrial landscape, with lumber camps up in the forests with choppers, splitters, and peelers felling trees, then donkey engines or oxen pulling the logs down river gulches along skid roads to holding ponds or storage yards. Horse-drawn tramways and small locomotives moved materials to the steam-powered sawmills, after which the processed lumber continued to the coast for shipment from the doghole ports.

Doghole-port towns, like Caspar, Point Arena, Gualala, Little River, and Duncan's Landing, all trace their origins back to the sawmills and surrounding community infrastructure. Doghole-port operations were not isolated or independent ventures; they were units in a larger landscape that linked lumber mills with the shoreline shipment points. The resulting communities founded at these locations were social outposts. Population density near doghole ports led to associated facilities, such as stores, saloons, hotels, boardinghouses, schools, post offices, barns, livery, and blacksmith shops, to support the residents and visitors. Immigrants from Germany, Sweden, Italy, Ireland, Mexico, Russia, and China who worked the forests made the coastal towns a melting pot. The overlapping lumbering, ranching, and farming activities created doghole-port communities with varying sustainability and economic success.

Efforts to document and interpret the archaeological remains present at the doghole ports provide opportunities to capture the physical elements for better resource management. At the same time, these investigations revealed the larger role these small coastal indentations, now mostly abandoned and free of obvious remains, played in California's development. A closer look at the doghole-port locations found that, while efforts to return the areas to a natural state did wipe away much of the physical remains, these locations still have archaeological remains, including submerged cultural material, evidence of lumber chutes on the cliffs and surrounding rocks, roadbeds, and landscape alterations, that persist today.

I have been fortunate to experience other Gold Rush vessels after *Frolic* and *Winfield Scott* and have gained an even greater appreciation for how that event changed the world. The Gold Rush's massive population migration and resulting demand for goods and services in a short period of time led to economic and societal influence that reverberated widely, but that brought attention to the natural resources present within the state. Sonoma and Mendocino sawmills supplied millions of board feet of lumber that built San Francisco's businesses and residences and facilitated the waterfront's growth. Maritime commerce connected California to a global trade network; shipwrecks and hulks emblematic of that connection can be found in far-flung places and, most famously, under the streets of modern San Francisco.

Not all shipwrecks are hidden away underwater or in inaccessible locations. One of my favorite places linked to the Gold Rush is Tennessee Cove, the site of the shipwreck of the Panama-route steamship *Tennessee*. A 2 mi. long pathway in Mill Valley, California, ends at a beautiful sandy cove where *Tennessee* wrecked in 1853 after missing the entrance to San Francisco Bay. It is places like this where you can try and imagine what it was like for shipwreck survivors to come ashore after a disaster and wonder what to do next. The vessel's remains are mostly buried under the sand and offshore, but cultural material still sometimes reveals itself at low tide and on the beach to remind us of the *Tennessee*'s presence and the passengers and crew who were coming to California to strike it rich.

Before the Panama route allowed people a faster trip from the East Coast to the goldfields, sailing ships made the passage around Cape Horn, a long and perilous journey. A once-in-a-lifetime trip to the Falkland Islands in 2017 provided me an opportunity to visit the hulk of the bark *Vicar of Bray*, located in Goose Green, an example of the hundreds of sailing ships that participated in the Gold Rush. The project, led by James Delgado, sought to document that vessel's recently collapsed hull and to record its transition from hulk to shipwreck. *Vicar of Bray* stopped in San Francisco in 1849 and offloaded a variety of cargo, including iron retorts, or furnaces, used to process mercury, a key element for refining gold.

The bark ended up in the Falklands in 1870 for repairs and never left. Its last life was as a storeship for the Falkland Islands Company, who had a sheep-shearing station and slaughterhouse in picturesque Goose Green. Outfitted in dry suits and snorkeling gear, our team, including maritime archaeologists Amy Borgens and Matthew Lawrence, spent several days floating over the remains of that well-preserved Gold Rush–era sailing vessel. Sometimes you wonder how you got to a specific location or on a project, but it is all about good timing, taking chances, and the people you connect with. The Falkland Islands project was one of those occasions.

I have enjoyed being able to reflect on *Frolic* and where it has led me. I still have much to learn and hope the future provides more opportunities for exploration and education. I plan to continue my personal and working relationships with colleagues in California and those working on Gold Rush topics, and eventually would like to be living back in California near my family. Surprisingly, California does not have a dedicated maritime archaeologist working for any of the state agencies that deal with historic preservation or environmental protection, such as the Office of Historic Preservation, State Lands Commission, or State Parks. As a result, there are lost opportunities related to research, archaeological fieldwork, and resource management of California's underwater cultural heritage. NOAA's Office of National Marine Sanctuaries manages four sanctuaries around the Channel Islands, Cordell Bank, Greater Farallones, and Monterey Bay, but does not employ a maritime archaeologist within any of those sanctuaries or within the larger ONMS West Coast Region.

For a state that is so forward-thinking about protecting the ocean and natural resources, it still surprises me that such a submerged cultural-resource expertise gap exists. Other archaeologists have expressed similar sentiment about being disappointed in California's lack of attention to

DEBORAH E. "DEDE" MARX

maritime archaeology, both in academic institutions and at the state and federal level. A tremendous amount of work has gone on in the state on a variety of submerged sites, mainly shipwrecks, but that work in my opinion has focused more on a project-by-project basis and not on a wider long-term scale that is needed to make community connections and leave a lasting impact on resource management.

Fieldwork, undertaken as part of the National Historic Preservation Act Section 106 compliance or from a focused site-specific grant project is important, but it's only one component. These projects can sometimes overlook or neglect the interpretation, assessment, publication, or more in-depth research and analysis needed to tell the larger story.

The archaeologists and historians who have worked on and continued to work on *Frolic* have done so not because they are responsible for the legal management of the site, but rather for the realization that *Frolic*, both in a historical and archaeological context, is significant to the story of California and deserved the attention.

Thomas N. Layton

Thomas N. Layton, Ph.D., is Professor of Anthropology and President's Scholar, Emeritus, at San Jose State University. He was born in 1942 into an academic family. His father was a biochemistry professor, and his mother was a Holocaust survivor. He grew up in Maryland, Utah, and then Berkeley, California, where he graduated from Berkeley High School in 1961. He majored in anthropology at the University of California, Davis, completing his B.A. in 1965 and his M.A. in 1966. He entered Harvard in 1966, received his Ph.D. in 1971, and did a postdoctoral year in Middle Eastern archaeology. He was a visiting professor at Louisiana State University in 1972/1973 and served as Director of the Nevada State Museum in 1974. From 1975 to 1978 he taught at California

State University, Dominguez Hills, and then at San Jose State University from 1978–2003, where he served as department chair. A specialist in both historical and prehistoric archaeology, as well as oral history, he has published 5 books, produced 4 movies, written over 60 historical photo essays about San Jose, California, and was the recipient of the first James Deetz Book Award for accessible writing from the Society for Historical Archaeology.

Since 2002, he has been building an archive of historic South Bay (Santa

Figure 112. Thomas N. Layton, portrait by Robert Bain, 2012.

Clara Valley) images—now over 60,000 of them—for the Smith-Layton Archive at the Sourisseau Academy of State and Local History, San Jose State University. Tom plays bluegrass guitar and banjo. His current research, incorporating oral narratives describing over two centuries of family memories, is focused on the history of the Upper Kanawha River valley in southern West Virginia.

Thomas N. Layton

1 February 2021
San Jose, California

The *Frolic* shipwreck came into my life in July of 1984, when my San Jose State University archaeology field class students began finding blue-on-white potsherds in the Native American site that we were digging atop Three Chop Ridge in northern Mendocino County, California. Explaining those potsherds and their broader context would dominate my professional life for the next four decades.

But, my fascination with the past, leading me to Three Chop Village, extends back to my childhood—so I'll start my narrative there.

I was born on Friday, 13 November 1942, at St. Mary's Hospital in Rochester, New York, where my dad was working for Eastman Kodak. Dad referred to me as his "little weatherstrip to keep Daddy out of the draft." My dad was a great storyteller. He told me how, in the early 1780s, our family crossed the mountains from Virginia to the Kanawha River on the western Virginia frontier and how they pulled their wagons under a giant rock overhang that they named Camp Rock. He told me how the Indians drove deer off Deer Cliff, and how, as a kid, he had climbed the mountain across the river to see the Indian wall, so old that it had giant trees growing through it. He described his adventures

with his dog, Jack, and I named my little stuffed dog "Jack."

My continuous memories start at age four in Baltimore, where Dad became a professor at Johns Hopkins University. Dad's stories had already inspired in me a desire to touch the past. My first collection was composed of unusual pebbles, one of which contained a piece of fossilized bone. The mystery of that pebble was augmented by Dad's stories of dinosaurs!

Meanwhile, Alice Baker, my godmother, had given me an 1888 silver dollar, and my grandfather, Hugo Philip, gave me a 1947 silver peso, issued by the Philippines in honor of Douglas MacArthur. Those two coins and my fossil pebble were my treasures, kept safe inside my Swee-Touch-Nee tea tin, colored red and gold like a treasure chest. Soon I had my parents collecting 1943 steel pennies from their pocket change, and Dad gave me an 1859 Indian-head penny.

I was already fascinated by Indians and began collecting the cardboard sheets separating layers of Nabisco shredded-wheat biscuits. On each of these was printed an episode of Indian lore—"Injun-uity"—with pictures showing how to make such essentials as arrows, moccasins, and tepees, all explained by "Straight Arrow" himself!

By that time, Dad had pretty much run

Figure 113. Summer 1951: After attending "Science School" at Woods Hole, Massachusetts, I presented my first public lecture, Seashore Life, at Homewood Friends Meeting in Baltimore, Maryland. (Photo by Laurence L. Layton)

out of stories about West Virginia, and he began telling me stories from his reading of Herodotus, the first Greek historian (born 484 B.C.). I vividly recall how Egypt was saved from an Assyrian invasion by the desert mice who, the night before their planned attack, ate the Assyrians' bowstrings. And then there were the Amazon women, who cut off their left breasts so that they could draw their bowstrings unimpeded by their bodies.

At the end of World War II, Mom had learned that her own grandparents and other close relatives in Europe had been murdered by the Nazis, and that her closest friend, Annalisa Schmidt, for whom my sister Annalisa had recently been named, had been killed in a British bombing raid. I recall helping Mom fill postwar "care packages" for the Schmidt family and for several of Mom's high school classmates—boxes containing coffee, chocolate, peanut butter, sugar, shoes, gloves, and warm jackets, none of which were available in the devastation left by the war.

At the University of Maryland, Dad had become the mentor for several Jewish graduate students who were being treated badly by an anti-Semitic senior professor. Dad's reputation apparently followed him to Hopkins, where he soon accumulated a racially mixed team of graduate students: Mr. Das, from India; Miss Shook Yee Chan and Mr. Chow, from China; and Mr. Alonza Johnson, one of the very few African American graduate students at Hopkins. I vividly recall a Chinese dinner prepared at our house by Mr. Chow, and the crash of his gigantic iron cleaver reducing a whole chicken into tiny pieces. These early exposures to cultural diversity prepared me to feel comfortable with "Otherness." Meanwhile, my parents decided that we kids should receive religious instruction. They chose Homewood Friends Meeting in Baltimore because the Quaker emphasis was not on dogma, but on doing good.

In 1940, my grandparents, Hugo and Anita (Heilbut) Philip, had been able to complete their escape from the Nazis with a few pieces from the art collection that Grandpa had purchased during the 1920s. In 1947, with Dad finally established at a major university, Hugo and Anita presented us with several of those pieces, chosen to provide our household with some degree of elegance: *Die Erwachende* (the awakening), a bronze statue by Klimsch; an exact copy of Leonardo da Vinci's *Beatrice d'Este*, commissioned by Grandpa; a selection of German Expressionist prints, numbered and signed by Emil Nolde, Ernst Opler, and Max Liebermann; and a portrait of Albert Einstein that Dad later carried to Princeton, New Jersey, for Einstein to autograph. These works of art transported me back to an earlier time.

To provide us with summer vacations while continuing his research, Dad rented space at the Marine Biological Laboratory in Woods Hole, Massachusetts, where he enrolled me in "Science School" [the Children's School of Science]. Soon afterwards, as a nine-year-old fresh out of Science School, I gave my first lecture—on seashore life—at Homewood Friends Meeting.

For a long time, Dad had wanted to study the chemical basis of aging, and Hopkins provided him with the freedom to begin that research. Although Dad's research was going well at Hopkins, he felt that he needed more income to support our family, and so he left the university to take a much higher-paying government job—a decision that he would regret for the rest of his life.

The Army hired Dad to continue his research on wound healing—from chemical burns, atomic radiation, and exposure to nerve gases—at Dugway Proving Grounds in a remote desert valley in Utah. So we moved to the Mormon community of Tooele, about 60 mi. from Dad's work. Shortly after taking that job, two of Dad's superiors left, and he became chief of chemical warfare—a job clearly in conflict with our family's Quaker values.

For me, as a nine-year-old, our move to Utah was a fabulous opportunity. I could walk up the nearby canyon and catch trout. I watched Mexican neighbors build an adobe house. I read *The White Indian Boy*, about how in the late 1840s a boy about my age, from the next town, had been raised by the Indians. I imagined being a hunter and read everything I could find about trapping. Meanwhile, Dad was telling me stories of a cave being dug by archaeologists out in the desert near where he worked, where they were finding sandals thousands of years old. He pointed out the ancient beach terraces of pluvial Lake Bonneville and taught me to imagine ancient worlds.

It was in Tooele that I became interested in cars. My buddies and I would stand

THOMAS N. LAYTON

by the road and compete to be the first to identify each approaching car. In those days, each manufacturer had a distinctive grill and bumper design that changed with each model year, and I was able to identify almost any car built between 1930 and the early 1950s. One of the schoolteachers drove a 1930 Model A Ford, and at every opportunity I would carefully examine all the details of its design.

It was also in Tooele that I woke up to popular music. Every few months my parents would take us out for dinner at the Hillcrest Lounge, where I always ordered jumbo fried shrimp. The Hillcrest had a jukebox, and I would beg my parents for a nickel so I could listen to "Ghost Riders in the Sky."

As a third grader in Baltimore I had been a slow learner. When I entered fourth grade in Utah, all the kids were older than me, and I was doing poorly. My dad tried to help me with math, and I could feel his frustration. To this day I still feel his frustration whenever I make a mathematical calculation. My parents held me back, and I repeated fourth grade.

In 1954 Dad got a job as associate director of research and development at the Naval Powder Factory in Indian Head, Maryland, where the main research focus was on developing propellants for rockets and missiles. The move back to Maryland put me a year ahead of many of my classmates, so I was soon listed on the academic honor roll.

In Indian Head I developed a series of passionate interests—first as a coin collector, regularly going to the bank to get $10 bags of pennies, each one of which I examined for rare dates and mint marks. Then it was antique cars, encouraged by a neighbor who took me along to visit local junkyards to find parts for his vintage

Packard—a major formative event in my young life!

At age 13, I convinced Mom to drive me out to a farm where a rusted-out Model T Ford was for sale for $45. I can still picture those rotted wooden-spoke wheels!

I identified every neighborhood family with the make of the car that they drove. The Deskins drove a Hudson; the Skolniks, a Buick; and we Laytons drove a 1951 Cadillac. When we had a family reunion at our house, Dad's sister arrived in an Oldsmobile Rocket 88 and his brother in a two-tone 1954 Buick Century with a yellow body and a green roof. I fell in love with that car, and 22 years later I would purchase and restore a condor-yellow 1954 Buick convertible. Those early skills in recognizing and dating the annual stylistic changes in automobiles and the subtleties of American coinage would prepare me to see analogous subtleties in assemblages of artifacts.

I needed money to be able to pursue my hobbies. By the time I turned 13, I was earning money mowing lawns, catching crabs in the Potomac River and selling them to neighbors, and delivering the *Evening Star* newspaper to 45 houses. The price was $1.65 per month. When I collected the fees each month from my subscribers, many of them paid me with two $1 bills. I learned to take a long time digging through my pockets to find the 35¢ change—and, if I dug long enough, some of them would say: "Keep the change!" I recall my consternation when the subscription was raised to $1.95!

Every summer my parents would rent a beach cabin on the ocean where we would spend a couple of weeks. One summer we went to Rehoboth Beach in Delaware. Nearby was Coin Beach, where coins were said to wash in from some ancient shipwreck. I spent many hours looking for coins, but never found any. Sometimes we would take a picnic lunch to Calvert Cliffs beside the Chesapeake Bay, where fossilized sharks' teeth were eroding out of the cliff. I still have my coffee can full of sharks' teeth.

About this time, I discovered arrowheads in the fresh topsoil spread onto my junior high school baseball diamond. I found out where the dirt had come from and convinced Mom to drive me out to that hole in the woods—my first archaeological survey!

And then, there was rock-and-roll music! I traded my long-ignored violin for a guitar and taught myself to play it. Living in southern Maryland, it was an easy transition from rock-and-roll to country music, and it was late one night, with my ear to the radio, that I first heard the lonesome sound of a bluegrass banjo— and I was smitten. To play a five-string banjo, just like Earl Scruggs, became my ambition.

Old coins, antique cars, arrowheads, and bluegrass music all fed my passion to touch the past. I guess by then I was already preadapted to become an archaeologist.

It was about this time that I had my only religious epiphany. I had been baptized in a Congregational church, then attended a Quaker Sunday school in Baltimore, and then a Mormon young people's group in Utah, and, that Sunday morning, I was listening to the sermon in a Methodist church in southern Maryland. I recall that Reverend Andrew Gunn asked us all to bow our heads in prayer. I didn't. I looked around the room at all the bowed heads and suddenly realized that I was not one of them. That realization allowed me to appreciate the social function of religious traditions without becoming a slave to any

dogma—a perspective that has served me well as an anthropologist.

In 1957, Dad took a job with the U.S. Department of Agriculture, and we moved to the San Francisco Bay area—first to El Sobrante and then to Berkeley. It was in El Sobrante that I saw a 1930 Model A Ford convertible for sale just down the street, for $85. I had just turned 15. To this day I'm amazed that my parents gave me permission to buy it! Soon, my mother was ferrying me and a buddy and our toolboxes to local junkyards, where we were allowed to unbolt fenders and other parts for my restoration project.

At Berkeley High School I began to open up to the world. My most memorable class was semantics, in which Mr. Fitzgibbon, our teacher, deconstructed and explained Randall Jarrell's poem, "The Death of the Ball Turret Gunner." It introduced me to the power of language. I can still recite that poem from memory. As a junior, I knocked on doors as a neighborhood precinct captain in support of John F. Kennedy for President. In my spring of 1961 Berkeley High School graduation address, I told the audience that most of the Japanese members of my class had been born in "American concentration camps!"

Shortly after my graduation, my mother took me aside and revealed, almost apologetically, that she was Jewish. She and my father had hidden that fact to protect us four kids from racist taunts and from the Jewish quotas in private schools and social clubs, including the Quaker school that I might have attended had we remained in Baltimore.

I entered UC Berkeley in the fall of 1961. I was commuting from home. I was lonely, and I didn't have a major. I had enrolled in a physical anthropology course to cover part of the science requirement,

THOMAS N. LAYTON

Figure 114. Summer 1961: My Berkeley High School buddies helped me (fourth from left) rebuild the 1930 Model A Ford that is still parked in my garage. (Photo by David Wasley)

Figure 115. Summer 1964, northern Humboldt County, Nevada: My first archaeological expedition was composed of me, Kathy Branstetter, Dave Wasley (a buddy from high school), and my mother, Lisa Layton, who hiked up the canyon and discovered Smokey Creek Cave, which was to become my 1966 UC Davis master's thesis. (Photo by David Wasley)

and the old professor just plodded through the material. But, I thought: "Gosh, I'd like to go on an archaeological expedition." My buddy from high school French class at Berkeley High School was Steve Heizer, and his dad was an archaeology professor. So I went to see Dr. Heizer at his office. It was a long narrow office with him sitting far at the back. "Dr. Heizer," I said, "I'm Tom Layton. Steve and I know each other from high school, and I was wondering if you could use somebody on an archaeological dig. I can cook and do all kinds of stuff." Heizer barely looked up from what he was doing and said: "No!" And that's all he said! "No!"

I was doing poorly at Berkeley and earned a 1.6 grade point average that semester. My parents were concerned. But my mother had heard good things about the University of California, Davis campus. Mom and I climbed into our Volkswagen bus and drove up to Davis. It was raining, but, as we drove around the campus, a student said: "Hi, are you lost? If you give me a ride, I'll show you around." So we toured the campus with that student pointing out the important places, and while there I applied for admission. Fortunately, this was before the digital age, and, with classes about to start, I was accepted. I had moved into the dorm and was already attending classes before they received my transcripts. The dean called me to his office and explained that my GPA was too low to transfer to Davis. "But," he added, "since you're already here, I recommend you take some courses to get your GPA up." He recommended tennis!

My second semester in the dorms, my new roommate turned out to be an anthropology major. He was enrolled in an archaeology field class, so I enrolled, too! Every Saturday we were transported to the Miller Mound near Knight's Landing and were assigned 5 × 5 ft. units to excavate. We dug in 6 in. levels, shoveling directly into 1/4 in. mesh screens. Men dug and women screened. The goal among the men was to dig 5 ft. deep in a day, and I was proud to achieve that. We were not taught to take notes and received no instruction about the American Indians whose tools and burials we were excavating.

My roommate played banjo, and I played guitar and banjo, and I discovered that some of the other anthropology majors were into folk music. I went through several majors (pre-law, economics, and English) before settling on anthropology in my junior year. I had re-enrolled in the Saturday field archaeology dig course every semester since my sophomore year.

In the fall of 1962, my sister, Annalisa, moved into the dorm directly across the lawn from mine. The major benefit was that I got to meet all of her dorm-mates. My roommate and I accompanied many dorm sing-alongs.

In 1964, the summer of my junior year, I enrolled in a UCLA archaeology field class in Cedar City, Utah. It was an eye opener! I was no longer digging 5 ft. pits with a shovel. I was now scraping with a trowel and trying to see subtle soil-coloration changes marking the edge of a house or the circle of a fire pit. I learned stratigraphic excavation and how to take notes.

Later that summer, a graduate student at Davis invited me to assist him on a survey in northeastern California. He had recently written a master's thesis on Bare Cave in Surprise Valley. After completing our survey of sites eroding into Lake Britton, we visited Bare Cave, where the wife of the ranch manager told us about a

THOMAS N. LAYTON

cave on Smokey Creek about 30 mi. into Nevada.

When I got home to Berkeley I told my parents that I wanted to investigate that cave. I recruited my former pit partner from the Davis field class, but her mother wouldn't let her go unless my mother went as chaperone. My mom was eager to go, so, with the addition of a high school buddy, I had an expedition. We found the cave, but it didn't have much archaeological deposit. Mom didn't like the cave because there were bats flying in and out. One afternoon she took a hike up the canyon and found a better cave. We quickly dug a test pit into that one, revealing about 5 ft. of deposit, rich in projectile points and other flaked-stone tools.

The following summer, just after graduating, my professor, Dr. Martin Baumhoff, arranged for me to borrow a truck from the university motor pool. With an expedition of volunteers from Davis and a few more I recruited from a UCLA field class in Oroville and my mom as cook, we spent a week excavating Smokey Creek Cave. That site became my master's thesis, "The Archaeology of Smokey Creek Cave: Humboldt County, Nevada," completed in May of 1966.

One of the monographs I had read for my thesis research was written by John Cowles, an amateur who had excavated/pillaged Cougar Mountain Cave in the Fort Rock Valley of eastern Oregon. An obsidian-hydration-dating lab had been established at UC Davis, and I had received hydration measurements on the projectile points from Smokey Creek Cave for my thesis. The Cowles booklet illustrated some very early types of projectile points together with almost all of the more recent types for that region, and all of them were made of obsidian. I figured that

I might be able to work out a chronology if I could secure hydration measurements on those points—so I wrote to John Cowles, and he agreed for me to secure hydration measurements. He shipped me seven large frames containing most of the complete "exhibitable" points from the site.

The Cougar Mountain obsidian-hydration dates demonstrated that large-stemmed projectile points (now termed "Western Stemmed") were the earliest, and that the leaf-shaped points (Cascade) that a prominent archaeologist (B. Robert Butler) had touted as the earliest in the region, were significantly later. That was an important discovery, so I recruited a crew of my Davis classmates, borrowed a university truck through Dr. Baumhoff, and set off for a week in the Fort Rock Valley.

My goal was to find undisturbed deposits beneath where Cowles had stopped digging and to collect enough charcoal to radiocarbon date the earliest occupation at the site. We actually found some of that early deposit and laboriously picked out tiny flakes of charcoal with splinter forceps. Sadly, there was not enough charcoal to meet the minimum sample size for a radiocarbon date.

Over half a century later, in 2019, my colleague, Geoffrey Smith, at the University of Nevada, pulled those charcoal samples out of storage and, employing AMS (accelerator mass spectrometry) dating, requiring less than 50 mg of charcoal, was able to date two tiny fragments from our original sample (one from a basket), producing dates of over 12,000 years [B.P.]. Had we had access to that technology back in 1966 we would have secured among the earliest reliable carbon dates for human occupation in the New World!

In the fall of 1965, I applied for admission to university Ph.D. programs at

Figure 116. Summer 1967, northern Washoe County, Nevada: David Hurst Thomas and Jane Russell joined me for an archaeological survey in which we discovered and sampled most of the sites for my doctoral dissertation (Harvard 1970), and Dave's 1967 master's thesis at UC Davis. (Photo by Thomas Layton)

Columbia, Chicago, Harvard, UCLA, and, for insurance, Davis. I was accepted by UCLA and Davis, and, to my surprise, Harvard! My application letter to Harvard had stated that I wanted to study Paleolithic archaeology under Professor Hallam Movius.

I arrived at Harvard in September of 1966, and within a few minutes of meeting Movius I decided that I didn't want to study under him. Our elevator ride from the first floor of the Peabody Museum to his fifth-floor office seemed like the longest trip in my life. Movius came across as stern and inflexible. There seemed to be no joy in the man. Among his first questions to me was "Are you independently wealthy?" The anthropology department graduate-student list showed that some of his current students had been at work on their dissertations for over 10 years, and I immediately decided to change my focus

back to the Great Basin, where I could direct my own projects. When I told Movius, he replied: "So you're returning to the land of milk and honey!"

My decision was validated by a Movius joke then current among the graduate students. A Movius student was said to have made an appointment to talk with this professor. "Dr. Movius," he said, "my wife just had a baby and lost her job. I don't have enough to pay our rent or even buy books. I'll have to drop out of graduate school!" To which Movius thought for a moment and replied in his most fatherly tone: "My boy, sometimes even the most prudent of us must dip into our capital!"

After saying farewell to Movius, I needed a new dissertation advisor, and none of the faculty specialized in anything west of the Great Plains. But there was one old fellow who had worked in the Southwest during the 1930s, Dr. J. O. "Jo" Brew,

THOMAS N. LAYTON

the director of the Peabody Museum. Brew was a kindly, jolly old fellow, a great storyteller with a red nose, probably from drinking. I became Dr. Brew's only graduate student. I decided to expand on my master's thesis work at Smokey Creek Cave to include sites representing the entire span of human occupation in that region. Dr. Brew couldn't advise me on the archaeology, but I could write letters requesting permissions and support and he would sign them. Suddenly I had more freedom than any of my graduate-student colleagues.

I convinced the Nevada State Museum to cosponsor a summer 1967 Harvard-Nevada Expedition focused on discovery and test excavations at sites that showed promise. David Hurst Thomas, a UC Davis graduate student, asked if he could join the expedition and triple-screen one unit from each of the sites we tested. I had known Dave since his first archaeology field class at Davis, for which I had been the teaching assistant, after which he had volunteered for my Cougar Mountain Cave dig.

At that time most archaeologists were using 1/4 in. mesh screen to sift whatever they were excavating and rarely 1/8 in. mesh. A 1/4 in. screen might capture all the mountain sheep and deer bone, but what about rabbit, ground-squirrel, and bird bone? Dave's idea was to discover how much identifiable animal bone was being lost from each mesh of screen. He built a special screen with three stacked trays—1/4, 1/8, and 1/16 in. mesh. His plan was to calculate multipliers to correct for the loss of species through the 1/4 in. and 1/8 in. meshes. We discovered and tested enough sites for my doctoral dissertation, and Dave got enough data for his master's thesis.

Early in our field season we had a serious wreck. The rear wheels of our truck slipped onto the sandy shoulder of a road 125 mi. north of Reno. The truck rolled three times and landed on its roof. On its final roll I fell through the open door onto the ground. I recall feeling thankful that I was alive. Then the vehicle rolled back onto me with the cab pressing me into the ground. I tried to shout, but only had enough air in my lungs for a loud whisper. Dave and the uninjured crew members pushed and tilted the truck far enough for me to roll to safety. Following an ambulance ride to Reno, stitches to my scalp, bandages to my skinned back, and a week of recovery, we returned to the field with a replacement truck supplied by Dr. Baumhoff at Davis, who was now Dave's thesis advisor.

I wrote to Dr. Brew at Harvard describing the wreck and received a delightful, reassuring note in return:

Dear Tom,
Thank you for your letter and your preliminary report. I am very sorry to hear about your automobile accident. It actually takes me back into the past, because I had a Ford turn over on me during my first expedition in the Southwest. It still ran, too, after a new steering wheel was put on it, but I had to get along without a top (it was a phaeton). I was laid up in bed for a week with bruised muscles and had nine broken ribs which I did not discover until ten years later when they showed up in a routine X-ray taken by the Army. ...

With best wishes,
J. O. Brew
Director

In the middle of our field season Dave

Thomas and I made a trip to Austin in central Nevada to attend the first, and only, Austin Conference—intended to become an annual midseason, work-in-progress gathering of Nevada archaeologists, modeled after the Pecos Conference in the Southwest. It was on that trip that Dave first saw the Reese River valley that was to become one of his prime research areas for the rest of his career.

I returned to Nevada in the summer of 1968 with a field crew mostly recruited from family, friends from earlier expeditions, and Tom Beale, a Harvard undergraduate (who will appear later in this story). That summer we conducted major excavations at Hanging Rock Shelter and Silent Snake Springs, surface-collected an early assemblage from the beach terraces of pluvial Lake Parman, and mapped and tested Last Supper Cave.

By the end of the summer I had enough data for my doctoral dissertation and began to study for my Ph.D. oral examination. Anthropology department folklore had it that James Deetz had been asked to list all the California linguistic groups from Oregon south to the Mexican border. I memorized them all. In order to understand the history of American anthropology and archaeology I read all of the obituaries in the journals *American Antiquity* and *American Anthropologist*.

By that time Dr. Brew had retired, and Steven Williams, the new museum director and a specialist in Southeastern archaeology, had taken over as my advisor. It was in the dead of winter just after a heavy snowstorm that I met with my examining committee, mostly composed of junior faculty (Jeremy Sabloff, Geoffrey Brain, and Dena Dincauze) and my advisor, Steven Williams. I remember three of the questions. One was on the significance

of burins. That was easy. The committee members were mostly pottery specialists, and I knew my lithic technology better than any of them. Then Williams asked about the significance of the Kirk projectile point in Southeastern archaeology. I recalled the exact publication that presented that point type as a time marker.

Finally, after a few more questions, Williams asked me about Llewellyn Loud, an almost totally forgotten employee (actually a janitor/custodian) of the anthropology department at Berkeley. Loud had dug several archaeological sites for Kroeber in the summer of 1913, and I had read a small compilation of Loud's letters from the field to Kroeber: *An Anthropological Expedition of 1913 or Get It through Your Head or Yours for the Revolution*.

One of the goals of the oral exam was to plumb the depth of a student's knowledge, and I think Williams thought he had me on that one. But I proceeded to describe Loud's life in detail—including his socialist politics. Finally, Williams signaled me to stop, and they adjourned. They had me sit in the department office, down the hall from the meeting room. Periodically I could hear laughter from the meeting room. I sat there for what seemed an eternity. Finally, Dr Williams appeared, grinned, shook my hand, congratulated me, and apologized for having forgotten about me while they dealt with other business.

I decided to write my dissertation in California, where I had stored the collections and where it was warm. I rented a modern apartment in Davis and began writing in November of 1969. I turned in my final draft six months later, in May of 1970: *High Rock Archaeology: An Interpretation of the Prehistory of the Northwestern Great Basin*. I was a little too

Figure 117. Summer 1971, Tepe Yahya in southeastern Iran: I spent my postdoctoral year at Harvard as an instructor while studying Middle Eastern archaeology, before serving as an excavation supervisor at Tepe Yahya. (Photo by Thomas Layton)

late to graduate in 1970, so I received my diploma, written in Latin, in March of 1971.

When I had decided to focus on the Great Basin for my dissertation research I realized that I would end up as an expert on an obscure topic—and I had already decided that I would be more presentable on the job market if I had a second, more-prestigious regional specialty.

A few years earlier, Carl Lamberg-Karlovsky, a young Harvard professor, had begun excavations at Tepe Yahya in southeastern Iran, and I had recommended that he take Tom Beale from my Hanging Rock Shelter excavation onto that project. I knew Carl pretty well, having earlier served as a teaching assistant for one of his "General Education" courses. I decided to spend a postdoctoral year at Harvard reading Middle Eastern archaeology and auditing Carl's courses. Steve Williams got me an appointment as an anthropology instructor teaching a sophomore honor's tutorial with eight students, and that was enough to cover my rent in the graduate dorm. My plan was to join Carl's Tepe Yahya expedition. Carl's idea was that I would pair up with Richard Meadow, a second-year graduate student, to test another site, Tepe Nurabad, at the completion of the Yahya dig. We would have Richard's experience from two prior field seasons in Iran plus my Ph.D. degree to give us credibility with the Iranian Antiquities Service.

That expedition was my first trip outside the United States. I learned a great deal at Yahya, excavating a 10 × 10 m Bronze Age exposure replete with massive architectural remains. Sadly, the Yahya field camp was filthy—the wadi behind us was the village toilet—and I spent the summer fighting infections, bowel problems, diarrhea, and, eventually, hemorrhoids.

At the end of the season I weighed 128 lb., and it was a relief when Richard Meadow and I were denied the permit to dig Nurabad. The official explanation was that all Antiquities Service personnel would be at Persepolis looking after visiting royalty celebrating the 2,500th anniversary of the founding of the Persian Empire by Cyrus.

While I was in Iran, the bottom had dropped out of the academic job market. I sent out a multitude of job applications, but received no return requests for letters of recommendation. So, to bolster my resumé, I began writing articles based on my Cougar Mountain Cave research and my dissertation. Meanwhile, I applied for the Peace Corps and received an offer to do archaeology in Ghana. I was about to accept when Steve Williams, through his old-boy network, found me a job starting in January 1972 as a Visiting Professor at Louisiana State University (LSU).

I thoroughly enjoyed my year at LSU. I remember calling the roll on my first day and noticing the French names, most of which I could pronounce, and then coming to Hebert, an easy English name. "Is Mr. Hebert here?" After a long pause there came a shout from the back of the room—"A-bare!"—followed by loud laughter from the rest of the class.

The other visiting professor was a geographer from Ghana, about my age. As the most junior faculty, part of our duties was to expose the students to local cultures through a series of field trips. On one trip we arrived in the evening at a rural bar out in a swamp to attend a *fais do do*—a Cajun dance party. We followed the students as they entered the bar, but my African colleague was stopped—"No Blacks allowed!" So all the students had to troop back to the parking lot to eat somewhere else!

One of the brightest students in my Old World archaeology course was a handsome blond-haired guy who asked for additional reading material when we came to the Aryan-invasion hypothesis relating to northern India. I didn't know anything about him, but was impressed! At the end of the semester I was chatting with Dr. Haag, the senior archaeology professor, and he asked me how I'd done with David Duke. I told him that David was the most promising student in the class. Haag laughed and said that David had been the campus Nazi and was now an officer in the Ku Klux Klan! For the rest of my career, I imagined David someday announcing to the world that all he had achieved he owed to Tom Layton, his wonderful archaeology professor.

Midway through that first semester at LSU I was contacted by Don Tuohy at the Nevada State Museum. He told me that a group of local amateurs was planning to pillage Last Supper Cave that summer. He asked me to put together a proposal to dig the cave before the amateurs destroyed it. I knew from my 1968 test pit that the cave's dry deposits contained reed matting, basketry, and many other perishable artifacts. This was an extremely important site, perhaps the last unexcavated dry cave in Nevada. I quickly organized a joint field class for my LSU students and any students from the University of Nevada who might also wish to enroll.

The cave seemed so important that I included in my proposal the purchase of a high-quality 16 mm movie camera and enough color film to document the entire expedition—and a stipend for my girlfriend Grace to be camp director and cook. I brought five students from LSU and recruited two others from the University of Nevada.

There were two surprises when we began excavating. The first was that the numerous perishables were restricted to massive packrat nests all along the cave's perimeter walls. The second was that there was a basal deposit with an ancient stratum containing harvested shellfish and numerous Great Basin stemmed projectile points similar to those I had surface collected from the pluvial Lake Parman beach terraces.

The Nevada State Museum received great press coverage for this work, and following my return to LSU they asked me to become their museum director. I began work in January of 1974. Up to that time the museum (formerly the Carson City Mint) had exhibited collections of things bereft of any connecting ideas. I promised the trustees that I would try to modernize the exhibits. Although I had the support of the trustees, the museum curators were angry that none of them, all almost twice my age, had been selected for my job.

During my first six months I removed the button exhibit, removed the replication of a former senator's office, wrote legislation to bring the Nevada Archaeological Survey Reno and Las Vegas under the umbrella of the museum, established the survey lab in one of the vacated rooms, began restoration of our coin press to issue American Revolution Bicentennial medallions, and brought in convicts from the nearby state prison to scrape off a century of navy-gray paint from the woodwork in the entrance vestibule to reveal a dramatic vista of alternating "candy-cane" slats of pine and redwood.

As director of the museum, part of my duty was to be a steward of Nevada's antiquities and to issue permits for all archaeological investigations. At that time, the Bureau of Land Management wanted to dig out spring deposits on their lands in order to provide more water for cattle. They had hired graduate students of Robert Heizer at UC Berkeley to approve each spring for development if they found no archaeological remains on the surface. Since desert springs were likely to have a long history of use, I insisted that they do subsurface testing to determine if there were any buried deposits. Heizer, who had grown up in Nevada, complained to the governor. His complaints plus those of the museum curators upset the governor, and that upset the trustees.

I completed the second and final season at Last Supper Cave that summer with Jonathan Davis as field director. Davis, a geologist, did excellent work, figuring out the stratigraphy and identifying volcanic ash from the well-dated Mount Mazama eruption both inside and outside the cave.

I was proud of my accomplishments, but, one morning in November, as I ate breakfast, I heard over the morning newscast that I had resigned as director of the museum. Of course I hadn't resigned, so I continued going to work. A few weeks later the trustees voted to fire me and to prevent me from reporting on the Last Supper Cave excavations; there followed a legal battle.

I loaded up my station wagon, returned to California, borrowed my parents' Volkswagen camper, and drove to Mexico City. I had submitted a few job applications and a few months later received an offer to teach fulltime in a nontenure-track position at California State University, Dominguez Hills (located between Los Angeles and Long Beach) starting in the fall of 1975.

My major recreation at Dominguez Hills became the restoration of a 1954 Buick convertible, for which I was able to rent space in a facility operated by a Buick restorer. I haunted the auto wrecking yards around Los Angeles and found a fender to replace the mangled front fender on my car. The restorer advised me as I took apart and cleaned the engine. I then hired one of my students, whose father operated a body shop, to repair the dents and repaint the car to its original condor-yellow color, just like my Uncle Tom's car that I had fallen in love with as a kid back in 1954.

Eventually, after a year of negotiations, the Nevada State Museum allowed me to begin research on the Last Supper Cave collection. I began with a study of the ancient assemblage from the basal cultural level at the site. At the same time, I wrote an article reporting on the surface assemblage that I believed represented Indians hunting domestic cattle. That article, "Indian Rustlers of the High Rock," appeared in *Archaeology* magazine.

In the spring of 1978, I finished my first draft of a monograph describing the basal assemblage at Last Supper Cave and was offered a tenure-track position at San Jose State University. Things were finally looking up for me. Then, in May, my sister Annalisa received a secret message from our younger sister Deborah asking our help to escape from the Peoples Temple in Guyana.

My younger brother Larry had joined Jim Jones's Peoples Temple in 1967. He had then enticed Debby to join, and, together, they brought my mother into the group. It was during my three years at Dominguez Hills that my mother divorced my father, donated her half of the divorce settlement to Peoples Temple, and, in the fall of 1977, emigrated together with Debby to the Peoples Temple commune in Jonestown, Guyana.

Annalisa and I joined forces to help Debby escape. Two days after her return to the states, I put away my Last Supper Cave manuscript and began tape-recording Debby's Jonestown narrative. Then, I loaded up my station wagon, hauled my scant belongings to San Jose, and flew back to drive my Buick up to San Jose. I never returned to my Last Supper Cave manuscript!

Shortly after I arrived in San Jose, I had begun a four-year relationship with Linda King, an archaeologist teaching at a local community college. Linda had mentored Jim Delgado during his high school years, so I met Jim, then a college junior. Jim would later become an important contributor to my *Frolic* shipwreck research.

The fall semester at San Jose State began in mid-August, and I had to scurry to organize my classes, one of which was a Saturday field class in archaeology. While driving my Buick north from Dominguez Hills to San Jose I had heard over the radio that an archaeological site in the East San Jose foothills had been destroyed during the excavation of a swimming pool. I received permission from the owner for my students to screen the pile of tailings from that pool excavation.

Meanwhile, my sister Debby's narrative, together with the stories of other concerned relatives, convinced Congressman Leo Ryan to travel to Jonestown to investigate. The resulting 18 November 1978 murder of Congressman Ryan, the murder-suicide of 900 Jonestown residents, and my brother Larry's arrest and his subsequent trials for conspiracy in Ryan's murder, were to dominate my life for the next 25 years until Larry was paroled from prison in 2002.

THOMAS N. LAYTON

Rather than allow our family tragedy to consume me, I resolved to document what led our family into it and how we were dealing with the consequences. Some years earlier I had begun collecting family letters and documents, and my grandfather, Hugo Philip, had given me the family archive that he had spirited out of Nazi Germany, containing of over a thousand letters and documents recording our German Jewish past.

I was powerfully drawn to Grandpa's archive because, among the documents, I recognized Mom's handwriting, and there lay my best opportunity to discover Mom's life in Germany before her escape to the United States—a story that she had never revealed to me. I then asked several relatives who had survived the Holocaust to undertake a translation project, augmenting each document with an interlinear identification of the people mentioned and an explanation of the life events being described. The first document to be translated was my grandparents' 1914–1928 diary, revealing Mom's life from birth to age 13. That project would continue for over 20 years until most of the documents were translated.

But I was looking for more-complete stories, so, in 1983, I flew to Europe to interview Mom's few surviving relatives. When I returned home, delighted with what I had learned, Dad asked me why I was ignoring his family. Well, Dad's West Virginia ancestors hadn't preserved many documents, but from his earliest childhood Dad had listened to family gossip going back to the 1780s when his ancestors crossed the mountains into western Virginia. With a mind like sticky flypaper, Dad still remembered much of what he had heard back then.

Thereafter, on each of my Sunday visits with Dad I tape recorded an interview—always giving Dad the topic of the next week's interview so that he could organize his thoughts. I then hired one of my students to transcribe the tape, which I would edit for clarity and then return to Dad to correct and expand. The result was over 60 interviews preserving an American story to parallel the German Jewish story. Recording and editing the oral-history narratives of my father and the Holocaust-survivor relatives of my mother would, a decade later, provide me with the skills and inspiration to record the oral narratives of the *Frolic* wreck divers and archaeologists reported in this volume.

Following my move to San Jose State in 1978, I refocused my research from northwestern Nevada to the much more accessible Mendocino coast of California. I decided to test the linguistic hypothesis (based on dialect geography) that the ancestral Pomo had expanded west from the Clear Lake area toward the coast, displacing the ancestral Coast Yuki. During the 1981–1983 field seasons we excavated a series of sites near Albion on the central Mendocino County coast.

Then I turned my attention inland to determine the locations from which the Pomo made their seasonal trips to the coast to gather shellfish and other sea creatures from the offshore rocks. Dan Foster, an archaeologist with the California Department of Forestry, took me on a tour of inland sites that I might excavate. One of these was Three Chop Village, an archaeological site about 15 mi. inland from Fort Bragg with visible house-pit depressions. In 1984 my field class students excavated Chinese potsherds from Three Chop Village. That discovery led me to the *Frolic*, a China-trade vessel that had wrecked near Point Cabrillo in the summer of 1850.

I immediately realized that I might be able to trace the entire settlement system of that band of Pomo by identifying Chinese potsherds at their village sites, but to accomplish this I needed to know all the ceramic styles carried aboard the *Frolic*. So, I searched out all of the wreck divers who had pillaged the *Frolic* wreck site during the 1960s and 1970s, conducted oral histories of most of them, and convinced them to donate their collections to the *Frolic* shipwreck repository that I had established at the Mendocino County Museum.

I reported on Three Chop Village and its connection to the *Frolic* shipwreck in *Western Pomo Prehistory* (Layton 1990). By 1987 I had initiated a broader study of the *Frolic* and in 1989 wrote the first draft of "Drug Runner"—later published as *The Voyage of the* Frolic: *New England Merchants and the Opium Trade* (Layton 1997).

I shared my draft manuscript with colleagues in Mendocino County and, to my joy, the Ukiah Players Theatre group sought my help to write *Voices of the* Frolic, first performed in 1994 (Ukiah Players Theatre, 1998), a play in which, at the suggestion of Jim Delgado, their actors, each impersonating a character associated with the *Frolic*—Captain Faucon, a Mendocino Chinese woman, a woman settler who received a bolt of silk from the Indians, a wreck diver, a Pomo elder, and even the archaeologist—passed the same Chinese potsherd from one to the next as they told their part of the *Frolic* story.

The part of the Pomo elder was written and played by Linda Noel, of Koyongk'awi (Concow) Maidu descent. Linda would later be celebrated as poet laureate

Figure 118. Summer 1984: I conducted a San Jose State University archaeological field class at Three Chop Village in northern Mendocino County, California, where my students excavated Chinese porcelain sherds documenting the Mitom Pomo's 1850 salvage of the *Frolic* shipwreck, 12 mi. to the southwest at Point Cabrillo. (Photo courtesy Thomas Layton)

THOMAS N. LAYTON

Figure 119a. Tom Layton, San Jose State University 1993, displaying *Frolic* artifacts at a planning session for the 1994 exhibits to be staged at the Kelley House Museum, the Grace Hudson Museum, and the Mendocino County Museum. (Photo by Deanna Horvath.)

Figure 119b. James Delgado, director of the Vancouver Maritime Museum, and Richard Everett, curator of exhibits at San Francisco's National Maritime Museum, select *Frolic* artifacts for exhibit at three museums in Mendocino County. (Photo by Mark Rawitsch, 1993)

THOMAS N. LAYTON

Figure 120. Left to right: Wreck divers Larry Pierson, Vic LaFountaine, and Patrick Gibson join Tom Layton at the Grace Hudson Museum in Ukiah, California, for the 1994 gala opening of the three linked *Frolic* exhibits and the premier performance of Voices from the *Frolic* and Beyond: A Mendocino History Play. (Photo by Thomas Layton)

of Mendocino County. Linda's poetic description of the *Frolic* shipwreck, its consequences for the local Native American community, and the insensitivity of the archaeological community struck me to the core and made me painfully aware of my obligations to the Native Americans upon whose archaeological record I had built most of my career. Linda's narrative appears in this volume.

The *Frolic* play premiered with the opening of three linked museum exhibits—at the Grace Hudson Museum in Ukiah, the Kelley House Museum in Mendocino, and the Mendocino County Museum in Willits. To celebrate the exhibit and the opening of the play, the Mendocino Brewing Company issued its first bottling of *Frolic* Shipwreck Ale—inspired by a conversation of Richard Everett (Curator of Exhibits at the National Maritime Museum in

San Francisco) with the brewmaster of the Mendocino Brewing Company. When the Ukiah Players performed the play at the 1995 Society for California Archaeology annual meeting, I was awarded the society's Mark Harrington Award for Conservation Archaeology.

In 1998, Richard Everett and his colleagues at the National Maritime Museum staged a major exhibit, *Found! The Wreck of the* Frolic—*A Gold Rush Cargo for San Francisco.*

The *Frolic* Shipwreck Project moved me from prehistoric archaeology to what, for me, turned out to be a much more satisfying focus on the archaeology of the historic period. The *Frolic* shipwreck research resulted in a trio of books: *The Voyage of the* Frolic: *New England Merchants and the Opium Trade* (Layton 1997), *Gifts from the Celestial Kingdom: A Shipwrecked*

Cargo for Gold Rush California (Layton 2002), and *The "Other" Dixwells: Commerce and Conscience in an American Family* (Layton 2021).

In 2003–4, the *Frolic* wreck site was finally subjected to a systematic archaeological study. Dr. Sheli O. Smith of Napa Community College organized two summer field classes to document and map what remained of the *Frolic* on the seafloor, to investigate wreck-diver collections, and to prepare a digital catalog of all the *Frolic* collections. To accomplish this, Sheli partnered with Rob Edwards at Cabrillo College, Charles Beeker at Indiana University, and Annalies Corbin at East Carolina University, along with students from all four institutions. Indiana University took on the conservation of the recovered pieces, Annalies Corbin of PAST Foundation and Sheli produced a database of artifacts, and Sheli's Napa College students created the database of repairs on the *Frolic* during her lifetime from Heard Company documents supplied by me. In 2005 Sheli published Frolic *Archaeological Survey*, including the first detailed map of the *Frolic* wreck site (S. Smith 2005). In 2009, Charles Beeker and colleagues published "The 1850 Frolic Cannon: A Technical Conservation Report" (Beeker et al. 2009).

It took me nine years (2002–2011) to write *The Other Dixwells*. The initial focus was on George Dixwell, for whom the *Frolic* was built. Then the focus shifted to George's female relatives, his Chinese wife, and their Eurasian son. To give life to the story, I pressed the envelope of archaeological writing, employing the techniques of novelists: character development and dialogue. The resulting volume told the archaeological story as well as a slightly fictionalized version of the story in which I filled the cracks between the facts. The result was a book without a genre, and the manuscript sat on my desk until 2020, when Rebecca Allen and Annalies Corbin convinced the Society for Historical Archaeology to publish it.

Meanwhile, throughout my career at San Jose State, I worked hard trying to defend my brother Larry, first by attending his trial in Guyana and coauthoring *In My Father's House: The Story of the Layton Family and the Reverend Jim Jones* (1981)—my attempt to provide a sympathetic back story for Larry and to soften public prejudice against him during his forthcoming prosecution in the United States. Then, came years of negotiating with defense attorneys and, eventually, helping Debby negotiate with more attorneys preparing petitions for Larry's parole—all the while providing emotional support for Dad.

Throughout this, I was a faculty member at San Jose State, and one of my duties was university service, for which I was asked to serve on the board of the Sourisseau Academy for State and Local History. There I became friends with Edith Smith, the curator, who, against the wishes of the board, wanted to build a collection of historical documents. Before Edith died in 1999, she created a trust with me as the primary trustee, and to honor her wish I began to purchase historical photos for what has become a major archive of South Bay images. When Edith's money ran out in 2011, I created Les Amis de Sourisseau, a support group whose annual donations enabled me to continue purchasing important images from eBay as well as large accumulations from dealers and private collectors. In 2013, when that collection approached 60,000 images, the Sourisseau Board honored Edith and me

THOMAS N. LAYTON

by christening it as the "Smith-Layton Archive."

The culmination of my teaching career came as a result of three events. I had taken scuba-diving lessons, and in 1997 I was finally able to dive the *Frolic* shipwreck. On my first dive I slowly swam the entire length of the vessel. For my second dive they gave me fresh tanks, and I began to mark artifacts that we should collect. Somehow, they had mistakenly given me two almost-empty tanks, and I wasn't experienced enough to notice the low pressure on my gauge. I ran out of air. I didn't have the brainpower to detach my weight belt, and I passed out. Fortunately, my mouthpiece remained in place and I didn't inhale my lungs full of water. My dive partner found me on the bottom and dragged me to shore, where some other divers hooked me to an oxygen tank. I woke up on the beach with no memory beyond my initial discomfort from not having enough air. A search-and-rescue team strapped me to a stretcher and hauled me up the cliff. As I stared at the headliner of the ambulance, I searched my memory for details to see if I had experienced brain damage. I immediately realized that my survival was a gift, that my career had almost ended, and the rest of my life was simply icing on the cake! At that moment I decided to retire as soon as I reached my eligibility for Social Security.

The second determining event was San Jose State University honoring me with its top research award by designating me as the 2002–2003 President's Scholar. The third determining event was the Society for Historical Archaeology presenting me the first James Deetz writing award for *Gifts from the Celestial Kingdom*. I was then a little over 62, and I decided to retire from the university on a high note!

My retirement present, to me, was a 1940 Martin D-18 guitar!

Retirement and early mornings at my favorite coffee shop provided me with the time and place to write *The "Other" Dixwells: Commerce and Conscience in an American Family*, my third volume inspired by the *Frolic* shipwreck. Retirement also provided me the leisure to organize the gigantic backlog of my own family's translations and transcriptions that I had accumulated. To accomplish this I created *In Our Own Words*—a self-published family-history series now totaling over 22 volumes, each devoted to a different topic or period of time.

As I began assembling these family volumes, I became painfully aware of the declining number of documents written by family members over the past 30 years. During that period, both the telephone and an increasing reliance on electronic mail had replaced our family's long, newsy letters, and our centuries-long written record seemed to be coming to an end. So, in 2006, I introduced a new tradition of "Annual Reports" written by each of my siblings and their offspring. These thoughtful and nuanced annual essays have sustained our literary tradition up to the present, and they seem likely to continue well into the future.

Retirement led me to transfer several of my archaeological projects to younger scholars. Dr. Geoffrey Smith at the University of Nevada, Reno and his graduate students are now employing new analytic techniques to the artifacts that I excavated in 1973 at Last Supper Cave in northwestern Nevada. I had filmed those 1973 excavations, and in 2018—45 years later—my filmmaker colleague Tom Wohlmut and I were able to film the new generation of researchers and join the past to the present by introducing them to four of my students from 1973 in a movie titled *Last Supper Cave: Then and Now*.

There remained for me only a few more pressing professional obligations. The most important of these was to find a permanent home for the Layton Family Archive. Then, in 2017, my nephew David Layton Valentine, a professor at the University of California, Santa Barbara described the collection to the head of archives at the University Library—and she asked for the collection! Thus during the past several years I've been transferring the documents into acid-free folders and boxes and writing finding aids.

As I began the process of organizing and packaging the collection, I realized that I could create a more-lasting human connection between future researchers and the Layton family with a movie narrated by me and my siblings—a movie telling the story of our German Jewish and southern Appalachian origins; the convergence of those two disparate traditions with the 1941 marriage of my parents, Laurence and Lisa Philip Layton; and the family's subsequent survival through World War II, the Holocaust, and the Peoples Temple tragedy, to become fully engaged citizens of the 21st century. That movie, filmed by my colleague Tom Wohmut, will accompany our archive to Santa Barbara.

This brings me to 2022 and the fulfillment of my obligation to the wreck divers and archaeologists and several others whose labors over the past four decades contributed to the success of the *Frolic* Shipwreck Project. My portion of this volume—"Touching the *Frolic*"—presents each of their personal narratives leading to the *Frolic*—and, as a byproduct, a personalized history of underwater archaeology in California. I thank them for making this possible.

Epilogue

10 September 2023
16 May 2024

There are many things that become clear only in retrospect. In the summer of 1984, when we excavated those first few blue-on-white porcelain sherds from Three Chop Village, I could not have imagined that they would drag me from the silent world of prehistoric archaeology into the very noisy world of the historical period. Four decades later, I recognize that "touching" those *Frolic* potsherds abruptly changed the direction of my professional career.

As a prehistoric archaeologist I had focused on technology, foodways, and social change over thousands of years. Historical archaeology, however, demanded that excavated artifacts and features be interpreted in the context of well-dated historical events. For me, this was a kind of liberation in which I might expand and actually correct the historical record.

In 1992, eight years after I first "touched" the *Frolic*, I began excavation of an historically known Coast Yuki village site located on a ridge above DeHaven, a long-vanished late 19th-century lumber-mill company town. By then I had developed some interviewing skills after having recorded the oral histories of the members of my mother's Jewish family

THOMAS N. LAYTON

who survived the Holocaust. Thus, when we began recovering European American artifacts, I began searching for someone who might remember at least the final years of DeHaven. I found that person in Mark Walker, a well-known raconteur who had just turned 100 years old. Meanwhile, I tried unsuccessfully to find a Native American narrator who could tell the story of the local Indian community.

I began interviewing Mark Walker in 1992, the same year I began interviewing the wreck divers whose narratives appear in this volume. I had taken care to balance the perspectives of the wreck divers with the perspectives of archaeologists. I interviewed Mark for seven years, until his death at age 107. Mark remembered members of the Indian community, many of them by name, but his descriptions were from the point of view of the white community that had exploited the Indians for cheap labor. I am still deeply troubled that I have been unable to provide a first-person Native American narrative as a balance to Mark's narrative.

As I taped the wreck divers about the *Frolic* and Mark Walker about DeHaven, I was also recording my father's narrative of his southern West Virginia origins. I was able to partially balance Dad's perspective with the perspective of an aged African American woman who had been raised just up the "holler" from where Dad grew up.

In 2024, I am still transcribing and editing Dad's narrative—over 60 hours of tape—and have completed a movie distilled from the 42 archival boxes of family letters, diaries, and photos saved by my ancestors. The movie—*In Our Own Words: An American History*—presents three strands of the American experience: the story of German Jewish Europeans; the story of southern Appalachian Americans; and the story of their postwar melding, including two of my own siblings' participation in the Peoples Temple-Jonestown-Guyana tragedy.

As I prepare the last of those 42 boxes for transport to their forever home among the special collections of the University of California, Santa Barbara Library, I am thinking about the talismans that I've accumulated documenting my own life—the Swee-Touch-Nee tea box that held my earliest childhood treasures, the coffee can containing the sharks' teeth I collected from the beach at Scientist Cliffs on the Chesapeake Bay, my collection of Lincoln pennies, my collection of orphaned banjo necks inlaid with mother-of-pearl, and my 1930 Model A Ford roadster that I've just given to my long-time colleague, David Hurst Thomas and his son.

These talismans have attached me to my past, just as the brass porthole covers proudly exhibited on the living-room walls of the *Frolic*'s wreck divers validated their own lives. I now more fully recognize the personal sacrifice of the wreck divers who donated their collections to the *Frolic* Shipwreck Repository at the Mendocino County Museum, and I hope that, as they enter their 80s, they will relinquish the last of those emotionally charged treasures as well.

Looking back on the *Frolic* Shipwreck Project, I can see that I benefited by being a land-based prehistoric archaeologist with little knowledge of the maritime world and ignorant of the politics regarding pillaged collections, and thus feeling no hesitancy in engaging with the wreck divers.

And, strangely, I also benefited because the *Frolic* had lodged near shore, was broken up by the surf, and was pillaged repeatedly over the past 150 years. Had the *Frolic* sunk in deeper water and escaped pillage, she might have been studied by nautical archaeologists with their own priorities. They would have seen the *Frolic* as a Baltimore clipper and focused on her architecture and her final cargo. But, as busy professionals with many other wreck sites demanding their attention, it is unlikely that any of them could spend 40 years researching the people that framed the *Frolic*'s life. Blessedly, with tenure at a teaching university, I had the freedom to follow my own research passions, and I am deeply thankful that this serendipity of circumstances enabled me to undertake a project that changed my life.

THOMAS N. LAYTON

PART III

~

Visual Timeline, Detailed Timeline,
Bibliography, and Acknowledgments

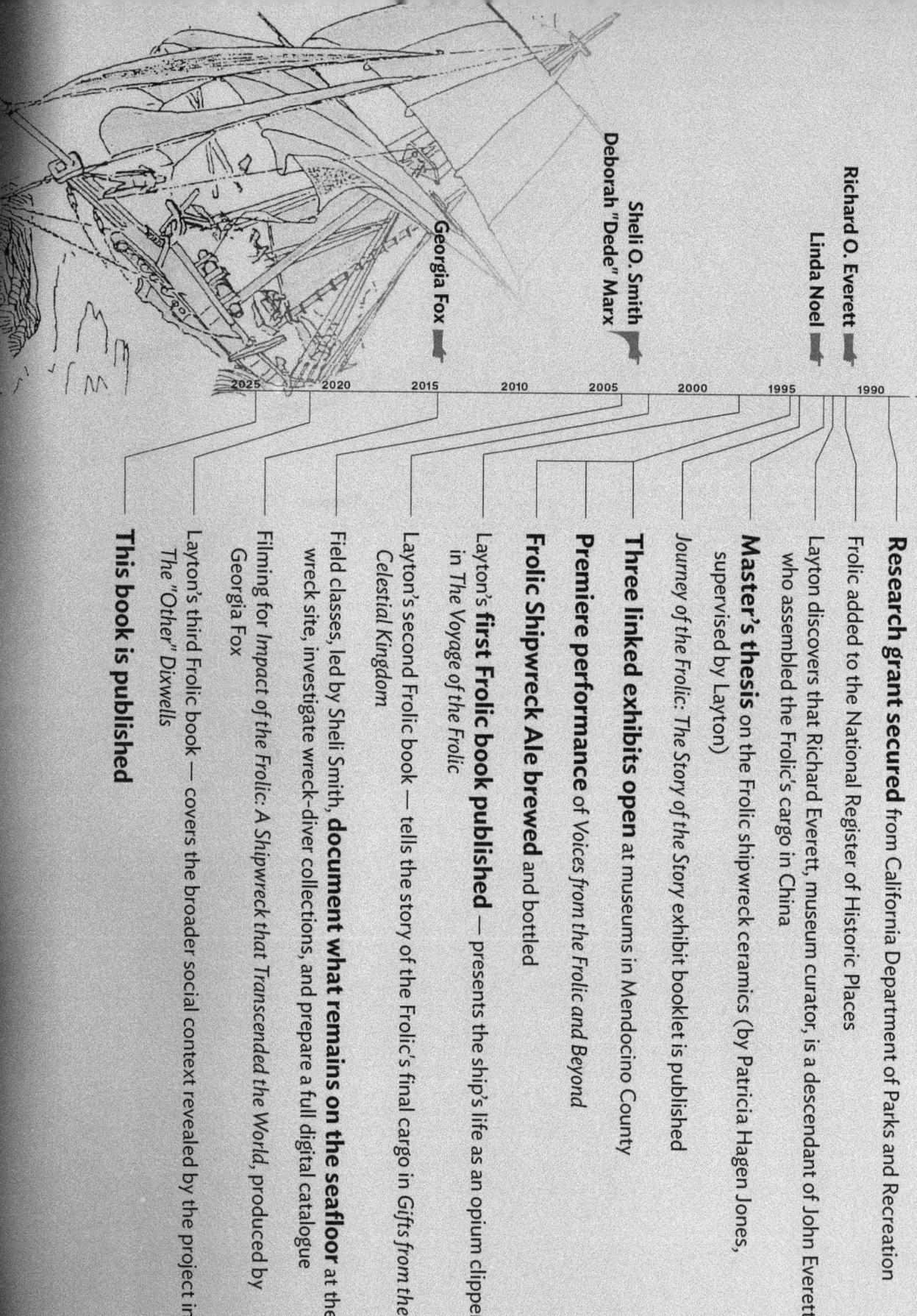

Richard O. Everett
Linda Noel
Sheli O. Smith
Deborah "Dede" Marx
Georgia Fox

2025 2020 2015 2010 2005 2000 1995 1990

Research grant secured from California Department of Parks and Recreation

Frolic added to the National Register of Historic Places

Layton discovers that Richard Everett, museum curator, is a descendant of John Everett, who assembled the Frolic's cargo in China

Journey of the Frolic: The Story of the Frolic exhibit booklet is published

Master's thesis on the Frolic shipwreck ceramics (by Patricia Hagen Jones, supervised by Layton)

Three linked exhibits open at museums in Mendocino County

Premiere performance of *Voices from the Frolic and Beyond*

Frolic Shipwreck Ale brewed and bottled

Layton's **first Frolic book published** — presents the ship's life as an opium clipper in *The Voyage of the Frolic*

Layton's second Frolic book — tells the story of the Frolic's final cargo in *Gifts from the Celestial Kingdom*

Field classes, led by Sheli Smith, **document what remains on the seafloor** at the wreck site, investigate wreck-diver collections, and prepare a full digital catalogue

Filming for *Impact of the Frolic: A Shipwreck that Transcended the World*, produced by Georgia Fox

Layton's third Frolic book — covers the broader social context revealed by the project in *The "Other" Dixwells*

This book is published

THE FROLIC
VISUAL TIMELINE

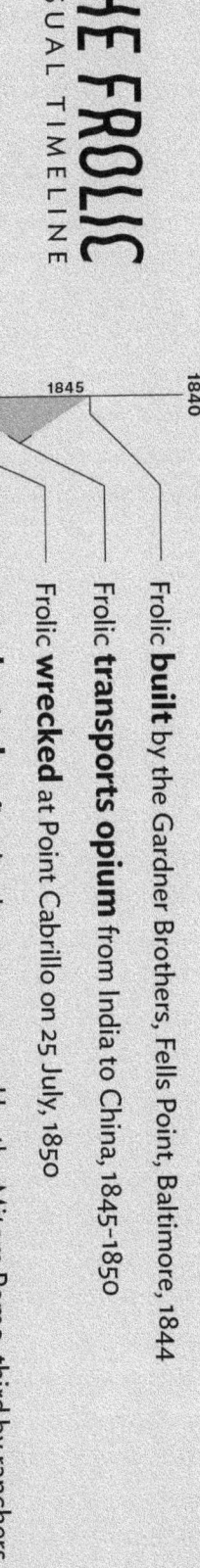

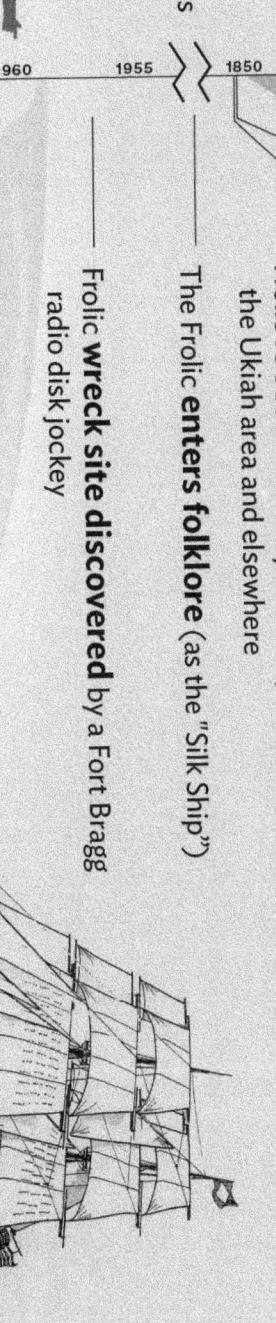

~100 years

1840   1845   1850   1955   1960   1965   1970   1975   1980   1985

Names on timeline:

Louis Dow "Louie" Fratis

James W. Kennon
Vilho "Bill" Kosonen

Larry J. Pierson

Clifton Bert "Cliff" Craft

David Buller

Thomas N. Layton
John W. Foster
James P. Delgado

Events:

Frolic **built** by the Gardner Brothers, Fells Point, Baltimore, 1844

Frolic **transports opium** from India to China, 1845–1850

Frolic **wrecked** at Point Cabrillo on 25 July, 1850

Frolic **looted** — first by the crew, second by the Mitom Pomo, third by ranchers from the Ukiah area and elsewhere

The Frolic **enters folklore** (as the "Silk Ship")

Frolic **wreck site discovered** by a Fort Bragg radio disk jockey

Modern **pillage begins** — Robert Nash hires divers (Larry Pierson and Patrick Gibson) to investigate wreck site and determine whether it is a Chinese junk

Cliff Craft **sets explosives** to break loose the congealed ballast pile

Thomas Layton excavates Three Chop Village and discovers blue-on-white "Chinese" potsherds from the Frolic shipwreck

Modern **research begins** — Layton meets John Foster and Jim Delgado at Frolic Cove

Frolic Detailed Timeline

1844	*Frolic* built by the Gardner Brothers, Fells Point, Baltimore.
1844–1850	*Frolic* transports opium from India to China.
1850 July 25	*Frolic* wrecked at Point Cabrillo.
1850	*Frolic* looted, first by her crew, second by the Mitom Pomo, third by ranchers from the Ukiah area and elsewhere.
1851 August 23	George Gibbs visits the ranch of George Armstrong Parker, near present-day Ukiah and reports seeing "huge china jars, camphor trunks, and lacquered ware in abundance."
1851 spring	Jerome B. Ford is sent up the coast by Harry Meiggs to salvage the *Frolic*'s cargo. He finds Indian women wearing silk shawls from the wreck, but nothing left to salvage. Ford reports the gigantic redwoods to Meiggs, and a lumber mill is established in 1852.
1852–1955	The identity and location of the *Frolic* is forgotten. It is remembered in local lore as the "Silk Ship."
Late 1950s	Don Pifer, a Fort Bragg radio disk jockey discovers the *Frolic* wreck site.
1960	Louie Fratis discovers the *Frolic* wreck site.
1965 June 30	Jim Kennon discovers the *Frolic* wreck site.
1965 fall	Jim Kennon meets with Mendel Peterson at the Smithsonian.
1966	Louie Fratis recovers one of the two *Frolic* cannons. This cannon is displayed for many years in the yard of the Kelley House Museum and is subsequently conserved by Charles Beeker at Indiana University. The cannon is now on display at the Point Cabrillo Lighthouse.
1966 March	Mendel Peterson visits Frolic Cove with Kennon and Kosonen.

1975	Robert Nash hires divers Larry Pierson and Patrick Gibson to travel with him from Los Angeles to investigate the wreck site and determine whether it is a Chinese junk.
1977 December	Larry Pierson and Patrick Gibson excavate and collect from the *Frolic*.
1978 August	Larry Pierson and Patrick Gibson excavate and collect from the *Frolic*.
1979 September	Larry Pierson and Patrick Gibson, Cliff Craft, and two others excavate and collect from the *Frolic*. Cliff Craft sets explosives to break loose the congealed ballast pile.
Before 1981	Richard Tooker discovers the *Daily Alta* article reporting the wreck of the *Frolic*. Several years later he passes the information to David Buller.
1981 March	Dave Buller begins to work with Jim Delgado on the SS *Tennessee* site.
1981 September	David and Steven Buller discover the *Frolic* wreck site. They make six trips to excavate and collect.
1984	Layton excavates Three Chop Village and discovers blue-on-white "Chinese" potsherds from the *Frolic* shipwreck.
1984	David Buller passes Richard Tooker's identification of the *Frolic* to Tom Layton.
Ca. 1985	Three Lanham brothers dive the *Frolic* wreck site. Bruce and Robert collect from the wreck, while younger brother Richard rigs and floats the *Frolic*'s second cannon. The next day Richard submerges the cannon in a creek on a private ranch near Mt. Diablo, where it remains, desalinizing, for about five years. In ca. 1990, Richard donates the cannon to the Mendocino County Museum.
1986 May	John Foster and Jim Delgado meet Tom Layton at Frolic Cove. They each make a short dive to view the wreck. Despite getting badly battered by the surf, they conclude that the site should be investigated.
1989	John Foster secures a California Department of Parks and Recreation grant to help support Layton's *Frolic* research trip to East Coast archives and also to fund an evaluation of the wreck site by David Buller. David attempts several dives over several months, but the water is too rough to do a systematic survey.
1989–1990	Layton researches the *Frolic* in Baltimore, Boston, Harvard,

	and Salem archives and writes the first draft of "Drug Runner."
1989 October 28	Jim Kennon interview No. 1.
1990	Jim Delgado and Tom Layton jointly write the National Register of Historic Places inventory and nomination form for *Frolic*.
1990	Thomas Layton presents the archaeological discovery of Chinese potsherds at a Native American archaeological site in Mendocino County, California, in *Western Pomo Prehistory* (Layton 1990), leading to the *Frolic* Shipwreck Project.
1991 May 16	*Frolic* is listed on the National Register of Historic Places.
1992 January 12	Cliff Craft interview.
1992 January 13	Larry Pierson interview.
1992	Layton discovers that Richard Everett, curator of exhibits at the National Maritime Museum in San Francisco, is a descendant of John Everett, who assembled the *Frolic*'s cargo in China.
1992	Patricia Hagen Jones (supervised by Thomas Layton) completes her master's thesis at San Jose State Univeristy: "A Comparative Study of Mid-Nineteenth Century Chinese Blue-and-White Export Ceramics from the *Frolic* Shipwreck, Mendocino County, California," later published in 1994 (Hagen Jones 1992, 1994).
1993 August 19–20	The *Frolic* Project team meets at Willits to discuss exhibit content, interpretation, design, and identification of specific voices of real people to tell the *Frolic* story. Jim Delgado suggests that each character hold the same piece of *Frolic* pottery to kick off his/her story.
1993 October	Layton hosts an exhibit-planning session with *Frolic* artifacts at San Jose State University.
1993	Richard Everett describes the *Frolic*'s cargo of Edinburg ale to the brewmaster of the Mendocino Brewing Company in Hopland. The result would be *Frolic* Shipwreck Ale.
1993 fall	The California Council for the Humanities grants the *Frolic* project $24,957 to support *Voices from the* Frolic *and Beyond*.
1994	Mark Howland Rawitsch publishes *Journey of the* Frolic: *The Story of the Story* (Rawitsch 1994). This booklet presents the back story of the three linked museum exhibits and of *Voices of the* Frolic: *A Mendocino History Play*.

1994 January	Actors audition for *Voices from the* Frolic *and Beyond*.
1994 January 21	David Buller interview.
1994 March 25	John W. Foster interview.
1994 April 9	James Delgado interview.
1994 July 9, August 5	Louie Fratis interviews.
1994 August 4	Jim Kennon interview No. 2.
1994 August 4	Bill Kosonen interview.
1994 September 26–27	David Buller's first mapping attempt.
1994 July	Three linked exhibits—each with an opening reception: Shipwreck! Impact of the *Frolic*, Kelley House Museum; From Canton to California, Mendocino County Museum; and The Wake of Change, Grace Hudson Museum.
1994 July	Premiere performance of *Voices from the* Frolic *and Beyond*.
1994 July 26	*Frolic* Shipwreck Ale brewed and bottled.
1995	*Frolic* Shipwreck Ale brewed and bottled.
1997	Thomas Layton presents the *Frolic*'s life as an opium clipper in *The Voyage of the* Frolic*: New England Merchants and the Opium Trade* (Layton 1997).
1997	Tom Layton dives the *Frolic*, nearly drowns, and is taken by search and rescue to a hospital in Fort Bragg for examination.
1998	Mark Howland Rawitsch and Kate Magruder present the script for *Voices from the* Frolic *and Beyond: A Mendocino History Play* (Rawitsch and Magruder 1998).
1998–1999	The San Francisco Maritime Museum presents Found! The Wreck of the *Frolic*—A Gold Rush Cargo for San Francisco (7 February 1998–31 January 1999). The exhibit was designed by curator of exhibits Richard Everett and his associates.
2002	Thomas Layton tells the story of the *Frolic*'s final cargo in *Gifts from the Celestial Kingdom: A Shipwrecked Cargo for Gold Rush California* (Layton 2002).
2003–2004	Sheli O. Smith of Napa Community College organizes two summer field classes to document what remains on the seafloor at the *Frolic* wreck site, to investigate wreck-diver collections, and to prepare a digital catalogue of all the *Frolic* collections. To accomplish this, Smith partners with Rob Edwards at Cabrillo College, Charles Beeker at Indiana University, and Annalies Corbin at East Carolina University, and with students from all four institutions. Indiana University

FROLIC DETAILED TIMELINE

takes on the conservation of the recovered pieces, the PAST Foundation produces the database of artifacts, and Napa College students create the database of repairs on the *Frolic* during her lifetime from Heard Company invoices supplied by Thomas Layton. Sheli Smith publishes Frolic *Archaeological Survey* in 2005 (S. Smith 2005b).

2013–2014   The Valene L. Smith Museum of Anthropology at Chico State University stages an exhibit: Into the Blue: Maritime Navigation and the Archaeology of Shipwrecks (December 2013– July 2014) featuring the *Frolic* shipwreck, curated by Georgia Fox.

2014   The Advanced Laboratory for Visual Anthropology at Chico State University films *Impact of the* Frolic: *A Shipwreck that Transcended the World*, 28 min., Matthew Ritenour, director, Georgia Fox, producer (Fox 2014).

2019   Sheli O. Smith conducts a reconnaissance dive at Frolic Cove for California State Parks and Recreation to ascertain whether the site can be used for park safety dive training.

2021   Thomas Layton presents the broader social context revealed by the *Frolic* Shipwreck Project in *The "Other" Dixwells: Commerce and Conscience in an American Family* (Layton 2021).

Bibliography

Aker, Raymond

    1965   *The Cermeño Expedition at Drakes Bay, 1595.* Drakes Navigators Guild, Palo Alto, CA.

Aker, Raymond, V. Aubrey Neasham, and Robert H. Power

    1974   The Francis Drake Controversy: His California Anchorage, June 17–July 23, 1579; the Debate: Point Reyes Peninsula/Drakes Estero; Bolinas Bay/ Bolinas Lagoon; San Francisco Bay/San Quentin Cove. *California Historical Quarterly* 53(3):203–292.

Allan, James M.

    1996   Fort Ross Cove: Historical and Archaeological Research to Identify the Remains of California's First Shipyard. Master's thesis, Maritime Studies Program, East Carolina University, Greenville, NC.

    1998   "Sheep in the Tunnel:" A Gold Rush Era Ship beneath Your Feet. *Society for California Archaeology Proceedings* 11:118–130.

    2007   "... So Many Ghastly Piles of Marine Debris": Discovery of the Whaling Ship *Candace* in Downtown San Francisco. *Society for California Archaeology Proceedings* 20:9–14.

Archeo-Tec

    1987   Hills Plaza: Archaeological Data Recovery Program. Manuscript, Archeo-Tec, Oakland, CA.

Ball David, Rosie Clayburn, Roberta Cordero, Briece Edwards, Valerie Grussing, Janine Ledford, Robert McConnell, Rebekah Monette, Robert Steelquist, Eirek Thorsgard, and Jon Townsend

    2017   Characterizing Tribal Cultural Landscapes. Volume I: Project Framework. Manuscript, U.S. Department of the Interior, Bureau of Ocean Energy Management, Pacific OCS Region, Camarillo, CA.

Barr, Bradley

2013   Understanding and Managing Marine Protected Areas through Integrating Ecosystem Based Management within Maritime Cultural Landscapes: Moving from Theory to Practice. *Ocean and Coastal Management* 84:184–192.

Bass, George F.

1966   *Archaeology under Water.* Frederick A. Praeger, New York, NY.

1976   *Archaeology beneath the Sea: A Personal Account.* Harper Colophon, New York, NY.

Becker-Collona, Andreina

1968   *Ancient Egyptian Literature.* University of California Extension, Berkeley.

Beeker, Charles D.

2000   Comparison, Analysis, and Recommendations for Steam Ship Pomona Establishment as an Underwater Historic Park. *Society for California Archaeology Proceedings* 13:44–48.

2005   *S.S. Pomona Shipwreck Project, Fort Ross State Historic Park, California.* California State Parks, Sacramento.

2006   An Underwater Historic Landscape at Emerald Bay State Park. *Society for California Archaeology Proceedings* 19:49–51.

2005   *S.S. Pomona,* Shipwreck, 20 December [Listed 31 January 2008]. National Register of Historic Places Registration Form, National Park Service, United States Department of the Interior, Washington, DC. NPGallery, National Park Service <https://npgallery.nps.gov/GetAsset/ccfbdd80-825d-46b4-97e3-3ef5e9942656>. Accessed 6 August 2023.

Beeker, Charles, and John Foster

2007   *Site Plan, S.S. Pomona Shipwreck Project, Fort Ross State Historic Park, California.* Indiana University Underwater Science Program, Bloomington.

Beeker, Charles, and Sheli Smith

2005   Crystal Cove F-4U Corsair Airplane Wreck, Scuba Maintenance and Survey Dive, Summer 2005, Close of Field Work Interim Report. Manuscript, Indiana University Underwater Science Program, Bloomington.

Beeker, Charles D., Frederick Hanselmann, Jessica Keller and Colleen McCloughlan

2009   The 1850 *Frolic* Cannon: A Technical Conservation Report. Manuscript, California Department of Parks and Recreation, Cultural Resources Division, Sacramento.

Berrocal, Maria Cruz, and Chen-hwa Tsang

2017a   *Historical Archaeology of Early Modern Colonialism in Asia Pacific: The Asia-Pacific Region.* University Press of Florida, Gainesville.

2017b   *Historical Archaeology of Early Modern Colonialism in Asia Pacific: The Southwest Pacific and Oceanian Regions.* University Press of Florida, Gainesville.

Borhegyi, Stephen D.

1968   Aqualung Archaeology. *Natural History* 67(3):120–125.

Bowers, Q. David

1999   *The Treasure Ship S.S. Brother Jonathan: Her Life and Loss, 1850–1865.* Bowers and Merena Galleries, Inc., Wolfeboro, NH.

Bullen, Isabel

1979   A Glimpse into the *Niantic's* Hold. *California History* 58(4):325–333.

Buller, David and Delgado, James P.,

1983   Losses of Major Vessels Within the Drakes Bay Survey Area. pp. 35-81. In Submerged Cultural Resources Inventory, Shipwreck Survey, Point Reyes National Seashore and Point Reyes--Farallon Islands National Marine Sanctuary, Larry Murphy, editor, National Park Service, Santa Fe, NM.

Buttolph, Phillip, and John D. DeMartini

2003   Intertidal and Subtidal Resource Survey in Point Cabrillo Reserve (July 9, 2003 to July 15, 2003). Report to California Department of Parks and Recreation, Sacramento, from Humboldt State University, Arcata, CA.

Byram, R. Scott

2013   *Triangulating Archaeological Landscapes: The U.S. Coast Survey in California, 1850–1895.* University of California, Contributions of the Archaeological Research Facility, Volume 65. Berkeley.

Cardone, Bonnie J., and Patrick Smith

1989   *Shipwrecks of Southern California.* Menasha Ridge Press, Birmingham, AL.

Carpenter, Scott L., and Laura A. Kim

1988   Underwater but not All Wet: The 1985 Lake Eleanor Archaeological Survey. *Society for California Archaeology Proceedings* 1:189–215.

Carrell, Toni (editor)

1984   *Submerged Cultural Resources Inventory: Portions of Point Reyes National Seashore and Point Reyes-Farallon Islands National Marine Sanctuary.*

National Park Service, Submerged Resources Center Professional Report
No. 3. Santa Fe, NM.

Chace, Paul G.

1983   Chinese Stone Anchor Research Design Validation. Paper presented at
the 16th Annual Conference on Historical and Underwater Archaeology,
Denver, CO.

Conrad, Cyler, and Allen G. Pastron

2014   Galapagos Tortoises and Sea Turtles in Gold Rush–Era California. *California History* 91(2):20–39.

Conrad, Cyler, Kenneth W. Gobalet, Kale Bruner, and Allen G. Pastron

2015   Hide, Tallow and Terrapin: Gold Rush-Era Zooarchaeology at Thompson's Cove (CA-SFR-186H), San Francisco, California. *International Journal of Historical Archaeology* 19(3):502–551.

Cooper, Diane

1995   From Small Ways to Big Business: The Growth of the Wooden Ship
Construction and Waterborne Industries Along the United States' Pacific
Coast, 1875-1900. Master's Thesis, Department of History, East Carolina
University, Greenville, NC.

Dana, Richard Henry

2004   *The Oxford Encyclopedia of American Literature*. Volume 1:347-349,
Oxford University Press. New York, NY.

Dames & Moore

1989   Archaeological Investigations at an 1851 Commercial Site along Howison's Pier, San Francisco, 343 Sansome Street. Manuscript, City and
County of San Francisco, Department of Planning, San Francisco, CA.

Del Cioppo, Nicholas J.

1988   Protecting California's Submerged History: Senate Bill 2199. In *Underwater Archaeology Proceedings from the Society for Historical Archaeology Conference, Reno, Nevada 1988*, James P. Delgado, editor, pp. 44–45. Society
for Historical Archaeology, Ann Arbor, MI.

Delgado, James P.

1979   No Longer a Buoyant Ship: Unearthing the Gold Rush Storeship *Niantic*.
California History 63(4):316–325.

1981   What Becomes of the Old Ships? Dismantling the Gold Rush Fleet of San
Francisco. *Pacific Historian* 25(4):1–9.

1983a   Underwater Archaeological Investigations of Gold Rush Era Steamships on the California Coast. In *Proceedings of the First Biennial Conference on Scientific Research in California's National Parks*, Charles Van Riper, L.D. Whitig and M.L. Murphy, editors. University of California Co-Operative Parks Studies Unit/National Park Service, Davis.

1983b   Water Soaked and Covered with Barnacles: The Wreck of S.S. *Winfield Scott*. *Pacific Historian* 27(2):5–21.

1984   Shipwreck Archaeology in California: New Discoveries, New Directions. In *Proceedings of the Joint Workshop New Frontiers*. California State Park Rangers Association, Park Rangers Association of California, and the Western Interpreters' Association, Santa Cruz.

1985a   Great Leviathan of the Pacific: The Saga of the Gold Rush Steamship *Tennessee*. Master's thesis, Maritime Studies Program, East Carolina University, Greenville, NC.

1985b   In the Midst of a Great Excitement: The Argosy of the Revenue Cutter *C. W. Lawrence*. *American Neptune* 45(2):119–131.

1985c   Skeleton in the Sand: Documentation of the Environmentally Exposed 1856 Ship *King Philip*. In *Proceedings of the Sixteenth Annual Conference on Historical Archaeology*, Paul F. Johnston, editor, pp. 30–36, Society for Historical Archaeology, Ann Arbor, MI.

1986a   Documentation and Identification of the Two-Masted Schooner *Neptune*. *Historical Archaeology* 20(1):95–108.

1986b   *The Log of the Apollo: Joseph Perkins Beach's Log of the Voyage of the Ship Apollo from New York to San Francisco, 1849*. Book Club of California, San Francisco.

1986c   The Maritime Connotations of the California Gold Rush: National Register of Historic Places Thematic Group Study. Manuscript, National Park Service, Washington, DC.

1986d   Underwater Archaeological Investigations of Gold Rush Era Steamships on the California Coast. In *Underwater Archaeology: The Proceedings of the Fourteenth Conference on Underwater Archaeology, 1983*, Calvin R. Cummins, editor, pp. 58–59. Fathom Eight, San Marino, CA.

1990a   Ships Were Constantly Arriving: The Hoff Store Site and the Business of Maritime Supply and Demand in Gold Rush San Francisco. In *The Hoff Store Site and Gold Rush Merchandise from San Francisco, California*, Allen G. Pastron and Eugene M. Hattori. editors, pp. 25–34. Society for Historical Archaeology, Ann Arbor, MI.

1990b   *To California by Sea: A Maritime History of the Gold Rush*. University of South Carolina Press, Columbia.

1991   The National Maritime Initiative: An Interdisciplinary Approach to Maritime Preservation. *Public Historian* 13(3):75–84.

1994 The Wreck of the S.S. *Tennessee. Journal of the West* 32(4):14–21.

1995 Ships as Buildings in Gold Rush San Francisco. *Mariners Museum Journal*, 2nd ser., 1:4–15.

2002a Maritime and Underwater Archaeology on the Pacific Coast. In *International Handbook of Underwater Archaeology*, Carol V. Ruppe and Jan Barstad, editors, pp. 221–246. Springer, New York, NY.

2002b The Gold-Rush Storeship *Niantic. Maritime Life and Traditions* 13:34–51.

2009 *Gold Rush Port: The Maritime Archaeology of the San Francisco Waterfront.* University of California Press, Berkeley.

2011 Ships on Land. In *The Oxford Handbook of Maritime Archaeology*, Alexis Catsambis, Ben Ford, and Donny L. Hamilton, editors, pp. 182–201. Oxford University Press, Oxford, UK.

2012 *Misadventures of a Civil War Submarine: Iron, Guns and Pearls.* Texas A&M University Press, College Station.

2013 The "Redwood Coast": The Maritime Cultural Landscape of the Northern California Coast from Bodega Bay to Mendocino." Manuscript, National Oceanic and Atmospheric Administration, Office of National Marine Sanctuaries Maritime Heritage Program, Silver Spring, MD.

2014 Pacific Graveyard: Adaptive Reuse, Recycling, and Abandonment in San Francisco's Maritime Graveyards, 1849–1959. In *The Archaeology of Watercraft Abandonment*, Nathan Richards and Sami Seeb, editors, pp. 119–136. Springer, New York, NY.

2017 The Archaeology of San Francisco's Gold Rush Waterfront, 1849–1851: Building a New Model of the 19th-Century Pacific Rim Maritime 'Frontier.' In *Historical Archaeology through a Western Lens*, Mark Warner and Margaret Purser, editors, pp. 32–50. University of Nebraska Press and Society for Historical Archaeology, Lincoln.

2021 SS *Tennessee*: A Near-Shore Shipwreck from the California Gold Rush. *Journal of Maritime Archaeology, Journal of Maritime Archaeology*, 16(4):445–476.

Delgado, James P., Marianne Babal, George Berry, Cheryl Jensen, Kirk Jensen, Greg Johnson, Gerry Long, and René Peron

1987 "Burned to the Waterline": A Report on the Archaeological Examination of the 1907 Steam Schooner Grays Harbor. Manuscript, Candlestick Point SRA, South San Francisco, CA.

Delgado, James P., and Robert L. Bennett

1981 Research Design for the Historical Archaeological Examination and Documentation of the 1848 Sidewheel Steamship Tennessee at Tennessee

Cove, Golden Gate National Recreation Area, Marin County, California. Manuscript, National Park Service, San Francisco, CA. Internet Archive <https://archive.org/details/DelgadoResearchDesignTennessee/page/n9/mode/2up>. Accessed 30 April 2023.

Delgado, James P., Amy Borgens, Deborah Marx, Matthew Lawrence, and David Eynon

2021   Archaeological Survey and Contextualization of the Barque *Vicar of Bray* (1841, Modified 1858–1859), Goose Green, Falkland Islands/Islas Malvinas. *Journal of Maritime Archaeology* 16:223–251.

Delgado, James P., Michael L. Brennan, Frank Cantelas, Kelley Elliott, Katherine L. C. Bell, Dwight Coleman, Allison Fundis, Jack Irion, Hans K. Van Tilburg, and Robert D. Ballard

2018   Telepresence-Enabled Maritime Archaeology in the Deep. *Journal of Maritime Archaeology* 13(2):97–122.

Delgado, James P., Michael L Brennan, Kelley Elliott, Russell E. Matthews, Megan Lickliter-Mundon, John G. Lambert, Frank Cantelas, and Robert V. Schwemmer

2018   Archaeological Survey of the Ex-USS *Independence* (CVL22). *Journal of Maritime Archaeology* 13(2):123–144.

Delgado, James P., Michael L. Brennan, Jan Roletto, Frank Cantelas, Russell Mathews, Kelly Elliott, Kai Vetter, Christopher Figueroa, Megan Lickliter-Mundon, and Robert V. Schwemmer

2017   Exploration and Mapping of USS *Independence*. *Oceanography* 30(1):834–835.

Delgado, James P., Frank Cantelas, and Robert V. Schwemmer

2016   Initial Archaeological Survey of the Ex-USS *Independence* (CVL-22). *Journal of Maritime Archaeology* 11(1):9–24.

Delgado, James P., and J. Candace Clifford

1990   *The National Maritime Initiative Inventory of Large Preserved Historic Vessels in the United States.* National Park Service, Washington, DC.

Delgado, James P., Kelley Elliott, Frank Cantelas, and Robert V. Schwemmer

2016   Assessment of the Deep Sea Wreck USS *Independence. Frontiers in Marine Science* 3. Frontiers: Frontiers in Marine Science <www.frontiersin.org/article/10.3389/fmars.2016.00080>. 20 April 2023.

Delgado, James P., Scott Green, Denise Jaffke, Matthew Lawrence, and Deborah Marx

2018   Maritime Cultural Landscape of Sonoma's Doghole Ports: Including the

Waters of Greater Farallones National Marine Sanctuary. Report on file with NOAA's Office of National Marine Sanctuary, Silver Spring, Maryland and California Department of Parks and Recreation, Sacramento, California.

2021 *Maritime Cultural Landscape of Sonoma's Doghole Ports.* California Department of Parks and Recreation, Cultural Resources Division, Publications in Cultural Heritage, Number 37. Sacramento.

Delgado, James P., and Stephen A. Haller

1989a *Shipwrecks at the Golden Gate.* Lexicos, San Francisco, CA.

1989b Submerged Cultural Resources Assessment: Golden Gate National Recreation Area, Point Reyes National Seashore, and Gulf of the Farallones National Marine Sanctuary. Manuscript, National Park Service, Washington, DC.

Delgado, James P., Frederick H. Hanselmann, and Dominique Rissolo

2011 The Richest River in the World: The Maritime Cultural Landscape of the Mouth of the Rio Chagres, Republica de Panama. In *The Archaeology of Maritime Landscapes*, Ben Ford, editor, pp. 233–246. Springer, New York, NY.

Delgado, James P., and Candace J. Clifford

1991 *Great American Ships.* Preservation Press, Washington, DC.

Delgado, James P. and Thomas N. Layton

1990 *Frolic*, Brig Shipwreck Site and Remains, 1990 [Listed May 1991] National Register of Historic Places Inventory/Nomination Form, National Park Service, United States Department of the Interior, Washington, DC NRHP #910005651991.

Delgado, James P., Russell E. Matthews, Megan Lickliter-Mundon, Michael L Brennan, and John G. Lambert

2018 USS *Independence*'s Aircraft. *Journal of Maritime Archaeology* 13(2):145–166.

Delgado, James P., Tomas Mendizábal, Frederick H. Hanselmann, and Dominique Rissolo

2016 *The Maritime Landscape of the Isthmus of Panamá.* University Press of Florida, Gainesville.

Delgado, James P., and Larry E. Murphy

1984 Environmentally Exposed Shipwreck Remains: Implications for a Natural Site Formation Process. Paper presented at the Fifteenth Annual Conference on Historical and Underwater Archaeology, Williamsburg, VA.

Delgado, James P., Larry E. Murphy, and Roger E. Kelly

1984   *Shipwreck Survey of a Portion of Ocean Beach, San Francisco, for the Revenue Cutter C. W. Lawrence.* National Park Service, San Francisco, CA.

Delgado, James P., and a National Park Service Maritime Task Force

1987   *Nominating Historic Ships and Shipwrecks to the National Register of Historic Places.* National Park Service, National Register Bulletin 20. Washington, DC. National Park Service <https://www.nps.gov/subjects/nationalregister/upload/NRB20-Complete.pdf>. Accessed 30 April 2023.

Delgado, James P., Allen G. Pastron, and Rhonda K. Robichaud

2007   "This Fine and Commodious Vessel": Archaeological Investigation of the Gold Rush Storeship General Harrison. Manuscript, Archeo-Tec, Oakland, CA.

Delgado, James P., Jan Roletto, Michael L. Brennan, Gary Williams, Christina Piotrowski, Guy Cochrane, Jamie Wagner, Ashley Marranzino, and Robert V. Schwemmer

2017   Mapping and Exploration of Deep-Sea Corals and Shipwrecks in the Greater Farallones National Marine Sanctuary. *Oceanography* 30(1):832–833.

Delgado, James P., and Robert V. Schwemmer

2016   Discovery and Identification of the Wreck of USS Conestoga (AT 54), Greater Farallones National Marine Sanctuary, California. Manuscript, NOAA's Office of National Marine Sanctuaries, Silver Spring, MD.

Delgado, James P., Robert V. Schwemmer, and Michael L. Brennan

2020   Shipwrecks and the Maritime Cultural Landscape of the Gulf of the Farallones. *Journal of Maritime Archaeology* 15(2):131–163.

Delsescaux, Jeffrey R.

2016   The Mystery of Bronze Anchors: The Monterey Bronze Anchor as a Case Study. *Society for California Archaeology Proceedings* 30:122–131.

2019   California's "Aquatic Assassin"—The Ex-German U-Boat UB-88: An Archaeological Resource from a World War I Naval Battlefield. *Society for California Archaeology Proceedings* 33:23–38.

Dickens, Robert

1998   Portuguese Shore Whalers in Nineteenth Century California. Master's thesis, Maritime Studies Program, East Carolina University, Greenville, NC.

Dodds, Tricia

 2014 Underwater Survey at Refugio State Beach. *Society for California Archaeology Proceedings* 29:282–285.

 2015 Diving into the Past: The F4U Corsair at Crystal Cove State Marine Conservation Area. *Society for California Archaeology Proceedings* 28:74–88.

 2016 Shipwrecks off California's Coast: Recent Discoveries in Greater Farallones National Marine Sanctuary. *Society for California Archaeology Proceedings* 30:132–141.

Dodds. Tricia, and Kirstin Hawley

 2019 Preliminary Investigations of the *Glenn Mayne* Shipwreck. *Society for California Archaeology Proceedings* 33:39–45.

Dodds, Tricia, and Denise Jaffke

 2014 Into the Blue: Underwater Archaeology in California State Parks. *Society for California Archaeology Proceedings* 28:188–196.

Elliott, Kelley

 2008 Contemporary Archaeological Examination of USS *Independence*, CVL-22. Master's thesis, School of Archaeology, University of Southampton, Southampton, UK.

Erlandson, Jon M.

 1993a California's Coastal Prehistory: A Circum-Pacific Perspective. *Society for California Archaeology Proceedings* 6:23–36.

 1993b The Historical Development of Santa Barbara Channel Archaeology. *Society for California Archaeology Proceedings* 6:221–232.

 1997 An Archaeology of the Pacific Rim. *Society for California Archaeology Proceedings* 10:103–109.

Esser, Kimberly

 1999 Inland Waterways of the California Delta: Identifying and Managing a Maritime Landscape. In *Underwater Archaeology, 1999*, Adrienne Askins Neidlinger and Matthew A. Russell, editors, pp. 17–20, Society for Historical Archaeology, Uniontown, PA.

Everett, Richard O.

 1997 Found! The Wreck of the *Frolic*—A Gold Rush Cargo for San Francisco. *Sea Letter* 53(Winter):4–9, National Maritime Museum Association, San Francisco, CA.

Faycurry, Jessica

 2018 Chutes and Landings: Maritime Communities and the Maritime Cultural

Landscape of the Sonoma Coast. Master's thesis, Department of Anthropology, Sonoma State University, Rohnert Park, CA.

Ferris, John

    1960   What's Doing in Diving? *Oakland Tribune* 29 December:40. Oakland, CA.

Field, Jason

    2017   Big Sur Doghole Ports: A Frontier Maritime Cultural Landscape. Master's thesis, Department of Anthropology, Sonoma State University, Rohnert Park, CA.

Fischer, George R., and Marion J. Riggs

    1969   *Prospectus for Underwater Archaeology.* Division of Archeology, Office of Archeology and Historic Preservation, National Park Service, Washington, DC.

Foster, John W.

    1981   Diving in Dogholes: The Prospects for Investigating Submerged Cultural Resources in Ft. Ross Cove. Paper presented at the annual meeting of the Society for California Archaeology, San Diego.

    1984   Schooners, Steamers and Spilled Cargo: A Preliminary Underwater Survey of Ft. Ross Cove, California. In *Underwater Archaeology: The Proceedings of the 13th Conference on Underwater Archaeology*, Donald H. Keith, editor, pp. 86–94. Fathom Eight , San Marino, CA

    1988a   The Brig *Sterling*: A Lost but not Forgotten Gold Rush Shipwreck on the Sacramento Waterfront. In *Archaeology in Solution: Proceedings of the Seventeenth Annual Conference on Underwater Archaeology*, John W. Foster and Sheli O. Smith, editors, pp. 100–103. California Department of Parks and Recreation, Sacramento.

    1988b   Stone Bowls from Goleta. Paper presented at the annual meeting of the Society for California Archaeology, San Diego.

    2001   Watching Cows and Fighting Devil-Fish: An Overview of History and Archaeology at the Site of the S.S. *Pomona*, Fort Ross State Historic Park. Paper presented at the California Council for the Promotion of History conference, Long Beach.

    2002   *Archaeology and History beneath the Sea: The Preservation, Management, and Interpretation of California's Heritage Resources.* California Department of Parks and Recreation, Sacramento.

    2016   A Bubble Slowly Rising: Shipwrecks and the Development of Nautical Archaeology in California. *Society for California Archaeology Proceedings* 30:161–174.

2019   Getting behind the Fish: The Need for Establishing Underwater Heritage Parks in California *Society for California Archaeology Proceedings* 33:46–57.

2020   Older than Dirt: The Enigmatic Anchor Stones of Palos Verdes. *Society for California Archaeology Newsletter* 54(2):17–19.

Foster, John W., Jack Hunter, and Jim Gilmore

1983   "New Fire from Old Guns": A Description and Tentative Interpretation of Five Iron Cannon from Goleta, California. Paper presented at 16th Annual Conference on Historical and Underwater Archaeology, Denver, CO.

Foster, John W. and eleven associates

2008   Frolic Cove Project: Inventory of Features—Resource Summary and Recommendations for Classification and Naming. Manuscript, California State Parks, Sacramento.

Foster, John W., Annalies Corbin, and Sheli O Smith

2009   The Clarksburg Shipwreck: A Gold-Rush Ghost in the Sacramento River. In *Advisory Council on Underwater Archaeology Proceedings, 2009*, Erika Laanela and Jonathan Moore, editors, pp. 255–261. Advisory Council on Underwater Archaeology.

Foster, John W., Charles Beeker, Deborah Marx, and Sheli O. Smith

2016   The Mini-Fleet of Emerald Bay: Recreational Watercraft. In *The Archaeology of Vernacular Watercraft*, Amanda M. Evans, editor, pp. 255–271. Springer, New York, NY.

Foster, John W., and Denise Jaffke

2016   Undersea Drones: Explorations of the S.S. *Tahoe* (1896–1940) by Mini-ROV with Citizen Science, Engineering and Archaeology. *Society for California Archaeology Proceedings* 31:49–57.

Friends of the *Frolic*

1993   June *Friends of the* Frolic *Newsletter*, No. 1, Mendocino County Museum.

1993   fall *Friends of the* Frolic *Newsletter*, No. 2, Mendocino County Museum.

1994   winter *Friends of the* Frolic *Newsletter*, No. 3, Mendocino County Museum.

1994   spring *Friends of the* Frolic *Newsletter*, No. 4 Mendocino County Museum.

1994   fall *Friends of the* Frolic *Newsletter*, No. 5, Mendocino County Museum.

Frost, Frank J.

1982   The Palos Verde Chinese Anchor Mystery. *Archaeology* 35(1):22–28.

Garrison, Ervan, and Jessica Cook Hale

2020   "The Early Days"—Underwater Prehistoric Archaeology in the USA and Canada. *Journal of Island and Coastal Archaeology* 16(1):27–45.

Gearhart, Robert L. II

1988   Cultural Resources Magnetometer Survey and Testing, Great Highway/ Ocean Beach Seawall Project, San Francisco, *California*. Manuscript, Espey, Huston & Associates, Inc., Austin, TX.

Gearhart, Robert L. II, Clell Bond, and Steven Hoyt (editors)

1990   California, Oregon and Washington Archaeological Resource Study, 6 vol. Manuscript, United States Department of the Interior, Minerals Management Service, Pacific OCS Region, Camarillo, CA.

Gilmore, Jim, and Jack Hunter

1983   The Guns of Goleta: A Source Book of Information to Date. Manuscript, California Department of Parks and Recreation, Sacramento.

Goggin, John M.

1960   Underwater Archaeology: Its Nature and Limitations, *American Antiquity* 25(3):348–354.

Grech, Chris

2007   Rediscovery of Airship USS *Macon*: The First Archaeological Survey within the Boundaries of the Monterey Bay National Marine Sanctuary. In *Oceans 2007: On the Edge of Tomorrow*, pp. 1–10. Marine Technology Society, Vancouver, BC.

Gusick, Amy E., Tricia Dodds, Denise Jaffke, Marco Meniketti, and David Ball

2019   Defining Maritime Cultural Landscapes in California, *California Archaeology* 11(2):139–164.

Hagen-Jones, Patricia

1992   A Comparative Study of Mid-Nineteenth Century Chinese Blue-and-White Export Ceramics from the *Frolic* Shipwreck, Mendocino County, California. Master's thesis, Department of Anthropology, California State University, San Jose.

1994   *A Comparative Study of Mid-Nineteenth Century Chinese Blue-and-White Export Ceramics from the* Frolic *Shipwreck, Mendocino County, California*. University of South Carolina, South Carolina Institute of Archeology and Anthropology, Volumes in Historical Archaeology, No. 29. Columbia.

Hanna, Warren L.

1979   *Lost Harbor: The Controversy over Drake's California Anchorage*. University of California Press, Berkeley.

Heizer, Robert F.

1941   Archaeological Evidence of Sebastian Rodriquez Cermeño's California Visit in 1595. *California Historical Society Quarterly* 20(4):315–328.

1972   *California's Oldest Historical Relic?* Robert H. Lowie Museum of Anthropology, University of California, Berkeley.

Hill, Frederic B.

2016   *Ships, Swindlers, and Scalded Hogs: The Rise and Fall of the Crooker Shipyard in Bath, Maine*. Down East Books, Landham, MD.

Hillman, Raymond W.

1985   Historical Report on Hermit's Cove (aka Candlestick Cove) and Vicinity, San Francisco, California. Manuscript, Candlestick Park SRA, South Francisco, CA.

Hohenthal, W. D.

1969   Adán Eduardo Treganza, 1916–1968. *American Antiquity* 34(4):462–466.

Hough, Trevor Harrison

2018   Tomol's and the "Carrying Many People" Indigenous Control of the Sea in the Santa Barbara Channel. Master's thesis, Maritime Studies Program, East Carolina University, Greenville, NC.

Hudson, D. Travis

1974   17th Century Spanish Shipwreck. *Artifact: Newsletter of the San Luis Obispo County Archaeological Society* 9(10):2–3.

1976   *Marine Archaeology along the Southern California Coast*. San Diego Museum Papers, Number 9. San Diego, CA.

1979   A Charmstone from the Sea off Point Conception, California. *Journal of California and Great Basin Archaeology* 1(2):363–367.

Hudson, D. Travis, and Peter C. Howorth

1985   A Preliminary Survey on Sensitive Marine Archaeological and Historical Sites Located within the Boundaries of the Channel Islands National Marine Sanctuary, Vol. 1–4. Manuscript, Channel Islands National Marine Sanctuary and Channel Islands National Park, National Oceanic and Atmospheric Administration, and U.S. National Park Service, Ventura, CA

Hunter, Jack G.

1979   A Cultural Resource Reconnaissance Study of Proposed Dredging and Construction Areas at Mission Bay Harbor, California. Manuscript, U.S. Army Corps of Engineers, Environmental Planning Section, Los Angeles, CA.

1981   Preliminary Onshore Magnetometer Survey of Goleta Beach Cannon Discovery Site. Manuscript, Department of Anthropology, University of California, Santa Barbara.

Hunter, Jack G., and Franklin Fisher

1989   A Shipwreck Mapping and Recordation Reconnaissance of the Remains of the Steam Ship S.S. *Pomona*, Sonoma County. Manuscript, California Department of Parks and Recreation, Sacramento.

Hunter, Jack G., and John W. Foster

1997   Stone Anchors from Palos Verdes, California. In *The British Museum Encyclopaedia of Underwater and Maritime Archaeology*, James P. Delgado, editor, pp. 304–305. British Museum Press, London, UK.

Hunter, Jack, Steven P. Helmich, and Monica Reed

1984   Old Sacramento Waterfront Underwater Archaeological Survey. Manuscript, Sacramento Housing and Redevelopment Agency, Sacramento, CA.

Hunter, Jack G., and Larry J. Pierson

1980   A Detailed Cultural Resource Evaluation of Exposed Shipwrecks in the Los Angeles Harbor Deepening Project Landfill Area South of Terminal Island, California. Manuscript, U.S. Army Corps of Engineers, Los Angeles, CA.

Hykelma, Mark

2018   Part 1: Archaeology, History and the Stabilization of the Franklin Point Historic Shipwreck Cemetery (CA-SMA-207/H). In *Shipwrecks and Lime Kilns: The Hidden History of 19th Century Sailors and Quarrymen of the Central Coast*, Christopher Corey, editor, pp. 1-69. Cultural Resource Division, California Department of Parks and Recreation, Sacramento.

James, Rick

2004   *The Ghost Ships of Royston*. Underwater Archaeological Society of British Columbia, Vancouver, BC.

James, Stephen R., Jr.

1986a   Submerged Cultural Resources Survey, Sacramento Embarcadero, Sacramento, California. Manuscript, Espey, Huston & Associates, Austin, TX.

1986b   Underwater Archaeological Investigations, "Docks Area" Sacramento, California. Manuscript, Espey, Huston & Associates, Austin, TX.

1987   The Barks *La Grange* and *Ninus*: Two Recent Additions to the Growing Number of Gold Rush Era Shipwreck Sites. In *Underwater Archaeology Proceedings from the Society for Historical Archaeology Conference, Savannah, Georgia, 1987*, Alan B. Albright, editor, pp. 21–26. Society for Historical Archaeology, Ann Arbor, MI.

Jewell, Donald P.

1961   Freshwater Archaeology. *American Antiquity* 26(3):414–416.

1964   Limnoarchaeology in California. In *Diving into the Past: Theories, Techniques and Applications to Underwater Archaeology*, J. Drenning Holmquist and A. Hillman Wheeler, editors, pp. 27–31. Minnesota Historical Society, St. Paul.

Kelly, Roger E.

1988a   Are Submerged Heritage Resources Protected in Pacific Rim Nations? In *Underwater Archaeology Proceedings from the Society for Historical Archaeology Conference, Reno, Nevada 1988*, James P. Delgado, editor, pp. 37–39. Society for Historical Archaeology, Ann Arbor, MI.

1988b   Going Overboard for Historical Archeology. *CRM Bulletin* 11(5&6):8–11.

2001   New Wine in Old Bottles: Changing Public Perspectives of Maritime Heritage in North America and the Pacific Rim. *Journal of the Australasian Institute for Maritime Archaeology* 25:79–82.

Kelly, Roger E., and Gary Franklin (editors)

2001   *Along the Shores of Time: Submerged Historic and Indigenous Resources in the Pacific Rim Region: Proceedings of an International and Interdisciplinary Conference Held at the United States Army Corps of Engineers San Francisco Bay Model Visitor Center, Sausalito, California*. National Park Service, San Francisco, CA.

Kennell, Henry

2019   Treasure Hunters, Adventurers, Sport Divers, and Archaeologists: Influences on Early Underwater Archaeology. Senior honors thesis, Department of History, University of Connecticut, Avery Point. OpenCommons@UConn, UCONN Library <https://opencommons.uconn.edu/srhonors_theses/617/>. Accessed 10 August 2023.

King, Thomas F., and W. F. Upson

1970   Protohistory on Limantour Sandspit: Archaeological Investigations at 4-Mrn-216 and 4-Mrn-298. In *Contributions to the Archaeology of Point*

Reyes National Seashore: A Compendium in Honor of Adan E. Treganza, R. E. Schenk, editor, pp. 114–194. San Francisco State College, San Francisco, CA.

Kortum, Karl, and Roger Olmsted

1971   *"... It Is a Dangerous Looking Place": Sailing Days on the Redwood Coast*. California Historical Society, San Francisco.

Layton, Thomas N.

1990   *Western Pomo Prehistory*. University of California, Los Angeles, Institute of Archaeology, Monograph 32. Los Angeles.

1995   The Journey of the *Frolic. Society for California Archaeology Newsletter* 29(1):1,3–5.

1997   *The Voyage of the* Frolic: *New England Merchants and the Opium Trade*. Stanford University Press, Stanford, CA.

1998   The Last Voyage of the Frolic. *Museum of California, Bicentennial Issue* 22(1):27-31, Oakland Museum of California.

2002   *Gifts from the Celestial Kingdom: A Shipwrecked Cargo for Gold Rush California*. Stanford University Press, Stanford, CA.

2021   *The "Other" Dixwells: Commerce and Conscience in an American Family*. Society for Historical Archaeology, Germantown, MD.

Lenihan, Daniel J.

2002   *Submerged: Adventures of America's Most Elite Underwater Archeology Team*. Newmarket Press, New York, NY.

Lenihan, Daniel J., Toni L. Carell, S. Fosberg, L. Murphy, S. L. Rahl, and J. A. Ware

1981   The Final Report of the National Reservoir Inundation Study, 2 vol. Manuscript, National Park Service, Southwest Cultural Resources Center, Santa Fe, NM.

Lickliter-Mundon, Megan

2018   *Aviation Archaeology: History, Theory, Practice and Direction*. Doctoral dissertation, Nautical Archaeology Program, Texas A&M University, College Station. University Microfilms International, Ann Arbor, MI.

Lickliter-Mundon, Megan, Bruce G. Terrell, Michael L. Brennan, and Robert V. Schwemmer

2015   2015 Mapping Survey and Conservation Assessment of the USS *Macon* Site. Manuscript, NOAA's Office of National Marine Sanctuaries, Maritime Heritage Program, Silver Spring, MD.

Lindstrom, Susan

  1990   Submerged Tree Stumps as Indicators of Mid-Holocene Aridity in the Lake Tahoe Basin. *Journal of California and Great Basin Archaeology* 12(2):146–157.

Lydecker, Andrew D. M.

  2010   Archaeological and Historical Investigation of an Historic Ferry in the Sacramento River at Clarksburg. In *ACUA Underwater Archaeology Proceedings, 2010*, Chris Horrell and Melanie Damour. editors, pp. 236–244. Advisory Council on Underwater Archaeology.

Marine Protected Areas

  2011   Recommendations for Integrated Management Using a Cultural Landscape Approach in the National MPA System. Marine Protected Areas <https://nmsmarineprotectedareas.blob.core.windows.net/marineprotectedareas-prod/media/archive/pdf/helpful-resources/mpafac_rec_cultural_landscape_12_11.pdf>. Accessed 30 April 2023.

Marshall, Don B.

  1978   *California Shipwrecks: Footsteps in the Sea*, Superior Publishing Co., Seattle, WA.

Marshall, Neil F., and James R. Moriarty

  1964   Principles of Underwater Archaeology. *Pacific Discovery* 17(5):18–25.

Marx, Deborah

  2002   " ... With the Speed of a Stag Hound": The Steamship *Winfield Scott*: A Case Study in Early United States Steam Navigation. Master's thesis, Maritime Studies Program, East Carolina University, Greenville, NC.

Marx, Robert F.

  1978   History of the Council of Underwater Archaeology. In *Beneath the Waters of Time: Proceedings of the Ninth Conference on Underwater Archaeology*, J. Barto Arnold III, editor, pp. vii–xi. Texas Antiquities Committee, Austin.

  1987   The Manila Galleon. In *Underwater Archaeology Proceedings from the Society for Historical Archaeology Conference, Savannah, Georgia, 1987*, Alan B. Albright, editor, pp. 1–2. Society for Historical Archaeology, Ann Arbor, MI.

Masters, Patricia M.

  1983   Detection and Assessment of Prehistoric Artifact Sites off the Coast of Southern California. In *Quaternary Coastlines and Marine Archaeology*, Patricia. M. Masters and Nicholas C. Flemming, editors, pp. 189–213. Academic Press, New York, NY.

1985   California Coastal Evolution and the La Jollans. *Oceanus* 28(1):27–34.

May, Ronald V.

1982   The Search for Fort Guijarros: An Archaeological Test of a Legendary 18th Century Spanish Fort in San Diego. *Fort Guijarros Quarterly* 1(10):1–22.

1985a   The Fort that Never Was on Ballast Point. *Journal of San Diego History* 36(2):121–136.

1985b   The Guns of Point Loma: America's First Sea Coast Artillery Defense in San Diego. In *The Military in San Diego*, pp. 26-36. Cabrillo Historical Association, San Diego, CA.

1985c   Schooners, Sloops and Ancient Mariners: Research Implications of Shore Whaling in San Diego. *Pacific Coast Archaeological Society Quarterly* 21(4):1–24.

1986   Dog Holes, Bomb-Lances and Devil-Fish: Boom Times in the San Diego Whaling Industry. *Journal of San Diego History* 36(2):73–90.

1988   A Preliminary Report on the Summer–Fall 1988 Archaeological Field Season at Ballast Point, San Diego. *Fort Guijarros Quarterly* 2(3):4–25.

1990   Discovery at the Ballast Point Whaling Station: Archaeological Exposure of a Tryworks Oven in California. In *Underwater Archaeology Proceedings from the Society for Historical Archaeology Conference, Tucson, Arizona, 1990*, Toni L. Carrell, editor, pp. 119–124. Society for Historical Archaeology, Ann Arbor, MI.

1994   Field VIII Archaeology Report for the 1989–1993 Seasons. Manuscript, Department of the Navy, San Diego, CA.

1995   Evidence for the Physical Appearance of 18th Century Spanish Cannon Batteries in California. *Fort Guijarros Journal* 1:4–15.

1996   Research Design for the 1996 Investigation of the Interior Wall of a Spanish Cannon Battery, American Army Artifacts, and the Ballast Point Whaling Station Located on the United States Naval Submarine Base, San Diego. Manuscript, U.S. Navy, San Diego, CA.

McCann, Anna Marguerite, Joanne Bourgeois, Elaine K. Gazda, John Peter Oleson, and Elizabeth Lyding Will

1987   *The Roman Port and Fishery at Cosa: A Center of Ancient Trade*. Princeton University Press, Princeton, NJ.

McCarthy, Celia

1999   Training Walls and Ferry Slips Are not Sexy Lingerie. In *Underwater Archaeology, 1999*, Adrienne Askins Neidlinger and Matthew A. Russell, editors, pp. 11–16. Society for Historical Archaeology, Uniontown, PA.

McCaslin, Dan E., and James K. [Otto] Orzech

    1988   Romancing the Stones: The Worked Stone Objects off the Palos Verdes Peninsula, Los Angeles, California. In *Archaeology in Solution: Proceedings of the Seventeenth Annual Conference on Underwater Archaeology*, John W. Foster and Sheli O. Smith, editors, Coyote Press, Salinas, CA.

McClellan, Whitney

    2015   "Tell Me What You Eat and I'll Tell You Who You Are": The Zoorachaeological Analysis of Four Nineteenth-Century San Francisco Maritime Households. Master's thesis, Department of Anthropology, Sonoma State University, Rohnert Park, CA.

Meighan, Clement W.

    1950   Excavations in Sixteenth Century Shellmounds at Drake's Bay, Marin County. *Papers on California Archaeology* 6–9(5):27–32. Berkeley.

    2002   The Stoneware Site, a 16th Century Site on Drakes Bay. In *Essays in California Archaeology: A Memorial to Franklin Fenenga*, W. J. Wallace and F. A. Riddell, editors, pp. 62–87. Contributions of the University of California Archaeological Research Facility No. 60. Berkeley.

Meighan, Clement W., and Robert F. Heizer

    1952   Archaeological Exploration of Sixteenth-Century Indian Mounds at Drake's Bay. *California Historical Society Quarterly* 31(2):99–108.

Mendocino County Museum

    1993   *Friends of the* Frolic *Newsletter*, No. 1, June, Mendocino County Museum.

    1993   *Friends of the* Frolic *Newsletter*, No. 2, Fall, Mendocino County Museum.

    1994   *Friends of the* Frolic *Newsletter*, No. 3, Winter, Mendocino County Museum.

Meniketti, Marco

    1996   Bones in the Sand: Reconnaissance and Test Excavation of the 19th Century Barkentine *Jane L. Stanford*. *Society for California Archaeology Proceedings* 9:157–160.

    2014   Initial XRF Analysis of Chinese Ceramics from Spanish Shipwrecks on the Pacific Coast. *Society for California Archaeology Proceedings* 28:305–310.

    2017   The Wreck of the Galleon *San Agustin*: A Case Study in Economics, Exploration, and European Development of the Pacific Rim. Paper presented at the 50th Annual Conference on Historical and Underwater Archaeology, Fort Worth, TX.

2020   *Timber, Sail and Rail: An Archaeology of Industry, Immigration, and the Loma Prieta Mill*. Berghahan, New York, NY.

Meniketti, Marco, ed.

2023   *The Long Shore: Archaeologies and Social Histories of California's Maritime Cultural Landscapes*. Bergahn Books, NY.

Moriarty, James R.

1969   Marine Archaeology in Submerged Prehistoric Sites. *Ocean Magazine* 3(2):47–49.

1981   Marine Geology in the Solution of Problems in a Submerged Early Prehistoric Site. In *Underwater Archaeology: The Challenge before Us: The Proceedings of the Twelfth Conference on Underwater Archaeology*, Gordon P. Watts, Jr., editor, pp. 276–284. Fathom Eight, San Marino, CA.

Moriarty, James R. III, P. Gibson, and Larry Pierson

1975   Artifacts from Submarine Archaeological Sites. *Masterkey* 9(4):47–154.

Morris, Don P., and James Lima

1996   *Channel Islands National Park and Channel Islands National Marine Sanctuary, Submerged Cultural Resources Assessment*. National Park Service, Intermountain Cultural Resource Center Professional Papers, Number 56. Santa Fe, NM.

Muche, James F.

1978a   An Inundated Aboriginal Site, Corral Beach, California. In *Beneath the Waters of Time: Proceedings of the Ninth Conference on Underwater Archaeology*, J. Barto Arnold III, editor, pp. 101–108. Texas Antiquities Committee, Austin.

1978b   A Stone Vessel Located off Point Dune. *California Search* 2(10):15–19.

1978c   Two Associated Artifacts from Offshore San Nicolas Island. *California Search* 2(2):3–10.

1981   The Manila Galleon *San Pedro*: Subsequent Surveys. In *In the Realms of Gold: The Proceedings of the Ninth Conference on Underwater Archaeology, 1979*, Wilbur A. Cockrell, editor, pp. 45–55. Fathom Eight, San Marino, CA.

1982   F8A-39: An Inundated Aboriginal Fishing Site. In *Underwater Archaeology: The Proceedings of the Ninth Conference on Underwater Archaeology, 1980*, Calvin R. Cummings, editor, 107–111. Fathom Eight, San Marino, CA.

Muche, James F., and A. Lani Low Muche (editors)

   1984   *A Bibliography of Underwater Archaeology*. Fathom Eight, San Marino, CA.

Murphy, Larry E. (editor)

   1984   *Submerged Cultural Resources Survey: Portions of Point Reyes National Seashore and Point Reyes-Farallon Islands National Marine Sanctuary.* National Park Service, Submerged Resources Center Professional Report No. 2. Santa Fe, NM.

Olmsted, Nancy, and Adrian Praetzellis

   1993   The Archaeology of Buried Ships and Wharves. In Tar Flat, Rincon Point and the Shore of Mission Bay: Archaeological Research Design and Treatment Plan for SF-480 Terminal Separation Rebuild, Vol. 2, Adrian Praetzellis and Mary Praetzellis, editors, pp. 349–364. Manuscript, Sonoma State University, Rohnert Park, CA.

Olmsted, Roger, Nancy Olmsted, and Allen G. Pastron

   1977   San Francisco Waterfront: Report on Historical Cultural Resources for the North Shore and Channel Outfalls Consolidation Projects. Manuscript, Archeo-Tec, San Francisco, CA.

Owens, Joan, Producer and Director

   1997   *The Hunt for Amazing Treasures*, episode 10, part 2. Learning Channel, Andrew Solt Productions, Los Angeles, CA.

Panich, Lee M., GeorgeAnn DeAntoni, and Tsim D. Schneider

   2021   "By the Aid of His Indians": Native Negotiations of Settler Colonialism in Marin County, California, 1840–70. *International Journal of Historical Archaeology* 25(1):92–115.

Panich, Lee M., Tsim D. Schneider, and R. Scott Byram

   2018   Finding Mid-Nineteenth Century Native Settlements: Cartographic and Archaeological Evidence from Central California. *Journal of Field Archaeology* 43(2):152-165.

Pastron, Allen G., and Richard D. Ambro (editors)

   2007   Final Report on Archaeological Monitoring at the Broadway Family Apartments Project, San Francisco. Manuscript, Archeo-Tec, Oakland, CA.

Pastron, Allen G., Richard D. Ambro, and James P. Delgado

   2007   Archaeological Research Design and Testing/Treatment Plan for the 555

Washington Street Project, San Francisco. Manuscript, Archeo-Tec, Oakland, CA.

Pastron, Allen G., and James P. Delgado

1991   Archaeological Investigations at a Mid-19th-Century Shipbreaking Yard, San Francisco, California, *Historical Archaeology* 25(2):61–77.

Pastron, Allen G., and Eugene M. Hattori (editors)

1990   The Hoff Store Site and Gold Rush Merchandise from San Francisco, California. Society for Historical Archaeology, Ann Arbor, MI.

Pastron, Allen G., Jack Prichett, and Marilyn Ziebarth (editors)

1981   Behind the Seawall: Historical Archaeology along the San Francisco Waterfront, 3 vol. Report to San Francisco Clean Water Program, San Francisco, CA, from Archeo-Tec, Oakland, CA.

Péron, René

1988   Anthropological Perspectives in Nautical Archaeology. In *Underwater Archaeology Proceedings from the Society for Historical Archaeology Conference, Reno, Nevada 1988*, James P. Delgado, editor, pp. 53–55. Society for Historical Archaeology, Ann Arbor, MI.

Pettus, Roy E.

1981   A Marine Cultural Resources Survey Offshore from a Spanish Fort Site at Ballast Point, San Diego. Master's thesis, Department of Anthropology, San Diego State University, San Diego, CA.

1982a   Submerged Cultural Resources in San Diego, Casual Papers. *Cultural Resource Management* 1(1):72–87.

1982b   Underwater Archaeology Research in San Diego Bay Offshore from Fort Guijarros. In *Fort Guijarros, Tenth Annual Cabrillo Festival Historic Seminar*, Ronald V. May, Roy Pettus, and Stephen A. Colston, editors, pp. 23–60. Cabrillo Historical Association, San Diego, CA.

Pettus, Roy, James F. Muche, and A. Lani Low

1981   Fort Guijarros: A Composite Site. In *Underwater Archaeology: The Challenge before Us: The Proceedings of the Twelfth Conference on Underwater Archaeology*, Gordon P. Watts, Jr., editor, 292–297. Fathom Eight, San Marino, CA.

Pierson, Larry J.

1977   Pre-Columbian Voyages to the New World. In *Cabrillo and His Compatriots*, James R. Moriarty III, editor, pp. 1–21, Cabrillo Historical Association, San Diego, CA.

Pierson, Larry J., and James R. Moriarty III

1980   Stone Anchors: Asiatic Shipwrecks off the California Coast. *Anthropological Journal of Canada* 18:17–23.

1981   New Evidence of Asiatic Shipwrecks off the California Coast. In *Underwater Archaeology: The Challenge before Us: The Proceedings of the Twelfth Conference on Underwater Archaeology*, Gordon P. Watts, Jr., editor, pp. 87–95. Fathom Eight, San Marino, CA.

Pierson, Larry J., and Gerald L. Schiller

1989   Archaeological Resource Study: Morro Bay to Mexico, Revisited. In *Underwater Archaeology Proceedings from the Society for Historical Archaeology Conference, Baltimore, Maryland, 1989*, J. Barto Arnold, III, editor, pp. 19–20. Society for Historical Archaeology, Ann Arbor, MI.

Powers, Dennis M.

2006   *Treasure Ship: The Legend and Legacy of the S.S. Brother Jonathan*. Citadel Press, New York, NY.

Rawitsch, Mark Howland

1994   *Journey of the* Frolic: *The Story of the Story*. Mendocino County Museum, Willits, CA.

Roberts, Andrew P.

2008   *Great Republic*: A Historical and Archaeological Analysis of a Pacific Mail Steamship. Master's thesis, Nautical Archaeology Program, Texas A&M University, College Station.

Rockefeller, Camilla

2015   "Stronger than Family:" Framing Modern Seamen as the Figurative Descendants of 19th Century Mariners Buried at the Presidio of San Francisco. Master's thesis, Department of Anthropology, Sonoma State University, Rohnert Park, CA.

Rozaire, Charles

1962   Underwater Finds at Dana Point. *Masterkey* 36(2):77–78.

Rudmann, Brent

2000   The SS *Pomona*, a West Coast Innovation. *Society for California Archaeology Proceedings* 13:31–37.

Ruhge, Justin M.

1984   The Cannons of Goleta. *International Journal of Nautical Archaeology and Underwater Exploration* 13(4):297–304.

1987   The Goleta Cannon on Display. *International Journal of Nautical Archaeology and Underwater Exploration* 16(3):225–231.

Russell, Matthew A.

1996   An Historical and Archaeological Examination of Three Beached Shipwreck Scatters at Channel Islands National Park. Master's thesis, Maritime Studies Program, East Carolina University, Greenville, NC.

2004a   Beached Shipwrecks from Channel Islands National Park, California. *Journal of Field Archaeology* 29(3&4):389–384.

2004b   *Comet: Submerged Cultural Resources Site Report, Channel Islands National Park.* Submerged Resources Center Professional Reports, Number 17. Santa Fe, NM.

2009   Encounters at Tamál-Húye: The Archaeology of Cross-Cultural Interactions in Sixteenth-Century Northern California. *Society for California Archaeology Proceedings* 21:58–62.

2011   *Encounters at Tamál-Húye: An Archaeology of Intercultural Engagement in Sixteenth-Century Northern California.* Doctoral dissertation, Department of Anthropology, University of California, Berkeley. University Microfilms International, Ann Arbor, MI. eScholarship <https://escholarship.org/uc/item/40x2d7w2>. Accessed 16 April 2023.

Sanchez, J. P.

2001   From the Philippines to the California Coast in 1595: The Last Voyage of *San Agustin* under Sebastian Rodriquez Cermeño. *Colonial Latin American Historical Review* 10(2):223–251.

Schneider, Tsim

2018   Making and Unmaking Native Communities in Mission and Post Mission Era Marin County, California. In *Forging Communities in Colonial Alta California*, Kathleen L. Hull and John G. Douglas, editors, pp. 88–109. University of Arizona Press, Tucson.

2019   Heritage in-between: Seeing Native Histories in Colonial California. *Public Historian* 41(1):51–63.

Schwartz, Steven J.

1989   Evaluation and Documentation of the Steam Propulsion System of the Wrecked Ferry Boat Sierra Nevada. In *Underwater Archaeology Proceedings from the Society for Historical Archaeology Conference, Baltimore, Maryland, 1989*, J. Barto Arnold III, editor, pp. 137–140. Society for Historical Archaeology, Ann Arbor, MI.

1991   Evaluation of the Steam Propulsion System of the Wrecked Ferry Boat *Sierra Nevada. Society for California Archaeology Proceedings* 4:205–211.

Schwemmer, Robert V.

1999   Channel Islands National Marine Sanctuary: Presenting the Past through Cooperative Interpretation. In *Underwater Archaeology, 1999*, Adrienne Askins Neidlinger and Matthew A. Russell, editors, pp. 64–70. Society for Historical Archaeology, Uniontown, PA.

2005   History and Site Assessment of the Shipwreck *Cuba*. In *Sixth California Islands Symposium, Ventura, California*, David K. Garcelon and Catherin A. Schwemm, editors, pp. 155–180. Institute for Wildlife Studies, Eureka, CA.

Schwemmer, Robert V., and Fred Gamble

1999   *U.S. Pacific Coast Shipwreck Database*. Channel Crossings Post, Santa Barbara, CA.

Shangraw, Clarence, and Edward P. von der Porten

1981   *The Drake and Cermeño Expeditions' Chinese Porcelains*. Santa Rosa Junior College and the Drake Navigators Guild, Santa Rosa, CA.

Simoulin, Marianne

2000   The Archaeology of the Steam Ship *Pomona*: 1998 Underwater Survey. *Proceedings of the Society for California Archaeology* 13:38–43.

Simpson, Glenn D.

1998   Wreckers on the Bay: The Archaeological Potential of Historic Shipwrecks in the Humboldt Bay Region. *Society for California Archaeology Proceedings* 11:135–140.

2001   Evaluating Shipwreck Significance in the Humboldt Bay Region, Master's thesis, Department of Anthropology, Sonoma State University, Rohnert Park, CA.

Smith, Mary Hilderman

1981   An Interpretive Study of the Collection Recovered from the Storeship Niantic. Master's thesis, Department of Anthropology, San Francisco State University, San Francisco, CA.

Smith, Sheli O.

1991   *Emerald Bay Barges*. Los Angeles Maritime Museum. San Pedro, CA.

2002   Education. In *International Handbook of Underwater Archaeology*, Carol V. Ruppé and Janet F. Barstad, editors, p. 587. Kluwer Academic/Plenum, New York, NY.

2005a   Emerald Bay Mini-Fleet DPR 523 Site Record. Manuscript, PAST Foundation, Columbus, OH.

2005b   Frolic *Archaeological Survey*. Past Foundation, Columbus, OH.

2005c   *Frolic* Archaeological Survey 2003–2004. Manuscript, California State Parks, Sacramento.

2006   The Archaeological Survey of the Shipwreck *Frolic*. *Proceedings of the Society for California Archaeology* 19:43–48.

Smith, Sheli O., and Laurel H. Breece

2002   California State Marine Managed Areas: Cultural Resource Survey 2001/2002. Manuscript, Long Beach City College, Maritime Archaeology Certificate Program, Long Beach, CA.

Smith, Sheli O., Stephen R. James, Jr., James P. Delgado, Jack Hunter, and Monica Reed

1988   *La Grange: A California Gold Rush Legacy*. Underwater Archaeological Consortium, San Pedro, CA.

Snethkamp, Pandora E., R. E. Taylor, Louis A. Payen, Peter J. Slota, Jr., and Robert Maddin

1990   The Origin of the Goleta Cannons: Inferences of Age Based on Various Lines of Evidence. *Historical Archaeology* 24(2):82–91.

Sowden, Carrie E.

2006   A Shipping Crate from the 1865 California Shipwreck *Brother Jonathan*: Hardware from the Russell and Erin Manufacturing Company. Master's thesis, Nautical Archaeology Program, Texas A&M University, College Station.

Spitzer, Rebecca M.

2015   The Maritime Shipping Industry of the Geographic Region Bounded by Aptos and Aviso, California, 1850–1950. Master's thesis, Department of Anthropology, San José State University, San Jose, CA.

Stickel, E. Gary

1977   An Underwater and On-Land Cultural Resource Survey, Port San Luis, California. Manuscript, U.S. Army Corps of Engineers, Environmental Review Section, Los Angeles, CA.

1978   Archaeological Literature Survey and Sensitivity Zone Mapping of the Southern California Bight Area, Volume 1. Technical Report. Report to Bureau of Land Management, Washington, DC, from Science Applications, Inc., La Jolla, CA.

Stradford, Richard A.

  1998   Brigantine, Schooner, Houseboat: Journeys of the Galilee. *Society for California Archaeology Proceedings* 11:131–134.

Strother, Eric, Allen Estes, Aimee Arrigoni, James M. Allan, William Self, and James Delgado

  2007   Final Archaeological Resources Report: 300 Spear Street Project, San Francisco, California. Manuscript, William Self Associates, Orinda, CA.

Sullenberger, Martha

  1980   *Dogholes and Donkey Engines: A Historical Resources Study of Six State Park System Units on the Mendocino Coast.* California Department of Parks and Recreation, Sacramento.

Sunday Examiner and Chronicle

  1968   Sea Archaeologist John Huston Dies. *Sunday Examiner and Chronicle* 31 March:52. San Francisco, CA.

Taylor, Robert A., and Karen Cooley-Reynolds

  1982   Inundated Terrestrial Sites in California. In *Underwater Archaeology: Proceedings of the Ninth Conference on Underwater Archaeology, 1980,* Calvin R. Cummings, editor, pp. 112–116. Fathom Eight, San Marino, CA.

Throckmorton, Peter

  1987   *The Sea Remembers.* Weidenfeld & Nicolson, New York, NY.

Timbrook, Jan

  1985   Memorial to Dee Travis Hudson (1941–1985). *Journal of California and Great Basin Anthropology* 7(2):147–154.

Treganza, Adán E.

  1959   *The Examination of Indian Shellmounds in the Tomales and Drake's Bay Areas with Reference to Sixteenth Century Historic Contacts.* University of California, Phoebe A. Hearst Museum of Anthropology, Archaeological Archives Manuscript No. 283. Berkeley.

Treganza, Adán E., and Thomas F. King (editors)

  1968   *Archaeological Studies in Point Reyes National Seashore.* San Francisco State College Archaeological Survey, San Francisco, CA.

  1988   Underwater Archaeological Consortium 1988 LaGrange: A California Gold-Rush Legacy. Manuscript, California State Parks, Sacramento.

Ukiah Players Company

  1994   *Voices from the* Frolic *and Beyond: A Mendocino History Play*, Mark H.

Rawitsch, introduction, Kate Magruder, director's notes. Mendocino County Museum Grassroots History Publication Number Seventeen. Willits, CA.

Von der Porten, Edward P.

1968   *The Porcelains and Terra Cottas of Drakes Bay.* Drake Navigators Guild, Point Reyes, CA.

1972   Drake and Cermeño in California: Sixteenth Century Chinese Ceramics. *Historical Archaeology* 6:1–22.

Wagner, Henry R.

1924   The Voyage to California of Sebastian Rodriguez Cermeño in 1595. *California Historical Society Quarterly* 3(1):3–24.

1937   California as an Island Disappears. In *The Cartography of the Northwest Coast of American to the Year 1800*, Vol. 1, Henry R. Wagner, editor, pp. 144–147. University of California Press, Berkeley.

Warren, Daniel

1998   S.S. *Monumental City*: An Historical and Archaeological Study of the First Transpacific Screw Steamship. Master's thesis, Maritime Studies Program, East Carolina University, Greenville, NC.

William Self Associates

1996   *Historic Archaeology of the Muni Metro Turnback Project San Francisco, California.* William Self Associates, Orinda, CA.

1999   *Historic Archaeology of Tichenor's Ways, A Mid-19th Century Marine Railway and Drydock.* Coyote Press, Salinas, CA.

Wood, Virginia S.

1981   *Live Oaking: Southern Timber for Tall Ships.* Northeastern University Press, Boston, MA.

Wright, Steven, and Edward Von der Porten

2019   The History and Archaeology Relating to Drake, Cermeño and Vizcaino in Marin County. *Society for California Archaeology Proceedings* 33:93–96.

Frolic **Films and Television Programs**

Fox, Georgia (producer)

2014   *Impact of the* Frolic: *A Shipwreck that Transcended the World*, Matthew Ritenour, director. Video, Advanced Laboratory for Visual Anthropology, California State University, Chico, Chico. alvanthro, YouTube <https://www.youtube.com/watch?v=BSlkgXZHrrA>. Accessed 12 August 2023.

1997   *The Hunt for Amazing Treasures*, episode 10, part 2 [aired on the Learning Channel]. Video, Andrew Solt Productions, Los Angeles, CA.

Lindahl, Carl H., and Angela Martenez (producers)

2003   Gold Rush Disaster: *Frolic* Shipwreck, *Deep Sea Detectives*, season 1, episode 12 [aired on the History Channel, 11 November]. Video, Santo Domingo Film and Music Video, Santo Domingo, Dominican Republic.

Acknowledgements

This history is the product of cooperation between six wreck divers, now mostly deceased, six archaeologists, a museum curator, and a Native American poet. Tom thanks the wreck divers for donating their collections – over 2,500 artifacts – to the *Frolic* Repository at the Mendocino County Museum, and for trusting the project enough to dictate their life histories that appear here. He also thanks Samuel F. Manning who drew the original images illustrating the *Frolic's* life. Jim thanks the experts, a generation-and-a-half older, and all of those who are described in his narrative, who took the time to mentor him in things nautical and maritime. He also thanks and acknowledges all the friends and colleagues with whom he has had the privilege to work in the projects described in this narrative.

We thank Annaliese Corbin and Rebecca Allen for recommending this book project to the Society for Historical Archaeology where Ben Ford, Co-publications Editor; Richard Schaeffer, Copy Editor; and knic pfost with render jemis, Designers, have transformed our many texts and photos into a book that is far more than the sum of its parts. We thank Thomas Wohlmut of Purple Root Productions, LLC for enhancing the focus of several of these photos.

For the many photos that bring this book to life, we thank the archaeologists and divers who supplied images to illustrate their narratives. Other images were supplied by the Jim Kennon Family; the Bill Kosonen family; Patrick Gibson; Bruce Lanham; Richard O. Everett; Jerre Costa; Robert V. Schwemmer; the Phoebe A. Hearst Museum, University of California, Berkeley; the San Francisco Maritime National Historic Park, National Park Service; the Golden Gate National Recreation Area, National Park Service; the California Department of Parks and Recreation; the Institute of Nautical Archaeology; the Ocean Exploration Trust; the National Oceanic and Atmospheric Administration, Office of National Marine Sanctuaries; and the National Oceanic and Atmospheric Administration, Office of Ocean Exploration and Research.

Finally, Tom thanks Mabel Teruko Miyasaki, and Jim thanks Ann Goodhart, for their encouragement and their hard work in editing our initial drafts for this and for many earlier projects.

Thomas Layton, San Jose, California
James Delgado, Rockville, Maryland

www.ingramcontent.com/pod-product-compliance
Lightning Source LLC
Chambersburg PA
CBHW041532120626
46551CB00019B/2669

* 9 7 8 1 9 5 7 4 0 2 5 7 4 *